ONTOGENY OF LEARNING AND MEMORY

ONTOGENY OF LEARNING AND MEMORY

Edited by

NORMAN E. SPEAR

STATE UNIVERSITY OF NEW YORK AT BINGHAMTON

BYRON A. CAMPBELL

PRINCETON UNIVERSITY

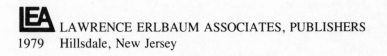 LAWRENCE ERLBAUM ASSOCIATES, PUBLISHERS
1979   Hillsdale, New Jersey

DISTRIBUTED BY THE HALSTED PRESS DIVISION OF

JOHN WILEY & SONS

New York   Toronto   London   Sydney

Lawrence Erlbaum Associates, Inc., Publishers
365 Broadway
Hillsdale, New Jersey 07642

Distributed solely by Halsted Press Division
John Wiley & Sons, Inc., New York

Library of Congress Cataloging in Publication Data

Main entry under title:

Ontogeny of learning and memory.

  Papers based on a conference held at the State
University of New York at Binghamton, June 21-23,
1977.
    Includes bibliographies and indexes.
    1. Learning, Psychology of–Congresses. 2. Me-
mory–Congresses. 3. Psychology, Comparative–
Congresses, 4. Animals, Infancy of–Congresses.
5. Infant psychology–Congresses. I. Spear,
Norman E. II. Campbell, Byron A., 1927-
III. New York (State). State University at
Binghamton.
BF318.O57   156'.3'1   79-19045
ISBN 0-470-26849-2

Printed in the United States of America

Contents

Preface

It has been more than 10 years since George Collier invited the two of us to have lunch with him at a New Brunswick Rathskeller. Since that time we have enjoyed innumerable dry martinis together while collaborating on our 1972 Psychological Review article and subsequently in keeping abreast of each others research. The June 1977 conference at SUNY-Binghamton, on which this book is based, was a natural outcome of our now long-standing friendship, and the exciting new developments that have occurred in the ontogeny of learning and memory in recent years. We are particularly pleased to see familiar faces from other areas of psychology show an interest in this field and extend a special welcome to Abe Amsel, Jerry Rudy and Eliott Blass.

The past 5 years have produced a remarkable change in the field. Where once only a few were actively doing research there are now a sizeable number who contribute regularly. The most dramatic developments have occurred in the analysis of neonatal learning. Where once it was thought that the earliest age at which learning could be established in the rat was around 12–15 days, it is now evident that some types of learning can occur immediately post-partum. For these new discoveries we have to credit young investigators like Jerry Rudy, Eliott Blass and Ted Hall who have developed ingenious new techniques for studying learning and other behaviors in infant rats.

The conference was held at SUNY-Binghamton on June 21 to 23, 1977 and supported by a grant from the SUNY Conversations in the Disciplines and funds provided by Dr. Arthur K. Smith, Provost for Graduate Studies and Research at SUNY Binghamton, and Lawrence Erlbaum Associates. The talks and discussions were relatively informal, and the manuscripts presented in this volume were prepared after the conference. While this allowed the participants to incorporate the comments of the audience, it also regrettably delayed publication.

Nonetheless we believe the volume to be timely and to reflect the rapidly changing state of the art.

That the chapters vary in length is a reflection of the particular author's role in the conference. Each meeting at the conference included a long and short presentation. One function of the shorter presentation was to promote discussion of the longer, but even for these relatively abbreviated addresses, the speaker was encouraged to present his or her own data and ideas. It will be seen that the chapters emphasize the latter, with good effect. Each of the chapters presents new information, and there is certainly no correlation between length and value of the chapters.

The chapters are ordered on a rough continuum based on the nature of the behavior under consideration. The first four chapters concern relatively simple behaviors exhibited almost inevitably by the animal within its own ecological niche. Chapters 5, 6, 7, and 8 concern more complex environmental episodes that require the animal to learn and remember after relatively brief periods. The last four chapters concentrate on "infantile amnesia" as it is classically defined—exaggerated forgetting shown by immature animals long after original learning, when the animal is an adult. Throughout the twelve chapters there is pervasive concern for analysis and a search for understanding beyond mere description of how behavior changes ontogenetically. Each chapter, however, stands alone as an important contribution to the literature; to paraphrase their content here could not do justice to the important message of each.

It is a pleasure to acknowledge the substantial help of colleagues at SUNY Binghamton in conducting the conference and preparing this book. For the conference, the convenient arrangements, smooth operations and relaxed atmosphere were achieved primarily through the skillful efforts of James Wolz with energetic support and guidance from John Magnotta. Aid in preparing the book was provided by Teri Tanenhaus, Wes Schryver and Greg Smith. Finally, the enthusiastic support of Larry Erlbaum and the congenial efficiency of Sandi Guideman and the entire LEA staff has, as always, our sincere gratitude.

N. E. S.
B. A. C.

ONTOGENY OF LEARNING AND MEMORY

1

The Sensorimotor and Motivational Bases of Early Behavioral Development of Selected Altricial Mammals

Jay S. Rosenblatt
Rutgers—The State University

The aim of this chapter is to propose a scheme of the relationship between sensorimotor and motivational processes during the early behavioral development of selected species of altricial mammals. It will serve as a background for the chapters that follow which deal with the ontogeny of learning and memory and which employ the same altricial species and the same patterns of behavior.

In focusing on the species-typical behavior patterns of the newborn to study the ontogeny of learning and memory, investigators have heeded the lessons of the past 20 years during which it has been shown that learning cannot be studied apart from natural patterns of adjustment in newborn. Failure to do so led Scott and his associates (Fuller, Easler, & Banks, 1950; James & Cannon, 1952; Scott, 1958) to propose that learning does not occur in the newborn puppy, and this proposal was extended to the newborn of many altricial species (Scott, 1958, 1962). This failure consisted of attempting to establish conditioned leg withdrawal to electric shock in young puppies; more recent studies of suckling and home orientation indicate clearly that newborn puppies are very capable of learning in these spheres even if they cannot learn to lift their legs to an auditory or visual stimulus until they are nearly 3 weeks of age (Scott, Stewart, & DeGhett, 1974; Stanley, Bacon, & Fehr, 1970).

The early response behavior of altricial newborn has three main focuses: the mother, the siblings, and the home or nest site. Because vision and audition are absent until some time later, newborn are limited during their first few weeks to thermotactile, olfactory, and gustatory sensory systems as their only means of responding to their environment. Their *effective environment*, as compared to the actual environment, therefore is limited to nearby objects and to the proximal stimulation they receive from them. Within this limitation they are capable of responding to the mother in suckling and nonsuckling situations, to siblings during huddling, and to the nest or home region in which they spend all their time. It is during the development of one or another of these functional patterns that early learning and memory have been studied.

The first section of this chapter reviews studies in these three areas of behavioral functioning in selected altricial species. The second section deals with the early sensory basis of these behavior patterns, confining itself to the thermotactile and olfactory stimuli available to altricial newborn during their early development. The third section discusses theoretical considerations stemming from the evidence reviewed with particular attention to the nature of motivational organization in the newborn.

To anticipate the findings: In reviewing how sensory stimuli serve the newborn in behavior toward the mother, siblings, and home region, it has been found that they have a dual function. Newborn become active and initiate behavior (i.e., motivational processes) when the normal stimulus conditions in which they live are disturbed, specifically with respect to thermal, tactile, and, later, olfactory stimulation. Their behavior is then guided by these same stimuli as they find their way to the mother and suckle from her, reach their siblings and huddle with them, and arrive in the home or nest and fall asleep. Motivation is therefore initially sensory-induced, but there is a close relationship in development between the sensory stimuli that induce motivation and those that stimulate the sensorimotor mechanisms that lead the newborn toward a source of stimulation. This close relationship between motivational and sensorimotor processes characterizes the earliest postnatal stage of behavioral organization among altricial newborn and serves as a starting point for later development.

I. EARLY BEHAVIORAL DEVELOPMENT IN ALTRICIAL NEWBORN

The early behavioral development of altricial newborn can be traced in their responses to the mother, siblings, and home or nest site (Rosenblatt, 1971, 1976). Although responses to the mother in suckling and nonsuckling encounters and to siblings during huddling (Alberts, 1978a; Cosnier, 1965) are quite obvious, home orientation often passes unnoticed because the newborn are rarely outside the nest or home site and, should they wander or be dragged out of the home, the mother usually retrieves them. In fact, retrieving itself often occurs in response to calls the young make when they are disturbed by finding themselves outside the nest (Noirot, 1972; Okon, 1972). I shall therefore review studies of home or nest orientation before dealing with the other two principal areas of newborn behavioral development.

A. Home Orientation

The original description of home orientation was based upon studies of kittens from birth to 3 weeks of age (Rosenblatt, 1971; Rosenblatt, Turkewitz, & Schneirla, 1969). The mother and littermates were removed from the home cage, and individual kittens placed first in the home region, then in a corner adjacent to the home and finally in a corner diagonally opposite it. The home region was usually located in a rear corner quadrant of the cage, 18 inches square, and was determined by observing where the mother nursed the kittens and where they huddled when she was absent. In addition kittens were placed in a freshly washed cage (field) similar to the home cage but in only one corner of this cage. Tests lasted 3 minutes in each corner of the home cage and 2 minutes in the field. Before being placed in each test situation the kittens were placed on a cool floor to start them vocalizing.

The kittens' movements and vocalizations were used to describe their behavior during the tests. The kind of movements they performed (e.g., pivoting, crawling, etc.) and their location, at 15-second intervals, were recorded. Their vocalizations were rated by intensity or frequency; intensity measures ranged from low to peak and included medium- and high-intensity vocalization. Finally, the kittens were described as sleeping, resting, or having withdrawn into a corner based upon fairly reliable indices of these kinds of behavior.

The implication of the foregoing measures of home orientation is that it consists not only of locomotion between two areas of the home cage but also of how kittens respond emotionally to the region in which they find themselves. Are they calm or disturbed? If they are calm in one region and disturbed in another, we know first of all that they can distinguish between the two regions and, further, that they feel more comfortable in one than in the other. Movement, sleeping or resting, and vocalization can be used to determine a kitten's emotional state: A kitten that starts vocalizing then falls asleep in the home region a short time after entering it is obviously more comfortable in the home region that in the field, where it remains immobile, withdraws into a corner, and continues to vocalize loudly. It is important to recognize that home orientation involves both a kitten's direction of movement in relation to a source of stimulation and its emotional response to being in the presence or absence of the stimulus.

Home orientation is defined as (a) the tendency for kittens to remain in the home when placed there and (b) their tendency to crawl to the home when placed in either the adjacent or diagonal corner. The second definition implies that kittens leave all outlying cage regions and, conversely, that once they have entered the home they remain there.

In reviewing studies on orientation in other animals such as rats, hamsters, and puppies, we find that few have been described as studies of nest or home orientation, with the notable exceptions of the studies on the rat by Altman and his group (see Altman & Sudarshan, 1975) and by Fleischer and Turkewitz (1979). Nevertheless we can usually relate the conditions of testing in these studies to those used in the kitten studies to show that in fact one or another aspect of the study of home orientation is involved in the former. As examples, open field (i.e., strange cage) tests of rats are comparable with respect to test conditions to the tests of kittens in freshly washed cages (Denenberg, 1969), and placing rats on nest material taken from the home cage is equivalent to placing them in the nest region (Tobach, 1977; Tobach, Rouger, & Schneirla, 1967).

1. *Home orientation in the kitten.*   Among kittens the tendency to remain in the home when placed there develops earlier (i.e., around the 3rd—4th day) than the ability to crawl to the home from the adjacent and diagonal corners of the home cage (i.e., around the 5th—6th day and the 13th—14th day, respectively) (Rosenblatt, 1971; Rosenblatt et al., 1969). Even before the kittens can orient to the home from these outlying regions, they can distinguish between them. Their behavior during the earliest stage, which we have called "regional differentiation," consists of low vocalization and resting in the home, compared to medium-to-high vocalization and pivoting, which occur in the adjacent and diagonal corners and are accompanied by occasional bursts of crawling for short distances. In the field, kittens pivot a little in place then back into the corner and vocalize at peak intensity throughout the remainder of the test. It is clear that at this early age (3—4 days) they can distinguish the field from the home and the home from outlying regions of the cage. They are most disturbed in the field, but even the adjacent and diagonal regions of the home disturb them to some extent.

After the 5th day kittens begin immediately to crawl toward the home when placed in the adjacent corner, but when placed in the diagonal corner they pivot near the starting place. Crawling toward the home involves first of all departure from the adjacent or diagonal corner, then adopting a path to the home (pathtaking), and, finally, entering the home and coming to rest, without vocalizing. The last stage has been labeled the "settling reaction." The settling reaction occurs almost immediately if kittens are placed directly in the home.

After it has become established during the first 2½ weeks, home orientation begins to decline, and by the end of the 3rd week it is no longer present: Kittens wander throughout the home cage (Rosenblatt, 1971). The waning of home orientation follows a characteristic pattern: First, kittens begin to leave the home region when started there and wander around the home cage. At the same time, however, they return to the home if started in the adjacent or diagonal corners. Only later does this behavior, too, begin to decline, and finally the kittens no longer return to the home. In the field, during this period, kittens begin to leave the starting place and cautiously explore the freshly washed cage, vocalizing less than earlier. They walk short distances away from the starting corner, nose-tapping on the floor at frequent intervals, and eventually explore the entire field cage.

2. *Home orientation in other altricial newborn.* The stage of *regional differentiation* in the rat has been studied by a number of investigators (Altman, Brunner, Bulut, & Sudershan, 1974; Altman & Sudarshan, 1975; Altman, Sudarshan, Das, McCormick, & Barnes, 1971; Bulut & Altman, 1974; Gregory & Pfaff, 1971; Salas, Schapiro, & Guzman-Flores, 1970; Sczerzenie & Hsiao, 1977; Tobach, 1977; Tobach et al., 1967). At an early age, between 3 and 8 days, pups show more activity, chiefly head-lifting, in nest material taken from their own home cages than in fresh nest material lacking the odors of the home nest. Placed between the home cage and a freshly washed cage, they tend to "point" with their heads and orient their bodies toward the home cage. Beginning about the 5th–6th day, if allowed to choose, they crawl toward home nest material and away from fresh nest material. Crawling toward the nest material is preceded by olfactory exploration—i.e., head-lifting and pointing toward the home nest material, together with sniffing (Welker, 1964)—and before crawling into the nest material the pups push their faces into it.

Fowler and Kellogg (1975) describe the behavior of rat pups placed in a thermal gradient during the first week, which can be related to thermal orientation to the home nest. In the first few days their behavior resembles that of kittens during the stage of regional differentiation: They become calm when placed directly in a warm region and remain there resting, and when placed in a cooler region at a distance they remain active but are unable to adopt a path from the cooler to the warmer region until they are older. Fowler and Kellogg (1975) provide a vivid description of the contrasting behavior of pups placed in the warm (I) and cool (II) chambers: "When placed in II animals that had been moving in the center compartment continued to move about. When placed in I the animals did not move. Animals 6 to 10 days of age showed a tendency to continue exploration in compartment II. They moved around, explored the edges of the box, and attemped to climb the walls. In the warm environment they moved less and often remained still for the whole time period . . . they rarely left the compartment once they had entered it [p. 742]."

As indicated in the foregoing, at the end of the first week pups begin to adopt a path to the warm chamber from a short distance away (15 cm), provided a rather steep thermal gradient lies between the two regions. Sczerzenie and Hsiao (1977) also found that crawling toward home nest material improved during this period, and a relationship between these two observations and nest orientation in the home cage is indicated by the findings of Fleischer and Turkewitz (1977) that pups tested in their home cages begin to orient from the adjacent to the home region after the 8th day, reaching 70% success on the 12th day. Diagonal-to-home orientation develops at about the same age, and on the 14th day pups reach the home from the diagonal corner in 70% of tests.

On the 9th day Altman et al. (1975) placed pups in a neighboring cage and found that they reached the home cage by passing through a narrow, funnel-shaped entrance in 50% of the tests. Latencies ranged initially from 2 to 3 minutes to traverse the 15- to 30-cm distance between the strange and home cages but declined to 1 to 2 minutes by the 12th day; by the 16th day 85% of the pups reached the home cage with latencies ranging from 30 to 40 seconds. They continued to orient to the home until the 21st day, when latencies were shortest— 10 seconds or less.

In the home cage tests, started in the nest site, reported by Fleischer and Turkewitz (1979), *settling* in the nest appeared in 80% of the pups from the 8th day on. Like kittens of a later age, however, rat pups begin to leave the nest corner at about the 10th day, after which there is a steady decline in the percentage that settle in the home when placed there; pups started outside the nest corner continue to return to the nest, however.

Campbell and his students have been pursuing a series of studies on the behavior of 10- to 25-day-old rat pups in an open field that can be related to the development of home orientation (Campbell & Raskin, 1978). Their early findings indicate that rat pups placed in a strange cage show a marked increase in activity between the 10th and 15th day, followed by a decrease in activity between the 16th and 25th day (Campbell & Mabry, 1972; Mabry & Campbell, 1974; Moorcroft, 1971). The initial interpretation of these findings was related to subcortical arousal and maturation of cortical inhibitory control, but it has been put in question by the finding that there is only a slight increase in activity from the 10th to 25th day in pups tested in shavings taken from their own home cages (Campbell & Raskin, 1978). This contrast between the behavior of pups in their own nest material and in fresh nest material is reminiscent of the contrast in the behavior of kittens in their home and in the freshly washed cage, but there is an important difference that may reflect species differences in responses to strange environments. In a comparable strange cage situation kittens become immobilized and huddle in one corner of the cage, vocalizing loudly, whereas rat pups appear to become *more active* in a strange cage up to age of 15 days. Fowler and Kellogg (1975) observed a similar high level of activity in rat pups confined to a cool chamber, and Hofer (1973a, 1973b, 1973c, 1975) and Tobach (1977) have reported greater activity in fresh nest material than in home nest material as pups grow older. Thermal factors were ruled out by Campbell and his students, because warming the strange cage did not prevent the rise and subsequent fall in activity described earlier (Moorcroft, Lytle, & Campbell, 1971). The rise in activity in the strange cage was prevented with equal effectiveness by odors from the nest and by contact with the mother or siblings, suggesting that pups respond to a combination of olfactory, thermal, and tactile stimuli (Campbell & Raskin, 1978; Randall & Campbell, 1976).

Finally, Campbell and Raskin (1978) examined the alternative hypotheses that the increase in activity arose either from fear of the strange cage or from curiosity and exploration. Pups, however, show little inclination to enter a strange cage joined to one in which there is home bedding and the anesthetized mother; after being placed in the strange cage they quickly enter and remain in the more familiar surroundings with home bedding and female. Clearly, as the authors indicate, "The hyperactivity elicited by the unfamiliar environment is a reflection of a fear or stress response rather than curiosity or exploratory behavior." These findings agree with Hofer's (1973a, 1973b, 1973c), which were that exploratory behavior increased, as did self-grooming, urination, and defecation, in 14-day-old pups separated from the mother in unfamiliar surroundings.

The decline in pup activity in the strange cage after the 15th day also needs to be explained in relation to the development of home orientation. It will be recalled that kittens begin to leave the starting corner in the strange cage once home orientation begins to decline in the home cage. Pups on the other hand become less active. The decline in disturbance produced by the strange cage appears to be expressed in opposite ways in these two species, and this parallels the different ways in which they express their disturbance during the earlier period, before the 15th day.

Among hamsters Leonard (1974) has shown the early development of a capacity to orient along a thermal gradient. This capacity may be related to nest orientation, because the nest is normally the warmest region of the home cage and is usually surrounded by a declining thermal gradient. For the first week or so hamster pups rapidly move along a 45-cm-long thermal gradient and come to rest in a thermal zone of 33°C. In the absence of a thermal gradient but with a thermal high point, pups placed at a distance are active, as during regional orientation, but are unable to reach the preferred thermal zone.

As thermal orientation declines in the week-old hamster, olfactory orientation to nest material arises, as shown originally by Devor and Schneider (1974) and confirmed by Alberts (1976), Cornwell (1975, 1976), and Gregory and Bishop (1975). These last two investigators have shown that the preference for home nest material over fresh nest material continues through the 16th day, somewhat longer than was found by Devor and Schneider, who reported its decline around the 13th day. It should be noted, however, that hamster pups have not been tested for the development of home orientation in their home cage and that most of the preference tests have opposed fresh nest material to home nest material, which would correspond in our kitten studies to a comparison between the home region in the home cage and a corner in the freshly washed cage. For this reason the phase of pathtaking has not been observed except perhaps in Leonard's study, which was confined to a thermal gradient.

Evidence of home orientation in puppies is scattered in several reports by Scott and his coworkers (Elliot & Scott, 1961; Scott, Stewart, & DeGhett, 1974) and consists mainly of what we have referred to as the "settling response." When removed from the nest box, puppies vocalize loudly and may be quieted by placing them in contact with a warm, soft surface (i.e., nesting material retaining the mother's warmth) or by returning them to the litter nest box itself. This response appears as early as the 6th to 8th day in some litters and by the 11th to 12th day in nearly all litters.

B. Huddling among Siblings

Huddling among preweanlings often cannot be distinguished from home orientation on the basis of observations of group aggregation alone, because huddles
form in the home and may, in fact, be mainly the home settling reaction by each
individual. The same, of course, may be said about home orientation, namely,
that it is really huddling, except that when mother and siblings are removed from
the cage the young still exhibit home orientation. There is in fact some evidence
among kittens that a precondition for huddling may be the settling response in
the home, because two kittens that come into contact with one another outside
the home often do not remain in contact (i.e., huddle); instead each remains
active until it reaches the home, when it may then huddle with its sibling. Hofer
(1972) has reported a similar phenomenon among rat pups.

Huddling, however, is not a passive response to another newborn; young do
not remain in contact with one another simply because they find themselves
together after a nursing or are responding to being in the home. As Welker
(1959) has shown among puppies and Cosnier (1965), Alberts (1978a) and
Alberts and Brunjes (1978) among rat pups, huddling is an active response of
the young to the stimulus characteristics of their siblings. Although it is common
among all species of altricial young, most of which give birth to more than a
single newborn, it has been studied in very few. It is in a sense so common that it
has been ignored, until recently!

If huddling is described in relation to group activity, there are three phases:
the coming together of the group, or *aggregation*; the activity within the huddle
once it has formed, or *maintenance* of the group; and the dispersion of the group,
or *scattering*. As one might suspect, the factors involved in aggregation,
maintenance, and scattering cannot be sharply separated.

Despite its group character, huddling during its various phases remains the
activity of individuals. Welker (1959) has shown that among puppies lowering
the ambient temperature causes individuals to increase their activity (Crighton &
Pownall, 1974) and that while crawling, contact with another puppy evokes
approach and further contact until all the young of a litter have come together
into a huddle. Increasing the ambient temperature causes the huddle to break up
and the puppies to scatter. Welker has shown that scattering is based on the
response of overly warm puppies to contact with littermates: On making nose
contact, each withdraws from the other and crawls away.

Cosnier (1965), using a fur-lined sleeve that had been warmed above the
outside floor temperature and one that was at the same temperature, tested rat
pups for entry into the sleeve by placing them at the entrance to it. Their
responses can be interpreted as huddling: Only when sleeve temperature was
above that of the floor did they crawl into it the length of their bodies, beginning
with the first day and continuing for 18 days. The sleeve obviously simulated
contact with a warm pup under conditions in which low ambient temperature have
cooled the floor surface below the surface temperature of the littermates.

Alberts (1978a) and Alberts and Brunjes (1978) have studied the individual basis of huddling directly, using an anesthetized target pup and an awake pup that seeks the other for huddling. Their studies confirm those of Cosnier by showing that huddling is based upon thermal and tactile stimulation during the early period. They have shown, moreover, that the huddle is maintained through continuous activity within it, in which each individual pup maximizes its contact with other pups when the ambient temperature is low and minimizes it when the temperature is high, short of scattering. Anesthetized pups, unable to respond, are found at the periphery of the huddle under low ambient temperatures, exposed to the cold, and are buried in the middle of the huddle under high ambient temperatures, therefore, receiving maximal additional warmth.

The function of huddling as a group thermoregulatory mechanism has been amply demonstrated by Cosnier (1965) and Alberts (1978b). At an age when they lack fully developed thermoregulation, pups reduce exposure of their body surfaces by huddling and thereby retain their body heat so as to remain at near-normal body temperature. As individuals and as a group, the amount of body surface that is exposed during huddling is directly proportional to the ambient temperature.

C. Suckling and Nonsuckling Responses to the Mother

Although suckling constitutes the principal response to the mother by newly born young, there are many times when the young seek and remain in contact with the mother without suckling. Moreover, even during attempts at suckling the young are responsive to many aspects of the mother that are not directly concerned with nipple-grasping and sucking. This is perhaps most clearly exemplified in kittens that have been isolated from the mother and littermates for the first week of life and then returned to them (Rosenblatt, Turkewitz, & Schneirla, 1961). These kittens are attracted to the mother by her licking and body contact, and although they may make contact with her a short time after rejoining her, it may be several hours before they begin to search for a nipple and suckle.

As with huddling, nonsuckling responses among altricial young are so common they have been largely ignored. The need to create artificial mothers to rear young has been the main impetus to study what maternal stimuli the young respond to, but of necessity such research emphasizes the static features of the mother, leaving the active features still to be investigated.

The newborn's earliest responses to the mother occur during parturition when she rests between deliveries, particularly toward the end of parturition, when most of the pups are present and several have already been cleaned, freed of birth membrane and placenta, and become active. In both the rat pup and kitten, suckling is sometimes initiated before parturition is completed (Holloway, Dollinger, & Denenberg, 1976; Schneirla, Rosenblatt, & Tobach, 1963), but more often it is initiated during what we have called the "postpartum resting interval'' (Schneirla et al., 1963). The mother is exhausted from the efforts of delivery, and after feeding and drinking she often lies down with her newborn in the home region and sleeps, thereby providing the young with their first good opportunity to locate and attach to nipples. Teicher and Blass (1977) have recently shown that this initial suckling is very much dependent upon the events of parturition itself, particularly the spread of amniotic fluid to the nipples. When the parturient mother was anesthetized and made available for suckling and her nipples washed thoroughly, 90% of the newborn failed to attach, compared to newborn attachment of 80% when the nipples retained amniotic fluid. Nipple attachment could be reinstated by replacing either amniotic fluid or an extract of the nipple wash; even taking saliva from the mother shortly after parturition— probably because it contained amniotic fluid licked by her—reinstated nipple attachment in newborn. Ewer (1959) proposed some time ago that kittens delayed their initial nipple attachment until the appearance of some special, attractive substance on the nipples during the first hour after birth, but she believed that this substance emanated from the nipple itself. The previously mentioned study suggests that the substance may be the product of parturition, as it is in the rat, but of course this would not account for a delay in nipple attachment; even the delay seems questionable, because Schneirla, et al., (1963) found no such delay postpartum in initial nipple attachment.

The use of brooders to rear rat pups, kittens, and puppies and to examine the responses of newborn rabbit young to artificial mothers has shown that thermotactile properties and the mother's body shape play important roles initially in the mother's general attractiveness to the young and that subsequently olfactory stimuli become important. A warm, moist, pulsating plastic tube proved very attractive to rat pups and elicited close contact, "hugging," and nuzzling (Thoman and Arnold, 1968). Warm, fur-textured surfaces also attract puppies, kittens, and rabbit young (Jeddi, 1970; Rosenblatt, et al., 1961; Toropova, 1961). Rounded, continuous surfaces are important in aiding kittens to locate the nipple for suckling; sharp angles, crevices, and discontinuous surfaces provide too many distractions to enable kittens freely to explore the entire surface where the nipple is located on the artificial mother (Kovach and Kling, 1967; Rosenblatt, 1971). Even when nuzzling on the mother's body surface, kittens often are distracted from the nipple region by the warm, moist crevices under her arms and legs and by similar features in her anogenital region. The full extent to which the various furry textures and the form and the shape of the mother's body, especially when she lies down to rest with her newborn, are important features that attract and guide young to her nipples has yet to be investigated systematically.

The thermal basis of the pup's response to the mother during nonsuckling and suckling behavior has recently been studied in some detail. Leon, Croskerry, and Smith (1978) have charted the 24-hour course of maternal and pup surface temperatures (taken at ventral sites at the sternum of both mother and pups) and of nest temperatures recorded under an ambient temperature of 22°C. Maternal ventrum temperature ranges between 37.5°C and 38.3°C, and nest temperature ranges between 33°C and 34°C; the latter temperature is maintained largely by the pups, whose surface temperature is within this range. Leon, et al., (1978) have shown that the mother tends to initiate contact with her pups in the nest when her ventral temperature reaches the low point of her normal range and that during the course of this contact, which usually involves nursing, her ventral temperature rises nearly 1°C, to the high point of her temperature range. At the same time nest temperature rises nearly 2°C, reflecting a rise in pup temperature. The female leaves the pups when their temperature and her ventral surface temperature at at the high points of their ranges.

Hofer, Shair, and Singh (1976) found that the ventral surface in lactating mothers (12th day of lactation) ranges in temperature from 31.5°C at the base of the tail to 36.5°C on both the neck and at various locations surrounding the two lines of six nipples each. The nipples themselves are somewhat cooler (36.1°C–36.4°C, than the surrounding fur, forming thereby a thermal microgradient; more peripheral and distant body regions are also at lower temperatures, forming larger thermal gradients to the nipple region.

Major alterations in the body and surface temperatures of anesthetized mothers do not, however, affect the pups' readiness to suckle from them. Hofer et al. (1976) lowered the ventral surface temperature 6°C before placing 12-day-old pups on the mother's ventrum and found that all the pups attached to nipples within 2 minutes. Blass, Teicher, Cramer, Bruno, and Hall (1977) lowered maternal ventral temperatures to 31°C and then to 28°C and found that pups 2 to 12 days of age are unaffected as far as nipple attachment is concerned but that pups 11 to 12 days of age have longer latencies to attach to nipples for suckling. Pups were placed in nose contact with the mother's ventrum at the start of these tests. It does appear therefore that when in close contact with the mother, thermal stimulation does not play a crucial role in nipple attachment. However, thermal stimulation may play a role in attracting pups to the mother from a short distance, because it is likely that a thermal gradient extends outward from the mother's body a short distance, as we have found among cats (Freeman and Rosenblatt, 1978a; and Jeddi, 1970) has reported among dogs and rabbits.

New features of the mother come into play early in development to stimulate suckling and other approaches to her. A number of studies have shown that maternal odors are important both at a distance and when young are in contact with the nipple (Alberts, 1976; Cheal, 1975). Rat pups distinguish these odors as early as the 3rd day and may show active approaches to them between the 3rd and 10th day (Blass et al., 1977; Hofer et al., 1976; Salas et al., 1970; Schapiro & Salas, 1970; Teicher and Blass, 1976; Tobach et al., 1967). Distance approaches to the mother after the 10th day may be largely olfactory-based, as the work of Nyakas and Endroczi (1970, 1973) and particularly the studies of Leon and Moltz (1971, 1972) and Leon (1975, 1978) have shown.

Among rabbit young, mice pups, puppies, and kittens, approaches to the mother on the basis of olfactory stimuli have been shown directly (Ivanitskii,) and indirectly through the response of young to maternal olfactory deposits or artificial odors (Fox, 1970; Rosenblatt et al., 1969; Scott et al., 1974).

II. SENSORY BASES OF EARLY BEHAVIORAL DEVELOPMENT

A. Transition between Thermotactile and Olfactory Bases of Early Behavioral Adjustments

After the 5th day, pups made anosmic with intranasal zinc sulphate fail to huddle with a warmed sibling (Alberts, 1978a; Alberts & Brunjes, 1978). Between the 5th and 10th day, pups make a transition in the sensory basis of huddling from primarily thermotactile stimulation to primarily olfactory stimulation. In the absence of pup odors, as for example when tested with a warmed plastic tube (37°C), they continue to huddle on the basis of thermotactile stimulation, but when odors are present they favor the olfactory stimulation as a basis for huddling (Alberts, 1978a; Alberts & Brunjes, 1978; Cosnier, 1965). In home orientation the transition from thermal orientation (Fowler & Kellogg, 1975) to olfactory orientation (Sczerzenie & Hsiao, 1977) also occurs between the 5th and 10th day.

On the other hand, in suckling olfactory stimulation is important from the beginning (Teicher & Blass, 1976, 1977). Pups placed with their noses to the nipple on the belly of anesthetized females grasp the nipple only if it is coated with amniotic fluid.

In the hamster pup, home orientation during the first week appears to be based solely on thermal and thermotactile stimulation, but after the 9th day olfactory stimuli become increasing effective (Alberts, 1976; Devor & Schneider, 1974). Pups are capable of responding to olfactory stimulation earlier, as Devor and Schneider and Cornwell (1975, 1976) have shown, and the recent study of Gregory and Bishop (1975) indicates that olfactory orientation to nesting material develops slowly between the 2nd and 6th day, reaching over 80% preference for that material on the 6th day and continuing until the 16th day.

As indicated earlier, thermotactile stimulation induces the settling response in week-old puppies (Scott et al., 1974), and there is no reason to doubt that huddling among puppies, as Welker (1959) has shown, and responses to the mother are based initially on thermotactile stimulation. Toropova (1961) has emphasized the importance of a soft, warm surface in eliciting suckling from puppies reared on an artificial mother. Somewhat similar conditions have been described by Jeddi (1970) as optimal for rabbit newborn; he has shown that these young prefer warmed metal tubing shaped like a nursing mother over a soft, woolly surface that has not been warmed if they are forced to choose between warmth and soft fur, which are normally combined in the actual mother. However, rabbit pups and puppies can be conditioned to olfactory stimuli placed on the mother's ventral body surface by about the 5th day (Fox, 1970; Ivanitskii (n.d.).

A recent study by Freeman and Rosenblatt (1978a) sheds some light on the developmental relationship between thermotactile and olfactory stimulation in home orientation among newborn kittens. Newly born kittens are capable of responding to a thermal gradient with a thermotaxic turning toward the warmth, and they exhibit the settling response when placed on a warm floor panel (Freeman and Rosenblatt, 1978a). They appear unable to orient along a gradient for long distances unless guided by tactile stimuli.

Kittens were tested in the home cage, emptied of the mother and littermates, with the home region varied in the following ways: The home was both warm and contained olfactory deposits (HW) or was cool with olfactory deposits (HC); the home region was cool but had olfactory deposits, and at the same time the diagonal corner was warmed (HC−DW); finally, the open field, or strange cage, had one region warmed (OW) and the kitten was placed in an adjacent corner. The kittens were tested at 2-day intervals starting on the 1st day and ending on the 15th day after birth. These various test conditions enabled us to determine whether kittens preferred thermal, olfactory, or the combination of thermal and olfactory stimuli in orienting to the home region.

Whether the home was warm (HW) or cool (HC), all the kittens that left the adjacent corner went to the home, and by the 7th day more than 50% of the kittens did so (Fig. 1.A, B). When the open field was warmed (OW), however, a small percentage of kittens reached the home between days 1 and 5, but there was not a significant increase over the next 10 days (Fig. 1.C). The kittens therefore appeared to use olfactory stimuli to orient to the home from an early age but may also have used thermal stimuli during the first 5 days, although for them it is not a very effective stimulus for home orientation. This conclusion was confirmed when kittens presented with olfactory stimulation in the home and warmth in the diagonal corner (HC−DW) nearly all chose the cool home region (Fig. 1.D) rather than the warmed diagonal corner.

The stimulus to which kittens respond in orienting to the home may not, however, be the one that they respond to in exhibiting the settling response while in the home. To investigate this possibility, kittens were tested by being placed directly in the home under the following conditions: The home region was warm (HW) or cool (HC), or an open-field corner was either warm (OW) or cool (OC). Since normally kittens do not leave the home region, we measured their activity and their vocalization frequencies in the home. A warm home (HW) evoked the least amount of activity between the 1st and 9th day, and vocalization frequency was also lowest in HW. When the home was cool (HC), activity and vocalization

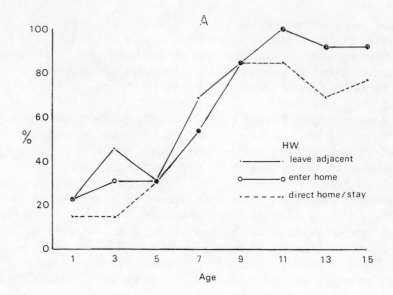

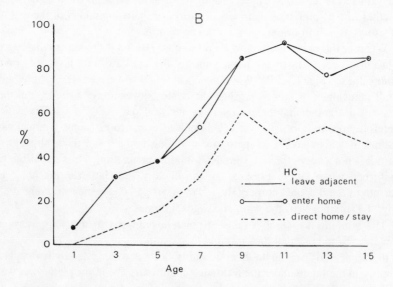

FIG. 1.1.   Home orientation performance of 1- to 15-day-old kittens under four experimental conditions. Kittens were placed in the adjacent corner at the start of the test. The experimental conditions were: (A) warm home region (HW), (B) cold home region (HC), (C) warm "home" in a freshly washed cage (OW), and (D) cool home region and warm diagonal region (HC-DW). Graphs show the

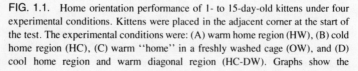

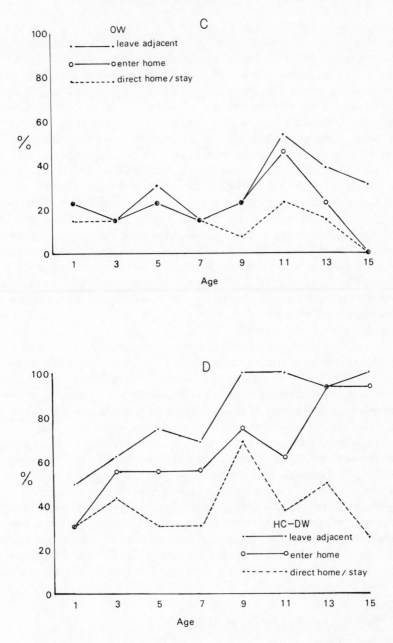

percentage of kittens ($n = 9$) that left the adjacent corner, entered the home during the test and remained there, and went directly to the home and remained there. (From Freeman and Rosenblatt, (1978a)—Copyright by Interscience Publishers. Reprinted by permission.)

frequency were high from the first day on. This was also true when kittens were placed in the cool open-field corner (OC). When the open field was warm (OW), activity during the first 7 days was minimal and equal to that in HW tests, but then it became greater, whereas vocalization frequency was greater by the 5th day and remained so thereafter.

Thus kittens prefer the combination of warmth and home odors in the home, exhibiting reduced activity and a low frequency of vocalization (i.e., the settling reaction). Although warmth alone is sufficient to evoke the settling reaction during the first 3 days, by the 5th day home odors are necessary as well, and without them kittens vocalize more frequently and become more active.

This study also provided some information on what stimulates kittens to leave a region, e.g., the adjacent region in tests started there. Kittens that were placed in the home region or a region of the open field under the various experimental conditions were observed for departures from these regions. During the first week, few of the kittens left any of the regions in which they had been placed. During the second week, however, 39% left the cool open-field region (OC) and 47% left the cool home (HC), whereas only 6% and 14% left the warm regions, HW and OW, respectively. Warmth appears to hold kittens in a region whereas coolness causes them to depart, and home odors do not seem to play a very important role in this response.

The study shows that thermal and olfactory stimuli are interwoven in the development of home orientation behavior in kittens. Departure appears to depend largely on thermal stimulation, but orientation to the home—that is, path-taking—is based largely on olfaction after the 3rd day. Settling in the home depends on a combination of thermal and olfactory stimulation from the 5th day on; before then it may be based mainly on thermal conditions.

The interrelationship in development between thermal and olfactory stimuli has not been examined in many other species. Alberts' (1978a; Alberts & Brunjes, 1978) studies on huddling in rat pups comes closest (see Fig. 8 in Alberts, 1976). In these studies it does appear that a warm plastic tube (substituting for a warm sibling) elicits huddling (or what might be called "settling" in contact with a littermate or the tube) at all ages between 5 and 20 days (Cosnier, 1965), even though reduced olfaction eliminates huddling during the same period. One might suggest that finding the sibling in the test arena is based on olfaction, but huddling with it, once it is located, may be based upon thermal stimulation.

B.   Olfactory Basis of Early Behavioral Adjustments

One established, olfaction plays a crucial role in the early behavioral adjustments of altricial young. Cheal (1975), Alberts (1976), and Rosenblatt (1976) have recently reviewed the role of olfaction in early behavioral development, and

Alberts has related it to the development of the olfactory system in the rat. All the evidence for olfactory function in mammalian young comes from studies of home orientation, huddling, and responses to the mother (see Alberts, 1976, for treatment of this subject in the rat). In dealing with the transition from thermotactile to olfactory function, we have already cited much of this evidence; however, certain points have yet to be established, and this section deals with these points.

As indicated earlier, suckling appears to be elicited by olfactory stimuli on the nipple at birth and in the first weeks, yet pups do not respond to maternal odor at a distance until the 10th day. Initially response at a distance appears to be based on her urine (Nyakas & Endroczi, 1970), but by the 14th to 16th day olfactory approaches to the mother are based upon maternal caecotroph odors (Leon & Moltz, 1971, 1972). Thus there appears to be a succession of maternal odors to which the young respond that is determined by the successive production by the mother of attractive odors. Maternal caecotroph does not become effective in attracting pups until the mother begins to excrete excessive amounts and the young ingest the excess and learn to approach the odor (Leon, 1978).

The odor in the nest to which young respond in orientation also appears to emanate from the mother, because several studies have shown that only nest material from lactating females, whether the pups' own mother or another mother, is effective in eliciting orientation; the odors of nonlactating females and of males are ineffective (Gregory & Pfaff, 1971; Schapiro & Salas, 1970; Sczerzenie & Hsiao, 1977).

Among hamster pups, nest odors from any lactating female are effective in contrast to nest odors from nonlactating females and males (Devor & Schneider, 1974; Gregory & Bishop, 1975).

Among kittens the olfactory basis of home orientation has recently been shown to be somewhat specific to the kitten's own litter (Freeman & Rosenblatt, 1978b). To investigate this question, 8-day-old kittens from litters born within a day of one another were tested first in their own home cages (emptied of the mother and littermates) and then in the cage of a strange mother and litter—or vice versa. Most of the kittens were successful in orienting to the home from the adjacent corner of their own home cages, but fewer than 50% could orient to the home in the cage of a strange mother and litter (Fig. 1.2). The fact that a number of kittens were successful in the strange cage and that those who were not successful did not act as though they were in an entirely alien environment suggests that the odors of a strange lactating female are somewhat familiar but not familiar enough to enable all the kittens to orient to the home as they are able to do in their own home cage.

Kittens that failed to orient to the home in the strange mother's cage were then placed with her and her litter for 48 hours in the expectation that they would learn to use the foster mother's odors to orient to the home at the end of this period. After 48 hours the kittens were again tested in their new home cages and in their original home cages. Surprisingly, the kittens failed to orient to the home in the new home cage, and in addition their ability to orient to the home in their original home cages was lost (Fig. 1.2)! They were returned to their original home cages for 24 hours, but at the end of that time they still has not regained their ability to orient to the home in this cage (Fig. 1.2).

These findings suggest that there are two components to maternal odor: one component that is common to all lactating females, to which kittens responded as familiar in the strange mother's cage, and a second component specific to each lactating female, which kittens appear to use in orienting to the home. We interpret these findings in relation to this two-component theory as follows: In the home cage, kittens made use of both components and could orient to the home, but in the strange cage only a somewhat familiar nonspecific component was present and an entirely unfamiliar specific component. Some kittens either used the nonspecific component to orient to the home in the strange cage or could respond to the specific component of the strange mother. When kittens were placed in strange mothers' cages they "searched" for the familiar specific component; not being able to find it, they gave up and did not learn the specific component of the new mother and litter. Further, when returned to their own mothers they no longer were responsive to her specific component and were unable to relearn it in 24 hours.

One additional finding in this study is of interest for an understanding of how litter-specific odor responsiveness develops. One group of kittens in this study

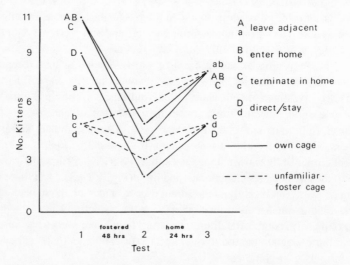

FIG. 1.2. Home orientation performance of 8- to 11-day-old kittens in their own home cages and unfamiliar home cages. Test 1 was done before fostered kittens had lived with the foster mother and litter, and Test 2 was done after they had lived with them for 48 hours. Test 3 was done after they had been returned to their own cages for 24 hours. (From Freeman and Rosenblatt, (1978b)—Copyright by Interscience Publishers. Reprinted by permission.)

were slow learners and by the 8th day were not yet able to orient to the home in their home cages. When they were tested on the 8th day in a strange mother's cage they showed no more distress than in their own home cages and also did not orient to the home region. Over the next 5 days they gradually developed orientation to the home in their home cages and at the same time began to show some distress in the strange mother's cage, where they were unable to orient to the home. These findings indicate that before kittens have developed home orientation on the basis of their own mother's odors, they do not show any differentiation between her odor and that of another lactating mother, but as home orientation develops this differentiation emerges simultaneously.

Leon (1975) has shown that rat pups also may respond to the maternal pheromone of a specific mother if mothers are fed diets that differ in ways that contribute to the odor of maternal caecotrophe. Pups reared by such mothers react only to the odor of their own mothers; they differ from kittens in that they show no positive response to the odors of strange mothers.

A number of studies have used artificial odors to demonstrate that odors can be learned and used to discriminate among the significant objects in the newborn's environment. In nearly all cases the odors are applied to the mother's ventrum so that the newborn are exposed to them during nuzzling and suckling. Ivanitskii (n.d.) showed that an artificial odor could be conditioned to the appearance of the mother and suckling, and Fox (1970) showed among puppies that an initially aversive artificial odor could be made positive by being associated with suckling during the first 5 days. Woll (cited in Rosenblatt, 1971) was able to teach 1- to 3-day-old kittens to suckle from one brooder nipple as against a second nearby painting the flanges surrounding the nipples with artificial odors and providing milk in only one of the nipples. Learning was rapid, and by 2 or 3 days of age, kittens nuzzled and attached to the positively reinforced nipple almost exclusively.

Recently, however, Leon, Galef, and Behse (1977) exposed rat pups to an artificial odor (e.g., peppermint extract) for 3 hours daily from the 1st to the 19th day postpartum after they had been removed from their mother. These pups therefore had no opportunity to associate the odor with the mother and siblings. At 21 days of age they were tested for their choice of peppermint as against no odor, and more than 70% chose the peppermint.

The process by which olfactory stimuli come to evoke responses to the home region, siblings, and mother includes association with nonolfactory stimuli and with simple exposure that familiarizes the young with an olfactory stimulus, reducing its fear-evoking and aversive properties.

III. SOME THEORETICAL CONSIDERATIONS

This review of the thermotactile and olfactory bases of home orientation, responses to the mother, and huddling with siblings during the early behavioral development of altricial mammalian young raises certain theoretical issues: the relationship between sensory maturation and behavioral development, sensory interrelationships during development, relationships among the three patterns of behavior, and motivational organization in the newborn.

A. Relationship between Sensory Maturation and Behavioral Development

Home orientation, huddling, and some features of the newborn's responses to the mother are initially dependent upon thermotactile stimulation and only gradually come under the control of olfactory stimulation. In the rat this control appears to be dependent on the gradual maturation of olfactory sensitivity, because before the 3rd day it has proved difficult to elicit olfactory-based responses (Alberts, 1976; Tobach, 1977). A similar situation exists in the newborn kitten with respect to home orientation. However, in both species studies have shown that from the beginning nipple attachment is under olfactory regulation (Teicher & Blass, 1976, 1977; Woll, cited in Rosenblatt, 1976). In the hamster olfactory response to nest odor was initially found only after the first week, although pups distinguished between different artificial odors the 3rd or 4th day (Cornwell, 1975, 1976; Devor & Schneider, 1974). It appears therefore that sensory maturation is only one factor in the integration of olfaction into behavioral development; the integration of olfaction into nipple attachment may be based on some initial effect of this stimulation that facilitates subsequent response to thermotactile properties of the nipple, whereas the same response plays no role in approaching the mother or siblings or in home orientation before the 3rd day. There is evidence in the studies of Gregory and Pfaff (1971) and Tobach (1977) that the initial response to olfactory stimulation is head-lifting and lowering, and only later (6 days of age) does forward crawling emerge as a predominant response to familiar odors. At this later age, therefore, it may be integrated into approaches toward the mother, siblings, and the nest. One cannot discount, also, that there is a prenatal basis in the neonate's response to amniotic fluid.

The relationship between sensory maturation and behavioral development is, thus not a direct one but depends in part on the pattern of behavior under study. Although neurophysiological studies can establish the age of onset of sensory capacities (Gottlieb, 1977), the actual integration of sensory functioning in behavioral development requires the analysis of particular behavior patterns as they change during development.

B. Sensory Interrelationships during Development

Closely related to the foregoing question is that of the nature of sensory interrelationships during development. Thermotactile and olfactory stimuli are related in different ways in different patterns of behavior. In the kitten, as we have shown, thermal and olfactory stimuli are interwoven during home orientation: Orientation is initiated largely on the basis of thermal stimulation, pathtaking is guided mainly by olfactory stimuli, and the settling reaction depends on a combination of thermal and olfactory stimuli. In the rat and kitten olfactory and tactile stimuli are involved in finding and grasping the nipple and sucking. The young are capable of locating nipples when the perioral region is desensitized but cannot grasp them, whereas they can grasp the nipple but cannot suck when the tongue is anesthetized (Anokhin & Shuleikina, 1977; Hall, unpublished). Olfactory-bulbectomized kittens have difficulty locating nipples on the mother, but when they are held to an artificial nipple they rapidly grasp it and suckle (Kovach & Kling, 1967). Rat pups also fail to suckle if they are made anosmic either by olfactory bulbectomy or intranasal lavage with zinc sulfate (Singh & Tobach, 1975; Singh, Tucker, & Hofer, 1976; Tobach, 1977; Tobach et al., 1967), but placed on the female's nipple or fed with an artificial nipple they are able to suckle and obtain milk. At later ages, however, bulbectomy and zinc sulphate treatment, though still exhibiting an effect on the duration of suckling, have much less of an effect on pup survival, indicating that dependence on olfaction during suckling has undergone a developmental change.

Alberts (1978a) and Alberts and Brunjes (1978) have shown that in the rat pup, huddling comes under the control of olfaction after the 5th day, and anosmic pups spend little time huddling with an anesthetized pup. It might appear that thermal stimulation has been succeeded entirely by olfactory stimulation in the pups' huddling response, yet in the presence of a warm tube simulating the temperature of a pup, 5- to 20-day-old pups show an *increase* in their tendency to huddle with the tube (Alberts & Brunjes, 1978; Cosnier, 1965). Similarly, in the hamster, the findings of Leonard (1974), Devor and Schneider (1974), and Alberts (1976) suggest that thermal orientation declines at about the end of the first week as olfactory-based response to nest odors develops. However, Leonard (1974) has also shown that under reduced ambient temperatures and with well-defined thermal zones, hamsters continue to orient on a thermal basis well into the second week. Similar findings have been reported with respect to thermal orientation in the rat (Cosnier, 1965). These findings indicate that thermal- and olfactory-based huddling and home orientation are also very likely interwoven in these newborn and that the relationship between the two may vary according to circumstances.

C. Relationships among the Three Patterns of Behavior

The three patterns of behavior I have been discussing are interrelated in their functional significance and in their stimulus determinants. All three serve the newborn in its efforts to maintain its temperature by bringing it directly into contact with a thermal source (mother), or a substitute source (siblings) that also provides insulation, or with the nest and home, which for some species provides additional insulation and in all is the site of huddling and contact with the mother. The network of functional interactions among these three patterns affecting nursing and other maternal care, protection against predators, and gradual widening of the newborn's zone of activity requires too extensive discussion for the present chapter.

Another form of interrelationship is based upon common sources of stimulation. The newborn's limited sensory capacities result in responses to relatively simple forms of stimulation—chiefly, thermal, tactile, and olfactory. It is likely that thermal stimuli are equivalent in their effect whether the source is the mother, siblings, or the home or nest. Olfactory stimuli emanate chiefly from the mother; responses to siblings and nest odors have been shown to be equivalent to responses to maternal odors among rats, hamsters, puppies, and kittens. Tactile stimuli seem to be effective through shape, texture, movement, and so forth, independent of the actual source of the stimuli but not of the thermal and olfactory stimuli that accompany them.

One consequence of the interrelationship among stimuli governing behavior patterns is that experience in one area of functioning may play an important role in the development of other patterns. For example, experience of maternal odor during suckling may play a role in huddling, because maternal odors have spread to the other siblings. The common odor shared by mothers in a colony of rats enables young to respond positively to all mothers, not only their own, a situation that contrasts sharply with colonies in which females feed on different diets, so that their odors differ sufficiently for young to respond positively only to their own mother's odor (Leon, 1975).

D. Motivational Organization in the Newborn

1. *The nature of suckling motivation.* Bindra (1969) has provided a structural model of motivation that will be useful in discussing motivational organization in the newborn and the problem of developmental changes in motivation. The model is shown in Fig. 1.3. A focal concept is the *central motive state* (CMS), which is defined as a central neural state produced by the interaction between the physiological state of the animal and incentive stimuli related to that state. The CMS "favors *selective attention* to a certain class of incentive stimuli and also creates a *response bias* in favor of a certain class of species-typical actions [p. 1081]." As shown in the figure, autonomic responses (i.e., emotional responses) may be viewed as manifestations of the CMS in the same manner as motor responses involved in postural and other action patterns.

The model as it stands depicts adult motivational organization in which the CMS for a particular motivational state, more or less highly specified by the combined influences of physiological state and incentive stimuli, makes use of highly developed perceptual and response processes and complexly organized autonomic responses in organizing the animal's behavior. An adaptation of this

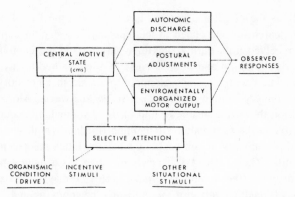

FIG. 1.3.   Scheme of motivational organization in mature animal postulated by Bindra (1969, p. 1073), showing interrelations of the central motive state (CMS) with internal organismic conditions and environmental incentive stimuli and sensory and motor mechanisms involved in the organization of response. (From Bindra, (1969)—Copyright by the New York Academy of Sciences. Reprinted by permission.)

model to deal with the development of motivation, starting with the newborn, would require modifications with respect to each of these component processes. The data I have reviewed and additional data on suckling provide some ideas as to the nature of these modifications.

In the newborn and young animal, CMS's are relatively nonspecific and are more dependent on external stimulation than in the mature animal. Evidence for this proposal comes from studies of suckling in newborn rats and kittens in which it has been shown that an internal physiological state corresponding to "hunger" in the mature animal plays no role in suckling during the first 10 days and perhaps longer in the rat pup and during the first 3 weeks in the kitten.

Hall, Cramer, and Blass (1977) found that during the first 10 days, rat pups deprived of suckling for 22 hours and those allowed to suckle shortly before testing with an anesthetized mother had similar short latencies to initiate suckling and that both improved at the same rate during this period. After that age, recently suckled pups had longer latencies than pups deprived of suckling, suggesting that perhaps at this age hunger and satiation play a role in whether suckling is initiated. One indication that this might not be the case—which we discuss later—was the fact that the pups that had not suckled overnight and therefore had been without food continued to suckle at the mother's nipples despite the fact that they received no milk during suckling!

Koepke and Pribram (1971) showed a similar phenomenon among kittens during the first 3 weeks after birth. Kittens that were being fed by intubation of milk directly into the stomach suckled as frequently and as long on the nipples of nonlactating females as kittens that received milk during their suckling and they exhibited the entire pattern of nipple-searching, including nuzzling and so forth, as frequently as the nipple-fed kittens. Even after the third week these kittens continued to search for and attach to the nipples of the dry females as often as kittens that received milk during suckling, but they did not continue to suckle long. Similarly, Anokhin and Shuleikina (1977) have noted highly active EEG patterns associated with vigorous attempts to suckle that are not different in satiated and "hungry" kittens during the first 2½ to 3 weeks. Moreover, during the same period they were unable to find medial hypothalamic neurons that are normally active at the termination of suckling (medial hypothalamic inhibitory neurons) and presumably inhibit suckling when the kitten has taken a sufficient amount of milk. They write: "The newborn kitten has a natural hyperphagia. The immaturity of the inhibitory system (Hm⁻) may also explain these peculiarities of feeding behavior of an intact newborn animal, namely, its particular greed for food. During the first day of its life the kitten sucks almost incessantly (natural hyperphagia) [p. 413]." According to their findings, inhibition of suckling by food intake does not mature until the third week. There is strong sensory input and EEG activity associated with nipple grasping and suckling, but there is no evidence that these would not appear in the absence of milk ingestion. The study of Koepke and Pribram (1971) has shown that the ingestion of milk during suckling does not begin to play a role in regulating the duration of suckling until after the third week and that the anticipation of obtaining milk does not play a role in initiating suckling even later.

Taken together, these findings in young rats and kittens indicate that there does not appear to be a physiologically based (e.g., hunger) contribution to the CMS; the CMS is largely stimulus-generated, and in the case of suckling the stimulus is a combination of oral factors that does not even include milk ingestion. Approach to the mother and nipple searching, grasping, and sucking are motivated by suckling deprivation rather than food deprivation. This motivation has recently been employed by several investigators to study early learning and retention in rat pups between the age of 7 days and weaning at 25 days of age. Kenny and Blass (1976) deprived pups of access to a lactating mother for 24 hours, then trained them to crawl through one of two arms of a Y maze to suckle from the dry teat of their anesthetized mother. The opportunity to suckle was an effective reward, promoting learning of the Y maze, whereas simply arriving at the mother and meeting a covered nipple was ineffective. Amsel, Burdette, and Letz (1976), using a 12-hour suckling-deprivation period in 10-day-old pups, measured the speed of crawling the length of a straight alley to reach an anesthetized mother's nipple and suck from it. Suckling-rewarded trials resulted in increased speed to cover the distance to the mother's teat, whereas nonrewarded trials extinguished this response and decreased speeds to those at the initiation of training. Furthermore, this study showed that exposing pups to the odor of the mother alone was not sufficient to promote learning or to retard extinction.

The fact that suckling a dry nipple is sufficient "reward" for learning to occur indicates that 12 and 24 hours of suckling deprivation, apart from the possible accompanying "hunger" from the food deprivation, could serve to motivate pups to crawl to the mother's nipple. There is the possibility that food deprivation is also a motivating factor in this situation and that pups were operating under both motivating conditions, only one of which was "rewarded" by suckling the nipple. Williams, Rosenblatt, and Hall (1977) have examined whether suckling deprivation is "motivating" by depriving 20-day-old pups of suckling as well as dish food and water for 20 hours (i.e., hungry and suckling-deprived pups), of suckling from the mother but with dish food and water available (i.e., pups that were not hungry but were suckling deprived), and of neither the mother nor dish food and water (i.e., neither hungry nor suckling-deprived pups) and compared their readiness to suckle from the dry nipples of an anesthetized mother. Only those pups that were deprived of suckling immediately attached to the nipples of the anesthetized mothers, whether or not they had fed from dishes; those that had suckled from the mother during the 20 hours were much less interested in attaching to nipples. The same has been found to be true of 25-day-old pups. Until they are weaned, therefore, pups are motivated to initiate suckling because of suckling stimulation, not because they are hungry.

Pups suckling a dry nipple can continue to suck almost interminably (Hall, unpublished), although normal suckling bouts on a lactating mother terminate after about 30 minutes. This suggests that although suckling is not initiated by hunger, it may be controlled with respect to its duration by milk ingestion. Two studies by Hall and Rosenblatt (in press) investigate this question.

Hall devised a method for feeding controlled amounts of milk to pups while they suckled from a dry nipple of an anesthetized mother. The tip of a catheter was passed through the pup's lower jaw and emerged at the upper surface of its tongue where small amounts of milk, equal to the amounts normally ejected by the mother, could be injected into the pup's throat. Pups responded to each milk injection by exhibiting the normal "stretch response" that accompanies natural milk ejections and swallowing (Drewett, Statham, & Wakerly, 1974). Using this procedure with pups 5, 10, 15, and 20 days of age, and testing the effects of 3 durations of suckling deprivation, pups were allowed to suckle and take milk until they released the nipple, after which they were observed for 3 minutes while an attempt was made to reattach them to the nipples.

The results of this study for an 8-hour suckling deprivation indicate that the factors that regulate the duration and termination of suckling undergo developmental changes between 5 and 20 days of age. Among 5- and 10-day-old pups the waning of the stretch response prevents further milk intake and results in pups releasing the nipple. As shown in Fig. 1.4, in more than 75% of the 5- and 10-day-old pups, waning of the stretch response preceded termination of

BEHAVIORS AT THE TERMINATION OF SUCKLING
(% OF PUPS)

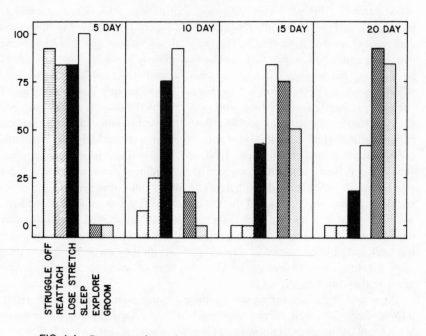

FIG. 1.4.   Percentage of pups showing various behaviors during the last two milk deliveries of diet by intraoral tube, while suckling from anesthetized mother. Behaviors observed during 3-minute posttermination interval. (From Hall and Rosenblatt, (1977). Suckling behavior and intake control in the developing rat pup. Journal of Comparative and Physiological Psychology, 91: 1232–1247. Copyright 1977 by the American Psychological Association. Reprinted by permission.)

suckling, and before waning, milk intake was more than twice the amount taken during ad lib suckling from the mother. Although nearly all the milk ingested was present in the pups' stomachs at the end of suckling, pups continued to suckle until the stretch response waned, and, in the case of 5-day-olds, milk was regurgitated from the mouth, blocking respiration, before the pups released the nipple. The 10-day-olds had equally full stomachs at the end of sucking, and milk dribbled from their mouths, but not until the stretch response waned did most of them give up the nipple. Termination of suckling is not regulated, therefore, in any direct way by stomach contents (i.e., distention), although stomach distention may influence waning of the stretch response (Glenn & Erickson, 1976).

The 15-day-old pups terminated suckling either as a consequence of the waning of the stretch response (40%, Fig. 1.4) or before the stretch response had waned (60%). Milk ingestion amounted to more than 8% body weight at termination of suckling, twice the amount normally taken during a suckling from the mother. The majority of these pups therefore responded to stomach load, but it proved to be a poor regulator of milk intake. This group may be considered a transition group in which waning of the stretch response continues to play a role in regulating the termination of suckling but stomach load appears to be the principal determinant.

The 20-day-old pups showed almost complete regulation of the termination of suckling by milk intake: Nearly all (65%, Fig. 1.4) terminated suckling before the stretch response had waned, when they had ingested about 5% of their body weight, the amount taken when suckling from the mother. The more recent study by Hall and Rosenblatt (in press), in which nutritive (half-and-half) and nonnutritive (saline) stomach preloads were given to 10- and 20-day-olds before they suckled on an anesthetized mother, indicates that it is not simply gastric distention that terminates suckling in 20-day-olds but some chemical or nutritional effect of the preload. Among 10-day-olds the nutritional difference between the preloads does not affect their milk intake differentially.

There were other differences between 5- and 10-day-olds compared to 15- and 20-day-olds following termination of suckling (Fig. 1.4). Among 5-day-olds and 10-day-olds, 75% and 25%, respectively, were ready to reattach to nipples almost immediately, but none of the 15- and 20-day-olds reattached when held to the nipple. Further, the younger pups engaged in little exploration or grooming after feeding, and most fell asleep within 3 minutes, whereas the 15- and 20-day-olds increasingly explored the surroundings and groomed, after which they fell asleep. By 20 days, pups were exhibiting the adult pattern of postingestion behavior.

Summarizing these findings, it appears that the motivating factor for the *initiation of suckling* throughout the first 25 days is oral–phatyngeal stimulation: At 20 days of age, when nutritive preload reduces the amount of milk ingested during subsequent suckling, it does not affect the latency for attaching to the nipple (Hall & Rosenblatt, in press). Between 10 and 15 days of age stomach loading by ingested milk begins to play a role in terminating sucking, and the effect appears to be based on distention rather than nutritional or osmotic factors (Drewett & Cordall, 1976). Earlier, ingested milk may play a role in the waning of the stretch response and swallowing; however, a large amount of milk is required to terminate suckling, and the most obvious effect is through the regurgitation of the excess milk that interferes with respiration. After 15 days of age nutritional factors rather than stomach load alone influences the termination of suckling. At all ages the ingestion of milk causes pups to become lethargic soon after terminating suckling. Hofer (1972) also found that 14-day-old pups preloaded with an overload of nonnutritive substance (Maalox) became behaviorally inactive (i.e., slept) for up to an hour after the preloading. Pups 5 to 15 days in the study by Hall and Rosenblatt (1977) fell asleep within 3 minutes of terminating feeding, probably owing to stomach load, because pups suckling a dry nipple can remain awake for long periods. With reduced milk ingestion, and when termination of suckling is under nutritive control, 20-day-olds are able to remain awake longer after terminating suckling and during this period exhibit exploration and grooming; eventually, however, they, too, fall asleep.

The CMS receives little contribution from a physiological state corresponding to hunger in the young rat; the principal influences on suckling are sensory ones. Throughout the suckling period oral–pharyngeal sensory stimuli regulate the initiation of suckling, largely through "suckling deprivation" and "suckling satisfaction"; termination of suckling is initially regulated by the waning of the stretch response after repeated elicitation by milk ingestion and, perhaps, through some as yet unidentified gastric distention effect on this response. Later, gastric filling and nutritional factors regulate the duration of suckling. Throughout, however, general arousal plays an important role in initiating suckling, and dearousal (i.e., sleep) plays an important role in making pups unresponsive to stimuli that normally activate suckling. Satinoff and Stanley (1963) and James and Rollins (1965) reported similar effects of gastric loading on arousal in puppies. In 20-day-old rat pups there is the first indication that the dearousal effect of gastric loading can be modulated by nutritional factors so as to have a more specific effect on suckling, allowing other activities (i.e., exploration, grooming) to be spared, at least for a short period after terminating.

2. *Motivational bases of huddling and home orientation.* During an early stage, as we have seen, huddling and home orientation are based on thermotactile stimulation. There is some ambiguity in the term "thermal responsiveness": Some investigators have taken the term to mean thermoregulation (Leonard, 1974) and have referred to this stage as "physiological" (Alberts & Brunjes, 1978). The implication is that responsiveness is not mediated by thermal receptors but by the direct effect of ambient thermal conditions on surface and core temperature. The fact that thermal orientation often leads a newborn into a warm ambient temperature and that this in turn results in an increase in body temperature (Alberts, 1978a; Cosnier, 1965; Fowler & Kellogg, 1975; Jeddi, 1970) points only to the outcome not to the mechanism of thermal orientation. It is implied, however, that the motivating condition is a thermoregulatory one—a lowered core temperature that activates the newborn to find a warmer region.

Freeman and Rosenblatt (1978a) view thermal orientation as a sensory-based phenomena in which thermal receptors, concentrated largely around the mouth and nose region in the kitten, respond to thermal stimulation by evoking approach toward warmth and withdrawal from cold. Welker (1959) applied heat from a lamp to puppies and found an immediate response that would be unlikely if increase in body temperature were the basis of the response. Among rat pups warmth and cold evoke responses of which the latencies are too short to reflect changes in body temperature, although it is quite clear that over a period such changes do take place and are associated with increased ultrasonic calling (Allin & Banks, 1971; Okon, 1971).

In cats, thermal receptors are responsive to prolonged stimulation by cold and warm stimuli, and the effect is such that under continued cold stimulation thresholds for response to cold increase whereas those for warmth decrease; the converse threshold changes occur under prolonged warm stimulation (Kenshalo, Duncan, Weymark, 1967; Kenshalo, Hensel, Graziade, & Fruhstorfer, 1971). Thus animals exposed to cold are highly sensitive to slightly warmer stimuli and those exposed to warmth are highly sensitive to slightly cooler stimuli. Such animals are able to orient towards a species-typical thermoneutral zone solely on the basis of thermosensory stimulation.

Thermotactile stimulation is therefore a source of stimulation for huddling and home orientation that can function like nipple stimulation in the scheme proposed in Fig. 1.5 as a major input to the CMS underlying these patterns of behavior. In the case of huddling, separation from the huddle exposes the newborn rat to a lowered ambient temperature than the huddle (Alberts, 1978b; Cosnier, 1965) and provides the stimulating condition motivating it to become active. In the case of early home orientation (Fowler & Kellogg, 1975), removal from the nest exposes the newborn to a lower ambient temperature and has the same motivating effect. The behavior that follows is determined largely by situational factors that differ in huddling and home orientation. The huddle is likely to produce a thermal gradient extending a short distance, and the newborn coming into contact with this gradient is able to orient toward the huddle and crawl to it. Unless the thermal gradient to the nest is quite steep, the newborn is likely to pivot a good deal before picking up the "thermal trail to the home." Under both conditions, however, arrival at the huddle and at the nest terminate the activity, and the settling reaction occurs.

Cooling therefore plays two roles: First, it establishes a CMS (in combination, perhaps, with the state of arousal resulting from its effect on body temperature) that instigates newborn activity, and second, it heightens sensory responsiveness to slightly warmer temperatures and therefore guides the newborn toward the source of warmth. Like oral stimulation during suckling, cooling during huddling and home orientation plays a role in determining the newborn's sequence of responses to reach warmth.

At an early age in all the species I have discussed, olfactory stimuli associated with the mother, siblings, and home region acquire the same motivating and incentive properties as stimuli associated with suckling and as thermotactile stimuli associated with huddling, home orientation, and nonsuckling responses to the mother (Alberts, 1976; Cheal, 1975; Rosenblatt, 1971). I have traced how

MOTIVATIONAL   ORGANIZATION
OF   FEEDING   IN   THE   NEWBORN

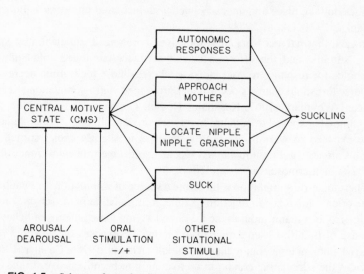

FIG. 1.5.   Scheme of postulated motivational organization at an earlier stage of development in an altricial newborn. The scheme depicts the motivational organization of suckling in the rat pup during the first 2 to 3 weeks. Note modifications in organismic condition (arousal to dearousal), incentive stimuli (oral stimulation +/−), and selective attention (stimulus sensitivity).

olfactory stimuli from the mother gradually are incorporated in the kitten's pattern of home orientation, and Alberts (1976) and Alberts and Brunjes (1978) and Devor and Schneider (1974) have traced this process in the huddling of rat pups and in the hamster's nest orientation, respectively. As discussed earlier, the process underlying the growth of effectiveness of olfactory stimuli as motivating and incentive stimuli in the newborn's responses to its environment has not yet been studied extensively, and the available evidence allows the possibility that simple exposure to odors is sufficient to establish their potency (Leon et al., 1977). Whatever the mechanism underlying the development of responses to olfactory stimuli from species mates, it is clear that apart from inherently aversive olfactory stimulants and those that at high concentrations become aversive, odors gain their effect through experience (Freeman & Rosenblatt, 1978b; Leon, 1975), which may be the reason why individual recognition is often mediated by odors among animals. It is this distinction between odors and thermal stimuli that Alberts and Brunjes (in press) have in mind when they refer to the one as psychological and the other as physiological.

In the scheme shown in Fig. 1.4 olfactory stimulation would be the incentive stimulus that activates the CMS and simultaneously serves in orienting the young toward the incentive (i.e., the mother, siblings, and nest or home region). In reality it is the absence of familiar odor that serves as the motivating stimulus in all the olfactory-based responses that we have discussed, and it is the presence of such odors that quiets animals and causes them to come to rest. To reach the incentive they must follow the olfactory trail, and in this sense olfaction serves both as instigator and orienter in the behavior of the young animal.

An important issue is whether olfactory stimulation has any specific responses associated with it or whether it is chiefly an orienting stimulus that enables a young animal to reach a significant feature of its environment where it then responds on the basis of thermotactile stimulation. There are indications that the latter is the case in the kitten during home orientation (Freeman & Rosenblatt, 1978a) and in the rat pup during huddling after the 5th day (Alberts, 1978a; Alberts & Brunjes, 1978), and it may be the case in the pup's response to maternal pheromone, as a recent study by Nyakas and Endroczi (1973) suggests. If this is the case, olfaction-based motivational organization may represent an advance in motivational development in that it would be less directly linked with any particular pattern of response and would therefore be available to several different behavior patterns and several different developing motivational systems—as in fact has been found to be true with respect to the young animal's response to the mother, siblings, and nest among rats.

3. *Autonomic responses (emotional responsiveness).*   Thus far we have referred mainly to sensorimotor manifestations of motivational states (CMS), although earlier we noted that these could not be separated from autonomic responses manifest through vocalization and kinds of movements indicating distress or calm in newborn. In his scheme in Fig. 1.3 Bindra (1969) gives equal importance to autonomic discharge and sensorimotor response as representatives of CMS. The difficulty of observing such autonomic responses compared to the ease of observing sensorimotor responses has retarded our understanding of how these responses are involved in early behavioral development.

Hofer and his associates (Hofer, 1972, 1975) have pioneered the study of autonomic responses and their significance in early reactions of rat pups to the mother. As early as 4 days of age prolonged separation from the mother (i.e., 24 hours) results in profound autonomic reactions characterized chiefly by an immediate reduction in cardiac rate, which declines even further as the separation continues. The reaction is most marked in 14-day-old pups, in which heart rate declines nearly 20% in 2 hours and 40% over 12 hours. This finding presented the opportunity to study the nature of stimulation from the mother, which maintains the pup's normal cardiac rate, and to investigate the mechanism underlying stimulational control of this autonomic response.

After thermal factors were ruled out by the finding that maintaining pups at normal nest temperature did not prevent the precipitous decline in cardiac rate, feeding was investigated, and it was found that introducing a single tube feeding of milk at the end of 2 hours, when cardiac rate had already declined significantly, reversed the trend and caused an acceleration to near-normal heart rate, which persisted for as long as 4 hours when 2.0 ml of milk was given. Koch and Arnold (1976) have subsequently shown that contact with a nonlactating mother is additive with tube feeding in its effect on cardiac rate and that the two cause a greater increase than either alone.

In a more recent study Compton, Koch, and Arnold (1977) have shown that in 10-day-old rat pups maternal odor may function equivalently to feeding in reversing the cardiac deceleration that follows maternal separation. At the end of 2 hours of maternal separation pups were exposed in an olfactory chamber to the odor of their own mother, that of a nonlactating female, or no odor at all. Only pups presented with maternal odor showed cardiac acceleration, which was maintained by repeated presentation of the odor at 15-minute intervals. It should be noted that the pups had been separated from the mother by removing them from the nest and placing them in the olfactory chamber, raising the possibility that not only were responses to the mother being investigated but an aspect of nest orientation behavior was also involved, although as we have noted the two may not differ with respect to the essential stimulus component that defines the nest for the pup.

In a significant statement referring to their earlier work Compton et al. (1977) note, "Since it has been shown that hourly feedings (by intubation) and the presence of a nonlactating foster mother do constitute sufficient conditions to maintain a high cardiac rate, some form of tactile stimulation would appear to contribute to the maintenance of a normal cardiac rate [p. 772]." They suggest therefore that the developmental background for the effectiveness of maternal odor in maintaining cardiac function may be tactile and perhaps thermotactile in association with the gastric factor that Hofer and his associates have found to have a direct effect on cardiac activity via sympathetic pathways. There are, however, few studies that have investigated this and other autonomic responses in response to thermal and tactile stimuli, especially during suckling, huddling, and home orientation. That this would be a fruitful line of research is indicated in studies that have shown that huddling maintains a high metabolic rate in rat pups, implicating therefore a variety of autonomic thermoregulatory responses (Alberts, 1978b; Cosnier, 1965).

We are familiar with attempts at tracing continuity in behavioral development through sensorimotor mechanisms that change as a result of sensory and motor maturation and various kinds of experience. Less familiar is the role of autonomic responses to sensory stimuli in behavioral development. Yet is it likely that sensorimotor responses are associated with autonomic responses during all phases of behavioral development and that they have both nonspecific feedback relations with CMS's and specific contributions to ongoing sensorimotor responses.

SUMMARY

The sensorimotor processes and motivational basis during early behavioral development among altricial newborn of selected mammalian species were analyzed through an examination of the development of home or nest orientation, huddling among siblings, and suckling and nonsuckling responses to the mother. The newborn's earliest behavioral adjustments are organized in relation to thermotactile stimuli, and their physical and social environment is highly structured in these sensory modalities in the form of thermal gradients and various textures, shapes, and surfaces; by responding to these forms of stimulation the newborn is able to adjust to the most significant objects in its proximal social environment. Early in development olfactory-based responses appear in each of these areas of the newborn's functioning; the earliest evidence of olfactory functioning is in suckling. Olfactory stimuli are interwoven with thermotactile stimuli in the organization of each of these patterns of behavior, and there is evidence that olfaction gains its importance by simple exposure and by association with these earlier forms of stimulation. The integration of these sensory stimuli differs in each of these patterns of behavior and the age at which olfactory-based responses are established varies in the different areas.

The motivational organization of the newborn was discussed in relation to the scheme proposed by Bindra (1969) for the mature animal. Suckling in the rat and to a lesser extent in the kitten was analyzed to determine the characteristics of motivational organization in this area of functioning and its relationship to other areas of newborn functioning. During the first 3 weeks suckling is not based on a specific physiological state of hunger but is organized in relation to peripheral oral stimulation that elicits the responses of nipple grasping sucking and the stretch reflex (swallowing). The ingestion of milk during suckling does not directly regulate readiness to feed but does indirectly regulate the newborn's motivational state by its arousal/dearousal properties, both behaviorally and physiologically. Suckling motivation (CMS) is strongly dependent on peripheral sensory stimulation and its absence for initiating and terminating the pattern of behavior.

The motivational bases of huddling and home or nest orientation are initially dependent on motivational states induced by thermotactile stimuli, chiefly the absence of warmth (i.e., cooling) and the absence of contact with soft tactile stimuli. At later ages olfactory-based motivational states begin to play a role, and both unfamiliar odors and the absence of familiar odors motivate the young animal's behavior.

Autonomic responses (emotional responses) are an aspect of the newborn's response to thermotactile and olfactory stimulation and are closely related to the motivational state induced by this stimulation.

During early developmental motivational processes and sensorimotor responses are closely related because of the dual role that sensory stimuli play in inducing motivational states and in eliciting and guiding the newborn's responses to the significant objects in its environment.

ACKNOWLEDGMENTS

The research reported in this article and the writing of the article were supported by USPHS Grant MH-08604 to J. S. Rosenblatt and a Biomedical Research Support Grant. Dr. Warren G. Hall did all of the jointly cited research on suckling in rat pups while a Postdoctoral Training Fellow at the Institute of Animal Behavior supported by MH-05067 except for that cited with Christina Williams, currently a graduate student. I am indebted also to Dr. Natalie C. G. Freeman who did the research on home orientation in kittens and to all three for discussions that led to the ideas presented in this article. Publication number 288 of the Institute of Animal Behavior.

REFERENCES

Alberts, J. R. Olfactory contributions to behavioral development in rodents. In E. Doty (Ed.), *Mammalian olfaction: reproductive processes and behavior.* New York: Academic Press, 1976.

Alberts, J. R. Huddling by rat pups: Multisensory control of contact behavior. *Journal of Comparative and Physiological Psychology,* 1978, *92,* 220−230. (b)

Alberts, J. R. Huddling by rat pups: Group behavioral mechanisms of temperature regulation and energy conservation. *Journal of Comparative and Physiological Psychology,* 1978, *92,* 231−245.

Alberts, J. R. & Brunjes, P. C. Ontogeny of thermal and olfactory determinants of huddling in the rat. *Journal of Comparative and Physiological Psychology,* 1978, *92,* 897−906. (a)

Allin, J. T., & Banks, E. M. Effects of temperature on ultrasound production by infant albino rats. *Developmental Psychobiology,* 1971, *4,* 149−156.

Altman, J., Brunner, R. L., Bulut, F. G., & Sudarshan, K. The development of behavior in normal and brain-damaged infant rats, studies with homing (nest-seeking) as motivation. In A. Vernadakis & N. Weiner (Eds.), *Drugs and the developing brain.* New York: Plenum Press, 1974.

Altman, J., & Sudarshan, K. Postnatal development of locomotion in the laboratory rat. *Animal Behaviour,* 1975, *23,* 896−920.

Altman, J., Sudarshan, K., Das, G. D., McCormick, N., & Barnes, D. The influence of nutrition on neural and behavioral development. III. Development of some motor, particularly locomotor patterns during infancy. *Developmental Psychobiology,* 1971, *4,* 97−114.

Amsel, A., Burdette, D. R., & Letz, R. Appetitive learning, patterned alternation, and extinction in 10-d-old rats with non-lactating suckling as reward. *Nature,* 1976, *262,* 816−818.

Anokhin, P. K. & Shuleikina, K. V. System organization of alimentary behavior in the newborn and the developing cat. *Developmental Psychobiology,* 1977, *10,* 385−419.

Bindra, D. A unified interpretation of emotion and motivation. *Annals of the New York Academy of Sciences,* 1969, *159,* Art. 3, 1071−1083.

Blass, E. M., Teicher, M. H., Cramer, C. P., Bruno, J. P., & Hall, W. G. Olfactory, thermal and tactile controls of suckling in preaudial and previsual rats. *Journal of Comparative and Physiological Psychology,* 1977, *91,* 1248−1260.

Bulut, F. G., & Altman, J. Spatial and tactile discrimination learning in infant rats motivated by homing. *Developmental Psychobiology*, 1974, *7*, 465–473.

Campbell, B. A., & Mabry, P. D. Ontogeny of behavioral arousal: A comparative study. *Journal of Comparative and Physiological Psychology*, 1972, *81*, 371–379.

Campbell, B. A., & Raskin, L. A. The ontogeny of behavioral arousal: Role of environmental stimuli. *Journal of Comparative and Physiological Psychology*, 1978, *92*, 176–184.

Cheal, M. Social olfaction: A review of the ontogeny of olfactory influences on vertebrate behavior. *Behavioral Biology*, 1975, *15*, 1–25.

Compton, R. P., Koch, M. D., & Arnold, W. J. Effect of maternal odor on the cardiac rate of maternally separated infant rats. *Physiology and Behavior*, 1977, *18*, 769–773.

Cornwell, C. A. Golden hamster pups adapt to complex rearing odors. *Behavioral Biology*, 1975, *14*, 175–188.

Cornwell, C. A. Selective olfactory exposure alters social and plant odor preferences of immature hamsters. *Behavioral Biology*, 1976, *17*, 131–137.

Cosnier, J. *Le comportement grégaire du rat d'élevage (Étude éthologique)*. Unpublished doctoral dissertation, University of Lyon, 1965.

Crighton, G. W., & Pownall, R. The homeothermic status of the neonatal dog. *Nature* (London), 1974, *251*, 142–144.

Denenberg, V. H. Open-field behavior in the rat: What does it mean? *Annals of the New York Academy of Sciences*, 1969, *159*, Art. 3, 852–859.

Devor, M., & Schneider, G. E. Attraction to home-cage odor in hamster pups: Specificity and changes with age. *Behavioral Biology*, 1974, *10*, 211–221.

Drewett, R. F., & Cordall, K. M. Control of feeding in suckling rats: Effects of glucose and of osmotic stimuli. *Physiology and Behavior*, 1976, *16*, 711–717.

Drewett, R. F., Statham, C., & Wakerley, J. B. A quantitative analysis of the feeding behaviour of suckling rats. *Animal Behaviour*, 1974, *22*, 907–913.

Elliot, O., & Scott, J. P. The development of emotional distress reactions to separation in puppies. *Journal of Genetic Psychology*, 1961, *99*, 3–22.

Ewer, R. F. Suckling behavior in kittens. *Behaviour*, 1959, *15*, 146–162.

Fleischer, S. F., & Turkewitz, G. Effects of neonatal stunting on the physical growth and behavioral development of rats: II. Early and late effects of large litter rearing. *Developmental Psychobiology*, 1979, *12*, 137–147.

Fowler, S. J., & Kellogg, C. Ontogeny of thermoregulatory mechanisms in the rat. *Journal of Comparative and Physiological Psychology*, 1975, *89*, 738–746.

Fox, M. W. Reflex development and behavioral organization. In W. A. Himwich (Ed.), *Developmental neurobiology*. Springfield, Ill.: Thomas, 1970.

Freeman, N. C. G., & Rosenblatt, J. S. The interrelationship between thermal and olfactory stimulation in the development of home orientation in newborn kittens. *Developmental Psychobiology*, 1978a, *11*, 437–457.

Freeman, N. C. G., & Rosenblatt, J. S. Specificity of litter odors in the control of home orientation among kittens. *Developmental Psychobiology*, 1978b, *11*, 459–468.

Fuller, J. L., Easler, C. A., & Banks, E. M. Formation of conditioned avoidance responses in young puppies. *American Journal of Physiology*, 1950, *160*, 462–466.

Glenn, J. F., & Erickson, R. P. Gastric modulation of gustatory afferent activity. *Physiology and Behavior*, 1976, *16*, 561–568.

Gottlieb, G. Ontogenesis of sensory function in birds and mammals. In E. Tobach, L. R. Aronson, & E.Shaw (Eds.), *The biopsychology of development*. New York: Academic Press, 1971.

Gregory, E. H., & Bishop, A. Development of olfactory-guided behavior in the golden hamster. *Physiology and Behavior*, 1975, *15*, 373–376.

Gregory, E. H. and Pfaff, D. W. Development of olfactory-guided behavior in infant rats. *Physiology and Behavior*, 1971, *6*, 573–576.

Hall, W. G. Unpublished manuscript, available from Research Section, North Carolina Division of Mental Health, Box 7532, Raleigh, North Carolina 27611.

Hall, W. G., Cramer, C. P., & Blass, E. M. The ontogeny of suckling in rats: Transitions towards adult ingestion. *Journal of Comparative and Physiological Psychology*, 1977, *91*, 1141–1155.

Hall, W. G., & Rosenblatt, J. S. Suckling behavior and intake control in the developing rat pup. *Journal of Comparative and Physiological Psychology*, 1977, *91*, 1232–1247.

Hall, W. G., & Rosenblatt, J. S. Development of nutritional control of food intake in suckling rat pups. *Behavioral Biology*, in press.

Hofer, M. A. Physiological and behavioural processes in early maternal deprivation. In CIBA Foundation Symposium 8, *Physiology, emotion and psychosomatic illness*. New York: Elsevier, 1972.

Hofer, M. A. The effects of brief maternal separations on behavior and heart rate of two week old rat pups. *Physiology and Behavior*, 1973, *10*, 423–427. (a)

Hofer, M. A. The role of nutrition in the physiological and behavioral effects of early separation on infant rats. *Psychosomatic Medicine*, 1973, *35*, 350–359. (b)

Hofer, M. A. Maternal separation affects infant rat's behavior. *Behavioral Biology*, 1973, *9*, 629–633. (c)

Hofer, M. A. Studies on how early maternal separation produces behavioral change in young rats. *Psychosomatic Medicine*, 1975, *37*, 245–264.

Hofer, M. A., Shair, H., & Singh, P. Evidence that maternal ventral skin substances promote suckling in infant rats. *Physiology and Behavior*, 1976, *17*, 131–136.

Holloway, W. R., Dollinger, M. J., & Denenberg, V. H. *The parturitional environment and later growth and development in the rat*. Paper presented at the meeting of the Eastern Regional Conference on Reproductive Behavior, Saratoga Springs, June 1976.

Ivanitskii, A. M. The morphological investigation of development of conditioned alimentary reaction in rabbits during ontogenesis. *Works Higher Nervous Activity, Physiology Series*, n.d., *4*, 126–141.

James, W. T., & Cannon, D. J. Conditioned avoiding response in puppies. *American Journal of Physiology*, 1952, *168*, 251–253.

James, W. T., & Rollins, J. Effect of various degrees of stomach loading on the suckling response in puppies. *Psychological Reports*, 1965, *17*, 844–846.

Jeddi, E. Comfort de contact et thermorégulation comportementale. *Physiology and Behavior*, 1970, *5*, 1487–1493.

Kenny, J. T., & Blass, E. M. Suckling as incentive to instrumental learning in preweanling rats. *Science*, 1976, *196*, 898–899.

Kenshalo, D. R., Duncan, D. G., & Weymark, C. Thresholds for thermal stimulation of the inner thigh, footpad, and face of cats. *Journal of Comparative and Physiological Psychology*, 1967, *63*, 133–138.

Kenshalo, D. R., Hensel, H., Graziadei, P., & Fruhstorfer, H. On the anatomy and physiology and psychophysics of the cat's temperature-sensing system. In R. Dubner & Y. Kawamura (Eds.), *Oral–facial sensory and motor mechanisms*. New York: Appleton-Century-Crofts, 1971.

Koch, M. D. & Arnold, W. J. Maternal and nutritional factors in maintenance of infant rat cardiac rate following maternal separation. *Physiology and Behavior*, 1976, *16*, 521–527.

Koepke, J. E., & Pribram, K. H. Effect of milk on the maintenance of sucking behavior in kittens from birth to six months. *Journal of Comparative and Physiological Psychology*, 1971, *75*, 363–377.

Kovach, H. A., & Kling, A. Mechanisms of neonate sucking behavior in the kitten. *Animal Behaviour*, 1967, *15*, 91–101.

Leon, M. Dietary control of maternal pheromone in the lactating rat. *Physiology and Behavior*, 1975, *14*, 311–319.

Leon, M. Filial responsiveness to olfactory cures in Rattus Norvegicus. In J. S. Rosenblatt, R. A.

Hinde, E. Shaw, & C. G. Beer (Eds.), *Advances in the study of behavior*. New York: Academic Press, 1978.

Leon, M., Croskerry, P. G., & Smith, G. K. Thermal control of mother-young contract in rats. *Physiology and Behavior*. 1978, *21*, 793−811.

Leon, M., Galef, B. G., Jr., & Behse, J. H. Establishment of pheromonal bonds and diet choice in young rats by odor pre-exposure. *Physiology and Behavior*, 1977, *18*, 387−391.

Leon, M., & Moltz, H. Maternal pheromone: Discrimination by pre-weanling albino rats. *Physiology and Behavior*, 1971, *7*, 265−267.

Leon, M., & Moltz, H. The development of the pheromonal bond in the albino rat. *Physiology and Behavior*, 1972, *8*, 683−686.

Leonard, C. M. Thermotaxis in golden hamster pups. *Journal of Comparative and Physiological Psychology*, 1974, *86*, 458−469.

Mabry, P. D., & Campbell, B. A. Ontogeny of serotonergic inhibition of behavioral arousal in the rat. *Journal of Comparative and Physiological Psychology*, 1974, *86*, 193−201.

Moorcroft, W. H. Ontogeny of forebrain inhibition of behavioral arousal in the rat. *Brain Research*, 1971, *35*, 513−522.

Moorcroft, W. H., Lytle, L. D., & Campbell, B. A. Ontogeny of starvation-induced behavioral arousal in the rat. *Journal of Comparative and Physiological Psychology*, 1971, *75*, 59−67.

Noirot, E. Ultrasounds and maternal behavior in small rodents. *Developmental Psychobiology*, 1972, *5*, 371−387.

Nyakas, C. & Endroczi, E. Olfaction guided approaching behavior of infantile rats to the mother in maze box. *Acta physiologica Academiae scieniarum hungaricae*, 1970, *38*, 59−65.

Nyakas, C., & Endroczi, E. Learning and memory as a function of age and food deprivation in young rats. *Acta Physiologica Academiae Scientiarum Hungaricae*, 1973, *41*, 163−173.

Okon, E. E. The temperature relations of vocalization in infant golden hamsters and Wistar rats. *Journal of Zoology*, 1971, *164*, 227−237.

Okon, E. E. Factors affecting ultrasound production in infant rodents. *Journal of Zoology*, 1972, *168*, 139−148.

Randall, P. K., & Campbell, B. A. Ontogeny of behavioral arousal in rats: Effect of maternal and sibling presence. *Journal of Comparative and Physiological Psychology*, 1976, *90*, 453−459.

Rosenblatt, J. S. Suckling and home orientation in the kitten: A comparative developmental study. In E. Tobach, L. R., Aronson, & E. Shaw (Eds.), *The biopsychology of development*. New York: Academic Press, 1971.

Rosenblatt, J. S. Stages in the early behavioural development of altricial young of selected species of non-primate mammals. In P. P. G. Bateson & R. A. Hinde (Eds.), *Growing points in ethology*. Cambridge: Cambridge University Press, 1976.

Rosenblatt, J. S., Turkewitz, G., & Schneirla, T. C. Early socialization in the domestic cat as based on feeding and other relationships between female and young. In B. F. Foss (Ed.), *Determinants of infant behaviour*. London: Methuen, 1961.

Rosenblatt, J. S., Turkewitz, G., & Schneirla, T. C. Development of home orientation in newly born kittens. *Transactions of the New York Academy of Sciences*, 1969, *31*, 231−250.

Salas, M., Schapiro, S., & Guzman-Flores, C. Development of olfactory bulb discrimination between maternal and food odors. *Physiology and Behavior*, 1970, *5*, 1216−1264.

Satinoff, E., & Stanley, W. C. Effect of stomach loading on sucking behavior in neonatal puppies. *Journal of Comparative and Physiological Psychology*, 1963, *56*, 66−68.

Schapiro, S., & Salas, M. Behavioral response of infant rats to maternal odor. *Physiology and Behavior*, 1970, *5*, 815−817.

Schneirla, T. C., Rosenblatt, J. S., & Tobach, E. Maternal behavior in the cat. In H. L. Rheingold (Ed.), *Maternal behavior in mammals*. New York: Wiley, 1963.

Scott, J. P. Critical periods in the development of social behavior in puppies. *Psychosomatic Medicine*, 1958, *20*, 42−54.

Scott, J. P. Critical periods in behavioral development. *Science*, 1962, *138*, 949–958.

Scott, J. P., Stewart, J. M., & DeGhett, V. J. Critical periods in the organization of systems. *Developmental Psychobiology*, 1974, *7*, 489–513.

Sczerzenie, V., & Hsiao, S. Development of locomotion toward home nesting material in neonatal rats. *Developmental Psychobiology*, 1977, *10*, 315–321.

Singh, P. J., & Tobach, E. Olfactory bulbectomy and nursing behavior in rat pups (Wistar DAB). *Developmental Psychobiology*, 1975, *8*, 151–164.

Singh, P. J., Tucker, A. M., & Hofer, M. A. Effects of nasal $ZnSO_4$ irrigation and olfactory bulbectomy on rat pups. *Physiology and Behavior*, 1976, *17*, 373–382.

Stanley, W. C., Bacon, W. E., & Fehr, C. Discriminated instrumental learning in neonatal dogs. *Journal of Comparative and Physiological Psychology*, 1970, *70*, 335–343.

Teicher, M. H., & Blass, E. M. Suckling in newborn rats: Eliminated by nipple lavage, reinstated by pup saliva. *Science*, 1976, *193*, 422–425.

Teicher, M. H., & Blass, E. M. The role of olfaction and amniotic fluid in the first suckling response of newborn albino rats. Science, 1977, *198*, 635–636.

Thoman, E. B., & Arnold, W. J. Incubator rearing of infant rats without the mother: Effects on adult emotionality and learning. *Developmental Psychobiology*, 1968, *1*, 219–222.

Tobach, E. Developmental aspects of chemoception in the wistar (DAB) rat: Tonic processes. *Annals of the New York Academy of Sciences*, 1977, *290*, 226–269.

Tobach, E., Rouger, Y., & Schneirla, T. C. Development of olfactory function in the rat pup. *American Zoologist*, 1967, *7*, 792–793.

Toropova, N. V. Technique of artificial feeding of puppies in the early postnatal period. *Pavlov Journal of Higher Nervous Activity*, 1961, *11*, 137–138.

Welker, W. I. Factors influencing aggregation of neonatal puppies. *Journal of Comparative and Physiological Psychology*, 1959, *52*, 376–380.

Welker, W. I. Analysis of sniffing in the albino rat. *Behaviour*, 1964, *22*, 223–244.

Williams, C. L., Rosenblatt, J. S., & Hall, W. G. *Changing oral factors in the development of suckling*. Paper presented at the meeting of the International Society for Developmental Psychobiology Meeting, Anaheim, November 1977.

2

Motivation, Learning, and Memory in the Ontogeny of Suckling in Albino Rats

Elliott M. Blass, John T. Kenny, Michael Stoloff,
John P. Bruno and Martin H. Teicher
The Johns Hopkins University

W. G. Hall
North Carolina Department of Mental Health

INTRODUCTION

Two strategies have evolved for studying the ontogeny of motivational, associative, and retentive mechanisms in altricial species. One is based on the view that altricial neonates are incompletely formed adults whose motivational, associative, and retentive capacities are likewise primitive. Differences between neonatal and adult performances are thus seen as quantitative only. The infant is thought to live in an overdetermined, protective environment that, through the mother and her nest, meets all its nutritional, hydrational, eliminative, and thermal needs. No environmental pressures are thought to foster either behavioral flexibility or concomitant associative development during the immediate perinatal period. As the neonate's sensorimotor capabilities mature and it becomes increasingly liberated from mother and nest, so, too, "intellectual" capacities develop. Accordingly, at about the time of weaning or shortly thereafter the juvenile has caught up with and is essentially indistinguishable from the adult, as judged by its performance on a number of traditional animal-learning tasks—shock avoidance, for example. It follows therefore that a major task of this approach is to chart the course of adult development and to relate changes in performance to those in neurological and neurochemical ontogeny. The impressive progress attained through this approach has been documented by Campbell and Coulter (1976), and the most recent findings of a number of its leading advocates are admirably presented in the present volume.

An alternative approach rests on the facts that the infant's world is dynamic (Schneirla, 1965); that infants, indeed fetuses (Bradley and Mistretta, 1975), detect and respond to select environmental alterations; and that altricial neonates, within days after birth, can modify their behavior for long periods of time in response to certain environmental contingencies (see Chapter 7). This approach, as most recently discussed by Gottlieb (1976a, 1976b), favors identifying and analyzing the effects of specific, naturally occurring events on the expression of behavior. These events may simply maintain the behavior in question, may facilitate the appearance but not the form of a succeeding behavioral stage, or may actually determine the characteristics of the succeeding behavior.

We have followed this strategy in our efforts to understand the determinants of suckling in albino rats. Suckling lends itself nicely to this form of analysis. It expresses the synchronization of infant and mother positions and motor patterns. It spans the period of rapid infantile growth and differentiation characterized by quantitative and qualitative alterations in sensory (almost all altricial mammals start to see and hear *during* this period) and motor development. The infant's responses toward some of the stable environmental stimuli also change. During the first 7 to 10 days after delivery, the rat mother makes herself readily available to her young, hovers over them, retrieves wayward pups, attends to the nest, and generally spends a great deal of time with the litter. Her behavior gradually changes so that by the third or fourth week postpartum she actively avoids and fends off her active and aggressive preweanlings (Rosenblatt & Lehrman, 1963). Despite all these changes, suckling remains the predominant behavior of awake pups, at least during the first weeks postpartum, and diminishes gradually thereafter, terminating at weaning, when all nutritional and hydrational demands are satisfied by feeding and drinking.

What are the bases of suckling behavior? Are the internal events determining its occurrence and duration analogous to those controlling adult ingestion? What are the external controls? Do they change during the course of ontogeny, especially with the onset of vision, or do they remain invariant? How do the animals' suckling experiences affect future suckling? Do they have any effect at all? Do they simply maintain future suckling or do they affect the range of stimuli that will elicit it? How can we account for the paradox of weaning, where a behavior with a rich history of positive reinforcement no longer occurs?

Our laboratories have undertaken three closely related analytic programs aimed at understanding the different levels of complexity of the suckling act and how each level changes throughout ontogeny. At the simplest level we have sought to identify the proximal environmental stimuli that release, direct, and terminate the consummatory aspect of the suckling act and to discover how the controls exerted by these specific, identifiable stimuli change during development. The second level of analysis is concerned with the appetitive components of suckling—that is, those factors that influence the animal's approach to the dam, more specifically to her nipple region, from a distance. The consummatory and appetitive analyses document the animal's steady state behavior at any given point in time. By comparing behaviors from point to point we can identify periods of behavioral change and seek the possible behavioral events, if any, that may either precipitate or determine the form of change. This is the task of the third approach.

In order to prepare the reader for the bulk of this chapter, which concerns progress realized along the second and third paths, we will briefly summarize that of the first approach. A more complete report of this aspect of our research has recently appeared (Blass, Hall, & Teicher, in press). We have identified the external and internal controls of suckling behavior and their changes during development by anesthetizing the dam and allowing her nondeprived and suckling-deprived (4–24 hour) pups to locate and attach to her nonlactating nipples. This paradigm has allowed us to manipulate the mother's sensory characteristics to reveal that olfaction is the dominant sensory modality for suckling elicitation. Specifically, Teicher (1977), Teicher and Blass (1976, 1977), and Blass, Teicher, Cramer, Bruno, and Hall (1977) have shown that removing a scent from the anesthetized mother's ventrum virtually eliminates nipple attachment in her young of all ages; and reinstating a vacuum distillate of the wash or of rat pup saliva reinstates suckling to prewash levels. Hofer, Shair, and Singh (1976) have found that washing the anesthetized mother's ventrum eliminates nipple attachment. Blass et al. (1977) and Teicher (1977) have also shown that altering the thermal (by cooling, cf. Hofer et al., 1976), tactile (by shaving), or both qualities of the anesthetized mother generally did not interfere with nipple attachment.

Our laboratories have also studied the development of internal controls over suckling. Hall and Rosenblatt (1977), for example, have demonstrated that nutritional factors do not appear to exert control over nipple attachment or intake volume until about 15 days of age and appear to reach adult levels of sensitivity at about 20 days of age. Likewise, Drewett and Cordall (1976) and Bruno (1977) have demonstrated that the anorexogenic action of cellular dehydration on suckling follows a remarkably similar time course of development. Finally, cholecystokinin, a gut hormone thought to be a potent inhibitor of feeding in adult rats (Antin, Gibbs, Holt, Young, & Smith, 1975), does not influence intake volume until about 15 days of age and reaches adult levels of sensitivity at about 3 weeks of age (Blass, Beardsley, & Hall, 1979). In short, three independent lines of evidence converge on the conclusion, in regard to the consummatory aspects of suckling, that neither nipple attachment nor intake volume is influenced by internal stimuli that are powerful inhibitors of normal adult feeding behaviors. All three controls seem to develop simultaneously, appearing at about 15 days of age and attaining adult levels of control at about 3 weeks postpartum.

THE ANALYSIS OF APPETITIVE BEHAVIOR

The second level of analysis is concerned with the infant's behavior when it is removed from the immediate stimulation provided by the mother. This is assessed by allowing rats of different ages to choose different aspects of the mother for contact. By using a Y maze we (Kenny & Blass, 1977) have allowed the infants to inform us which aspects of the mother provide incentives sufficient to support instrumental learning throughout ontogeny and which aspects of the mother become differentially preferred during ontogeny. We are thus exploiting the infant's impressive associative capacities (Amsel, Burdette, & Letz, 1976) to identify age-related preferences independent of immediate proximal stimulation. Stated differently, this series of experiments identifies and analyzes the appetitive and motivational aspects of suckling. The first two levels of analysis study the characteristics of suckling at a given age and the transitions from age to age. The third seeks to learn how specific, biologically relevant experiences maintain, permit, faciliate, or determine the changes in suckling behavior that are the hallmark of rats at a particular chronological age.

The analysis of appetitive behavior has been considerably simplified through the development of the Y maze (Kenny & Blass, 1977) shown in Fig. 2.1. Rats 7 to 24 days of age are placed in the start box and are allowed to approach the Y portion of the maze. In our initial experiments they chose between the opportunity to suckle a nonlactating nipple on one side of the maze or to root into the ventrum covered with a thin layer of gauze. The gauze prevented nipple access but

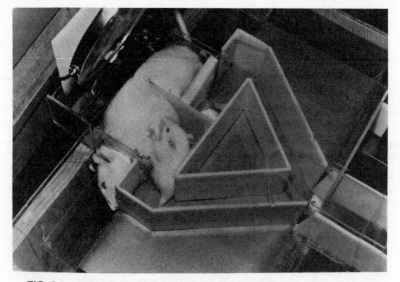

FIG. 2.1. Photograph of Y maze utilized to study appetitive behavior in neonatal rats.

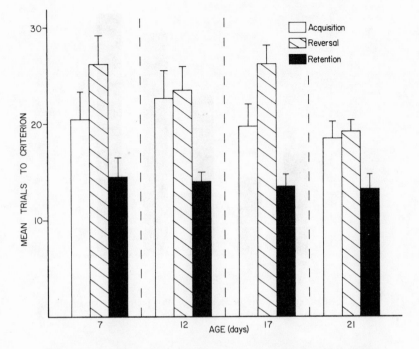

FIG. 2.2. Acquisition, reversal, and retention performances of neonatal rats of various ages. "Correct" response was rewarded with 30 seconds suckling from a nonlactating nipple. Criterion was 8 of 10 correct responses with a ceiling of 50 trials. (From Kenny and Blass, ©(1977) by the American Association for the Advancement of Science.)

allowed the odors on the ventrum to reach the pup at the start box and choice point. Fig. 2.2 makes a number of points concerning motivational, associative, and retentive mechanisms in rats 7 to 23 days of age. First, a nonlactating nipple provides sufficient incentive for 24-hour deprived rats to move toward, locate, and remember its position in the maze. Thus rats as young as 7 days of age are motivated to suckle. They performed an operant that permitted the occurrence of a consummatory response (Teitelbaum, 1966, pp. 566–567).

In regard to associative capabilities during development, even 7-day-old rats, whose neurological and neurochemical development is primitive and whose encephalization process has barely begun, solved a spatial (left–right) discrimination problem. Moreover, there were no age-related improvements in either acquisition, reversal, or retention performances. The fact that 7-day-old rats reversed their learned preference strongly suggests that animals of this age are at least as capable as older rats in inhibiting certain classes of response tendencies and that the search for putative "inhibitory" neurotransmitters or systems must start in even younger animals (see Chapter 8).

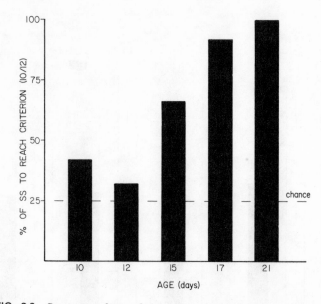

FIG. 2.3. Percentage of rats of various ages that preferred a lactating to a nonlactating nipple. Each column represents 12 rats.

But let us return to the development of appetitive, motivated behavior. Recall from our earlier discussion that the nascent internal controls over nipple attachment and intake volume emerge at about two weeks postpartum and seem to attain adult levels of sensitivity over these consummatory components of suckling shortly before the third week. We now ask whether there are aspects of the appetitive components that follow a similar developmental time course. To answer this question Kenny, Stoloff, Bruno, and Blass (in press) utilized a tongue cannula described by Hall and Rosenblatt (1977) to allow experimental injection of a small bolus of milk into the posterior third of the tongue, the area where milk is normally delivered by the mother. Thus, pups so equipped, when choosing the mother's ''lactating'' nipple in the maze, received a 0.05-ml pulse of milk delivered for 10 seconds during the 30-second suckling bout. When choosing the ''nonlactating'' side, the pups suckled a nonlactating nipple for 30 seconds. If the internal stimuli that control appetite develop in parallel with the consummatory controls, then rats younger than 15 days of age should not prefer the lactating over the nonlactating teat. Starting at about Day 15, however, they should. Figure 2.3 demonstrates this sequence of development. Rats 10 and 12 days of age did not perform above chance levels even though they are capable of discrimination learning (Fig. 2.2). As shown in Fig. 2.3, 67% of the 15-day-old rats chose the lactating side. Preference for the lactating nipple is unanimous by 21 days postpartum.

Thus, two aspects of the infant's perception of its mother are revealed. First, there is a hierarchy of preferred activities that the baby will engage in vis-à-vis the mother. Suckling is preferred to rooting into the gauze-covered fur at all ages studied. The neonates demonstrate their clear knowledge of nipple position and the anticipation of suckling, because they learn the side of the maze that provides the opportunity to suckle; and when the side is reversed, they follow to the reversed position. Second, appetitive and consummatory components appear to develop in parallel. Until about 15 days of age nipple attachment appears to be determined, in large part, by the sensory characteristics of the dam. Intake volume is controlled by the availability of the mother and her milk supply. In short, the mother and not the young are rate-limiting volume ingestion (see Blass et al., 1979; Hall & Rosenblatt, 1977, for a fuller discussion). Likewise, appetite toward the nipple is not contingent upon milk delivery in rats 10 and 12 days of age. The appetite appears to be for the opportunity to suckle and not necessarily to obtain nutrient. Starting at about two weeks of age, however, and especially thereafter, the nipple is perceived *also* as a nutritive source.

THE ROLE OF EXPERIENCE IN THE ONTOGENY OF SUCKLING AND INGESTIVE BEHAVIORS

Kenny, et al. asked whether suckling and milk delivery had to occur, when internal controls were starting to affect appetitive behavior, in order for the lactating nipple preference to develop. Stated differently, they sought to determine whether the ingestive act had to occur during the appearance of the hunger system in order for this system to gain control over suckling behavior. Hogan (1973, 1977) has demonstrated that the hunger system in chicks must be paired with the pecking act in order for chicks to discriminate food from sand. Accordingly, rats at 11 days of age were removed from their mothers and raised on an intragastric infusion pump (see Hall, 1975a, 1975b, for complete details) until 16 days of age, at which time the food delivery system was disengaged and a tongue cannula installed. The rats were then deprived for 24 hours and provided the opportunity to suckle from a nonlactating nipple on one side of the maze and a "lactating" nipple on the other. Figure 2.4 demonstrates first that both the appetitive and consummatory components of the suckling act survived the 6-day abstinence from suckling—that is, the rats ran down the alley and attached to the available nipples. Second, Fig. 2.4 shows that the hunger system gains control over preference even though it had not been linked with any form of ingestion during its development. Specifically, in contrast with the behavior of 12-day-old rats (left histogram), 17-day-old rats unanimously chose the lactating side whether normally raised with the mother and litter from the 11th through the 17th day postpartum or in total isolation from them (N = 16). Thus the albino rat does not need to practice the already *well developed* suckling act in order for it

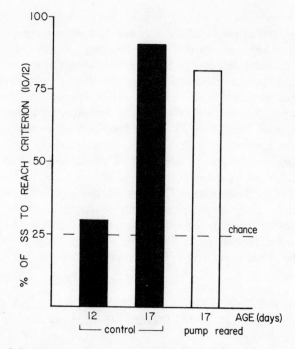

FIG. 2.4. Preference for a lactating nipple of 12- and 17-day-old rats reared normally (*shaded columns*) or isolation-reared for Days 11–17 (*open column*).

to be maintained, at least for a 6-day abstinence, nor must it be exercised in order for the age-related transition to occur and to occur at approximately the same time as in normally raised rats.

Despite the resistance of the well-practiced suckling act to deterioration with lack of practice, there is an abundant agricultural literature on the difficulties of reestablishing suckling in precocial species after a brief period of mother–infant separation during the first few days postpartum. Although William James (1890) suggested that the interesting issue here was the loss of suckling behavior, most studies have focused on the effects of this separation on maternal behavior (this also is an interesting choice, because many mothers—goats, for example—viciously reject their young after separation).

As a first step toward identifying the effects of isolation on suckling, Hall (1975a) separated the young from their mothers at either 2, 5, 10, or 15 days postpartum and studied their nipple attachment behavior in three situations at 5, 10, 15, and 20 days of age respectively. In the simplest paradigm (pups-on-nipple) the pups were hand-held in contact with a well-suckled nipple of their anesthetized mother and allowed to attach to it (this is essentially the procedure devised by Drewett, Statham, & Wakerley, 1974). In a second test, developed by Hall, Cramer, and Blass (1975, 1977), pups were placed in contact with the ventrum of their anesthetized mother, who was lying supine in a trough placed in a standard mouse breeder cage (see Hall et al., 1977, for complete details) where they were allowed to locate and attach to the nipples (pups-on-mother test). In the third test they were returned to their normal nonanesthetized mother and siblings in the nest. In all cases their performance was judged against that of their untreated or sham-operated littermates.

The outcome of this manipulation was clearcut. Rats separated from their dams at 5, 10, or 15 days of age and tested 5 days later were essentially indistinguishable from normal on all three measures utilized by Hall (1975a). The consequences of longer periods of separation were not determined. In contrast, however, even 2 to 3 days of separation was disastrous for the youngest rats studied. Only 25% of these rats attached on the pups-on-mother test, 60% on the pups-on-nipple test, and none of the pups attached to the awake mother in the nest for at least 2 days; then attachment did occur, and all the pups survived. We should note that attachment failure did not reflect poor maternal care. The mothers did not appear to distinguish between the returned and control siblings and appeared equally attentive to all. Thus the suckling act must be practiced by albino rats during the first 5 days of life in order for it to survive normally. Once it has developed sufficiently under normal circumstances (seemingly by Day 5 postpartum), it resists the 5-day, experimenter-imposed separation.

Kenny, Hall, and Blass (unpublished data, 1977) sought to identify the events necessary for the maintenance of suckling in rats separated from their mothers for the 3rd and 4th days postpartum. All experimental rats were removed from their mothers on the morning of Day 2, had an intragastric tube installed under clean surgical conditions (Hall, 1975a, 1975b), and were individually housed in shavings-lined styrofoam cups that floated in a temperature-controlled water bath. They were fed continuously through the gastric tube a liquid diet that closely approximated the composition of rat milk. The pups were randomly assigned to the following conditions: *No Suckling Experience* (NSE). These pups were reared as just described. Their only handling consisted of the morning maintenance of insuring intragastic tube patency. *Pups on Ventrum* (POV-12). These pups were also treated as outlined in the foregoing, and in addition they were allowed to explore and familiarize themselves with the mother's ventrum during 12, 5-minute exposures each on Days 3 and 4. They were never permitted to nipple attach, however. Attachment was thwarted by gently nudging the pups from the nipple each time contact was made. *Pups on Nipple* (PON). These pups were hand-held at the nipple and, once attached, were allowed 60 min of continuous suckling on each of Days 3 and 4. *Pups on Nipple-12* (PON-12). Pups were treated as in the foregoing except that 12 5-minute exposures were given each on Days 3 and 4 postpartum. After each 5-minute exposure, rats were gently disengaged from the nipple and allowed immediately to reattach, which they always did within 30 sec. *Pups on Mother-6* (POM-6). The isolated pups were exposed to the anesthetized, supine mother in groups of 3, 6 times each on

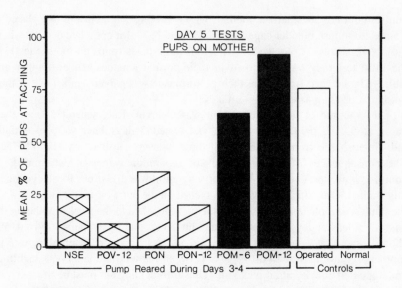

FIG. 2.5.   Percentage of rats attaching to the nipples of their anesthetized mother (POM test) following various treatments on Days 2–5 postpartum (see text for abbreviations).

Days 3 and 4 postpartum and allowed to nipple attach. Each exposure was of a 10-minute duration. *Pups on Mother-12* (POM-12). Pups were treated as in POM-6 except that 12 exposures, each of 5-minute duration, were given each of the 2 isolation days. On the 5th day postpartum, 2 full days after separation from the mother and siblings in the nest, all pups were studied in both the POM and PON paradigms and their performances compared with those of unoperated and sham intragastric-tube-operated littermates. To summarize, these manipulations fractionated normal nipple attachment into its components of search without attachment (POV-12) and attachment without search (PON) and synthesized them into the natural and spontaneous suckling act (POM) but without the benefit of maternal assistance.

Figure 2.5 demonstrates how the rats in the various treatments fared in the POM test. The histogram on the extreme left (NSE) replicates Hall's (1975a) major finding that total separation from mother and siblings for Days 3 and 4 postpartum markedly affects nipple seeking and attachment behaviors. The adjacent column (POV-12) indicates that exposure to, rooting in, and investigation of the mother that do not culminate in nipple attachment are not sufficient to preserve suckling during the interim. The two PON columns clearly demonstrate the ineffectiveness of nipple attachment and extensive suckling in the maintenance of the nipple location that is demanded by the POM test and under normal circumstances in the nest. The final two experimental columns (POM-6, POM-12) in Fig. 2.5 demonstrate the sufficient conditions for preserving suckling during the 2-day separation period. Only when the rat has associated the acts of nipple search and location with those of nipple attachment does suckling appear to be normal at 5 days of age. Note that maintenance here does not reflect attachment duration per se, because pups in all conditions save NSE suckled for essentially equal periods of time.

If the suckling of rats in the POM-6 and POM-12 conditions was truly normal at 5 days of age, then it should survive until 10 days of age even if no additional suckling experience is provided during the 5-day interval. This prediction did not hold, because the number of rats from the POM-6 and -12 conditions that attached in the POM test dropped precipitously to 12% and 29%, respectively. None of the pups from the other conditions that were tested on Day 10 were able to attach. In comparison, as Hall (1975a) demonstrated, control animals separated for the first time at 5 days of age suckled normally on Day 10. Thus although we were able to identify the events that sustained suckling until Day 5, we must conclude that this suckling is more fragile than normal suckling and is insufficient to withstand the additional 5-day separation. This basis for this insufficiency is not immediately apparent. It may reflect our failure to provide the POM pups with enough exposure on Days 3 and 4 postpartum. Alternatively, the quality of the therapy that we provided differed from normal suckling in that it was not followed by milk ejection, a major natural consequence of nipple attachment. There is some reason to believe that deprived rats in this age range can respond to milk loads. According to Thoman, Wetzel, and Levine (1968), the activity of deprived rats decreased when hand-held for orogastric intubations only when the intubations were nutritive. It is not clear at this stage whether the diminution reflects association with the removal of hunger signals or with the removal of the general malaise attendant on deprivation, or whether this is even a legitimate distinction in the young animal. In any event, the foregoing alternatives are currently being investigated.

Figure 2.6 presents the outcome of these manipulations on the simpler act of nipple attachment alone. The behavioral profile resulting from the experimental treatments is quite similar to that of Fig. 2.5. As would be expected, pups in the NSE group were most affected, although their performance was better than on the more complex task, which demanded nipple location. Their performance of 67% attachment was not significantly improved by exposure to the mother (POV-12). Note that the PON experiences, in which each of the 2 nipple attachments was followed by 1 hour of uninterrupted suckling, did not improve performance either, but the PON-12 regimen did. This fact again speaks to the importance of practice for maintaining the sensorimotor sequence of tongue extension, nipple licking, and erection culminating in nipple attachment. It is not surprising, therefore, that the performance of rats in the POM-6 group, which did not practice the consummatory aspects of suckling as much as rats in the PON-12 group, was not as impressive as that of the PON-12 rats. These results emphasize the specificity of each component of the suckling act. There was no interaction between performance on the two types of tests. On the one hand, performance of the POM-6 group was approximately midway between the PON and PON-12

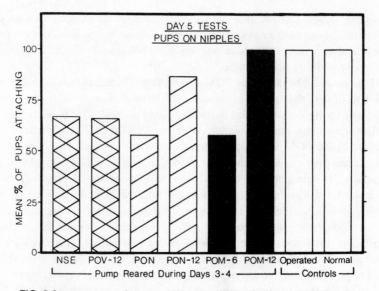

FIG. 2.6.   Percentage of rats attaching to the nipples of their anesthetized mother (PON test) following various treatments on Days 2–5 postpartum (see text for abbreviations).

rats, reflecting their intermediate attachment experience. On the other hand, there appears to be no transfer from nipple attachment per se to nipple location, because the performance of PON-12 rats on the POM test was no better than that of the NSE group. Finally, as expected, rats in the POM-12 group were normal in their attachment to the nipple when brought into contact with it for the first time by the experimenter.

The foregoing studies represent the beginning of an analytic series that may reveal the contribution of suckling experience in the maintenance and determination of subsequent suckling behavior. Even now we can see that the suckling experiences gleaned during the first 5 days postpartum maintain suckling at that stage and permit attachment to occur later on. Moreover, suckling during the first 10 days postpartum permits both the appetitive and consummatory components to come under internal control at about 15 days of age. The events that transpire during these early days, in addition to permitting the expression of these changes, may determine the actual form of the suckling act—for example, the classes of stimuli that will elicit suckling, but this remains to be assessed.

A PUTATIVE ROLE FOR ASSOCIATIVE MECHANISMS IN SUCKLING DEVELOPMENT

We could not help wondering why the suckling system required such a high level of complexity for its maintenance. After all, if suckling were simply a reflex, it should not require any practice at all. The experiments on sensory controls of suckling provide a framework for analyzing the putative contribution of associative mechanisms. Recall that Teicher and Blass (1976) and Blass et al. (1977) demonstrated that pup saliva, in the presence of a nipple, is sufficient to elicit rooting, licking, and, eventually, attachment. This raised three issues. First, it seemed difficult to believe that the rat was "hard-wired" genetically to respond to its own saliva. Saliva is a blood filtrate and should reflect the particular diet that the mother rat is eating. Because rats are scavengers and omnivores and live in widely varied climates and habitats, one would not predict that the saliva of their offspring would be uniform from locale to locale. Second, what elicits the infant rat's very first nipple attachment when its own saliva could not possibly have been deposited on the nipple? Third, does control shift from the stimuli that determine the first suckle to the pups' saliva? The first and third considerations suggest the possibility of an associative contribution. As will be seen immediately, the second consideration also makes this demand.

In regard to the events surrounding the albino rat's very first suckling act, Teicher and Blass (1977) utilized a between-subjects design to demonstrate that a substance has to coat the nipple in order for suckling to be elicited at birth; that either amniotic fluid or parturient mother's saliva is a remarkably effective elicitor of first suckling; and that these substances are uniquely effective, because a host of biologically relevant substances, including virgin female saliva and parturient mother's urine, fail to elicit attachment when painted on washed nipples. It is likely that the cue is contained in the amniotic fluid and not in the parturient female's saliva per se. The amniotic fluid is licked and swallowed by the mother during parturition (Rosenblatt & Lehrman, 1963), and she deposits it on her mammae during the interbirth interval. This is an exciting finding, because it raises the possibility that the fetal tasting[1] and swallowing of the amniotic fluid may be affecting the animal's initial major postnatal behavior.

Regardless of the behavioral or genetic origins of initial attachment, one is still faced with the problem of how suckling gets transferred from amniotic to saliva fluid control. Teicher's (1977) first step in this analysis holds considerable promise for solving this problem. Teicher divided his litters at birth into two groups. One group was first tested (PON) on the unwashed parturient mother. The second test was given after nipple lavage and the third test after an extract of the wash was returned. Rats in the second group were tested twice only: first,

---

[1]It may also be smelling it as well. The vomeronasal organ is remarkably mature histologically at birth. This structure is thought to be the mammalian analogue to the reptilian Jacobson's organ, which is capable of detecting odors in a liquid medium. Additionally, dendritic bundle formation within the olfactory bulbs shows a remarkable degree of prenatal development, surpassing bundle formation in all other neural substrates save the spinal chord (Scheibel & Scheibel, 1975). It has been postulated that these bundles serve as a memory site for olfactory codes related to nipple attachment (Scheibel & Scheibel). Such neural events, as yet barely explored, provide an exciting mechanism through which the prenatal environment may set the stage for the manifestation of important postnatal behaviors.

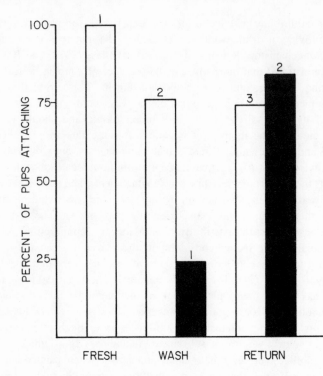

FIG. 2.7.   Percentage of newborn rats attaching to the nipples of their anesthetized mother. Superscript above each column represents the neonate's first, second, or third suckling experience ever. FRESH = unwashed mother, WASH = following nipple lavage, RETURN = following wash and return of wash–distillate to nipples. Note that first suckling experience protects neonates against effects of nipple lavage.

following nipple lavage; second, after the return of the wash distillate to the nipple.

Figure 2.7 demonstrates the percentage of rats that attached under these regimens. The open column on the extreme left indicates that 100% of the rats attached to their mother's unwashed teats. The middle set of histograms demonstrates that the initial suckling experience spared 60% of these rats from the catastrophic effects of nipple lavage. Note that the wash was effective, because it virtually eliminated attachment in rats for which this was the first suckling experience. The final columns indicate that rats that did not attach to the washed nipple upon their first suckling exposure were not incapacitated but were responding to the properties of the nipple. They attached when a distillate of the nipple wash extract was returned to the nipples. Teicher showed in subsequent experiments that when the mother's entire ventrum was washed, suckling was totally eliminated even in rats that had previously suckled on the unwashed mother.

These constitute an exciting set of findings. At the very least, they suggest that the infant's very first suckling experience alters its behavior either by sensitizing it to respond to lower concentrations of amniotic fluid—maternal saliva or by forming an association between the suckling act and some other odor coating the mother. These data suggest that the search for the structure and function of associative and retentive mechanisms must start at birth or before.

GENERAL DISCUSSION

The progress documented in this chapter reflects the complexity of the suckling act in albino rats, particularly the contribution of experience toward its expression. We have described the maintenance function of suckling, have identified those aspects of the suckling act that contribute to this maintenance, and have indicated the development of suckling independence, i.e., when the act no longer has to be practiced in order to be maintained.

One could easily be tempted to invoke the concept of "critical periods" to explain these findings. This temptation should be resisted for a number of reasons. First, an approach emphasizing retention of previous experiences is probably more profitable as an investigatory and explanatory paradigm. Such an approach takes into account the infant's presumed limited memory capacity. It also demands that we recognize that the mother's sensory qualities are rapidly changing during the first 5 days postpartum. The mother and her nest are no longer saturated with birth fluid, and her mammae are becoming fuller and better developed. The data presented in Figs. 2.5 and 2.6 support the importance of nipple location *and* attachment and suggest that the suckling act must be practiced to be maintained. We believe, therefore, that the events underlying the development and maintenance of suckling in albino rats can be analyzed through traditional associative paradigms, classical conditioning in particular.

The second objection to the critical period notion stresses the view that Schneirla and Rosenblatt (1963) expressed in a different context. The events occurring during a particular time frame must be seen within the ontogenetic history of that act. The vital importance of the amniotic fluid as a suckling releaser in the newly born rat and the sensitization by the rat's very first suckling experience provide identifiable links in the ontogenetic chain of suckling events. The factors that occur during the 3 to 5 days postpartum must be viewed as continuous with these earlier links.

The data presented here require that suckling be treated as a complex appetitive motivated act and no longer be accorded the status of a reflex, despite its elicitation by an apparently narrow range of chemical stimuli. We do not know the events that channel the rat into the control of this narrow spectrum. But the facts that suckling must be practiced to be sustained and that rats 7 days of age learn an operant that provides them with the opportunity to suckle suggest that this behavior has the qualities of flexibility that characterize adult ingestive behavior.

The data that we have presented are consonant with the paradigm presented by Gottlieb for analyzing the effects of prenatal (1976a) and postnatal (1976b) experiences on subsequent function. To Gottlieb's categories of *maintenance*, *facilitation*, and *induction* effects of experience on function, we add the category of permission. Permissive is defined here as an experience at one stage of development that allows the manifestation of a later, qualitatively different developmental stage. It does not speak to the events that determine the characteristics of the later stage. Rats that lived with their mother for the first 5 days postpartum and were then maintaned by intragastric infusion until 20 days of age were remarkably similar in their nipple attachment behavior to their normally raised siblings. It is possible, of course, that the appearance of typical 20-day-old behavior might have been induced, and this is currently under investigation. Regardless, the permissive concept is consistent logically, and our preliminary data provide tentative support for its empirical validity.

Finally, we would like to place this report within the framework of systemogenesis provided by the Russian embryologist P. K. Anokhin. Anokhin (1964), in summarizing three decades of embryological research, explicitly provided the cornerstone for his analytic approach: "At birth an animal must already be equipped with adaptive activities capable of sustaining the newborn in its new environment." Anokhin then proceeded to demonstrate how the often unique sensorimotor and perceptual *systems* that typify species develop and become ready for when they are needed. We suggest that Anokhin's concept of systemogenesis be extended temporally and experientially. Temporally, we would assert that the developing animal *at any point in time* must be already equipped with activities that allow it to utilize that new environment. For example, the weanling must be able either to learn the spatial relationship between burrow and feeding site or to utilize cues that allow communication between the two sites. In this regard we raise the speculation that the specific associative experiences gained by the infant from its interactions with its mother and siblings are utilized in a general manner to maintain, permit, facilitate, or induce the appearance or form of the broader motivational and associative systems that are not necessarily related to the preceding behaviors in any obvious fashion. A compelling example is provided by Harlow's famous experiments (1963) on the effects of neonatal social experiences on adult sexual and maternal behavior. In regard to the present findings, the unexpected and remarkable complexity of the suckling act encourages us to seek its consequences in the natural and spontaneous behaviors of juvenile and adult rats.

ACKNOWLEDGMENTS

We thank David S. Olton for his insightful comments on an earlier draft of this article. This work was supported by NSF grant BMS75-01460 and NIH grant AM 18560 to Dr. Elliott M. Blass.

REFERENCES

Amsel, A., Burdette, D. R., & Letz, R. Appetitive learning, patterned alternation, and extinction in 10-day-old rats with nonlactating suckling as reward. *Nature*, 1976, *262*, 816−818.
Anokhin, P. K. Systemogenesis as general regulator of brain development. In W. A. Himwich & H. E. Himwich (Eds.), *Progress in brain research, the developing brain* (Vol. 9). Amsterdam: Elsevier, 1964.
Antin, J., Gibbs, J., Holt, S., Young, C., & Smith, G. P. Cholecystokinin elicits the complete behavioral sequence of satiety in rats. *Journal of Comparative and Physiological Psychology*, 1975, *89*, 784−790.
Blass, E. M., Beardsley, W., & Hall, W. G. *Age-dependent inhibition of suckling by cholecystokinin. American journal of physiology*, 1979.
Blass, E. M., Hall, W. G., & Teicher, M. H. The ontogeny of suckling and ingestive behaviors. In J. N. Sprague & A. N. Epstein (Eds.), *Progress in psychobiology and physiological psychology* (Vol. 8). New York: Academic Press, in press.
Blass, E. M., Teicher, M. H., Cramer, C. P., Bruno, J. P., & Hall, W. G. Olfactory, thermal, and tactile controls of suckling in preaudial and previsual rats. *Journal of Comparative and Physiological Psychology*, 1977, *91*, 1248−1260.
Bradley, R. M., & Mistretta, C. M. Fetal sensory receptors. *Physiological Reviews*, 1975, *65*, 352−382.
Bruno, J. P. Body fluid challenges inhibit nipple attachment in preweanling rats. Paper presented at the meeting of the Eastern Psychological Association, April 1977.
Campbell, B. A., & Coulter, X. The ontogenesis of learning and memory. In M. R. Rosenzweig & E. L. Bennett (Eds.), *Neural mechanisms of learning and memory*. Cambridge, Mass.: MIT Press, 1976.
Drewett, R. F., & Cordall, K. M. Control of feeding in suckling rats: Effects of glucose and of osmotic stimuli. *Physiology and Behavior*, 1976, *16*, 711−717.
Drewett, R. F., Statham, C., & Wakerley, J. B. A quantitative analysis of the feeding behavior of suckling rats. *Animal Behavior*, 1974, *22*, 907−913.
Gottlieb, G. Early development of species-specific auditory perception in birds. In G. Gottlieb (Ed.), *Neural and behavioral specificity: Studies on the development of behavior and the nervous system*. New York: Academic Press, 1976. (a)
Gottlieb, G. The roles of experience in the development of behavior and the nervous system. In G. Gottlieb (Ed.), *Neural and behavioral specificity: Studies on the development of behavior and the nervous system*. New York: Academic Press, 1976. (b)
Hall, W. G. Weaning and growth of artificially reared rats. *Science*, 1975, *190*, 1313−1315. (a)
Hall, W. G. *The ontogeny of ingestive behavior in the rat*. Unpublished doctoral dissertation, The Johns Hopkins University, 1975. (b)
Hall, W. G., Cramer, C. P., & Blass, E. M. Developmental changes in suckling of rat pups. *Nature*, 1975, *258*, 318−320.
Hall, W. G., Cramer, C. P., & Blass, E. M. The ontogeny of suckling in rats: Transitions toward adult ingestion. *Journal of Comparative and Physiological Psychology*, 1977, *91*, 1141−1155.

Hall, W. G., & Rosenblatt, J. S. Suckling behavior and intake control in the developing rat pup. *Journal of Comparative and Physiological Psychology*, 1977, *91*, 1232–1247.

Harlow, H. F., Harlow, M. K., & Hansen, E. W. The maternal affectional system of rhesus monkeys. In H. L. Rheingold (Ed.), *Maternal behavior in mammals*. New York: Wiley, 1963.

Hofer, M. A., Shair, H., & Singh, P. Evidence that maternal ventral skin substances promote suckling in infant rats. *Physiology and Behavior*, 1976, *17*, 131–136.

Hogan, J. A. Development of food recognition in young chicks: II. Learned association over long delays. *Journal of Comparative and Physiological Psychology*, 1973, *83*, 367–373.

Hogan, J. A. The ontogeny of food preferences in chicks and other animals. In L. M. Barker, M. Best, & M. Domjan (Eds.), *Learning mechanisms in food selection*. Waco, Tex.: Baylor University Press, 1977.

James, W. *Principles of psychology*. New York: Henry Holt, 1890.

Kenny, J. T., & Blass, E. M. Suckling as an incentive to instrumental learning in pre-weanling rats. *Science*, 1977, *196*, 898–899.

Kenny, J. T., Hall, W. G., & Blass, E. M. Unpublished data, 1977.

Kenny, J. T., Stoloff, M., Bruno, J. P. & Blass, E. M. The ontogeny of preference for nutritive over nonnutritive suckling in the albino rat. *Journal of Comparative and Physiological Psychology*, in press.

Rosenblatt, J. S. & Lehrman, D. S. Maternal behavior of the laboratory rat. In H. L. Rheingold (Ed.), *Maternal behavior in mammals*. New York: Wiley, 1963.

Scheibel, M. E., & Scheibel, A. B. Dendrite bundles, central programs and the olfactory bulb. *Brain Research*, 1975, *95*, 407–421.

Schneirla, T. C. Aspects of stimulation and organization in approach/withdrawal process underlying vertebrate behavioral development. In D. S. Lehrman, R. A. Hinde, & E. Shaw (Eds.), *Advances in the study of behavior* (Vol. 1). New York: Academic Press, 1965.

Schneirla, T. C., & Rosenblatt, J. S. "Critical" periods in the development of behavior. *Science*, 1963, *139*, 1110–1115.

Teicher, M. H. *Suckling in the developing rat: The importance of olfaction and a putative nursing pheromone*. Unpublished doctoral dissertation, The Johns Hopkins University, 1977.

Teicher, M. H., & Blass, E. M. Suckling in newborn rats: Eliminated by nipple lavage, reinstated by pup saliva. *Science*, 1976, *193*, 422–425.

Teicher, M. H., & Blass, E. M. First suckling response of the newborn albino rat: The roles of olfaction and amniotic fluid. *Science*, 1977, *198*, 635–636.

Teitelbaum, P. The use of operant methods in the assessment and control of motivational state. In W. K. Honig (Ed.), *Operant behavior: Areas of research and application*. New York: Appleton-Century-Crofts, 1966.

Thoman, E., Wetzel, A., & Levine, S. Learning in the neonatal rat. *Animal Behavior*, 1968, *16*, 54–57.

3 The Stimulus Control of Locomotor Persistence in Rat Pups

Paul M. Bronstein
Trenton State College

My interest in understanding learning from a developmental perspective attracted me in turn to the sequence of behavioral changes that unfolds during a rat's progression from birth to weaning. At the conclusion of the second postnatal week, rats display behavioral changes that rapidly bring them to a weanling state of maturity. The eyes open and become functional at this time, feeding on solid foods is noted, and adult forms of locomotion are also seen (Altman & Sudarshan, 1975; Babicky, Parizek, Ostadalova, & Kolar, 1973; Galef & Clark, 1972).

Rosenblatt & Lehrman (1963) reported an intense burst of locomotion in rat pups between Weeks 2 and 3, and this phenomenon seemed worthy of study for three reasons. First, the locomotor activity of 2-week-olds might indicate a style of learning typical of that age group. Bolles (1970), for instance, has suggested that knowledge of the response hierarchies of an animal species is one requirement for predicting the relative ease with which different tasks are learned. Furthermore, at least part of the explanation of developmental changes in rats' avoidance learning lies in age-related differences in reactions to unconditioned aversive stimuli (Bronstein & Hirsch, 1976) and to neutral cues paired with those noxious events (Hinderliter & Riccio, 1977). Documentation of reliable sequences of behavioral development will likely permit the further understanding of relationships between species-specific response dispositions and learning.

Second, the onset of walking might reflect learning that had occurred within the litter prior to the second week postpartum. The dam, for instance, could be

This paper was presented as part of the Symposium on the Ontogeny of Learning and Memory held at the State University of New York at Binghamton on June 21–23, 1977.

training her offspring to persist in locomotor activity either by social facilitation or by intermittently reinforcing germinal walking movements (perhaps by providing food and warmth in a response-contingent fashion).

Third, this pattern of behavioral development could reflect ongoing physiological maturation, and a functional analysis of the onset of adult-like locomotion might contribute to an understanding of the physiological control of this behavior. It has been speculated, for instance, that age-related changes in the function of the hippocampus and other forebrain structures are responsible for many of the behavioral transitions occurring during the rat's third postnatal week (Altman, Brunner, & Bayer, 1973; Campbell, Lytle, & Fibiger, 1969; Douglas, 1972).

SPONTANEOUS ACTIVITY

Our initial investigations were of the open-field activity of rats of different ages (Bronstein, Neiman, Wolkoff, & Levine, 1974). A prior report (Feigley, Parsons, Hamilton, & Spear, 1972) had shown that 2-week-old rats display unusually persistent nose-poking activity; we then demonstrated that this effect was also observable in the open field. It was found that 15-day-old animals walked and reared at a nearly invariant rate throughout our half-hour test. By Day 21, however, the pups showed the adult pattern of behavior; they reduced their locomotion significantly after being in the open field only 5 minutes.

We next attempted to discover some of the factors accounting for the behavioral persistence of 2-week-old rats. Three hypotheses were of interest: First, pups' locomotor persistence could be due to incomplete maturation, as suggested by Altman et al. (1973), among others. According to this theory, pups do not possess adequate neural functioning to permit them to restrict motor activity once initiated. More broadly, however, this supposed "lack of inhibition" is but one of an array of hypotheses whereby rats aged about 2 weeks are thought of as having some general capacity or quality (learned or innate) that differentiates them from other age groups. It is also possible to account for the persistent open-field and nose-poke activities of 2-week-old rats by hypothesizing that this age group is less susceptible to muscular fatigue than are animals just 1 week older.

A second, general explanation for the elevated and persistent activity is that the 15-day-old pups might be reacting to social isolation. Their locomotion might be elicited in reaction to separation from some aspect of the maternal nest.

A final possibility occurring to us was that the 15-day-old animals might be hyperexploratory (cf. Welker, 1971). That is, the investigation of external cues might be a main determinant of pups' persistent locomotion. Associated with this idea of age-related differences in exploratory behavior is the abstraction, common in this literature, that the persistent locomotion of 2-week-old rats represents a habituation failure—i.e., a deficit in learning (e.g., Parsons, Fagan, & Spear, 1973). Anthropomorphically, then, 21-day-old animals could be learning relatively rapidly that the novel testing chamber was a stable, unthreatening, uninteresting place; they explore a while but abandon their quest after a few minutes. The 2-week-old pup, on the other hand, might be having difficulty with some aspect of this learning process.

Clearly, the utility of this exploration-based hypothesis for age-related activity changes hinges on having some clear notion of which stimuli the animals are pursuing as well as on being able to measure that search process. My initial hypothesis was that the hyperactive pup was actually engaged in exploration. I then proceeded to investigate some of the stimulus conditions that might maintain that behavior.

EXPLORATORY BEHAVIOR

Our main strategy in studying the development of exploration has been to observe and analyze age-related changes in spontaneous alternation. Several lines of evidence suggested this approach. First, the existing literature unambiguously showed that weanlings, unlike adults, do not alternate above chance levels (e.g., Douglas, Peterson, & Douglas, 1973). Second, spontaneous alternation has been studied for decades and the phenomenon seemed thoroughly understood. Douglas (1966) showed that rats alternate solely by the use of extramaze spatial cues and the avoidance of their own odor trails. It seemed likely therefore that difficulties in using these two classes of stimuli might account for the alternation failure and, perhaps, for the persistent activity of 2-week-old pups. A third reason for analyzing spontaneous activity was that this behavior appeared relatively unaffected by peripheral, muscular fatigue (Dember, 1961). The lack of alternation among juveniles would therefore likely indicate the incomplete development of some central process. Finally, the failure of young rats to show spontaneous alternation might have accounted for the deficit among juveniles in acquiring a spatial discrimination (Bronstein & Spear, 1972).

Our studies of alternation led to three conclusions. First, we replicated the known developmental trend (Bronstein, Dworkin, & Bilder, 1974). Adult levels of alternation were attained by Day 25; younger animals exhibited only chance performance. Second, the young pups seemed to be turning randomly, showing neither alternation nor perseveration. Finally, we found that Douglas's theory is not adequate to explain alternation in rats (Bronstein, Dworkin, Bilder, & Wolkoff, 1974). When shaken in a horizontal plane between turns in a T maze, Douglas (1966) abolished the tendency of his adult subjects to alternate. This finding serves as the primary evidence for the use of extramaze spatial cues in spontaneous alternation. Our repeated failure to replicate Douglas's results was surprising and, furthermore, undermined the theoretical base of our studies.

Another approach (Palese & Bronstein, 1976) defined exploration as an entry into a relatively novel arm of a cross maze. Rats aged 16 to 30 days were tested for 30-minute trials with both the amount of ambulation and the patterning of arm entries being recorded. The nonattenuating activity of 16-day-olds differentiated them from other age groups. There was absolutely no evidence, however, that the younger pups patterned their movements any differently than older animals.

SOCIAL ISOLATION

At this point we were left with a robust and reliable phenomenon, the persistent locomotion of 2-week-old rats. We had been totally unsuccessful, however, in analyzing this distinctive age-related behavior pattern. Our only new insight was that the most widely accepted account of spontaneous alternation in adults (Douglas, 1966) was, at the very least, incomplete. We therefore switched orientations and hypothesized that the persistent activity of 15-day-old rats was a consequence of separation from the maternal nest or litter. It followed then that the behavior of 2-week-olds should be more like that of 3-week-olds if the younger pups were tested along with some stimuli usually found in the nesting environment. Specifically, isolated pups aged 15 days postpartum are not fully capable of adult thermogenesis, but more complete homeothermic regulation is typical of animals just a few days more mature (Adolph, 1957; Okon, 1971). Furthermore, Alberts (1978a, 1978b) has shown that rat pups normally use social behavior (huddling with their littermates and dam) to maintain their body temperatures when confronted by a cool environment. The isolated juvenile is an animal separated from aspects of its normal environment that are essential for thermoregulation. Therefore the locomotion of various age groups was assessed as a function of ambient temperature. We hypothesized a three-way interaction between subjects' age, ambient temperature, and minutes of testing. We suspected that 15-day-olds would show a marked activity decrement only when the temperature of the test apparatus was similar to that of the nest. Older pups were expected to show their typical activity decrement regardless of the environmental temperature.

In a recent study (Bronstein, Marcus, & Hirsch, 1978), pups of 15, 18, and 21 days were placed into small open fields (each about 25-cm-square), and these chambers, in turn, were enclosed in incubators set at either 22.8°C, 27.8°C, or 37.2°C. Test duration was 30 minutes, and the animals were each observed for 5 seconds per minute; interobservation interval was 55 seconds. Each rat was tested only once, and each of 11 litters contributed 1 pup to each of the 9 experimental conditions.

The behavior of each subject was noted on a nominal scale during each observation, and, for the most part, the pups were either walking or lying inactively. Other responses (e.g., grooming or rearing) occurred only rarely. All figures depict the percentage of times that the walking response was observed. As seen in Fig. 3.1, lower levels of ambulation were associated with older subjects as well as with pups tested in warmer environments. Furthermore, there was a reliable interaction of these two variables: An elevation of ambient temperature was most effective in eliminating the walking of 15-day-olds, whereas the older pups were least affected by temperature variations.

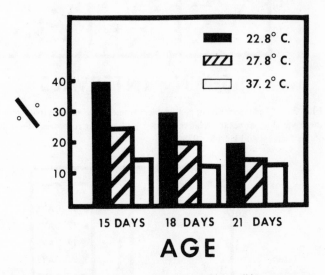

FIG. 3.1.   The percentage of observations during which walking responses were noted as a function of age and environmental temperature. (From Bronstein, Marcus, and Hirsch, 1978.)

Figure 3.2 is a description of the Age × Temperature × Blocks interaction. All groups of 18- and 21-day-olds showed a within-session drop in locomotion; the 15-day-old pups tested at the two cooler temperatures persisted in their initial levels of activity; and the youngest group tested in the warmest condition exhibited a striking depression of locomotion. In addition, essentially the same results were obtained when pups were tested longitudinally on alternate days, beginning at Day 15; these data are seen in Fig. 3.3. Only the juveniles aged 15, 17, or 19 days and tested in the cool environment (22.8°C) displayed the activity persistence seen in prior studies. The younger pups in the warmer environment as well as all groups of older pups showed reliable within-session decrements of locomotion.

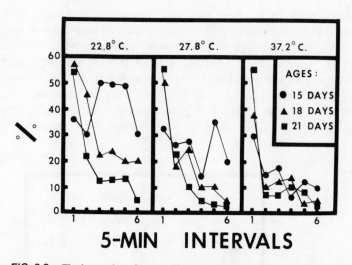

FIG. 3.2.   The interaction of age, ambient temperature, and intratrial intervals as these variables affect the relative frequency of walking responses. (From Bronstein, Marcus, and Hirsch, 1978.)

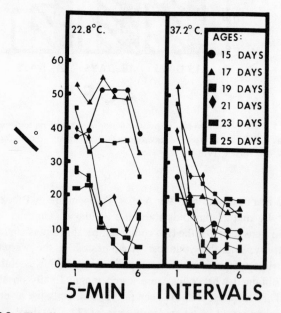

FIG. 3.3.   The effects of age, ambient temperature, and intratrial blocks upon the relative frequency of walking responses in a longitudinal investigation. (From Bronstein, Marcus, and Hirsch, 1978.)

GENERAL DISCUSSION

As research on the development of animal learning has intensified over the last decade, several authors have commented on the seeming inability of young rats to withhold responses. Pups are deficient at passive-avoidance learning (e.g., Riccio, Rohrbaugh, & Hodges, 1968); they fail to alternate in a T maze (Kirkby, 1967); they show an exaggerated partial reinforcement extinction effect (Amsel & Chen, 1976); and finally, isolated juveniles display heightened and/or persistent bar-pressing (Goodrick, 1975), nose-poking (Feigley et al., 1972), or walking (Bronstein, Neiman, Wolkoff, & Levine, 1974; Campbell et al., 1969). This collection of observations, together with their presumed neurological determinant—the functional immaturity of the rat's forebrain—has led to the theoretical formulation that altricial juveniles of mammalian species are either generally aroused or are lacking in their ability to inhibit responses (Altman et al., 1973; Campbell et al., 1969).

In this chapter I have attempted to analyze some of the functional stimulus— response relationships resulting in the developmental syndrome just described. This approach provides further operational meaning to presumed failures of behavioral inhibition. From these data it appears that 2-week-old pups, although active, are insensitive to several treatments used to define exploration in adults. These juveniles turn randomly in T mazes and do not show any greater preference for novel maze arms than that seen in other age groups. Furthermore, the determinants of spontaneous alternation in adults now seem too variable and uncertain to permit the use of this task as a model for assessing exploration in juveniles (Bronstein, Dworkin, Bilder, & Wolkoff, 1974).

Some further understanding of behavioral development was achieved when we manipulated an environmental variable (ambient temperature) with some known ecological validity. It has been found that 2-week-old rats are not *generally* aroused but seem to be responding with heightened activity to the absence of certain specific stimuli usually found in the nest. Encounters with either familiar odors (Campbell & Raskin, 1978) or sources of warmth (Bronstein et al., 1978; Goodrick, 1975; Randall & Campbell, 1976) will significantly reduce this isolation-induced locomotion. Furthermore, 2-week-old pups approach familiar odors (Leon, 1974) or thermoneutral temperatures (Fowler & Kellogg, 1975) when these are distributed in a graded manner throughout a test environment. In short, it is no longer possible to consider rat pups' heightened loco-motion as indicative of general arousal; the elevation in motor activity is specific to certain situations. Isolated pups could be searching for important thermal or olfactory stimuli, because locomotion ceases when contact with adequate cues is established.

ACKNOWLEDGMENT

This research was supported by Grants MH22027-01 and MH26372-01 from the National Institute of Mental Health.

REFERENCES

Adolph, E. F. Ontogeny of physiological regulations in the rat. *Quarterly Journal of Biology*, 1957, *32*, 89–137.

Alberts, J. R. Huddling in rat pups: Group behavioral mechanisms of temperature regulation and energy conservation. *Journal of Comparative and Physiological Psychology*, 1978, *92*, 220–230. (a)

Alberts, J. R. Huddling in rat pups: Multisensory control of contact behavior. *Journal of Comparative and Physiological Psychology*, 1978, *92*, 231–245. (b)

Altman, J., Brunner, R. L., & Bayer, S. A. The hippocampus and behavioral maturation. *Behavioral Biology*, 1973, *8*, 557–596.

Altman, J., & Sudarshan, K. Postnatal development of quadruped posture and locomotion in rats. *Animal Behaviour*, 1975, *23*, 896–920.

Amsel, A., & Chen, J. S. Ontogeny of persistence: Immediate and long-term persistence in rats varying in training age between 17 and 65 days. *Journal of Comparative and Physiological Psychology*, 1976, *90*, 808–920.

Babicky, A., Parizek, J., Ostadalova, I., & Kolar, J. Initial solid food intake and growth of young rats in nests of different sizes. *Physiologica Bohemoslovaca*, 1973, *22*, 557–566.

Bolles, R. C. Species-specific defense reactions and avoidance learning. *Psychological Review*, 1970, *77*, 32–48.

Bronstein, P. M., Dworkin, T., & Bilder, B. H. Age-related differences in rats' spontaneous alternation. *Animal Learning and Behavior*, 1974, *2*, 285–288.

Bronstein, P. M., Dworkin, T., Bilder, B., & Wolkoff, F. D. Repeated failures in reducing rats' spontaneous alternation through the intertrial disruption of spatial orientation. *Animal Learning and Behavior*, 1974, *2*, 207–209.

Bronstein, P. M., & Hirsch, S. M. Ontogeny of defensive reactions in Norway rats. *Journal of Comparative and Physiological Psychology*, 1976, *90*, 620–629.

Bronstein, P. M., Marcus, M., & Hirsch, S. M. The ontogeny of locomotion in rats: The influence of ambient temperature. *Bulletin of the Psychonomic Society*, 1978, *12*, 39–42.

Bronstein, P. M., Neiman, H., Wolkoff, F. D., & Levine, M. J. The development of habituation in the rat. *Animal Learning and Behavior*, 1974, *2*, 92–96.

Bronstein, P. M., & Spear, N. E. Acquisition of a spatial discrimination in rats as a function of age. *Journal of Comparative and Physiological Psychology*, 1972, *78*, 208–212.

Campbell, B. A., Lytle, L. D., & Fibiger, H. C. Ontogeny of adrenergic arousal and cholinergic inhibitory mechanisms in the rat. *Science*, 1969, *166*, 637–638.

Campbell, B. A., & Raskin, L. A. The ontogeny of behavioral arousal: Role of environmental stimuli. *Journal of Comparative and Physiological Psychology*, 1978, *92*, 176–184.

Dember, W. N. Alternation behavior. In D. W. Fiske & S. R. Maddi (Eds.), *Functions of varied experience*. Homewood, Ill.: Dorsey, 1961.

Douglas, R. J. Cues for spontaneous alternation. *Journal of Comparative and Physiological Psychology*, 1966, *62*, 171–183.

Douglas, R. J. Pavlovian conditioning and the brain. In R. A. Boakes & M. S. Halliday (Eds.), *Inhibition and learning*. New York: Academic Press, 1972.

Douglas, R. J., Peterson, J. J., & Douglas, D. P. The ontogeny of a hippocampus-dependent response in two rodent species. *Behavioral Biology*, 1973, *8*, 27–38.

Feigley, D. A., Parsons, P. A., Hamilton, L. W., & Spear, N. E. Development of habituation to novel environments in the rat. *Journal of Comparative and Physiological Psychology*, 1972, *79*, 738–746.

Fowler, S. J., & Kellogg, C. Ontogeny of thermoregulatory mechanisms in the rat. *Journal of Comparative and Physiological Psychology*, 1975, *89*, 738–746.

Galef, B. G., Jr., & Clark, M. M. Mother's milk and adult presence: Two factors determining initial dietary selection by weanling rats. *Journal of Comparative and Physiological Psychology*, 1972, *78*, 220–225.

Goodrick, C. L. Adaptation to novel environments in the rat: Effects of age, stimulus intensity, group testing, and temperature. *Developmental Psychobiology*, 1975, *8*, 287–296.

Hinderliter, C. F., & Riccio, D. C. *Species-specific defense reactions: A developmental comparison in rats*. Paper presented at the meeting of the Eastern Psychological Association, Boston, April 1977.

Kirkby, R. J. A maturational factor in spontaneous alternation. *Nature*, 1967, *215*, 784.

Leon, M. Maternal pheromone. *Physiology and Behavior*, 1974, *13*, 441–453.

Okon, E. E. The temperature relations of vocalization in infant golden hamsters and Wistar rats. *Journal of Physiology* (London), 1971, *164*, 227–237.

Palese, R. P., & Bronstein, P. M. Exploration and spontaneous activity in young rats. *Bulletin of the Psychonomic Society*, 1976, *7*, 352–354.

Parsons, P. J., Fagan, T., & Spear, N. E. Short-term retention of habituation in the rat: A developmental study from infancy to old age. *Journal of Comparative and Physiological Psychology*, 1973, *84*, 545–553.

Randall, P. K., & Campbell, B. A. Ontogeny of behavioral arousal in rats: Effect of maternal and sibling presence. *Journal of Comparative and Physiological Psychology*, 1976, *90*, 453–459.

Riccio, D. C., Rohrbaugh, M., & Hodges, L. A. Developmental aspects of active and passive avoidance learning in rats. *Developmental Psychobiology*, 1968, *1*, 108–111.

Rosenblatt, J. S., & Lehrman, D. S. Maternal behavior of the laboratory rat. In H. L. Rheingold (Ed.), *Maternal behavior in mammals*. New York: Wiley, 1963.

Welker, W. I. Ontogeny of play and exploratory behaviors: A definition of problems and a search for new conceptual solutions. In H. Moltz (Ed.), *The ontogeny of vertebrate behavior*. New York: Academic Press, 1971.

4

Ontogeny of Habituation and Sensitization in the Rat

Byron A. Campbell and Donald J. Stehouwer
Princeton University

Virtually all species of animals cease responding to stimuli that are of little biological consequence (Wyers, Peeke, & Herz, 1973). This process, typically described as habituation, allows the animal to respond to those aspects of the environment that are novel or of potential survival importance while at the same time preventing the fatigue and distraction that would result from continued responding to inconsequential stimuli. Thus habituation is of vital importance, because it allows the animal to attend and respond to biologically important stimuli with maximal economy. The simplicity and fundamental importance of habituation may explain why habituation is the first form of learning to emerge phylogenetically and why it has been retained throughout evolution.

The simplicity and generality of habituation also suggest that it may appear very early during ontogenesis. If this is the case, then habituation paradigms may provide a powerful tool for studying the ontogeny of infrahuman mammalian learning and memory. This approach has already proven to be of great value for studying cognitive and perceptual development in the human infant (Cohen, 1976; Jeffrey, 1976).

The research that follows was further inspired by the recent rapid advances in our understanding of habituation in spinal neurons (Thompson & Glanzman, 1976), invertebrates (Kandel, 1976), and in intact adult rats (Wagner, 1976). During the past decade these investigators and their co-workers have produced an enormous increase in our knowledge of the neural and behavioral processes underlying the phenomenon of habituation and its counterpart, sensitization.

In infrahuman mammals, research on the ontogeny of habituation has been complicated by the use of diffuse behaviors such as exploration of an open field (e.g., Bronstein, Neiman, Wolkoff, & Levine, 1974) or adaptation to a testing

67

environment (e.g., Bronstein & Dworkin, 1974; Feigley, Parsons, Hamilton, & Spear, 1972). In these instances not only are the responses ambiguous but so are the eliciting stimuli, because they are myriad and controlled by the subject rather than the experimenter. Effective study of habituation requires a response that can be reliably elicited, well defined in terms of the response itself, and, optimally, one whose underlying neuronal circuitry is known. Few, if any, studies on the ontogeny of infrahuman habituation meet these simple requirements. The studies that come closest are those by File and Plotkin (1974) and File and Scott (1976), who studied habituation of head-turning elicited by an air puff to the back of 1- to 19-day-old rats. Unfortunately the initial frequency of responding to the air puff varies considerably as a function of age, making it a somewhat unsatisfactory stimulus for studying the ontogeny of habituation.

With these considerations in mind, we chose to study habituation of the electric shock-induced limb-withdrawal response in the developing rat. Several compelling reasons dictated this choice. First, the limb-withdrawal response emerges very early in the developmental sequence, at about 16 days of gestation (Narayanan, Fox, & Hamburger, 1971; Vaughn & Grieshaber, 1973); second, it is well defined in relation to both the response and the eliciting stimulus; and third, it has been widely used in neurophysiological studies of habituation in adult mammals (see Griffin, 1970; Thompson & Glanzman, 1976).

METHODOLOGICAL STUDIES[1]

Apparatus

For this research we first placed the young rats in fabric harnesses that allowed free limb movement and then suspended them over a movement-recording device in a thermoneutral chamber, as shown in Figure 4.1. A grounded indifferent electrode ran the length of the subject's back, and a fine wire electrode passed around the subject's paw. Leg flexions were transduced by inducing a current in a coil via a magnet tied to the stimulated paw (Fig. 4.1). The output of the transducer was amplified and used to trigger a relay, the number of relay closures being recorded on electromagnetic printout counters.

Shock-Withdrawal Thresholds

Our first concern was to compare the sensitivity and reactivity to electric shock of preweanling rats at different stages of development. To determine withdrawal-response thresholds, a measure of shock sensitivity, we stimulated the forelimb

---

[1]These studies are described in somewhat greater detail in Stehouwer (1977) and Stehouwer and Campbell (1978).

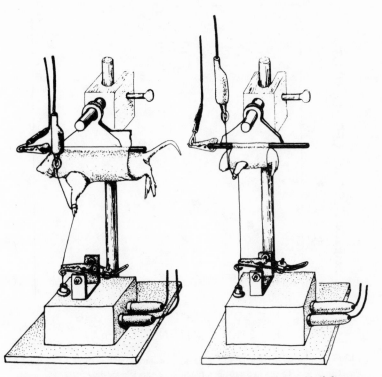

FIG. 4.1. Schematic representation of 3- (*right*) and 15-day-old (*left*) rats suspended in habituation apparatus. The shock source is connected via alligator clips to an indifferent electrode on the subject's back and to a stimulating electrode around the forepaw. A fine thread connects the stimulated forepaw to the motion transducer, whose output is amplified by a solid-state amplifier. (*not shown*).

of 3- and 15-day-old rats 10 times at 45-second intervals with shock intensities ranging from no shock to 0.16 mA. In all of our experiments the shocks were 35 msec. long, supplied by an AC constant-current shock source. The data from this experiment are shown in Fig. 4.2. It was found that 3-day-old rats displayed a considerably higher level of spontaneous responding than 15-day-olds but showed a parallel increase in the frequency of responding as a function of shock intensity. The response threshold was defined as the shock intensity that elicited a level of responding midway between spontaneous withdrawal-response levels and 100% responding (Campbell & Masterson, 1969). Since 3-day-old rats responded at a spontaneous rate of 24% and 15-day-olds at a rate of 8%, the midpoint values were 62% and 54%, respectively. The associated shock threshold intensities eliciting response 62% and 54% of the time were calculated to be 0.12 mA for both the 3-day-old and 15-day-old pups. These data indicate that sensitivity of the withdrawal response to electric shock does not change with age in the preweanling rat.

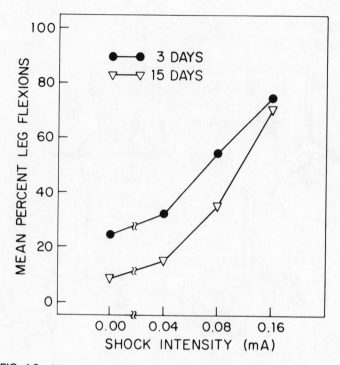

FIG. 4.2.   Mean percentage of leg flexions occurring within 1 second of shock
onset in 3- and 15-day-old rats as a function of shock intensity.

Reactivity to Shock

The next experiment was designed to assess changes in reactivity to shock, using
the same procedure but including a wider range of shock intensities and adding 6-
and 10-day-old subjects. In addition to recording the simple occurrence of
limb-withdrawal following shock, we recorded limb activity as a function of time
during the first 30 seconds following shock and the total number of responses
occurring during the entire 45-second period between shocks.

The likelihood that a response would occur was directly related to shock
intensity, and, as in the first experiment, flexion activity at lower shock levels
was inversely related to age. All pups at all ages responded to all shocks at the
two highest intensities. There were, however, dramatic differences in the total
number of responses that were elicited in animals of different ages, particularly
at the higher intensities. The 10- and 15-day-olds responded only a few times
during the entire interstimulus interval (ISI), even at the highest shock intensity.
The 3- and 6-day-olds, in contrast, responded frequently during the ISI, their
activity being directly related to shock intensity (Fig. 4.3).

Responding during the ISI was not randomly distributed, as Fig. 4.4 clearly
shows. In the younger pups there was a great deal of limb withdrawal activity

immediately following shock, gradually tapering off to baseline levels 15 to 20 seconds after shock. The older pups responded consistently to the shock but only during the first interval following shock.

Direct observation of the pups further clarified these age-related differences. The 3- and 6-day-olds repeatedly flexed the stimulated limb while squirming and wriggling in the harness. This behavior commenced with shock onset and continued long into the interstimulus interval. Similar generalized responses to localized stimuli in fetal and neonatal rats have been previously reported (Narayanan et al., 1971; Stelzner, 1971). The 10- and especially the 15-day-olds did not show this behavior, presumably because of maturation of (inhibitory) integrating mechanisms that modulate or control diffuse neuronal activity. At these ages, shocks elicited relatively discrete withdrawal responses, which were occasionally followed by attempts to scratch the stimulated area with the ipsilateral hindlimb. These observations and interpretations concur with those of

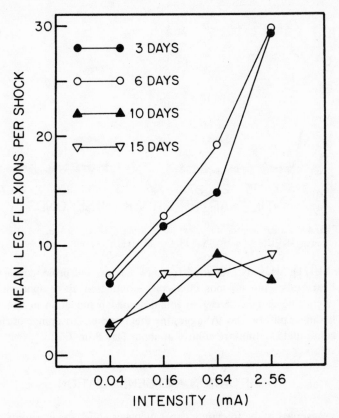

FIG. 4.3.   Mean number of leg flexions occurring during the entire 45-second interstimulus interval in 3-, 6-, 10-, and 15-day-old rats as a function of shock intensity.

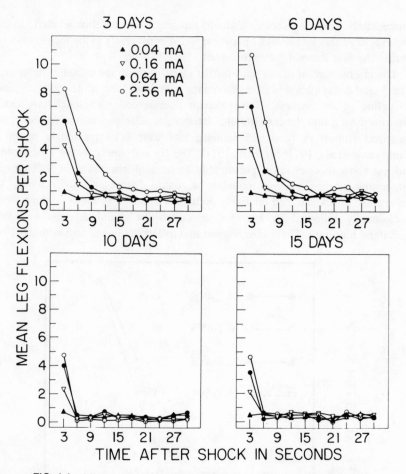

FIG. 4.4.   Mean number of leg flexions occurring in successive 3-second periods
following shock in 3-, 6-, 10-, and 15-day-old rats as a function of shock intensity.

Stelzner (1971), who also reported repeated flexion and prolonged activity in
neonatal rats following noxious cutaneous stimulation up to approximately 8
days of age. File and Scott (1976) found a sudden reduction in head-turning
elicited by an air puff on Day 9, suggesting that responses to a range of cutaneous
stimuli come under inhibitory control at about Day 8 or 9.

HABITUATION AND SENSITIZATION

The data presented in the foregoing experiments establish the feasibility of using
the shock-elicited forelimb-withdrawal response as a behavioral procedure for
studying habituation in the developing rat. Of primary importance is the finding

that the threshold for the withdrawal response does not change with age. Similarly, the qualitative changes in the behavior associated with the painful stimulus at different ages are not such as to preclude the use of limb withdrawal as a response for studying habituation. Even though the duration and pattern of responding during the interstimulus interval changes with development, the initial response to shock is always a rapid reflexive withdrawal of the forelimb. Thus we have identified a response that is reliably elicited by a known, quantifiable stimulus and whose basic underlying neural circuitry is relatively well understood.

Habituation and Dishabituation as a Function of Age

Having established the feasibility of using forelimb withdrawal as a response for studying habituation ontogenetically, our next step was to determine whether repeated stimulation produced habituation of the response. Three critical characteristics of habituation, as identified by Thompson and Spencer (1966), were examined in the present experiment. First, does occurrence of the withdrawal response decline as a negative exponential function of stimulus presentation? Second, is the rate and amount of response decline directly proportional to frequency of stimulation? Third, does presentation of an intense stimulus following habituation result in reappearance of the original response (dishabituation)? A further purpose of this experiment was to study the effects of age on these characteristics of habituation.

To this end we administered a 0.18-mA shock stimulus repetitively at interstimulus intervals ranging from 1.0 to 8.0 seconds to 3-, 6-, 10- and 15-day-old rats. After 160 stimuli, a 2.0-mA dishabituating shock stimulus was delivered in place of a 0.18-mA shock, following which 40 additional 0.18-mA shocks were administered.

The results of this experiment are shown in Fig. 4.6. Initially the shock stimuli produced a high level of responding at all ISI's. With continued stimulation the frequency of responding declined systemically at the shorter ISI's for all age levels. For the longer ISI's the decline in responding became less and less pronounced during development until at 15 days of age there was only a slight decline after the first 10 trials at the 8.0-second ISI.

In general the results of this research are in close agreement with the defining features of habituation listed by Thompson and Spencer (1966). The percentage of shocks eliciting the withdrawal response declines exponentially with repeated stimulation, the amount of habituation is proportional to frequency of stimulation, and strong shock produces marked dishabituation.

Two of the three characteristics studied changed markedly during development. First, at 3 days of age the pups habituated rapidly to all frequencies of stimulation, but later in development pronounced habituation occurred only at the higher frequencies. These results suggest that 3-day-old pups habituate more

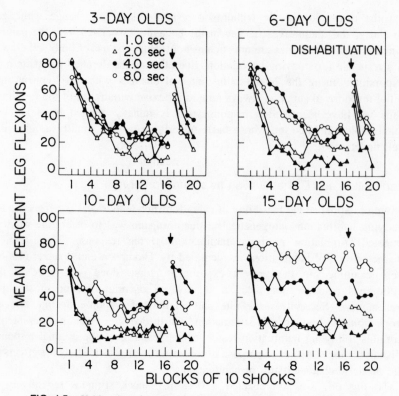

FIG. 4.5.   Habituation of the forelimb-withdrawal response to repeated shock in
3-, 6-, 10-, and 15-day-old rats with 1.0-, 2.0-, 4.0-, and 8.0-second interstimulus
intervals. Arrows in the top-right corners indicate insertion of a single intense
stimulus (dishabituation) into the habituation series.

easily than older pups and that the interstimulus interval would have to be increased well beyond 8.0 seconds to attenuate habituation in these young animals.

The effect of the strong dishabituating shock also changed as a function of
age. The 3- and 6-day-old pups responded vigorously to the strong shock and
were more responsive to subsequent weak shocks. Dishabituation was considerably less in the 10-day-olds and was virtually absent in 15-day-old pups.
These differences parallel those of the last experiment, showing that rats are very
responsive to a strong stimulus when very young but as they grow older become
much less so.

Locus of Dishabituation

In the preceding experiment the dishabituating stimulus was presented to the
same locus as the habituating stimulus. It is therefore possible that the resulting
restoration of responding is due either to specific facilitation of the withdrawal-

response pathway or to an increase in generalized arousal (sensitization), as postulated by Thompson and Spencer (1966) and Kandel (1976). If dishabituation in the present experiments is specific to the response pathway stimulated, then stimulation of a different site should be ineffective. However, if dishabituation reflects an increase in generalized arousal, the site of stimulation should be of little importance. In this experiment, rat pups were habituated as previously, given a strong shock to the contralateral hindlimb, and then tested for dishabituation.

Comparison of Figs. 4.5 and 4.6 shows that stimulation of the contralateral limb is just as effective in producing dishabituation as stimulation of the original site. As in the previous experiment, the 3-day-old subjects showed a large response increment, whereas 15-day-olds showed virtually none.

These results show that dishabituation does not depend on direct stimulation of the habituated site, suggesting that the strong shock produces dishabituation through generalized arousal rather than through specific response facilitation.

Response Amplitude and Latency during Habituation

Although we have described the general pattern of responding during habituation and dishabituation during development in the preweanling rat, the binary

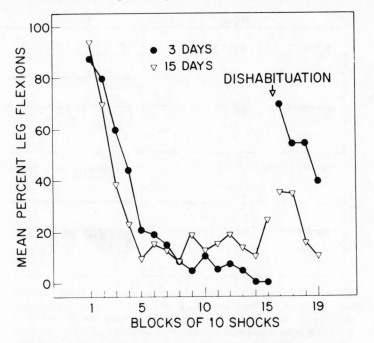

FIG. 4.6. Dishabituation of the forelimb-withdrawal response in 3- and 15-day-old rats following a single intense stimulus delivered to the contralateral hindlimb.

measure of response occurrence (relay closure) does not provide a full description of the withdrawal response during habituation. It does not show, for example, whether the response declines in amplitude as it becomes less frequent or whether response latencies change as a function of age, habituation, or shock intensity.

In order to obtain this information we recorded the amplified output of the motion transducer on a Grass polygraph. Relay closures, the response measure used in our other experiments, were also recorded on the polygraph. High-speed (50 mm/sec) records were used to determine latencies, and low-speed (50 mm/min for the 1.0-second ISI groups; 5 mm/min. for the 8.0-second groups) records were used to display changes in amplitude and likelihood of responding for the entire session.

Representative low-speed records (Fig. 4.7) show that during habituation there is a gradual waning of response amplitude. Furthermore there is close correspondence between the response decline measured directly from the transducer and that measured as a decline in the probability of a relay closure. Not surprisingly, response amplitudes were greater in the 15-day-olds than in the 3-day-olds.

Response latencies from shock onset for those trials on which a response was recorded were measured to the nearest 5 msec. from high-speed records and are

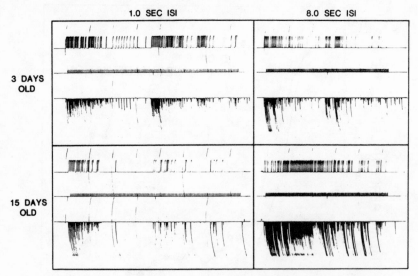

FIG. 4.7.   Polygraph records of a typical habituation session in 3- and 15-day-old rats, with shock stimuli presented at 1.0- or 8.0-second intervals. Each upward deflection in the top trace represents a recorded relay closure. Downward deflections in the bottom trace reflect response amplitude. Each deflection in the center trace represents a stimulus presentation, the downward deflection in the middle of the session marking the delivery of a strong dishabituating shock.

presented in Table 4.1. This table shows that latencies decrease with development but do not change during the course of habituation. In both 3- and 15-day-old animals the response latencies to the intense dishabituating shocks were much shorter than to the mild shocks. In the case of the 15-day-olds the response latencies to the dishabituating stimulus were too short to be measured accurately at the paper speed used, but all were 5 msec or less. Response latencies to the first 5 weak stimuli following dishabituation did not differ from those occurring prior to dishabituation.

Because responses to the mild shocks in the sampled periods did not differ in latency, these data were combined to generate the frequency distributions shown in Table 4.1. It is clear that latencies were much longer in the 3-day-olds than in the 15-day-olds and that the latencies of the 3-day-olds were longer when stimulated at 1.0-second intervals than at 8.0-second intervals.

This experiment shows that habituation of the flexor-withdrawal response in neonatal rats parallels a decline in the amplitude of the response and that latency to respond does not change during the course of habituation. When the response latencies to weak shock stimuli are compared with those elicited by the intense dishabituating stimulus, it is obvious that the former are much slower. A not unexpected finding is the observation that 15-day-old rats have response latencies two to three times shorter than 3-day-olds. This is probably due to increased myelination of axons in the response pathway (Jacobson, 1970) or maturation of some other aspect of neural or muscular function.

Further analysis indicated that the response latencies of the 3-day-olds were much more variable at the 1.0-second interstimulus interval than they were at the 8.0 ISI. The 15-day-olds did not show this difference. The greater variability of latencies in the 3-day-old, 1.0-second ISI condition may be due to the superimposition of elicited responses on a more variable background of interstimulus response. When high levels of interstimulus responding are present, the shock stimulus is about as likely to occur during the extension phase as in the flexion phase. Coincidence of extension and shock onset may be incompatible with flexion and thereby lengthen response latency. Conversely, stimulation

TABLE 4.1
Median Latency of Response (in msec)

		Trials			
Age	Interval	1-10	51-60	Dishabituation	101-105
3 days	1.0 sec	90	100	22.5	95
	8.0 sec	50	55	15	60
15 days	1.0 sec	20	25	5	20
	8.0 sec	30	12.5	5	20

during flexion may lead to spuriously short latencies. Similarly, response amplitudes may be either reduced or augmented.

Habituation as a Function of Age

The preceding experiments have shown that both reactivity to suprathreshold shock and the amount of response decline to repeated shock stimulation (at low frequencies) decrease with age. The fact that suprathreshold shocks elicit more responding in younger than in older rats suggests that a given shock is subjectively more intense in the younger rats.

In order to assess the possibility that differences in subjective intensity are responsible for differences in habituation during development, we varied stimulus intensity in this experiment to examine its effect on habituation. It is well documented that the amount of responding to stimuli of different intensities depends not only on the amount of habituation that has accrued to each intensity but also on differences in the immediate eliciting value of the stimuli. Using auditory startle stimuli of different intensities, Davis and Wagner (1968) showed that weak stimuli produced a greater response decrement within a session but that strong stimuli produced greater habituation as subsequently measured on standard test stimuli. Therefore we examined habituation in 3-, 6-, 10-, and 15-day-old rats using either 0.09-mA shocks or 0.18-mA shocks, half of the pups being tested with 0.09-mA shocks and half being tested with 0.18-mA shocks.

Because the differences in habituation that we observed during development are also dependent on the frequency of stimulation and since this variable may interact with stimulus intensity, we varied stimulus frequency as well as stimulus intensity. As is the case with stimulus intensity, measurement of habituation to different frequencies of stimulation depends not only on differences in habituation but also on the short-term effects of the previous stimulus (Davis, 1970). To assess habituation at different frequencies one must administer a test at a constant interval following habituation in order to eliminate this confounding. Because our data showed that there are no detectable effects of even a very strong stimulus after 30 sec (Fig. 4.4), we habituated pups to stimuli presented at either 2.0- or 4.0-second intervals and then tested them 30 sec after the habituation series. Half of each group at each frequency and each training intensity were tested at 0.09 mA and half at 0.18 mA.

The results of this experiment (Fig. 4.8) showed that as before there was a lesser response decline in the 15-day-old pups than in the younger pups when the stimuli were 0.18-mA shocks delivered at 4.0-second intervals. Reducing either stimulus intensity or the interval between stimuli attenuated this difference. At all ages less intense stimuli or more frequent stimulation resulted in a greater response decline. This result does not support the possibility that the developmental decrease in habituation results from a reduction in subjective intensity. On the contrary, it shows that stimuli of lesser intensity produce a greater within-session decrement.

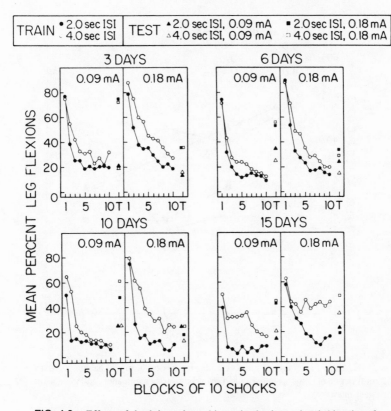

FIG. 4.8.   Effects of shock intensity and interstimulus interval on habituation of the forelimb flexion responses in 3-, 6-, 10-, and 15-day-old rats. Thirty seconds after completion of the habituation series, one-half of the subjects trained at each intensity were given 10 additional shocks at either the same intensity or the other intensity.

The effect of varying stimulus intensity during habituation on subsequent test performance can be seen in Fig. 4.9, which shows mean percent leg flexions for the 10 test trials. As described, half of the subjects in each training shock intensity were retested at that intensity and half at the other intensity. The results shown in Fig. 4.9 are the combined (averaged) frequencies of responding for both shock intensities. As expected, more habituation was seen in the high-intensity groups than the low-intensity groups. Frequency of shock stimulation had little effect during this habituation test. These data suggest that the amount of habituation, independent of other confoundings, changes very little with age and that if anything the older pups habituate slightly more than the younger ones. The deviant data point found at 15 days of age is believed to be a sampling artifact rather than an exception to the rule, because a replication of this part of the experiment showed that, as with all of the other groups, the more intense habituation stimulus yielded greater habituation on the test. These data also show

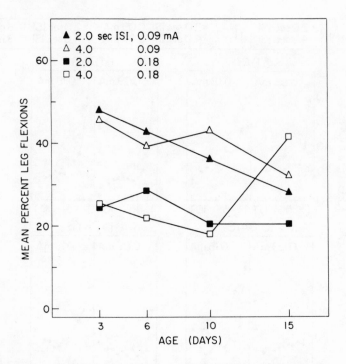

FIG. 4.9. Percentage of shocks eliciting leg flexion during the habituation test as a function of stimulus intensity and frequency during habituation, collapsed across test intensity.

that even though stimulus frequency influences performance during the habituation series, it has little effect on the amount of habituation as measured by the remote test.

To summarize, the results of this experiment suggest that the process of habituation does not vary appreciably as a function of age even though the observed decline in responding is not as great in the older subjects. The underlying mechanism for this apparently paradoxical finding may lie in the process of sensitization, a phenomenon closely linked to habituation and the subject of investigation in the following section.

Sensitization

The last experiment showed that even though responding at 15 days of age declined less than at 8 days of age, the amount of habituation as assessed on a remote test was about the same from 3 to 15 days of age. If habituation of the response is indeed the same for pups 3 to 15 days of age, then there must be another, facilitating process that is present in 15-day-olds but not in 3-day-olds. Groves and Thompson (1970) proposed that reiterated stimuli produce response sensitization as well as habituation. If this idea, which has since gained considerable experimental support (see Kandel, 1976; Thompson & Glanzman, 1976) is correct, then the higher response level of 15-day-old rats during the habituation session may result from greater response sensitization in these subjects. Observing response sensitization directly is difficult, because the two processes are said to act simultaneously to influence a common response. If, however, the two processes occur at different rates or reach their asymptotic levels of at different times, it may be possible to see the emergence of one of the processes by simply extending the length of the session. For example, if sensitization continues to increase after habituation has reached an asymptote, then one may see a sensitization-induced increase in responding after many shock presentations. Supportive evidence for this possibility was reported some time ago by Groves, Lee, and Thompson (1969).

To examine this possibility we gave pups 500 0.18-mA shocks at 4.0-second intervals instead of the usual 100 to 160 shocks. As in previous experiments, we

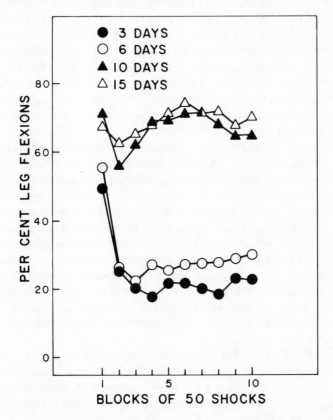

FIG. 4.10.   Percentage of shock stimuli eliciting leg flexions in 3-, 6-, 10-, and 15-day-old rats during an extended habituation series (500 stimulus presentations).

tested pups at 3, 6, 10 and 15 days of age. The results of this experiment can be seen in Fig. 4.10, which shows the percentage of shocks that were effective in eliciting forelimb withdrawal in blocks of 50 trials. It is quite clear that, as before, frequency of responding did not decline as much in the older pups as it did in the younger ones. Most interesting, however, is the fact that 10- and 15-day-old rats reached a response minimum during the second block (50th–100th shock) and then showed a consistent increase in responding during the next 4 blocks (100th–300th shock). Responding of 3- and 6-day-olds, in contrast, declined to a steady, low level after about 100 shocks and stayed at that level throughout the remainder of the session. They showed no evidence of a response increase like that seen in 10- and 15-day-old pups. These data suggest that sensitization can compensate for habituation but that sensitization does not emerge until between 6 and 10 days of age in the rat.

The inference that sensitization is responsible for the failure of 10- and 15-day-old rats to habituate in this experiment requires further explanation. Although we did not discuss it previously, dishabituation is thought by many investigators (e.g., Kandel, 1976; Thompson & Spencer, 1966) to result from "short-term" sensitization and not simply from removal of habituation. Similarly the perseverative behavioral activity (arousal) that occurs following shock is typically viewed as an index of short-term sensitization (e.g., Kandel, 1976, p. 635). Since these measures of short-term sensitization decline sharply between 6 and 10 days of age, the same period during which the "sensitization" shown in Fig. 4.10 emerges, it is apparent that these behavioral changes must reflect different underlying mechanisms.

"Long-term" sensitization, the counterpart to short-term sensitization, may account for the difference. Short-term sensitization is typically described as a brief state of arousal induced by a strong stimulus, or an unconditioned response to an emotional event. Long-term sensitization, in contrast, appears to be an acquired increase in reactivity that requires repetition to reach a maximum. It persists, as implied by its descriptive label, for an indefinite period as do other learned responses. Whether or not this is a form of "nonassociative" learning is moot, since the role of the US and other contextual cues have not been carefully evaluated. Our assumption here is that repeated presentation of shock results either in conditioning distress to contextual cues or that each shock becomes a predictive fear-arousing stimulus for subsequent shock. The acquired anxiety then summates with shock-induced withdrawal to produce greater responding.

We should also note that we are not happy with short-term and long-term sensitization as descriptive labels for these two phenomena, because they imply a continuity between the two processes that may not exist. Nonetheless we shall use these terms for the remainder of the chapter in deference to convention in the habituation literature.

Spontaneous Recovery and Rehabituation

Spontaneous recovery is a phenomenon common to both habituation and extinction of conditioned responses. If repeated trials with either procedure are followed by a rest interval, the criterion response tends to return toward pretraining levels, with the degree of return determined at least in part by the strength of original habituation or extinction. Given this basic relationship, spontaneous recovery can be used further to compare the amount of habituation developed by repetitive shock stimulation in rats of different ages. Rehabituation following a recovery interval can be used in the same manner.

In the following experiment the time required for a habituated response to return to preshock levels was measured in 3-, 6-, 10- and 15-day-old rats. Habituation was produced by administering 150 0.18-mA electric shocks to the forepaw at 1.0-sec intervals. This frequency of stimulation was chosen because it produced an approximately equal decline in responding in pups of all ages (see Fig. 4.5). Following habituation, pups at each age were divided into 4 groups and then tested for recovery by giving them an additional 100 shocks 10, 40, 160, or 640 seconds later.

During the initial habituation series the older pups habituated slightly more rapidly than the younger ones, but the asymptotic levels were comparable for all ages (Fig. 4.11, left panel). To show rate of recovery from habituation, the percentage of shocks eliciting a withdrawal response during the first 10 stimulus presentations of the test session were plotted as a function of recovery interval.

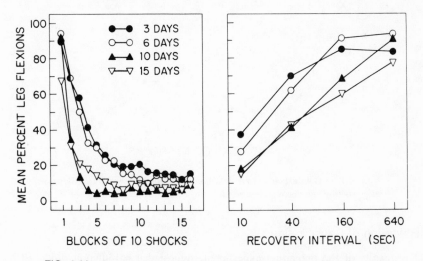

FIG. 4.11.   Spontaneous recovery from habituation as measured by percentage of shocks eliciting leg flexion during a 10-shock test series in 3-, 6-, 10-, and 15-day-old rats. The recovery intervals ranged from 10 to 640 seconds.

Although these data show that older pups required slightly longer to recover, the differences are minimal and tend to emphasize the invariance of recovery from habituation as a function of age rather than a major developmental trend.

To explore further the ontogenetic differences in persistence of habituation, we compared rehabituation of all pups at the 640-sec recovery interval with their performance during the original habituation series. No savings of habituation were observed with this measure. Instead there was a slight elevation in the asymptotic level of responding at all ages. These data are shown in Fig. 4.12. Our failure to find age-related differences in either spontaneous recovery from habituation or rehabituation following a 640-second recovery interval suggests again that the strength of habituation does not vary systematically as a function of age.

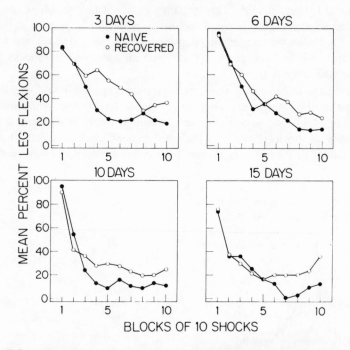

FIG. 4.12.   Habituation and rehabituation of the forelimb-withdrawal response after a 640-second recovery interval in 3-, 6-, 10-, and 15-day-old rats.

Retention of Sensitization

The results of the preceding experiment suggest that habituation produced by repetitive noxious stimulation is a transient phenomenon in all pups. Sensitization in contrast has been described as "a more or less permanent increment in an innate reaction upon repeated stimulation" (Razran, 1971, p. 58). The next experiment explored long-term retention of sensitization in developing animals as a function of age.

Because spaced training is presumed to produce greater sensitization than massed training (Kandel, 1976) we gave 3-, 6-, 10-, and 15-day-old rats 4 series of 150 0.18-mA shocks at 4.0-second intervals in lieu of the single 500-shock series shown in Fig. 4.10. A 1-hour interval separated successive series. A test series identical to the initial 150-stimulus series was administered 18 h after the end of training. Comparisons of performance on the test and initial training session are shown in Fig. 4.13.

From these data it is evident that 3- and 6-day-old pups show little residual effect of prior exposure to electrical stimulation of the forelimb. Responding during the test session is neither enhanced nor depressed, indicating that neither habituation nor sensitization is retained over the 18-hour period. In contrast, both the 10- and 15-day-old pups show significantly elevated levels of responding 18 hours later, suggesting again that sensitization to electric shock stimulation is a more permanently retained behavior.

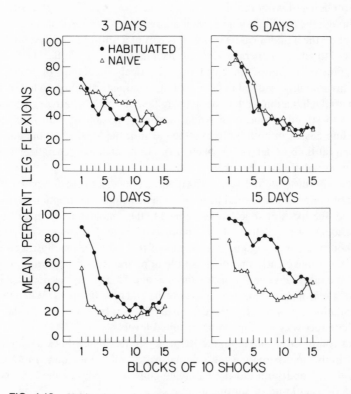

FIG. 4.13.   Habituation and rehabituation of the forelimb-withdrawal response following an 18-hour retention interval in 3-, 6-, 10-, and 15-day-old rats.

It is also important to emphasize, in considering the results of this study, that the experimental design could have lead to either sensitization or habituation. The four age groups were all given 600 relatively mild inescapable shocks and then administered an additional 150 shocks 18 hours later in order to assess the lasting effects of the initial stimulation. Give this paradigm, retention of either habituation or sensitization could have emerged after the 18-h retention interval. As noted, sensitization to electrical stimulation is without question the behavior that persists over the retention interval.

Generalization of Habituation

In studies of habituation in spinal and invertebrate animals habituation is typically specific to the sensorimotor pathway being stimulated (Groves & Thompson, 1970). The gill withdrawal response of *Aplysia*, for example, can be elicited by stimulation of either the siphon nerve or the branchial nerve, but habituation is specific to the pathway stimulated (Kandel, 1976). Repeated stimulation of the siphon nerve to the point of habituation does not affect the ability of the branchial nerve to elicit gill withdrawal.

Although the forelimb of a neonatal rat cannot easily be stimulated at different loci to elicit the withdrawal response, it is part of a sensorimotor system that may allow us to study generalization of habituation in a similar fashion. Our observation of the pups indicated that electrical stimulation of one forelimb almost invariability resulted in flexion of the contralateral limb in what seemed to be a partial elicitation of the stepping reflex. If this is the case it should be possible to stimulate one limb while measuring flexion of both forelegs until responding ceases in both limbs and then to shift the locus of stimulation to the contralateral limb to determine whether or not habituation generalizes from one locus of stimulation to the other.

To this purpose we delivered 150 0.18-mA shocks to the forepaw of 3- and 15-day-old pups at 1.0-second intervals. Then, without interruption of the shock sequence, the locus of shock was switched to the contralateral forepaw, and 100 more shocks were delivered. Responses of both forepaws were recorded throughout the entire session. The results of this experiment, illustrated in Fig. 4.14, show quite clearly that there is little or no transfer of habituation from one limb to the other. Frequency of flexion in 3- and 15-day-old rats declined in both limbs to a reasonably stable asymptote by the end of 150 shocks. When the locus of stimulation was shifted to the contralateral limb, both age groups showed an immediate recovery of responding to initial levels.

With continued stimulation, the frequency of flexion to shock declined in the second limb, approximating the original pattern of habituation. In 15-day-old groups the second limb did not habituate quite as rapidly as the first, possibly because of a build-up of sensitization.

It is thus certain that habituation derived from stimulation of one limb does not generalize to the contralateral limb even though that limb responded almost

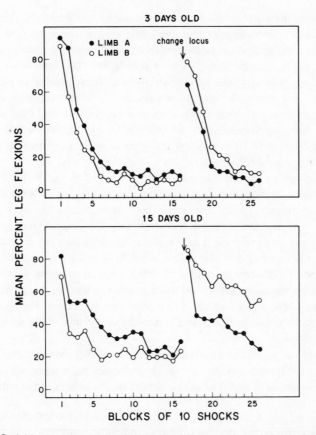

FIG. 4.14. Test for transfer of habituation following a change in locus of shock stimulation. Limb A was first stimulated at 1.0-second intervals until habituation was complete. Without interrupting the shock sequence, the locus of shock was then switched to Limb B. Responses from both Limb A and Limb B were recorded throughout the entire session. The left and right forelimbs were counterbalanced for order, half of the pups stimulated first on the left forelimb and half of the pups stimulated first on the right forelimb.

as frequently to the contralateral stimulation as the ipsilateral limb during the initial habituation series. This suggests that habituation of the forelimb-withdrawal response is stimulus- but not response specific. The finding that the previously habituated limb also responded vigorously as soon as the locus of shock was changed demonstrates again that fatigue plays little or no role in habituation of the withdrawal response, even in the youngest pups.

Localized vs. Generalized Reactivity to Shock

Until the last series of experiments we have measured the forelimb flexor response to shock as a discrete, perhaps reflexive reaction to shock. The finding that both forelimbs are almost equally activated by application of electric shock to only one forelimb suggests that even mild electric shock may be eliciting a diffuse set of motor and emotional responses, all of which decline as the animal habituates to the painful stimulation. If this is the case, then other responses elicited by the painful stimulation should show a parallel decline in frequency of occurrence. For example, audible vocalizations, which are also elicited by electric shock, may undergo habituation in a manner similar to the withdrawal response. Because vocalizations are elicited by electric shock but involve a different musculature, it is an ideal response to study in conjunction with the forelimb-withdrawal response.

In the following experiment, which was conducted by Dr. V. Haroutunian in our laboratory, habituation of vocalizations and the forelimb-withdrawal response were measured simultaneously. There were 200 electric shocks delivered to the forepaw at 4.0-second intervals following the general procedure used in the preceding experiments. Limb-withdrawal responses were automatically recorded as before on printout counters. Audible vocalizations occurring within 1 sec of shock onset were manually recorded via a microphone located ½ inch from the rat's snout and connected to an amplifier—loudspeaker system outside the chamber. The results of this experiment can be seen in Fig. 4.15, which shows without question that vocalizations habituate in concert with the withdrawal response.

This and the preceding experiment offer convincing evidence that the whole spectrum of responses elicited by shock undergoes habituation simultaneously and at about the same rate. From these results we can conclude that habituation to

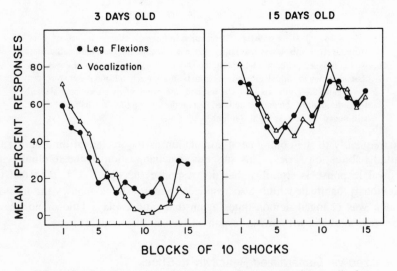

FIG. 4.15.   Percentage of shocks eliciting leg flexion and audible vocalizations in 3- and 15-day-old rats.

electric shock is stimulus-specific and response-general. Withdrawal of the stimulated and nonstimulated limb and vocalizations all show nearly identical rates of habituation, and changing the locus of shock restores responding. This stimulus specificity and response generality suggest that habituation to electric shock is more likely to be occurring in sensory pathways than in motor systems. In other words the rats behave as though they are becoming progressively less perceptive of the specific stimulus.

Forebrain Modulation of Behavior

An increasingly popular notion is that during the course of ontogenesis the forebrain gradually assumes greater and greater control of both generalized and reflexive behaviors. This view can be traced back to the early observations of Sir John Hughlings Jackson (cf. Taylor, 1931–1932), who proposed that function does not reside in any given region of the brain but is instead represented several times at different levels of the nervous system. Higher levels of the nervous system were said to have evolved slowly and to appear later during the course of ontogenesis. These late-developing structures were said to mediate function in a more finely tuned fashion and to inhibit lower, earlier developing regions of the brain. Damage to higher centers released the lower levels from inhibition, causing a regression to the lower, more premature level of function. A classic example of this sequence is the disappearance of reflexive nursing behaviors (e.g., rooting and suckling) during development and the reappearance of those behaviors following damage to the frontal lobes.

More recently this model has been used to characterize the course of behavioral arousal during development and the onset of reactivity to various neurotransmitter agonists and antagonists (cf. Mabry & Campbell, 1977). From these and related studies it is evident that many of the lesions and drugs that have their primary locus of action in the forebrain have little or no effect on behavior until the animal is 10 to 15 days of age or older. For example, anticholinergic agents do not increase behavioral arousal until the rat is 20 to 25 days of age (Campbell, Lytle, & Fibiger, 1969), and lesions of the hippocampus and cortex produce no visible effect on starvation-induced locomotor activity until the animals are about 15 or 20 days of age, respectively (Moorcroft, 1971). Similarly, frontal lesions do not produce hyperphagia until approximately 60 days postnatally (Kolb & Nonneman, 1976) indicating that some forebrain functions are very slow to appear in the developmental sequence.

Given our long-standing interest in the role of the forebrain in modulating behavior in the developing animal and what appears to be the generalized nature of responding elicited by electric shock, we undertook a series of preliminary studies to assess the effects of precollicular decerebration on the forelimb-with-drawal response at different stages of development. Our general expectation was that the forebrain would play a gradually increasing role in the control of shock-induced behavior. Of the previously presented data the strongest evidence suggesting that late-maturing structures might play such a role was observed in the study demonstrating that flexions continued much longer after intense, widely spaced shocks in the neonate than in the adult. Our hypothesis was that late-maturing structures acted to control or inhibit the intense neuronal activity induced by electric shock. It is also possible that the emergence of long-term sensitization is mediated by maturation of rostral brain structures.

To examine these possibilities we decerebrated 5-, 10-, 15-, and 20-day-old rats and then compared them to sham-operated controls using our standard habituation procedure for the forelimb-withdrawal response. The transections were performed by trephining the skull and inserting a wire knife to the base of the brain case. The cuts were completed by lateral and dorsal sweeps of the knife, maintaining gentle contact with the brain case. The transections passed just anterior to the superior colliculi dorsally and the mammillary bodies ventrally. The decerebrations were performed 2 to 3 hours prior to testing. This interval allowed recovery from the ether anesthesia and preceded severe physical deterioration of the animals.

The habituation series consisted of 100 0.18-mA shocks delivered to the forepaw at 2.0-second intervals followed by a 2.0-mA dishabituating shock and 50 more 0.18-mA shocks to assess rehabituation. Following testing, the pups were sacrificed and their brains examined to verify the level and completeness of the transection.

Although rigorous neurological tests were not administered, there were marked age-dependent effects of the transections that could be observed as soon as the pups recovered from the anesthesia. The transected 5-day-olds were indistinguishable from controls in terms of their gross behavior. Locomotion was normal in both form and level, and normal postures and righting reflexes were maintained. In pilot studies most of these pups survived until they were sacrificed two days later. However, suckling was abolished and they became emaciated.

The 15- and 20-day-old decerebrate pups differed markedly from their controls. From the time the pups recovered from anesthesia they were clearly hyperactive. They walked continuously in circles ranging from a few inches in diameter for some pups to a few feet in diameter for others. The walking had an automatic appearance, being very constant in rate. When the pups encountered an obstacle they walked over it if possible, never altering their stride. If the object was too high to walk over they reared and attempted to climb over it. In an enclosed chamber these pups persisted in trying to climb any wall that was encountered.

This "obstinate progression" (cf. Bailey & Davis, 1942) predominated for 1 to 2 hours following surgery. After this time they became less active, although they still moved in response to tactile stimulation. This relative quiescence characterized the period 2 to 4 hours following surgery. After about 4 hours of recovery the behavior changed again. The pups frequently had bursts of intense activity characterized by jumping produced by very powerful bilateral thrusts of the hindlimbs. These episodes, lasting 30 to 60 seconds, could be triggered by any sudden auditory or tactile stimulus. If several pups were together in an enclosed chamber, a loud clap of the hands was sufficient to trigger intense jumping in at least one of the pups. The animal invariably contacted one of the quiescent pups, which then started jumping, and the chain reaction continued.

This jumping differed from normal jumping in that it was very intense, was not goal-directed, and occurred continuously during the entire episode. Curiously, it was not possible to re-elicit a jumping episode until several minutes after termination of the previous one. After a jumping episode many but not all of the pups assumed a rigid, contorted posture that included extension of the limbs and a 60° to 90° twisting of the trunk, so that the hindlimbs were nearly parallel to the ground and the forelimbs pointing vertically upward.

Similar generalized hyperactivity interrupted by bursts of intense activity and "triggered" responses has been reported in the decerebrate kitten by Bignall and Schramm (1974). Davis and Gendelman (1977), in a study of habituation of the acoustic startle response in adult rats, reported that "handling the decerebrate during the postoperative recovery period frequently elicited hyperreflexia, whereby the rats would thrash around in the recovery cage. (p. 560)" They also noted the occurrence of this behavior without any obvious eliciting stimulus.

The 10-day-old decerebrate pups shared some behavioral anomalies with the older animals but failed to display others. These pups showed some of the increased extensor tonus seen in older pups, and some of the animals displayed the "automatic" locomotion described earlier for the older animals. However, all pups of this age failed to show the frantic jumping and contortions of the older pups.

The major results of this study are presented in Fig. 4.16, which shows the effects of decerebration on habituation and dishabituation in 5-, 10-, 15- and 20-day-old rats. Not surprisingly, the 15- and 20-day-old decerebrate pups were more likely to respond to the initial stimuli during habituation than their intact littermates. More striking, however, was the persistence of the withdrawal response throughout the session. At 20 days of age most of the animals responded to nearly every shock in the series, and none showed any appreciable tendency to habituate to the shock. These results are consistent with those of Davis and Gendelman (1977) and of Sharpless and Jasper (1956), who found that decerebrations retarded habituation of the startle response in the rat and auditory-evoked responses in the cat, respectively.

The limb-withdrawal responses of the older (15- and 20-day) decerebrate pups appeared to be much more vigorous and of greater magnitude than in intact pups. Somewhat surprisingly there was little shock-elicited perseverative responding during the interstimulus interval. In a further experiment in which we administered 2.0-mA shocks at 45-second intervals, a tabulation of intertrial responses indicated no significant differences in perseverative responding between intact

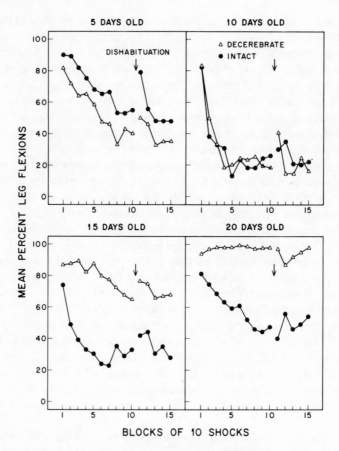

FIG. 4.16.   Percentage of shocks eliciting the forelimb-withdrawal response in 5-, 10-, 15-, and 20-day-old decerebrate pups and in intact littermates. Arrows indicate the insertion of a single intense stimulus into the habituation series.

and decerebrate 15- and 20-day-old rats. Given the intense and prolonged activity that occurs either spontaneously or following auditory or tactile stimulation in the recovery cage, this lack of perseverative activity was unexpected. Either the restraining characteristics of the canvas sling or the length of the postoperative period prior to testing may contribute to this difference. As noted earlier, maximum reactivity to auditory and tactile stimulation occurred 4 or more hours after surgery, but the animals were tested approximately 2 hours postoperatively. We should emphasize again, however, that the older decerebrates continued to react to nearly every shock during the 100 shock series, whereas the intact pups showed marked habituation to the shock. In addition an intense shock did not produce dishabituation in either 10- or 15-day-old rats. Taken together these results indicate that decerebration does not produce a simple regression to an earlier level of functioning. The behavioral profile obtained from the older decerebrates bears little relationship to the pattern of responding shown by 5-day-old neonates.

It was not surprising to find that decerebration had no effect on habituation of 5-day-old rats, because forebrain structures mature relatively slowly in the altricial rat. In addition, no gross behavioral changes were observed following the transection in those pups. It was, however, somewhat surprising to see no effect on habituation at 10 days of age, because these pups did show some behavioral changes similar to those observed in 15- and 20-day-olds. Furthermore, many of the ontogenetic changes in habituation and sensitization first appeared at 10 days, and it was our hypothesis that these changes reflected functional maturation of the forebrain. However, it should be noted that the observed behavioral changes following transections at 10 days were slighter than those found in older pups. Furthermore, normal 10-day-olds are somewhat inconsistent in their habituation performance, at times resembling the younger pups and at others the older pups. Thus it seems likely that 10 days of age is a transitional period during which some behaviors are affected by the transection and others not.

CONCLUSIONS AND PERSPECTIVES

Habituation

Overall the results of these experiments are similar in most respects to those reported by others who have studied habituation and sensitization in species ranging from *Aplysia* to man. With repeated electrical stimulation the forelimb flexor response declines in both frequency and amplitude. The decline is directly proportional to frequency of stimulation, inversely related to shock intensity, specific to the sensory pathway stimulated, and dishabituation is produced by strong shock to either the same or different locus. These behavioral changes comprise a number of the major characteristics of habituation (Thompson & Spencer, 1966). Habituation thus appears to be a universal phenomenon that appears very early in the developmental sequence. In this regard these findings are very much in agreement with W. R. Thompson's (1972) conjecture of some years ago suggesting that habituation, because of its inherent simplicity as an adaptive behavioral process, should appear very early in the developmental sequence. It is not necessarily the first "learned" behavior to occur, however. As Rudy and Cheatle report in Chapter 7, long-lasting learned aversion to odors can be conditioned shortly after birth.

These results are also in partial agreement with those of File and Plotkin (1974) and File and Scott (1976), who described habituation of air-puff-elicited head-turning in the neonatal rat. Like us, they found that habituation to the stimulus decreased with age during the early stages of development, but unlike us they found that this trend reversed at 9 days of age, with the older animals showing increasingly rapid habituation. Although they tentatively linked this sequence of behavioral development to maturation of the central nervous system, it is also possible that peripheral changes such as receptor sensitivity, increasing skin thickness, or hair growth altered reactivity to the air puff.

Our results and those of File and Plotkin (1974) and File and Scott (1976) contradict the statement of Feigley et al. (1972) that habituation does not occur prior to 15 days of age in the rat. Their measure of habituation, however, was reactivity to novel environmental stimuli, many of which could not be processed prior to that age because of sense organ immaturity.

Empirically the most striking change we found during development was the apparent increase in resistance to habituation that emerged between days 6 and 10 postnatally. Further research suggested, however, that this failure to show a decline in responding to repetitive stimulation did not indicate a change in habituation per se, but reflected instead the maturation of an antagonistic process, long-term sensitization. Several experiments were conducted to assess the strength of habituation unconfounded by sensitization. All seemed to indicate that the degree of habituation induced by repetitive electrical stimulation of the forelimb was relatively invariant during the course of development. As a simple, or perhaps the simplest, form of learning this result is not unexpected. Phylogenetically there is little to suggest that habituation changes during the course of evolution, and it is therefore not surprising for it to remain unchanged during the course of postnatal ontogenesis in the rat.

Sensitization

The most unexpected findings obtained thus far in this research program were the changes in short-term and long-term sensitization that occurred during development. Short-term sensitization, as measured by perseverative reactivity to shock and the dishabituating effects of intense shock, are strongly present at 3 days of age postnatally, the first age examined. They remain unchanged for at least the next 3 days of development, but then between 6 and 10 days of age they begin to decline precipitously, and by 15 days of age there is little evidence of short-term sensitization.

This striking change in short-term sensitization during development almost certainly reflects maturation of the central nervous system, either within the spinal cord or in higher brain centers. The likelihood, however, is that the major changes mediating this transition are occurring within the spinal cord. As reported, high decerebrations do not lead to the reappearance of short-term sensitization, and in an experiment just completed we found that spinal transections did not produce an increase in short-term sensitization at any age. In a related experiment, blockade of pre- and postsynaptic inhibition with picro-toxin and strychnine in subconvulsant doses restored perseverative responding to its neonatal form in spinally transected 15-day-old pups but had no effect on 5-day-olds. This evidence strongly suggests that the attenuation of short-term sensitization during the course of normal development is due to the functional maturation of inhibitory circuits intrinsic to the spinal cord. These data conform with the suggestion made by Gilbert and Stelzner (1975) that the motor immaturity of the neonatal rat is due to a lack of local connections within the spinal cord rather than to a paucity of supraspinal control.

Of equal interest is the absence of long-term sensitization during the first 6 days of postnatal development and its rapid emergence between Days 6 and 10. Again the likelihood is that maturation of either the spinal cord or higher brain centers is responsible for the change. In this instance we are considerably less certain of the locus of central nervous system change mediating the transition. It would be intuitively pleasing to us, however, if sensitization were a "higher mental process" related to late-maturing supraspinal structures. Empirically, however, we have no evidence to support this conclusion.

It also should be noted that the emergence of long-term sensitization parallels development of the infant rat's ability to acquire shock-avoidance and escape responses. Although this may be simply a coincidence, it raises the possibility that what the neurobiologists call long-term sensitization and what behavioral psychologists infer to be conditioned fear may be similar or overlapping concepts.

Learning and Memory

The major implications of this research for the ontogeny of learning and memory are covered extensively in other portions of the chapter. Of particular importance is the early appearance of habituation and the somewhat later appearance of long-term sensitization.

Not emphasized is the ontogeny of memory, a major subject of this volume. To date, as is evident, we have focused on other aspects of habituation and sensitization in order to understand these basic processes before considering memory mechanisms. The single set of experiments dealing with memory resulted in retention of sensitization rather than habituation. The generality of this result is uncertain, since a parametric analysis of the effects of number of stimuli presented, stimulus intensity, and distribution of training is yet to be done. Kandel (1976) reported retention of sensitization with a few intense stimuli but retention of habituation with many mild stimuli. Similarly, File and Plotkin (1974) and File and Scott (1976) found retention of habituation rather than sensitization using an innocuous air puff as the eliciting stimuli.

One of the important differences between stimuli that produce long-term sensitization and those that produce long-term habituation seems to be their ability to produce pain. In this regard, electric shock is unique in that even at low levels shock stimulation is accompanied by a sensation of pain. This property of shock may explain why, in our studies, long-term retention was manifested as sensitization rather than as a savings of habituation.

It is also worth emphasizing once again that habituation and sensitization are specific to the sensorimotor systems stimulated. Generalizations from one sensory domain to another may be unwarranted, and certainly the age at which habituation and sensitization of a given response appear will be linked to the maturity of the underlying system, both peripherally and centrally.

Forebrain Modulation of Behavior

To some extent the heightened behavioral reactivity produced by precollicular transection in the 15- and 20-day-old pups can be viewed as support for the Jacksonian view of development. Removal of late-maturing levels of the nervous system leaves the animal in an unchecked hyperarousal state. Although this may reflect a regression to an earlier level of functioning, the decerebrate animal is quite unlike the neonate even though both can be assumed to have either nonfunctioning or minimally functioning forebrains. For example, the decerebrate 20-day-old does not habituate rapidly to repetitive shock as does the 3-day-old, nor does a single intense shock produce marked dishabituation as it does at 3 days of age. Similarly, intense shock does not produce the prolonged perseverative motor activity characteristic of the 3-day-old pup's reaction to shock. In short, decerebration does not produce a simple regression to an earlier, neonatal level of responding as might be predicted from the Jacksonian model. Although components of the neonatal state may be unearthed by the decerebration, it also appears that the transection results in a pathological state in which the remaining caudal brain systems function abnormally following the sudden removal of inputs from the forebrain.

SUMMARY

Response Characteristics

In response to mild electric shock applied to the forelimb, the neonatal rat displays a rapid flexion of that limb closely followed by flexion of the contralateral limb and less specific movements of the hindlimbs. In the neonates flexor—extensor activity continues for some time in all four limbs before quiescence returns. Discrete, audible vocalizations are also evoked by the onset of shock. As development proceeds, reactivity to the shock decreases, and the time course of the shock-induced activity becomes abbreviated. Response latencies decrease and response amplitudes increase, but response thresholds to electrical stimulation remain constant throughout the course of development. These developmental changes are summarized in the left panel of Fig. 4.17.

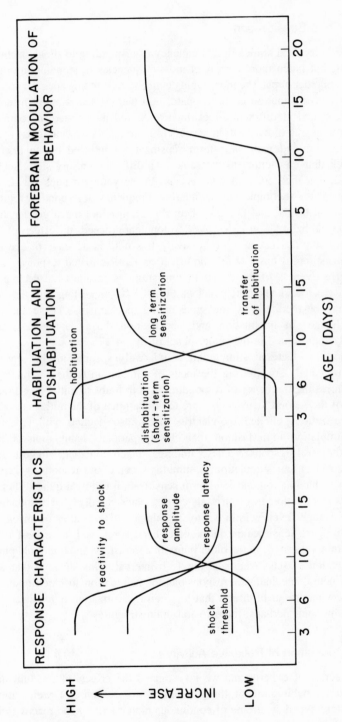

FIG. 4.17. Summary of the developmental changes in response characteristics (*left panel*), habituation and sensitization (*center panel*), and the effect of precollicular decerebrations (*right panel*).

Habituation and Sensitization

With repeated electrical stimulation, frequency of responding to shock declines (habituation), but much more rapidly at most frequencies of stimulation in the neonate than in older pups. The more rapid decline in responding does not appear to reflect greater habituation in the neonate, however. When pups of different ages are habituated at different shock intensities and then tested at common intensities, the degree of habituation appears to be roughly constant across ages. Dishabituation (an index of short-term sensitization) induced by an intense electric shock delivered either to the same or a different sensory site changes profoundly during the course of ontogenesis. In the youngest pups the strong shock produces almost complete dishabituation. Frequency of responding returns to prehabituation levels, and the rate of rehabituation is not much greater than that for the initial habituation series. As development proceeds the effects of the dishabituating stimulus become progressively less until at 15 days of age the dishabituating stimulus has virtually no effect on the habituated response. The decline in effectiveness of the dishabituating stimulus parallels the decline in reactivity to electric shock (left panel of Fig. 4.17), suggesting that the two processes may be mediated by the same neural mechanisms. These and the following changes in habituation and sensitization during ontogenesis are schematically represented in the center panel of Fig. 4.17.

Habituation to electrical stimulation is relatively specific to the sensory pathways stimulated. Transferring the locus of stimulation to the contralateral forelimb restores the frequency of responding in both limbs to initial levels, and habituation of the second locus is no more rapid than that of the initial site. The audible vocalizations elicited by electric shock also decline with repeated electrical stimulation in a fashion that closely parallels habituation of the forelimb-withdrawal response. These findings, taken together, suggest that habituation to electrical stimulation is stimulus-specific and response-general.

Retention of habituation and long-term sensitization follow a quite different time course. Habituation to electric shock dissipates rapidly, and responding returns to preshock levels within 15 to 20 minutes of cessation of shock in animals of all ages. Sensitization on the other hand is retained for at least 18 h (the longest interval tested) in the older pups. In contrast, 3- and 6-day-old pups show no retention of sensitization at the 18-h interval. This suggests that the sensory and neural mechanisms responsible for habituation to electric shock stimulation are mature at birth and that long-term sensitization is mediated by later-developing and, perhaps, more rostral brain structures.

Forebrain Modulation of Reflexive Activity

In the final series of experiments we investigated the effects of precollicular decerebration on habituation of the forelimb flexor response. Decerebration produced a stereotyped syndrome of continuous motor activity and reactivity in older animals but had no effect in the younger pups, suggesting that decerebration releases lower brain activity from late-maturing forebrain inhibitory functions in the Jacksonian sense. However, other aspects of neonatal behavior did not reappear following decerebration. Habituation did not occur rapidly, the effects of a strong dishabituating stimulus were minimal, and intense shock did not produce prolonged perseverative activity. These effects are the opposite of those seen in the 3-day-old neonate. In short, decerebration did not produce a simple repression to an earlier, neonatal level of responding as might be predicted from the Jacksonian model.

ACKNOWLEDGMENT

The authors express their thanks to the American Psychological Association for permission to use Figures 4.1—4.10 in this chapter. These figures were reproduced from Stehouwer and Campbell, 1978. © 1978, Journal of Experimental Psychology: Animal Behavior Processes.

REFERENCES

Bailey, P., & Davis, E. W. The syndrome of obstinate progression in the cat. *Proceedings of the Society for Experimental Biology and Medicine*, 1942, *51*, 1841.

Bignall, K. E., & Schramm, L. Behavior of chronically decerebrated kittens. *Experimental Neurology*, 1974, *42*, 519—531.

Bronstein, P. M., & Dworkin, T. Replication: The persistent locomotion of immature rats. *Bulletin of the Psychonomic Society*, 1974, *4*, 124—126.

Bronstein, P. M., Neiman, H., Wolkoff, F. D., & Levine, M. J. The development of habituation in the rat. *Animal Learning and Behavior*, 1974, *2*, 92—96.

Campbell, B. A., Lytle, L. D., & Fibiger, H. C. Ontogeny of adrenergic arousal and cholinergic inhibitory mechanisms in the rat. *Science*, 1969, *166*, 637—638.

Campbell, B. A., & Masterson, F. A. Psychophysics of punishment. In B. A. Campbell & R. M. Church (Eds.), *Punishment and aversive behavior*. New York: Appleton-Century-Crofts, 1969.

Cohen, L. B. Habituation of infant visual attention. In T. J. Tighe & R. N. Leaton (Eds.), *Habituation: Perspectives from child development, animal behavior and neurophysiology*. Hillsdale, N.J.: Lawrence Erlbaum Associates, 1976.

Davis, M. Effects of interstimulus interval length and variability on startle-response habituation in the rat. *Journal of Comparative and Physiological Psychology*, 1970, *72*, 177—192.

Davis, M. & Gendelman, P. M. Plasticity of the acoustic startle response in the acutely decerebrate rat. *Journal of Comparative and Physiological Psychology*, 1977, *91*, 549—563.

Davis, M., & Wagner, A. R. Startle responsiveness after habituation to different intensities of tone. *Psychonomic Science*, 1968, *12*, 337—338.

Feigley, D. A., Parsons, P. J., Hamilton, L. W., & Spear, N. E. The development of habituation to novel environments in the rat. *Journal of Comparative and Physiological Psychology*, 1972, *79*, 443—452.

File, S. E., & Plotkin, H. C. Habituation in the neonatal rat. *Developmental Psychobiology*, 1974, *7*, 121—127.

File, S. E., & Scott, E. M. Acquisition and retention of habituation in the preweanling rat. *Developmental Psychobiology*, 1976, *9*, 97—107.

Gilbert, M., & Stelzner, D. J. The pattern of supraspinal and dorsal root connections in the lumbo-sacral spinal cord of the newborn rat. *Neuroscience Abstracts*, 1975, *1*, 747.
Griffin, J. P. Neurophysiological studies into habituation. In G. Horn & R. A. Hinde (Eds.), *Short-term changes in neural activity and behavior*. Cambridge: Cambridge University Press, 1970.
Groves, P. M., Lee, D., & Thompson, R. F. Effects of stimulus frequency and intensity on habituation and sensitization in acute spinal cat. *Physiology & Behavior*, 1969, *4*, 383–388.
Groves, P. M., & Thompson, R. F. Habituation: A dual-process theory. *Psychological Review*, 1970, *77*, 419–450.
Jacobson, M. *Developmental neurobiology*. New York: Holt, Rinehart & Winston, Inc., 1970.
Jeffrey, W. E. Habituation as a mechanism for perceptual development. In T. J. Tighe & R. N. Leaton (Eds.), *Habituation: Perspectives from child development, animal behavior and neurophysiology*. Hillsdale, N.J.: Lawrence Erlbaum Associates, 1976.
Kandel, E. R. *Cellular basis of behavior: An introduction to behavioral neurobiology*. San Francisco: Freeman, 1976.
Kolb, B., & Nonneman, A. J. Functional development of prefrontal cortex in rats continues into adolescence. *Science*, 1976, *193*, 335–336.
Mabry, P. D., & Campbell, B. A. Developmental psychopharmacology. In L. L. Iverson, S. D. Iverson, & S. H. Snyder (Eds.), *Handbook of psychopharmacology* (Vol. 7). New York: Plenum Press, 1977.
Moorcroft, W. H. Ontogeny of forebrain inhibition of behavioral arousal in the rat. *Brain Research*, 1971, *35*, 513–522.
Narayanan, C. H., Fox, M. W., & Hamburger, V. Prenatal development of spontaneous and evoked activity in the rat (Rattus norvegicus albinus). *Behavior*, 1971, *40*, 100–134.
Razran, G. *Mind in Evolution*. Boston: Houghton-Mifflin, 1971.
Sharpless, S. K., & Jasper, H. Habituation of the arousal reaction. *Brain*, 1956, *79*, 655–680.
Stehouwer, D. J. Habituation of the limb-withdrawal response in the developing rat. Unpublished doctoral dissertation, Princeton University, 1977.
Stehouwer, D. J., & Campbell, B. A. Habituation of the forelimb-withdrawal response in neonatal rats. *Journal of Experimental Psychology: Animal Behavior Processes*, 1978, *4*, 104–119.
Stelzner, D. J. The normal postnatal development of synaptic end-feet in the lumbrosacral spinal cord and of responses in the hindlimb of the albino rat. *Experimental Neurology*, 1971, *31*, 337–357.
Taylor, J. *Selected writings of John Hughlings Jackson* (Vols. I and II). London: Hodder & Stoughton, 1931–1932.
Thompson, R. F., & Glanzman, D. L. Neural and behavioral mechanisms of habituation and sensitization. In T. J. Tighe & R. N. Leaton (Eds.), *Habituation: Perspectives from child development, animal behavior and neurophysiology*. Hillsdale, N.J.: Lawrence Erlbaum Associates, 1976.
Thompson, R. F., & Spencer, W. A. Habituation: A model phenomenon for the study of neuronal substrates of behavior. *Psychological Review*, 1966, *73*, 16–43.
Thompson, W. R. Storage mechanisms in early experience. *Minnesota Symposium on Child Psychology*, 1972, *6*, 97–127.
Vaughn, J. E., & Grieshaber, J. A. A morphological investigation of an early reflex pathway in developing rat spinal cord. *Journal of Comparative Neurology*, 1973, *148*, 177–209.
Wagner, A. R. Priming in STM: An information processing mechanism for self-generated or retrieval-generated depression in performance. In T. J. Tighe & R. N. Leaton (Eds.), *Habituation: Perspectives from child development, animal behavior and neurophysiology*. Hillsdale, N.J.: Lawrence Erlbaum Associates, 1976.
Wyers, E. J., Peeke, H. V. S., & Herz, M. J. Behavioral habituation in invertebrates. In H. V. S. Peeke and M. J. Herz (Eds.), *Habituation, Vol. 1: Behavioral studies*. New York: Academic Press, 1973.

5 Development of Learning and Memory Processes in Infant Mice

Z. Michael Nagy
Bowling Green State University

INTRODUCTION AND BACKGROUND

Developmental Approach to Learning and Memory

Among the many diverse approaches utilized by psychologists in their attempts to understand learning and memory processes better, one that has received rather belated attention is the ontogenetic or developmental approach. This approach involves the longitudinal and cross-sectional study of learning and memory capabilities, beginning at the very earliest ages of an organism and continuing through adulthood. It is well known that a number of organisms, particularly altricial mammals such as man, dogs, cats, rats, and mice, are born with a relatively immature central nervous system (CNS). Marked changes in brain structure, organization, and function continue postnatally through the infantile period and even extend into adulthood in some species (Himwich, 1970). Thus the developmental approach, which emphasizes the parallels between the emergence of structure and function in the maturing organism, may well provide us with insights concerning the underlying mechanisms of learning and memory that would not be possible by study of the adult alone. As Riesen (1971) has recently noted, "Less artificial or 'nonphysiological' than ablation, or even electrical or chemical stimulation techniques, growth of the organism provides alterations in brain that may be monitored and correlated with behavioral change [p. 60]."

The potential strength of the developmental approach rests on the fact that the maturation of neural CNS functions proceeds in a heterochronic fashion (Anokhin, 1964), beginning at the lower levels of the spinal cord and advancing up to the forebrain. In addition, the maturation of various structures and biochemical processes at particular levels of the CNS also proceeds at somewhat different rates (Himwich, 1970, 1973; Lanier, Dunn, & Van Hartesveldt, 1976; Paoletti & Davison, 1971; Sterman, McGinty, & Adinolfi, 1971; Tobach, Aronson, & Shaw, 1971; Vernadakis & Weiner, 1974, for recent and comprehensive reviews). These changes in CNS structure and function are paralleled by a progression of identifiable behavioral tendencies (Altman & Bulut, 1976; Bolles & Woods, 1964; Fox, 1965; Gottlieb, 1971) representative of particular periods in development within a given species. The emergence of distinctive response patterns, at least in theory then, should signal the functional consolidation and integration of specific CNS components involved in those response patterns.

Inadequacies of Early Research

Although comparative psychologists began around the beginning of this century to investigate the question of whether young animals learned as well as older ones, it has only been within the last 15 years that a clear picture of the relationship between age and learning/memory abilities has begun to emerge. Earlier studies yielded all possible conclusions: Younger animals were reported to learn faster, to learn at the same rate, and to learn more slowly than adults. In a review of this early literature, Campbell (1967) attributed these inconsistent and contradictory findings to the naive state of psychology at the time this research was conducted, when early investigators were unaware of, and subsequently failed to consider and control for, a number of variables that might have been expected to affect differentially learning and performance at various levels of maturity. For example, few investigators gave any consideration to the levels of reinforcement or motivation used in their studies, much less to the possibility that the roles of these factors vary with the different ages. In addition, little attention was paid to the effects of prior experience and/or learning upon later learning and memory, to the manner in which age-related unlearned behaviors might affect learning and performance, or to the selection of appropriate measures of learning and retention. Given the failure to consider these important variables, it is hardly surprising that all possible conclusions regarding the relationship between age and learning ability were reported.

In 1962, Campbell and Campbell provided the first set of unequivocal data concerning memory abilities of the rat as a function of age. In that study, 18-, 23-, 38-, 54-, and 100-day-old rats received a series of inescapable shocks in one of two sides of a black—white shuttlebox but no shocks in the other side. The rats were later retested for the amount of fear that had become associated with the shock side of the shuttlebox following intervals of 0, 7, 21, or 42 days. The results clearly demonstrated that retention of learned fear varied enormously as a function of age at original conditioning. Whereas older animals showed little loss of fear with increasing retention intervals, younger rats exhibited marked losses of fear. Although it was not possible to determine directly whether or not each group had acquired equivalent amounts of fear during conditioning owing to the fact that no response was required, the authors suggested that acquisition appeared approximately equal for all groups, because there was little difference among groups at the shortest retention interval. In addition, resistance-to-extinction data from another experiment revealed no age-related differences. Thus it was not likely that the age-related differences in retention were due to unequal amounts of learning at the various ages.

The failure of early studies investigating learning in young and adult animals to consider the possibility of differences in motivation levels as a function of age was also avoided in the Campbell and Campbell (1962) study. Following a series of experiments that demonstrated major differences in the effects of food and/or water deprivation at various ages (Campbell & Cicala, 1962; Campbell, Teghtsoonian, & Williams, 1961; Williams & Campbell, 1961), Campbell's group reported that shock appeared to induce equivalent levels of motivation across a wide range of ages in the rat (Campbell, 1967; Candland, Teghtsoonian, & Campbell, 1958). Thus the use of a shock level that was equally aversive across the age range employed by Campbell and Campbell allowed differences in motivation to be ruled out as a critical factor contributing to the relatively poor memory displayed by young rats. This finding was a major advance in the area of developmental learning and memory and was extremely influential in the studies with rats that followed, as evidenced by the fact that the majority of later research employed shock as a motivating stimulus at the early ages.

Recent Findings and Conclusions

Since 1962, a large number of experiments have been reported that attempted to determine the generalizability of the Campbells' findings of age-related memory deficits, or "infantile amnesia," to other kinds of learning tasks, particularly those involving instrumental learning. (Because extensive and up-to-date reviews covering a number of species are available in the literature, e.g., Campbell, 1967; Campbell & Coulter, 1976; Campbell, Riccio, & Rohrbaugh, 1971; Campbell & Spear, 1972; Spear, 1973; the studies cited in the present chapter should be considered as illustrative rather than comprehensive in scope. In addition, the major focus of attention in the present chapter will be on those studies involving lower mammals, particularly rodents.) For example, researchers have investigated age-related learning and/or memory abilities in simple shock-escape (Egger, 1974), discriminated shock-escape in single- (Campbell, Misanin, White, & Lytle, 1974) and double- (Smith, 1968) unit T mazes, active- (Feigley & Spear, 1970; Kirby, 1963; Riccio, Rohrbaugh, & Hodges, 1968) and passive- (Campbell et al., 1974; Feigley & Spear, 1970; Riccio et al., 1968; Riccio & Schulenburg, 1969; Schulenburg, Riccio, & Stikes, 1971) avoidance tasks, and light—dark discrimination tasks using food reinforcement (Campbell, Jaynes, & Misanin, 1968).

Overall, the results have been remarkably consistent. For the rat, the age-related memory function first reported by Campbell and Campbell (1962) for retention of acquired fear has been replicated on all of the tasks employed, with younger rats displaying considerably poorer memories of learned responses, particularly at the longer retest intervals, than adult animals. The hypothesis that such long-term memory deficits are due primarily to neurological immaturity at the time of original learning (Campbell et al., 1971; Campbell & Coulter, 1976; Campbell & Spear, 1972) has been especially appealing to investigators of behavioral development and has received recent additional support from cross-species studies using the guinea pig. Unlike the rat, the guinea pig undergoes the major portion of central nervous system (CNS) development during gestation (Dobbing & Sands, 1970; Flexner, 1955), and by most neurological and behavioral indices the newborn guinea pig appears comparable to the 30-40-day-old rat. When retested after various retention intervals following training on either escape or passive-avoidance tasks, young guinea pigs appear to remember as well as their adult counterparts (Campbell et al., 1974).

Whereas young rats consistently display poorer long-term memory than adults on a variety of learning tasks, differences in learning abilities appear task-specific. When the task requires a response to be made, most studies have found little difference among age groups in the rates of acquisition. When age-related deficits have been found, they have usually involved subjects less than 20 days of age, a stage of development where the more limited perceptual—motor abilities might be expected to result in performance deficits. Provided that the response is capable of being made equally well among age groups, Campbell and Coulter (1976) have tentatively concluded that a certain level of maturity *is not* a necessary condition for animals to acquire the basic response-reinforcement contingencies.

On tasks requiring the inhibition of a response, however, young rats have consistently been reported to acquire the task at a slower rate than adults (Feigley & Spear, 1970; Riccio et al., 1968; Schulenburg et al., 1971). Because there is evidence that inhibitory control develops more slowly and only after excitatory control in the rat, many investigators have attributed the poorer passive-avoidance learning by young rats to the relative lack of inhibitory control at those ages (see Campbell et al., 1971, for historical review of this literature). Experimental evidence showing the relatively slow development of inhibition of spontaneous activity in the rat (Campbell, Lytle, & Fibiger, 1969; Fibiger, Lytle, & Campbell, 1970) as compared to the guinea pig (Campbell & Mabry, 1972; Oakley & Plotkin, 1975) and the lack of age-related differences on passive-avoidance acquisition by the guinea pig (Campbell et al., 1974) is consistent with this conclusion. However, other possible reasons for the age-related deficit in passive-avoidance acquisition by the rat have been postulated (Campbell & Coulter, 1976) and are considered in a later part of this chapter.

Rationale and General Method for Our Research Program

Choice of the mouse as subject.   The purpose of the remaining portion of this chapter is to review some of the research from our laboratory that has been conducted in an attempt to trace the development of instrumental learning and memory capabilities in the mouse (*Mus musculus*). Although the mouse has been infrequently used as the subject for studies in the development of learning and memory, it has much to recommend it for this area of research. Aside from the practical aspects of being smaller and consequently less costly to rear and maintain than other rodents such as the rat, there is also available an extensive neurophysiological and biochemical literature (Green, 1966) for this species. In addition, the enormous variety of inbred and outbred strains that are currently available, many of which are known to differ in maturational rates of brain chemistry and behaviors (Fox, 1970; Fuller & Geils, 1972, 1973; Garrard, Harrison, & Weiner, 1974; Wahlsten, 1975), should allow for correlations between brain and behavioral development within the same species. Cross-species comparisons can also be readily made with the rat. Although it is a gross oversimplification to think of the mouse as a smaller version of the rat, it is known that both species undergo similar stages of postnatal CNS development. However, biochemical, morphological, electrophysiological (Agrawal & Himwich, 1970; Folch, Casals, Pope, Meath, LeBaron, & Lees, 1959; Kobayashi, Inman, Buno, & Himwich, 1963), and behavioral (Fox, 1965; Nagy, Murphy, & Ray, 1975) evidence suggests that the mouse matures at a somewhat faster rate than the rat.

Focus upon learning–memory development during brain "growth spurt" period. When we initiated this research project in 1968, our assessment of the then-current literature dealing with the development of learning and memory in rodents was that relatively little attention had been directed toward the question of when instrumental learning and retention abilities first become behaviorally evident during ontogeny. The majority of research had focused on the generality of the infantile amnesia effect, and in most of these studies the youngest age groups were typically weanlings, 20 to 25 days of age. It will be recalled that for tasks requiring a response to be made, rats at this age usually learn as rapidly as adults and also demonstrate retention of learning on several tasks that is equivalent to the adult for at least 24 hours. One might therefore conclude that mechanisms underlying a memory process for these tasks had sufficiently matured by 20 days of age to allow behavioral expression of that memory to be maintained for at least 24 hours. However, it is known that the period of most rapid CNS development, or the brain "growth spurt," is ending at about 20 days of age in the rat, with a major portion of physiological and biochemical brain development having already taken place (Davison & Dobbing, 1968; Dobbing, 1968). The first question we posed, then, was whether the onset of a 24-hour memory ability for certain simple tasks would become behaviorally evident during the brain growth spurt period, about 5 to 15 days of age in the rat and mouse. In other words would it be possible to determine two ages, perhaps only several days apart, at which learning could be demonstrated for both ages but 24-hour memory only for the latter within the brain growth spurt period?

A related question was whether or not it would be possible to utilize tasks and response measures that would allow us to examine the continuity of the learning and memory processes between this period of maturation and adulthood. It should be emphasized that we were not interested in the general question of when the capacity for instrumental learning per se develops. As Campbell and Coulter (1976) point out, many of the early conclusions that instrumental learning could not take place prior to a certain level of postnatal maturation (Cornwell & Fuller, 1961; Fuller, Easler, & Banks, 1950; James & Cannon, 1952) were based on dependent measures commonly used for the adult but that may have been beyond the limited sensory and response capabilities of the young puppy.

Recent evidence of instrumental learning capabilities at early ages.   More recent experiments that have required responses within the capability of the young organism and that provided reinforcements more relevant to that developmental stage have been successful in demonstrating instrumental learning at ages much younger than previously thought possible. For example, Stanley has demonstrated appetitive learning in the puppy within the first week of life when reinforcement was suckling an artificial nipple for milk (Stanley, Bacon, & Fehr, 1970), and Rosenblatt (1971, 1972, this volume) has demonstrated similar learning in the kitten. Rat pups can learn to traverse a runway for nonlactating suckling by 10 to 11 days of age (Amsel, Burdette, & Letz, 1976; Amsel, Radek, Graham, & Letz, 1977; Amsel, Chapter 8, this volume) and can learn a simple Y maze discrimination by 7 days of age for a similar reinforcement and retain that learning for at least two days (Kenny & Blass, 1977).

Shock as a motivating stimulus.   Because our primary interest was in determining whether or not learning and memory capabilities for instrumental responding developed within a very limited age range, 5 to 15 days of age, it was necessary to select a motivating stimulus that would allow for very rapid learning, preferably within a single training session of short duration. For this reason learning tasks such as the homing task developed by Altman and Bulut (1976) were not appropriate, because learning and retention of this task required a number of training days to become apparent. However, shock-motivated tasks provide for rapid learning with weanling and adult animals. In addition, the aversiveness of a particular level of shock has been reported to be relatively uniform in rats between 25 and 100 days of age (Campbell, 1967). Therefore we naturally turned to shock as a potentially useful motivating stimulus to study the development of learning and memory in mice.

Before proceeding with learning studies, however, it was first necessary to determine if a shock stimulus could be successfully used with very young mice. It was quite possible that even low levels of shock would prove incapacitating to our youngest groups and that they would be unable to make either approach or escape responses during the periods of shock exposure. Secondly, provided that very young mice were capable of responding to shock with reasonably coordinated responses, it was also necessary to determine whether or not the aversiveness of a particular level of shock resulted in similar behaviors during this age range of rapid morphological development. At 5 days of age the mouse pup is hairless, poikilothermic, functionally blind and deaf, and locomotes primarily by crawling on its stomach, usually pivoting in circles. By 15 days of age the mouse is thermoregulating to some degree, is capable of seeing and hearing, and is able to run upright on all four feet in a coordinated fashion. A phase of development with such major behavioral and biological change would seem likely to result in marked differences in responsivity to shock.

The procedure we employed was a modification of that reported by Campbell (1967). The apparatus was a small Plexiglas rectangular cage (16 cm × 5 cm × 7.5 cm) with a grid floor through which scrambled shock (60-Hz AC constant current) could be applied, and photocells and infrared light sources were mounted at either end of the cage so that crossings could be monitored. Basically, the breaking of one of the photobeams turned on shock and a timer, whereas breaking the alternate beam turned both off, providing "shock" and "safe" sides of the cage. If the mouse returned to the shock side after having escaped to the safe side, shock was again turned on until the pup escaped back to the safe side. However, because 5 to 9-day-old mice exhibit extremely low levels of spontaneous activity compared to older mice (Nagy et al., 1975), which might yield artificially high avoidance of the shock side following initial shock escape in this simple spatial preference task, the safe and shock sides of the cage were automatically alternated every 3 minutes during a 30-minute test session. Thus the mice could minimize the amount of shock received by quickly escaping the shock side following every 3-minute alternation and remaining on the safe side for the duration of the 3-minute period. If the mice remained on one side of the cage throughout the entire session or spent equal amounts of time on the safe and shock sides, a score of 50% preference for the safe side would be recorded (see Nagy, Murphy, & Ray, 1978, for a more detailed description). With increasing shock levels, the mice were expected to spend greater amounts of time on the safe side of the cage.

A total of 960 Swiss−Webster mice were tested over 8 levels of shock and 6 ages; each mouse was tested for only a single session at one of the ages and shock levels. By plotting the percentage of time spent on the safe side, it was possible to determine the relative aversiveness of each shock level for all age groups. Figure 5.1 presents the results of this experiment, and it is clear that there were no marked differences among the age groups in amount of time spent on the safe side at each shock level. Those differences that did occur were primarily for the two oldest age

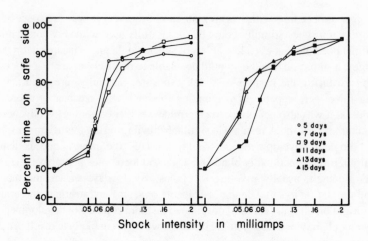

FIG. 5.1   Mean percent time of the 30-minute session spent on the safe side as a function of age and shock level. (From Nagy et al., 1978.)

groups, which showed somewhat higher preferences for the safe side than younger groups, at 0.05 and 0.06 mA. Although this difference might reflect differential sensitivity for shock at those low levels, it is more likely due to a change in the initial locomotor response to shock at these ages. Both 13- and 15-day-old mice usually run at the onset of shock, whereas younger mice tend to pivot in a circle before escaping. Subjected to higher shock levels, younger mice make fewer pivoting responses and escape more directly to the safe side.

The results of this experiment clearly showed that mice as young as 5 days of age are capable of escaping shock in spite of their rather limited locomotor abilities. In addition, all age groups responded to increasing levels of shock in a similar manner, spending more time on the safe side as shock levels became higher. Most age groups approached asymptotic avoidance of shock at about 0.1 mA, and all groups remained on the safe side between 85% to 89% of the session. Whether or not the equal amounts of time spent on the safe side by the different age groups actually reflect equal aversiveness or motivating properties of a particular level of shock is difficult to answer. It may well be that a particular level of shock was more motivating or painful for a younger group but that because of their more limited motor abilities they were unable to escape the shock side as quickly as older but less motivated mice. However, at least at the behavioral level we may conclude that time spent on the safe side is rather consistent for all age groups for a particular level of shock.

DEVELOPMENT OF INSTRUMENTAL LEARNING
AND MEMORY

Simple Escape Learning

Having determined that shock is a feasible motivating stimulus throughout the age range of the brain growth spurt period, we conducted a series of experiments on a simple escape task, the straight alley. Basically, the straight alley is a longer but narrower (22.8 cm × 3.2 cm × 6.4 cm) version of the chambers used to determine the aversiveness of shock in the previous experiment. A typical training trial began by placing the mouse pup into the start box for 3 to 5 seconds, then removing a door to the alley at the onset of shock. Shock continued until the mouse had reached the goal or 300 seconds had elapsed. If the mouse failed to reach the goal within this time, it was gently prodded to the goal and shock was terminated. The pup was then removed from the alley for a 45-second intertrial interval followed by replacement in the start box for the next trial. In most of the experiments a training session consisted of 25 trials with shock set at 0.1 mA, a level that the aversion experiment indicated would elicit consistent escape at all ages. Although several of our experiments used C3H mice and Wistar rats, the data reviewed in the present chapter are for the Swiss–Webster mouse unless otherwise noted.

Acquisition of escape behavior.   One of the surprising findings in our early experiments was that running speed, the measure most frequently employed to demonstrate learning with adult subjects on this task, did not increase over trial blocks in a single training session in mice 5 to 15 days of age (Nagy, Misanin, & Newman, 1970; Nagy, Misanin, Newman, Olsen, & Hinderliter, 1972; Nagy, Misanin, & Olsen, 1972). Yet it was apparent that the mice at all the ages tested were becoming more proficient at escaping shock over the training session. During the first few training trials the mice would typically engage in circling behavior, wall-climbing, and rolling over on their sides in an attempt to escape shock. By the last training trials, however, the frequency of these behaviors decreased dramatically, and the mice usually crawled or ran directly to the goal end of the alley. Thus it was clear that the mice were becoming more proficient in escaping shock but that this improvement was not reflected in escape latencies. Although space does not permit a complete explanation here, we concluded, on the basis of these and subsequent studies (Misanin, Haigh, Hinderliter, & Nagy, 1973; Misanin, Nagy, Keiser, & Bowen, 1971), that running speed at these early ages was a poor learning–performance measure for both mice and rats, because it seemed oversensitive to maturational changes and insensitive to behavioral changes within the training session. Because the frequency of the circling behavior appeared to reflect changes in escape performance, we chose it as our standard measure, operationally defined as a 180° turn away from the goal end of the alley, and termed this behavior a competing response. Figure 5.2 depicts the typical change in the frequency of competing responses over a training session in mice 3 to 11 days of age (each age group was tested for only a single session of 25 trials).

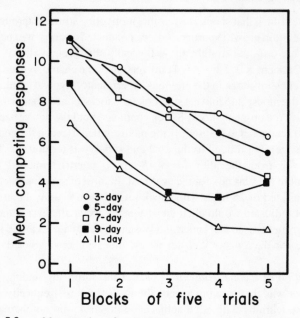

FIG. 5.2.   Mean number of competing responses made over blocks of five training trials as a function of age. (Adapted from Nagy, Misanin, Newman, Olsen, & Hinderliter, 1972.)

Retention of simple escape learning.   One of the first questions we sought to answer was whether or not this change in behavior would persist for some period of time. We (Nagy, Misanin, Newman, Olsen, & Hinderliter, 1972) trained separate groups of mice at 5, 7, and 9 days of age using the procedures previously described. Following training, each age group was divided into three retest groups and retrained following intervals of 1, 6, or 24 hours. The results are shown in Fig. 5.3. The left panel indicates the mean number of competing responses made during original training, and the right panel depicts the number made by the various retention groups during retraining. Comparisons between original training and retest indicated that for the 5- and 7-day-old mice, significantly fewer competing responses were made only during the 1-hour retention test. In contrast, 9-day-old groups made fewer competing responses than during original training at all of the retest intervals. It thus appeared that whatever was underlying the reduction in the number of competing responses persisted for at least 24 hours in the oldest group but for only 1 hour in the younger groups.

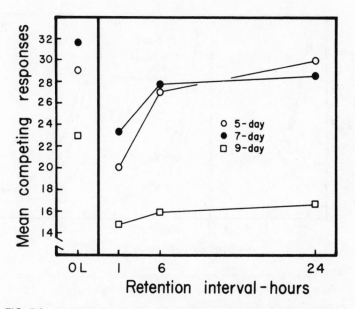

FIG. 5.3.   Mean number of competing responses made during original training (*left panel*) and retention testing (*right panel*) as a function of age and retention interval. (Adapted from Nagy, Misanin, Newman, Olsen, & Hinderliter, 1972.)

Effect of nonlearning factors on retention performance.   Although the results of the preceding studies suggested to us that the mice were learning to inhibit competing responses during the training session and were capable of remembering this learned inhibition for 24 hours by 9 days of age, it was also possible that nonlearning factors such as fatigue, habituation, sensitization, or some other aspect of the original shock-exposure session could account for the reduced number of competing responses made during the retention tests. In the following experiment (Ray & Nagy, 1974) we attempted to assess these possibilities. At each of three ages, 7, 9, and 11 days of age, littermates were assigned to one of three training conditions. In the first condition (Trained), mice were trained to escape in the straight alley with shock offset being contingent on reaching the goal on each trial. In the second condition (Yoked-shock), mice at each age received identical treatment as the trained group with the important exception that shock offset was predetermined for a given trial as the latency to escape by a matched littermate in the trained group on that trial. Mice in the third condition (Maturation control) received no treatment on the training day of their littermates. After 24 hours all groups received 25 training trials, shock offset being contingent on each mouse reaching the goal on every trial. The retention data are shown in Fig. 5.4. At none of the ages were the differences between the Yoked-shock and Maturation controls reliable, suggesting that previous shock exposure per se does not result in a reduced number of competing responses

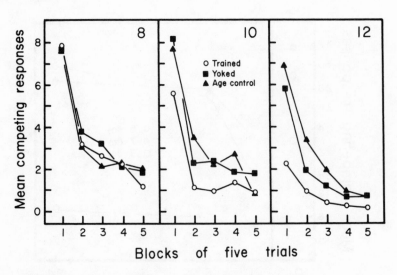

FIG. 5.4.   Mean number of competing responses made during 24-hour retention testing as a function of age and original training conditions.

during the retention test. In contrast, the Trained groups made significantly fewer competing responses than either the Yoked or Maturation control littermates at 10 and 12 days of age while failing to differ from these groups at 8 days of age. Because these results cannot easily be attributed to nonlearning factors during the original training session, it appears most likely that they represent the development of a memory process for prior escape training that emerges behaviorally between 7 and 9 days of age and persists for at least 24 hours.

Retention as a function of amount of training at 7 and 9 days of age.   Before one can conclude with some confidence that a 24-hour memory capability is emerging between 7 and 9 days of age for training on this task, a number of alternative possibilities must be accounted for. Because it is well known that degree of original learning is an important factor of memory, it may be the case that the 7-day-old mice failed to demonstrate 24-hour memory owing to insufficient learning. Therefore we conducted one study that varied the amount of original training on the straight alley to determine the effects upon 24-hour memory. In this experiment (Nagy & Mueller, 1973), 7- and 9-day-old groups received 0, 10, 25, or 40 training trials. As indicated in Fig. 5.5, both age groups continued to reduce the frequency with which competing responses were emitted as the number of training trials increased. After 24 hours following training, all groups, including the maturational control groups (0) that had received no original training, received 25 training trials. As clearly demonstrated in Fig. 5.6, those mice receiving training at 7 days of age failed to differ from one another or from the group with no prior training when retested 24 hours following original training. In marked contrast, mice trained at 9 days of age exhibited a direct

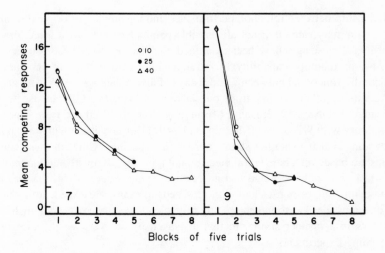

FIG. 5.5. Mean number of competing responses over blocks of five trials during original training as a function of age and amount of original training. (From Nagy and Mueller, © (1973) by the American Psychological Association. Reprinted by permission.)

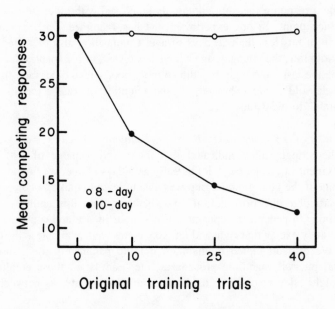

FIG. 5.6. Mean number of competing responses made during 24-hour retention tests as a function of age and amount of original training. (Adapted from Nagy and Mueller, © (1973) by the American Psychological Association. Reprinted by permission.)

relationship between retention performance and the amount of original training.

In summary, although not all possible parameters that might affect original learning at these ages have been examined, the data described herein suggest that a 24-hour memory capability for straight alley escape training becomes behaviorally functional between 7 and 9 days of age in the Swiss–Webster mouse. In addition, other reports from our laboratory with the C3H mouse (Nagy, Misanin, & Olsen, 1972; Nagy, Misanin, & Wetzel, 1973) and from Misanin's laboratory with Wistar rats (Misanin et al., 1971) are consistent with this finding, indicating that it is neither strain- nor species-specific. Although these conclusions are based on a behavioral measure not typically used with adult animals on this task, it should be noted that at least one study (Egger, 1974) that has used both competing responses and running speeds to examine escape learning in rats of different ages has found competing responses to decrease over training trials at all ages in a manner similar to that displayed by our very young mice in the preceding experiments.

Discriminated Escape Learning

We next turned our attention to the development of the acquisition and retention of escape training in the T maze. Not only was the T maze somewhat more complex than the simple straight alley escape task, but its use allowed us to examine a response measure commonly employed with older subjects, turns at the choice point. In one experiment that has examined T maze learning and retention in rats less than 20 days of age, Campbell et al. (1974) reported that 15-day-old rats, the youngest age which they tested, were capable of successfully learning the task, although they did so more poorly than older rats. In addition, the 15-day-old group exhibited 24-hour retention of escape training that was comparable to older rats.

Acquisition of discriminated escape behavior. Because our experiments with the straight alley indicated that mice were capable of within-session improvement in escape behavior as early as 5 days of age, we first attempted to determine if the young mouse pup was able to learn to make a choice-point turn in a particular direction and, if so, whether or not this ability varied with maturation. In general the apparatus was similar in size and construction to the straight alley except that right and left goal boxes were available at the end of the stem. We also attempted to maintain training parameters (i.e., shock level, intertrial interval, handling procedures, etc.) similar to those employed with the straight alley in order to facilitate comparison of results between the two tasks.

In one of the first experiments (Nagy & Murphy, 1974) mice received 25 training trials at 7, 9, 11, or 13 days of age, shock offset being contingent on reaching the goal arm opposite that chosen on the first training trial for each pup.

The acquisition data are shown in Fig. 5.7, where it can be seen that the 7-day-old group failed to show any improvement in the number of correct choice-point turns over the training session. All the older groups demonstrated significant within-session increases in correct turns, rate of improvement appearing to be directly related to age.

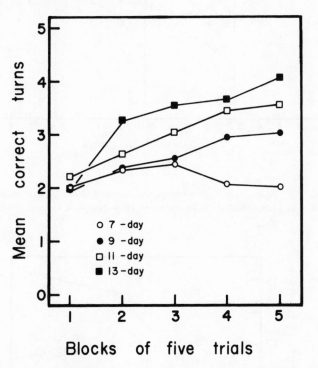

FIG. 5.7.   Mean number of correct choice-point turns during original training as a function of age and trial blocks. (From Nagy and Murphy, 1974.)

Development of memory for prior discriminated escape training.   Following training, each age group was divided into two groups and retrained 24 hours later. For one of the groups (Nonreversal) the correct goal arm remained the same as during original training. For the other group (Reversal) the formerly incorrect goal was now correct. Because the two retest groups had performed equally well within each age during original training, we hypothesized that memory of goal location during original training should interfere with relearning by the Reversal group at an age when that memory process was functionally mature.

As indicated in Fig. 5.8, the Reversal groups that were originally trained at 11 and 13 days of age made significantly fewer correct turns during the retention test than did their Nonreversal littermates, whereas there was little difference at the

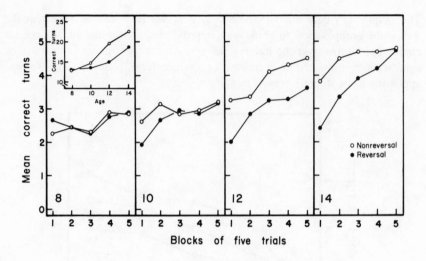

FIG. 5.8.   Mean number of correct choice-point turns during 24-hour retention testing as a function of age and retest group. (From Nagy and Murphy, 1974.)

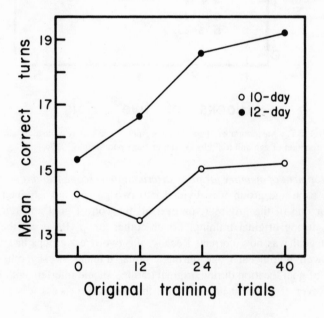

FIG. 5.9.   Mean number of correct choice-point turns made during 24-hour retention testing as a function of age and number of original training trials. (Adapted from Nagy, Pagano, and Gable, 1976.)

earlier ages between these groups. These results suggest the emergence of a 24-hour memory capability, at least within the confines of the parameters employed in this study, between 9 and 11 days of age, and lend support to an earlier experiment (Nagy & Sandmann, 1973) that arrived at a similar conclusion using a different paradigm.

Amount of prior training and the emergence of memory ability.   Finally, an experiment was conducted to determine whether 9-day-old mice might be capable of demonstrating 24-hour retention of T maze training if original training were continued beyond 25 training trials. In this study (Nagy, Pagano, & Gable, 1976) 9- and 11-day-old mice received 0, 12, 24, or 40 original training trials and were retested for 24 trials one day later. Figure 5.9 presents the total number of correct turns made during retest as a function of age and number of original training trials. Analyses of these data revealed that there were no differences among the groups retested at 10 days of age, indicating that prior training of up to 40 trials did not result in 24-hour memory of that training. In contrast, groups with 24 and 40 training trials at 11 days of age made significantly more correct turns during retest than did groups receiving 0 or 12 original training trials. Furthermore, all the 12-day-old groups with prior training made reliably more correct turns during retest than their younger counterparts, whereas the maturation control groups without prior training at the two ages did not differ from each other.

Differential development of two components of discriminated escape behavior.   In addition to recording correct turns at the choice point in the previous studies, we also recorded the number of competing responses made before reaching the choice point on each trial. If it is assumed that the reduction in the number of competing responses is indicative of learning to reach the choice point more efficiently, their inclusion in the choice-point data provides an interesting and systematic picture of the development of learning and retention abilities with increasing maturation. When trained at 7 days of age, the mice displayed a within-session decrease in competing responses but no increase in correct turns, suggesting that they were learning to reach the choice point more efficiently but were incapable of learning which way to turn at the choice point. When retested 24 hours later, trained pups did not differ from nontrained controls on either measure. At 9 days of age mouse pups showed both a decrease in the number of competing responses and an increase in the number of correct choice-point turns over training trials. Upon 24-hour retest, 10-day-old mice made fewer competing responses than controls but did not differ with respect to correct choice-point turns. This indicates that they were capable of remembering how to reach the choice point efficiently but not which way to turn. By 11 days of age the mice were capable of both increasing correct choice-point turns and decreasing competing responses; during retest, trained animals made more correct turns and fewer competing responses than nontrained controls, suggesting 24-hour memory of both escape components.

ALTERATION OF CNS MATURATION RATE

One of the major assumptions with which we are working in our research program is that the emergence or development of behaviors during ontogeny reflects the preceding maturation or integration of neural systems underlying these behaviors. If this assumption is correct, then our data would suggest that functional maturation of CNS processes underlying 24-hour memory of T maze training occurs between 9 and 11 days of age in a mouse. Manipulations that alter the rate of CNS maturation therefore would be expected also to have a corresponding effect on the age at which this memory capacity becomes behaviorally functional.

Acceleration of CNS Maturation

General effects of hyperthyroidism upon CNS maturation and behavior. The effects of the administration of thyroid hormones during the early postnatal period on later development have been widely studied. In general, early exposure to excess thyroid hormone has been reported to advance early stages of CNS maturation, as evidenced by the earlier development of adult-like electroencephalographic patterns (Schapiro & Norman, 1967), acetylcholinesterase levels (Schapiro, 1968), indexes of myelin formation (Schapiro, 1966; Walravens & Chase, 1969), and dendritic spine formation (Schapiro, Vukovich, & Globus, 1973), to mention only a few (for more comprehensive reviews see Balázs & Richter, 1973; Schapiro, 1971). In addition, behavioral, motoric, and sensory abilities are also advanced in thyroid-treated subjects (Davenport & Gonzalez, 1973; Eayrs, 1964; Schapiro, 1971). Although thyroid hormone administration has the effect of accelerating many processes during the early stages of ontogeny, it also appears to result in permanent deficits in cell numbers in the adult brain, presumably because of the premature termination of cell proliferation in the CNS (Balázs & Richter, 1973; Schapiro, 1971).

The effects of postnatal thyroid treatments on later learning abilities, however, have been unclear. Whereas Schapiro (1968) reported that thyroxine-injected rats learned an active-avoidance task better than controls at 16 to 18 days of age, Hamburgh, Lynn, and Weiss (1964) found no effect of thyroid administration on learning an escape task at 20 to 28 days of age, and Eayrs (1964) found deficits in a closed-field test when rats were tested at 100 days of age. Davenport and Gonzalez (1973) found no differences between thyroxine-injected and control rats on passive- and active-avoidance learning when trained at 19 to 20 days of age but poorer performance by thyroxine animals on the passive-avoidance task at 35 to 36 days of age and on a closed-field maze at 70 to 85 days of age.

Although the results of these experiments may appear to be at odds with one another, it is also possible that they simply reflect the early acceleration of maturation and the later consequential CNS deficiencies caused by early hyperthyroidism. Thyroxine-treated rats appear to learn better than controls when tested before weaning age, are equal to them just after weaning, but poorer when tested at later ages. This pattern corresponds to the suggestion that thyroxine-induced acceleration of CNS maturation also results in a decrease in adult behavioral plasticity (Schapiro, 1968, 1971). Because the deficits appear to occur primarily after weaning age, we decided to explore the possibility that early thyroxine treatment would result in the earlier emergence of T maze learning and 24-hour memory in mice, abilities shown by our previous studies to emerge behaviorally well before weaning age.

Effects of hyperthyroidism upon learning—memory of discriminated escape behavior. In this experiment, James Murphy, as part of his M.A. thesis (Murphy & Nagy, 1976), injected half of the mice from a number of litters with thyroxine (1μg/g body weight) and half with an equivalent volume of saline at 1, 2, and 3 days of age. At 7, 9, 11, or 13 days of age half of each of these groups were trained to escape to the goal opposite their first-trial preference in a T maze, and the remaining half were trained to escape in a straight alley. These latter groups served as controls in that they were trained to escape shock but were not provided the opportunity to make choice-point turns during original training. After 24 hours all groups were retrained on the T maze. Figure 5.10 presents the mean number of correct turns made by the T maze-trained mice during both original training and retention tests (each session consisted of 24 trials); data for control groups are presented for the retest day. Although not shown in this figure, within-session performance during original training for both the T maze and straight alley groups was comparable for each age to that indicated in Figs. 5.8 and 5.3, respectively. There were also no differences in performance during original training between thyroxine-treated and saline control mice within any of the ages.

Examination of the retest scores for saline-treated mice provides results similar to our previous data. Significant 24-hour retention was first evident when original training took place at 11 days of age, with younger saline-injected mice failing to differ from controls originally trained on the straight alley. Hyperthyroid mice that had received original training on the T maze, however, made more correct turns than controls when retested at 10 days of age and older. Because there were no differences between thyroxine- and saline-treated mice within each age during original training, these results suggest that there is about a 2-day acceleration in the behavioral appearance of a 24-hour memory capability in thyroxine-treated mice. It is also interesting to note that thyroxine-treated mice made fewer correct turns than saline controls at 14 days of age, notwithstanding the reliable retention effects demonstrated by both groups at this age. Although the addition of several older groups would be necessary to confirm this finding, these data suggest that the thyroxine-induced premature termination of CNS development may be occurring at an early age in mice and thereby affecting their learning ability on the T maze.

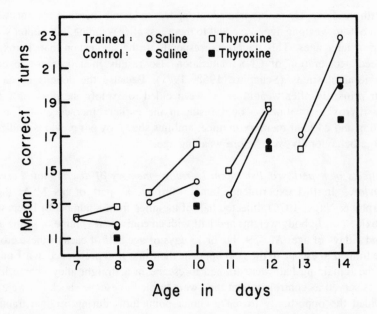

FIG. 5.10. Mean number of correct choice-point turns during original training and 24-hour retention testing as a function of age, thyroxine or saline treatments, and prior training conditions. (Adapted from Murphy and Nagy, 1976.)

Retardation of CNS Maturation

Encouraged by our success in accelerating the behavioral emergence of a memory capacity with thyroxine administration, we sought to determine whether or not the retardation of CNS maturation would result in a corresponding delay of memory development. Because it has been suggested that undernutrition during the brain growth spurt period has particularly severe and long-lasting detrimental consequences (Dobbing, 1970, 1971), we attempted to determine if undernutrition would also result in the delayed emergence of memory functioning.

General effects of undernutrition on CNS maturation and behavior. The developmental deficits produced by early postnatal undernutrition are widespread, affecting numerous CNS structures and behavioral capacities. For example, nutritional deprivation during preweanling development has been found to impede the morphological growth of the whole brain (Dobbing, 1968) and, in certain late-developing brain regions, to produce severe deficits in both cell number (Altman & McCrady, 1972; Bass, 1971) and axonal proliferation (Cragg, 1972). The maturation of numerous biochemical processes, including the accumulation of myelin components (Benton, Moser, Dodge, & Carr, 1966; Chase, Dorsey, & McKhann, 1967; Williamson & Coniglio, 1971), RNA synthesis capacities (de Guglielmone, Soto, & Duvilanski, 1974), and the development of various neurotransmitters and their associated enzymes (Mourek, Agrawal, Davis, & Himwich, 1970; Rajalakshmi, Kulkarni, & Ramakrishnan, 1974; Sereni, Principi, Perletti, & Sereni, 1966), is retarded in undernourished infants as is the attainment of adult-like CNS electrical patterns (Myslivecek, 1970; Salas & Cintra, 1975).

In addition to the extensive CNS deficits produced by early nutritional deprivation, the maturation of many sensory and rudimentary behavioral capacities is also delayed. Eye-opening and ear-unfolding, for example, occur at a later age for undernourished than for normally nourished rodents (Smart & Dobbing, 1971). The developmental appearances of certain reflexes are delayed by early undernutrition (Bush & Leathwood, 1975; Smart & Dobbing, 1971) as are the maturation of locomotor abilities (Altman, Sudarshan, Das, McCormick, & Barnes, 1971; Frankova, 1968) and adult-like swimming patterns (Salas, 1972).

Many of the deficits caused by early undernutrition, such as decreases in body weight, DNA, RNA, and protein content (Winick & Noble, 1966), decreases in cell size and number in various brain regions (Dobbing, Hopewell, & Lynch, 1971), and alterations in acetylcholinesterase activity (Adlard & Dobbing, 1972), persist into adulthood despite later rehabilitation. Attempts to assess the effects of early undernutrition on later behaviors, however, have provided generally ambiguous and contradictory results, with various studies reporting increases, decreases, or no effects on exploratory activity (Rech & Weichsel, 1973; Slob, Snow, & de Natris-Mathot, 1973; Smart, 1974) and learning abilities (Barnes, Cunnold, Zimmermann, Simmons, MacLeod, & Krook, 1966; Bush & Leathwood, 1975; Guthrie, 1968; Slob et al., 1973). Little research, however, has been directed toward examination of early learning and memory abilities. In view of the widespread CNS developmental deficits that early undernutrition causes, it would be indeed surprising if the emergence of learning and memory abilities was unaffected.

Development of learning—memory in postnatally undernourished mice.   In our experiment (Nagy, Porada, & Anderson, 1977) mouse pups were assigned at birth to foster mothers in litter sizes of 6 or 16 in order to produce normally nourished and undernourished subjects. At 9, 11, or 13 days of age, each pup was trained on the T maze for 24 trials, followed by a similar retention session 24 hours later. In addition, littermate controls without prior training or shock exposure also received training at the retest ages of their trained littermates. Figure 5.11 shows the mean number of correct choice-point turns during training and retest for the trained groups and during the retention day test for the control groups. It should be pointed out that there were no within-session differences between the normally nourished and undernourished mice at any of the ages. The 11- and 13-day-old groups demonstrated reliable increases in correct turns during

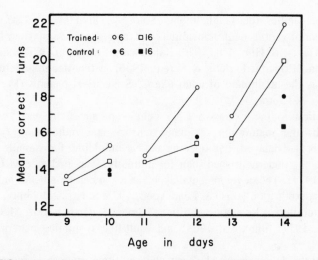

FIG. 5.11.   Mean number of correct choice-point turns made during original
training and 24-hour retention testing as a function of age, litter size, and prior
training conditions. (Adapted from Nagy, Porada, and Anderson, 1977.)

training; both 9-day-old groups showed only slight improvement. Thus differences in retention scores between the normally nourished and undernourished
groups cannot easily be attributed to differences in original learning. As in
our previous research, normally nourished mice failed to demonstrate significant 24-hour retention effects when retrained at 10 days of age, whereas groups retrained at 12 and 14 days of age made more correct choice-
point turns than did their respective controls. In contrast, undernourished mice
did not show significant 24-hour memory of prior training until retested at
14 days of age.

The results of this experiment suggest that undernutrition before and during
the brain growth spurt period delays the emergence of 24-hour memory of prior T
maze training for about 2 days. This 2-day delay is of particular interest, because
we found in two additional studies (Nagy et al., 1977) that the procedure of
rearing mice in large litters, resulting in body-weight deficits of 35% to 40%,
also produces about a 2-day delay in the development of adult-like swimming
behaviors and about a 3-day delay in the attainment of peak levels of spontaneous
activity, both unlearned behaviors thought to be indexes of CNS maturation
level. It has been suggested that the decline in spontaneous activity following
attainment of peak levels during ontogeny reflects the development of telen-
cephalic cholinergic and serotonergic inhibitory systems that appear to modulate
locomotor arousal (Campbell, Lytle, & Fibiger, 1969; Mabry & Campbell,
1974; Nagy et al., 1975), and the delay of such an activity decline in our
undernourished mice is consistent with previous reports of decreased cell
proliferation (Fish & Winick, 1969) and dendritic growth (Bass, 1971) in the

forebrain, as well as the delayed maturation of cholinergic functioning (Adlard & Dobbing, 1971; Eckhert, Barnes, & Levitsky, 1976) in undernourished rodents.

Taken together, the results of these experiments provide evidence that a 24-hour memory capacity for prior T maze training develops between 9 and 11 days of age in the mouse. Furthermore these data are consistent with the hypothesis that the emergence of this memory capability is reflecting the functional maturation of underlying processes, because manipulations that result in the general acceleration or retardation of CNS maturation rates also have corresponding effects on the ontogenetic appearance of 24-hour memory for this learning task.

ONTOGENY OF INHIBITORY CONTROL ON A PASSIVE-AVOIDANCE TASK

Previous Studies

The one learning situation in which acquisition has proven to be particularly difficult for young rats is the passive-avoidance task. Whether trained for a single trial (Riccio et al., 1968) or to some performance criterion (Campbell et al., 1974; Feigley & Spear, 1970; Riccio & Schulenburg, 1969; Riccio et al., 1968; Schulenburg et al., 1971), young rats learn to withhold a response more slowly than do adults. As noted in an earlier section of this chapter, this age-related learning deficiency has been generally attributed to the relatively poor inhibitory abilities of the immature rat. However, Campbell and Coulter (1976) have suggested that such deficiencies may also be due to age-related differences in either the strength of motivation underlying the response to be inhibited or in the ability to learn associations between response and punishment. Unfortunately the evidence to date has not been sufficient to attribute clearly the age-related passive-avoidance deficiencies shown by rats to any of the three possibilities.

In addition, the lack of inhibitory control hypothesis faces another challenge when the behaviors of very young rats and mice are examined on several tasks that appear to involve inhibitory processes. For example, the decrease in competing responses during training trials (Nagy, Misanin, Newman, Olsen, & Hinderliter, 1972) and the extinction of running for nonnutritive suckling (Amsel et al., 1976) appear to require some level of inhibitory control. Although most developmental studies of passive-avoidance learning have used 15- to 16-day-old rats as the youngest age group, with all older groups reported to acquire the task more rapidly, Riccio and Schulenburg (1969) reported that 10-day-old rats acquire the passive-avoidance task more rapidly than 15-day-old subjects. Unfortunately the Riccio and Schulenburg study provided neither short-term retention data nor adequate control groups to determine whether their 10-day-olds were actually learning to inhibit the response or whether their behavior may have been due to nonlearning effects of the shock and/or handling procedure per se. In fact, the lack of appropriate control groups has been evident in almost all the developmental research on the passive-avoidance task.

Passive-Avoidance Learning and Retention as a Function of Age in Mice

With these considerations in mind, Donald Ray, as part of his Ph.D. dissertation (Ray & Nagy, 1978), conducted the following experiment in order to examine the development of learning and memory for passive-avoidance training in the mouse. In general the study consisted of training mice at 7, 11, 15, 19, or 100 days of age on a passive-avoidance task and subsequently retesting them either 1 or 24 hours later. Because of the limited sensory and motor abilities of the youngest groups, we developed a step-off task for this study. Basically the apparatus consisted of a square Plexiglas chamber with a circular pedestal platform located in the center, slightly above a grid floor. The size of the chamber, platform, and grid spacing, as well as the distance from the pedestal to the grid floor, were roughly proportional to the size of the mouse at the various ages. In addition, because 7- and 11-day-old mice are relatively inactive (Nagy & Ritter, 1976), a controlled low level of vibration was applied to the pedestal in order to promote the step-off response in our youngest groups (lest the reader have visions of mice being violently shaken off the platform, allow me to assure you that a low level of vibration was chosen based upon pilot studies that indicated that even 5-day-old mice can easily remain on the platform for up to 5 minutes if they choose to do so). The same level of vibration was used for all age groups in this study.

The experimental design required five groups of animals at each age to account for possible confounding effects of nonlearning factors. In our primary experimental group (Trained) the mouse was positioned so that all four feet were on the platform at the beginning of a trial. After 1 second, pedestal vibration and a running timer were activated. A trial ended when the mouse stepped off the platform (all four feet in contact with the grid floor) or remained on the platform for a maximum latency of 120 seconds. If the mouse stepped off the platform it received a 3-second shock of 50 volts from a 150-kΩ fixed-impedance source (Nagy, Murphy, & Ray, 1978, have found this shock level to be equally aversive from at least 5–15 days of age). Following shock or a maximum latency, the mouse was removed for a 30-second intertrial interval and then replaced on the pedestal for the start of the next trial. All Trained mice received repeated trials until they achieved the criterion of remaining on the pedestal platform for two consecutive maximum latency trials.

Four groups served as controls in order to partial out the effects of shock, vibration, and handling upon performance. Each subject in each of these groups was a like-sexed littermate of a Trained mouse and received the control treatment at the same age. Mice in the first control group, performance control (PC), were exposed to the same aspects of the training situation as their Trained littermates except they were not shocked for stepping off the platform. They were placed on the platform, it vibrated, and they were allowed to step down and explore the chamber for the same amount of time as their Trained littermate had spent in the chamber on each trial. The second control group, handling control (HC), was treated identically to the PC group except there was no platform vibration. The efficacy of the vibrating platform in promoting step-off responses was evident in comparisons between the HC and PC groups, particularly at 7 and 11 days of age. Whereas mice in the HC groups tended to remain on the platform for increasingly longer times over the session, mice in the PC groups continued to step off the platform with either the same or shorter latencies. The remaining two groups received various aspects of the training trial, but they were not allowed to make a step-off response. For both groups a cylinder surrounded the pedestal platform and prevented the response. The third control group, yoked shock vibration (YSV), was placed on the platform, received an amount of vibration on each trial equal to their Trained littermate, and was then hand-placed on the grid floor where a 3-second shock was administered. Finally, the last control group, yoked vibration (YV), received treatment identical to the YSV group on each trial except that shock never followed their placement upon the grid floor.

Following training to criterion the Trained mice were assigned to either a 1- or 24-hour retest group and were retrained to criterion at that time. In addition, each of the Trained mouse's littermates in the four control groups was assigned to the same retest interval and was later trained to avoid shock passively by remaining on the vibrating platform for two consecutive 120-second training trials. The mean numbers of trials to achieve criterion are shown in Fig. 5.12. Examination of the left panel, which depicts mean scores during original training as a function of age for the Trained mice, clearly indicates that the relative difficulty of this task forms an inverted U-shaped function over the ages tested. Whereas mice of all ages were able to achieve criterion, the 15-day-old groups experienced the most difficulty, with both younger and older mice learning the task in fewer trials. The center panel shows the mean trials to criterion for all groups during the 1-hour retest session, and it is obvious that all age groups of mice with previous training required significantly fewer trials to re-achieve criterion than any of the controls, which did not differ among themselves within any age. The right panel illustrates trials to criterion during the 24-hour retests. The only significant differences within age occurred at 20 and 100 days of age, when previously trained mice required reliably fewer trials to achieve criterion than controls. As with the 1-hour data, there were no differences among controls within any age. Although the 24-hour retention data suggest that a 24-hour memory capability emerges between 15 and 19 days of age, these findings must be considered as preliminary, because it is quite possible that variations in training parameters,

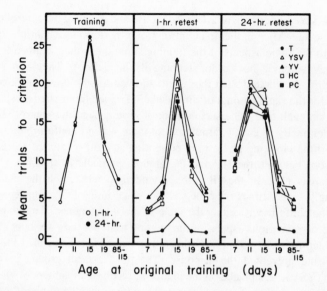

FIG. 5.12. Mean trials to criterion during original training (*left panel*), 1-hour
retention (*center panel*), and 24-hour retention (*right panel*) testing of a passive-
avoidance response as a function of age, retention interval, and training procedure.
(From Ray and Nagy, 1978.)

such as shock duration (Schulenburg et al., 1971), may affect retention of
passive-avoidance training at these ages.

The results of this experiment are strikingly clear and extremely relevant to
previous interpretations of age-related deficits in acquisition of the passive-
avoidance task. First, it should be noted that our training data with mice between
15 and 100 days of age are consistent with previous reports with the rat: The
youngest group showed the poorest acquisition and appeared relatively unable to
inhibit a punished response compared to older groups. However, the fact that
groups younger than 15 days of age were able to learn the task and did so more
readily than 15-day-old mice suggests that the hypothesis of lack of inhibitory
capability at the early ages due to immaturity of the frontal areas is not a
completely adequate explanation for the passive-avoidance acquisition deficits
found in previous studies. Although it is true that the younger groups are much
less active than 15-day-olds and may therefore require less inhibitory control to
suppress the step-off response, comparison of the Trained and control groups at
the 1-hour retest makes it clear that some level of inhibitory control is functional
even at 7 days of age. In addition, these comparisons also indicate that the
retention effects are unlikely to be due to nonlearning factors associated with
shock and/or handling during the training session and suggest that even our
youngest mice are capable of acquiring an association between a response and
punishment. Because the original training data are virtually identical in form to

the spontaneous activity levels evidenced in a nonshock situation at these ages for mice (Nagy et al., 1975) and are similar to rats (Campbell et al., 1969; Moorcroft, Lytle, & Campbell, 1971), the present findings are consistent with the suggestion by Campbell and Coulter (1976) that the passive-avoidance acquisition deficit may be due to age-related differences in the strength of motivation underlying the response to be inhibited. In other words inhibitory control is not absent at 15 days of age but is simply overshadowed by a stronger, age-related excitatory process.

CONCLUDING REMARKS

In general the data reviewed in the preceding pages indicate that marked changes in the abilities to acquire and remember adult-like responses involved in certain kinds of instrumental learning tasks occur during the brain growth spurt period and suggest that physiological and biochemical processes underlying these behavioral expressions achieve a level of functional maturity or integration during this period. In particular our data provide important new information pertaining to the age-related abilities of very young altricial rodents to acquire an association between a response and punishment and to retain associations formed between a response and reinforcement.

On the passive-avoidance task we found that the ability to learn to withhold a step-off response to a common criterion varied as an inverted U-shaped function between 7 days of age and adulthood, with poorest acquisition occurring at around 15 days of age. Because our 7-day-old groups achieved criterion as rapidly as adults, and comparisons with control groups during the 1-hour retest indicated that this behavioral change could not easily be accounted for by non-learning factors, the hypothesis that very young organisms are incapable of acquiring an association between a response and punishment appears to be in error, as does the extreme hypothesis that animals at these ages lack any inhibitory control at all. Although the relative ease with which the mice in our experiment were able to learn to inhibit responding varied as a function of age, all age groups achieved criterion. Perhaps the most plausible explanation at the present time for our data, as well as for those data previously reported by other investigators, is that the ability to learn to withhold a response varies as a function of the strength of motivation underlying that response at a particular age (Campbell & Coulter, 1976). At the very early ages the strength of motivation appears dependent on the relative maturational states of excitatory and inhibitory systems, with the interaction of the relative strengths of these systems either facilitating or interfering with the behavioral expression of that response.

The retention data derived from the straight alley and T maze are of particular interest. Mice trained on each of these escape tasks do not appear capable of remembering training for a 24-hour interval until they are 9 and 11 days of age, respectively, in spite of the fact that an improvement in performance can be demonstrated during original learning at earlier ages. Although only several training parameters have been examined thus far, our results are consistent with the hypothesis that the development of these memory capabilities reflects the maturation of underlying memory processes rather than the inability to learn during training. Indeed the findings that manipulations resulting in the general acceleration and retardation of CNS maturation rates had corresponding effects upon the emergence of 24-hour memory for T maze training provide rather strong support for this hypothesis. In each case the treatments affected memory capabilities while having little effect upon learning abilities within age groups. When learning differences were noted between treated and control groups, their occurrence during ontogeny was after the emergence of a 24-hour memory capability.

The hyperthyroid and undernutrition manipulations of course affect many aspects of CNS functioning and are probably of limited use in attempting to specify those related to the emerging memory capabilities. What is needed now are treatments that affect maturing physiological and biochemical CNS processes much more selectively and the determination of the effects of these treatments on developing memory capabilities.

ACKNOWLEDGMENT

The research reported in this chapter was supported by grants from the National Science Foundation (GB-30456) and the National Institute of Child Health and Human Development (HD-09145).

REFERENCES

Adlard, B. P. F., & Dobbing, J. Vulnerability of developing brain. III. Development of four enzymes in the brains of normal and undernourished rats. *Brain Research*, 1971, *28*, 97–107.

Adlard, B. P. F., & Dobbing, J. Vulnerability of developing brain. VIII. Regional acetylcholinesterase activity in the brains of adult rats undernourished in early life. *Journal of Nutrition*, 1972, *28*, 139–143.

Agrawal, H. C., & Himwich, W. A. Amino acids, proteins, and monoamines of developing brain. In W. A. Himwich (Ed.), *Developmental neurobiology*. Springfield, Ill.: Thomas, 1970.

Altman, J., & Bulut, F. G. Organic maturation and the development of learning capacity. In M. R. Rosenzweig & E. L. Bennett (Eds.), *Neural mechanisms of learning and memory*. Cambridge, Mass.: MIT Press, 1976.

Altman, J., & McCrady, B. The influence of nutrition on neural and behavioral development. IV. Effects of infantile undernutrition on the growth of the cerebellum. *Developmental Psychobiology*, 1972, *5*, 111–122.

Altman, J., Sudarshan, K., Das, G. D., McCormick, N., & Barnes, D. The influence of nutrition on neural and behavioral development. III. Development of some motor, particularly locomotor patterns during infancy. *Developmental Psychobiology*, 1971, *4*, 97–114.

Amsel, A. The ontogeny of appetitive learning and persistence. Chapter 8, this volume.

Amsel, A., Burdette, D. R., & Letz, R. Appetitive learning, patterned alternation, and extinction in 10-d-old rats with non-lactating suckling as reward. *Nature*, 1976, *262*, 816−818.

Amsel, A., Radek, C. C., Graham, M., & Letz, R. Ultrasound emission in infant rats as an indicant of arousal during appetitive learning and extinction. *Science*, 1977, *197*, 786−788.

Anokhin, P. K. Systemogenesis as a general regulator of brain development. In W. A. Himwich & H. E. Himwich (Eds.), *Progress in brain research*. (Vol. 9) *The developing brain*. Amsterdam: Elsevier, 1964.

Balázs, R., & Richter, D. Effects of hormones on the biochemical maturation of the brain. In W. Himwich (Ed.), *Biochemistry of the developing brain* (Vol. 1). New York: Marcel Dekker, 1973.

Barnes, R. H., Cunnold, S. R., Zimmermann, R. R., Simmons, H., MacLeod, R. B., & Krook, L. Influence of nutritional deprivation in early life on learning behavior of rats as measured by performance in a water maze. *Journal of Nutrition*, 1966, *89*, 399−410.

Bass, N. H. Influence of neonatal undernutrition on the development of rat cerebral cortex: A microchemical study. In R. Paoletti & A. N. Davison (Eds.), *Chemistry and brain development*. New York: Plenum Press, 1971.

Benton, J. W., Moser, H. W., Dodge, P. R., & Carr, S. Modification of the schedule of myelination in the rat by early nutritional deprivation. *Pediatrics*, 1966, *38*, 801−807.

Bolles, R. C., & Woods, P. J. The ontogeny of behaviour in the albino rat. *Animal Behaviour*, 1964, *12*, 427−441.

Bush, M., & Leathwood, P. D. Effect of different regimens of early malnutrition on behavioral development and adult avoidance learning in Swiss white mice. *British Journal of Nutrition*, 1975, *33*, 373−385.

Campbell, B. A. Developmental studies of learning and motivation in infra-primate mammals. In H. W. Stevenson, E. H. Hess, & H. L. Rheingold (Eds.), *Early behavior: Comparative and developmental approaches*. New York: Wiley, 1967.

Campbell, B. A., & Campbell, E. H. Retention and extinction of learned fear in infant and adult rats. *Journal of Comparative and Physiological Psychology*, 1962, *55*, 1−8.

Campbell, B. A., & Cicala, G. A. Studies of water deprivation in rats as a function of age. *Journal of Comparative and Physiological Psychology*, 1962, *55*, 763−768.

Campbell, B. A. & Coulter, X. The ontogenesis of learning and memory. In M. R. Rosenzweig & E. L. Bennett (Eds.), *Neural mechanisms of learning and memory*. Cambridge, Mass.: MIT Press, 1976.

Campbell, B. A., Jaynes, J., & Misanin, J. R. Retention of a light−dark discrimination in rats of different ages. *Journal of Comparative and Physiological Psychology*, 1968, *66*, 467−472.

Campbell, B. A., Lytle, L. D., & Fibiger, H. C. Ontogeny of adrenergic arousal and cholinergic inhibitory mechanisms in the rat. *Science*, 1969, *166*, 637−638.

Campbell, B. A., & Mabry, P. D. Ontogeny of behavioral arousal: A comparative study. *Journal of Comparative and Physiological Psychology*, 1972, *81*, 371−379.

Campbell, B. A., Misanin, J. R., White, B. C., & Lytle, L. D. Species differences in ontogeny of memory: Indirect support for neural maturation as a determinant of forgetting. *Journal of Comparative and Physiological Psychology*, 1974, *87*, 193−202.

Campbell, B. A., Riccio, D. C., & Rohrbaugh, M. Ontogenesis of learning and memory: Research and theory. In M. Meyer (Ed.), *Second Western Washington symposium on learning: Early learning*. Bellingham, Wash.: Western Washington State College Press, 1971.

Campbell, B. A., & Spear, N. E. Ontogeny of memory. *Psychological Review*, 1972, *79*, 215−236.

Campbell, B. A., Teghtsoonian, R., & Williams, R. A. Activity, weight loss, and survival time of food-deprived rats as a function of age. *Journal of Comparative and Physiological Psychology*, 1961, *54*, 216−219.

Candland, D. K., Teghtsoonian, R., & Campbell, B. A. A method of equating intensity of traumatic stimulation for rats of different ages. Paper presented at the meeting of the Eastern Psychological Association, Philadelphia, April 1958.

Chase, H. P., Dorsey, J. & McKhann, G. M. The effect of malnutrition on the synthesis of a myelin lipid. *Pediatrics*, 1967, *40*, 551–559.

Cornwell, A. C., & Fuller, J. L. Conditioned responses in young puppies. *Journal of Comparative and Physiological Psychology*, 1961, *54*, 13–15.

Cragg, B. G. The development of cortical synapses during starvation in the rat. *Brain*, 1972, *95*, 143–150.

Davenport, J. W., & Gonzalez, L. M. Neonatal thyroxine stimulation in rats: Accelerated behavioral maturation and subsequent learning deficit. *Journal of Comparative and Physiological Psychology*, 1973, *85*, 397–408.

Davison, A. N., & Dobbing, J. The developing brain. In A. N. Davison & J. Dobbing (Eds.), *Applied neurochemistry*. Philadelphia: Davis, 1968.

de Guglielmone, A., Soto, A. M., & Duvilanski, B. H. Neonatal undernutrition and RNA synthesis in developing rat brain. *Journal of Neurochemistry*, 1974, *22*, 529–533.

Dobbing, J. Vulnerable periods in developing brain. In A. N. Davison & J. Dobbing (Eds.), *Applied neurochemistry*. Philadelphia: Davis, 1968.

Dobbing, J. Undernutrition and the developing brain. In W. A. Himwich (Ed.), *Developmental neurobiology*. Springfield, Ill.: Thomas, 1970.

Dobbing, J. Undernutrition and the developing brain: The use of animal models to elucidate the human problem. In R. Paoletti & A. N. Davison (Eds.), *Chemistry and brain development*. New York: Plenum Press, 1971.

Dobbing, J., Hopewell, J. W., & Lynch, A. Vulnerability of developing brain: VII. Permanent deficit of neurons in cerebral and cerebellar cortex following early mild undernutrition. *Experimental Neurology*, 1971, *32*, 439–447.

Dobbing, J., & Sands, J. Growth and development of the brain and spinal cord of the guinea pig. *Brain Research*, 1970, *17*, 115–123.

Eayrs, J. T. Endocrine influence on cerebral development. *Archives de Biologie*, 1964 *75*, 529–565.

Eckhert, C. D., Barnes, R. H., & Levitsky, D. A. Regional changes in rat brain choline acetyltransferase and acetylcholinesterase activity resulting from undernutrition imposed during different periods of development. *Journal of Neurochemistry*, 1976, *27*, 277–283.

Egger, G. J. Escape learning: Acquisition and extinction rates as a function of age in rats. *Developmental Psychobiology*, 1974, *7*, 281–288.

Feigley, D. A., & Spear, N. E. Effect of age and punishment condition on long-term retention by the rat of active- and passive-avoidance learning. *Journal of Comparative and Physiological Psychology*, 1970, *73*, 515–526.

Fibiger, H. C., Lytle, L. D., & Campbell, B. A. Cholinergic modulation of adrenergic arousal in the developing rat. *Journal of Comparative and Physiological Psychology*, 1970, *72*, 384–389.

Fish, I., & Winick, M. Effect of malnutrition on regional growth of the developing rat brain. *Experimental Neurology*, 1969, *25*, 534–540.

Flexner, L. B. Enzymatic and functional patterns of the developing mammalian brain. In H. Waelsch (Ed.), *Biochemistry of the developing nervous system*. New York: Academic Press, 1955.

Folch. J., Casals, J., Pope, A., Meath, J. A., LeBaron, F. N., & Lees, M. Chemistry of myelin development. In S. R. Korey (Ed.), *The biology of myelin*. New York: Hoeber, 1959.

Fox, M. W. Reflex-ontogeny and behavioural development of the mouse. *Animal Behaviour*, 1965, *13*, 234–241.

Fox, M. W. Reflex development and behavioral organization. In W. A. Himwich (Ed.), *Developmental neurobiology*. Springfield, Ill.: Thomas, 1970.

Frankova, S. Nutritional and psychological factors in the development of spontaneous behavior in the rat. In N. S. Scrimshaw & J. E. Gordon (Eds.), *Malnutrition, learning, and behavior*. Cambridge, Mass.: MIT Press, 1968.

Fuller, J. L., Easler, C. A., & Banks, E. M. Formation of conditioned avoidance responses in young puppies. *American Journal of Physiology*, 1950, *160*, 462–466.

Fuller, J. L., & Geils, H. D. Brain growth in mice selected for high and low brain weight. *Developmental Psychobiology*, 1972, *5*, 307–318.

Fuller, J. L., & Geils, H. D. Behavioral development in mice selected for differences in brain weight. *Developmental Psychobiology*, 1973, *6*, 469–474.

Garrard, G., Harrison, G. A., & Weiner, J. S. Genetic and environmental factors determining the morphological maturation of the mouse and its relationship with weight growth. *Journal of Embryology and Experimental Morphology*, 1974, *31*, 247–261.

Gottlieb, G. Ontogenesis of sensory function in birds and mammals. In E. Tobach, L. R. Aronson, & E. Shaw (Eds.), *The biopsychology of development*. New York: Academic Press, 1971.

Green, E. L. (Ed.). *Biology of the laboratory mouse* (2nd ed.). New York: McGraw-Hill, 1966.

Guthrie, H. A. Severe undernutrition in early infancy and behavior in rehabilitated albino rats. *Physiology and Behavior*, 1968, *3*, 619–623.

Hamburgh, M., Lynn, E., & Weiss, E. P. Analysis of the influence of thyroid hormone on prenatal and postnatal maturation of the rat. *Anatomical Record*, 1964, *150*, 147–162.

Himwich, W. A. (Ed.). *Developmental neurobiology*. Springfield, Ill.: Thomas, 1970.

Himwich, W. (Ed.) *Biochemistry of the developing brain* (Vol. 1). New York: Marcel Dekker, 1973.

James, W. T., & Cannon, D. J. Conditioned avoidance responses in puppies. *American Journal of Physiology*, 1952, *168*, 251–253.

Kenny, J. T., & Blass, E. M. Suckling as incentive to instrumental learning in preweanling rats. *Science*, 1977, *196*, 898–899.

Kirby, R. H. Acquisition, extinction, and retention of an avoidance response in rats as a function of age. *Journal of Comparative and Physiological Psychology*, 1963, *56*, 158–162.

Kobayashi, T., Inman, O., Buno, W., & Himwich, H. E. A multidisciplinary study of changes in mouse brain with age. In J. Wortis (Ed.), *Recent advances in biological psychiatry* (Vol. 5). New York: Plenum Press, 1963.

Lanier, L. P., Dunn, A. J., & Van Hartesveldt, C. Development of neurotransmitters and their function in brain. In S. Ehrenpreis & I. J. Kopin (Eds.), *Reviews of neuroscience* (Vol. 2). New York: Raven Press, 1976.

Mabry, P. D., & Campbell, B. A. Ontogeny of serotonergic inhibition of behavioral arousal in the rat. *Journal of Comparative and Physiological Psychology*, 1974, *86*, 193–201.

Misanin, J. R., Haigh, J. M., Hinderliter, C. F., & Nagy, Z. M. Analysis of response competition in discriminated and nondiscriminated escape training of neonatal rats. *Journal of Comparative and Physiological Psychology*, 1973, *85*, 570–580.

Misanin, J. R., Nagy, Z. M., Keiser, E. F., & Bowen, W. Emergence of long-term memory in the neonatal rat. *Journal of Comparative and Physiological Psychology*, 1971, 77, 188–199.

Moorcroft, W. H., Lytle, L. D., & Campbell, B. A. Ontogeny of starvation-induced behavioral arousal in the rat. *Journal of Comparative and Physiological Psychology*, 1971, *75*, 59–67.

Mourek, J., Agrawal, H. C., Davis, J. M., & Himwich, W. A. The effects of short-term starvation on amino acid content in rat brain during ontogeny. *Brain Research*, 1970, *19*, 229–237.

Murphy, J. M., & Nagy, Z. M. Neonatal thyroxine stimulation accelerates the maturation of both locomotor and memory processes in mice. *Journal of Comparaive and Physiological Psychology*, 1976, *90*, 1082–1091.

Myslivecek, J. Electrophysiological parameters in undernourished developing brain: Dog and rat. In S. Kazda & V. H. Denenberg (Eds.), *The postnatal development of phenotype*. Prague: Academia, 1970.

Nagy, Z. M., Misanin, J. R., & Newman, J. A. Anatomy of escape behavior in neonatal mice. *Journal of Comparative and Physiological Psychology*, 1970, *72*, 116–124.

Nagy, Z. M., Misanin, J. R., Newman, J. A., Olsen, P. L., & Hinderliter, C. F. Ontogeny of memory in the neonatal mouse. *Journal of Comparative and Physiological Psychology*, 1972, *81*, 380–393.

Nagy, Z. M., Misanin, J. R., & Olsen, P. L. Development of 24 hour retention of escape learning in neonatal C3H mice. *Developmental Psychobiology*, 1972, *5*, 259–268.

Nagy, Z. M., Misanin, J. R., & Wetzel, B. Inception of a 24-hr memory capacity in two mouse strains. *Developmental Psychobiology*, 1973, *6*, 521–529.

Nagy, Z. M., & Mueller, P. W. Effect of amount of original training upon onset of a 24-hour memory capacity in neonatal mice. *Journal of Comparative and Physiological Psychology*, 1973, *85*, 151–159.

Nagy, Z. M., & Murphy, J. M. Learning and retention of a discriminated escape response in infant mice. *Developmental Psychobiology*, 1974, *7*, 185–192.

Nagy, Z. M., Murphy, J. M., & Ray, D. Development of behavioral arousal and inhibition in the Swiss–Webster mouse. *Bulletin of the Psychonomic Society*, 1975, *6*, 146–148.

Nagy, Z. M., Murphy, J. M., & Ray, D. Relative aversion thresholds for shock in infant mice. *Developmental Psychobiology*, 1978, *11*, 261–270.

Nagy, Z. M., Pagano, M. R., & Gable, D. Differential development of 24-h retention capacities for two components of T-maze escape learning by infant mice. *Animal Learning and Behavior*, 1976, *4*, 25–29.

Nagy, Z. M., Porada, K. J., & Anderson, J. A. Undernutrition by rearing in large litters delays the development of reflexive, locomotor, and memory processes in mice. *Journal of Comparative and Physiological Psychology*, 1977, *91*, 682–696.

Nagy, Z. M., & Ritter, M. Ontogeny of behavioral arousal in the mouse: Effect of prior testing upon age of peak activity. *Bulletin of the Psychonomic Society*, 1976, *7*, 285–288.

Nagy, Z. M., & Sandmann, M. Development of learning and memory of T-maze training in neonatal mice. *Journal of Comparative and Physiological Psychology*, 1973, *83*, 19–26.

Oakley, D. A., & Plotkin, H. C. Ontogeny of spontaneous locomotor activity in rabbit, rat, and guinea pig. *Journal of Comparative and Physiological Psychology*, 1975, *89*, 267–273.

Paoletti, R., & Davison, A. N. (Eds.). *Chemistry and brain development.* New York: Plenum Press, 1971.

Rajalakshmi, R., Kulkarni, A. B., & Ramakrishnan, C. V. Effects of pre-weaning and post-weaning undernutrition on acetylcholine levels in rat brain. *Journal of Neurochemistry*, 1974, *23*, 119–121.

Ray, D., & Nagy, Z. M. *The relationship between dendritic growth of cortical neurons and the ontogeny of conditioned and unconditioned reflex control.* 1974, Manuscript in preparation.

Ray, D., & Nagy, Z. M. Emerging cholinergic mechanisms and the ontogeny of response inhibition in the mouse. *Journal of Comparative and Physiological Psychology*, 1978, *92*, 335–349.

Rech, R. H., & Weichsel, M. E., Jr. Brain cell number and motor activity in rats subjected to neonatal undernutrition. *Life Sciences*, 1973, *13*, 1077–1087.

Riccio, D. C., Rohrbaugh, M., & Hodges, L. A. Developmental aspects of passive and active avoidance learning in rats. *Developmental Psychobiology*, 1968, *1*, 108–111.

Riccio, D. C., & Schulenburg, C. J. Age related deficits in acquisition of a passive avoidance response. *Canadian Journal of Psychology*, 1969, *23*, 429–437.

Riesen, A. H. Problems in correlating behavior and physiological development. In M. B. Sterman, D. J. McGinty, & A. M. Adinolfi (Eds.), *Brain development and behavior.* New York: Academic Press, 1971.

Rosenblatt, J. S. Suckling and home orientation in the kitten: A comparative developmental study. In E. Tobach, L. R. Aronson, & E. Shaw (Eds.), *The biopsychology of development.* New York: Academic Press, 1971.

Rosenblatt, J. S. Learning in newborn kittens. *Scientific American*, 1972, *227*, 18–25.

Rosenblatt, J. S. Sensory and motivational basis of early behavioral adjustments. Chapter 1, this volume.

Salas, M. Effects of early malnutrition on the development of swimming ability in the rat. *Physiology and Behavior*, 1972, *8*, 119–122.

Salas, M., & Cintra, L. Development of the electrocorticogram during starvation in the rat. *Physiology and Behavior*, 1975, *14*, 589–593.

Schapiro, S. Metabolic and maturational effects of thyroxine on the infant rat. *Endocrinology*, 1966, *78*, 527–532.

Schapiro, S. Some physiological, biochemical, and behavioral consequences of neonatal hormone administration: Cortisol and thyroxine. *General and Comparative Endocrinology*, 1968, *10*, 214–228.

Schapiro, S. Hormonal and environmental influences on rat brain development and behavior. In M. B. Sterman, D. J. McGinty, & A. M. Adinolfi (Eds.), *Brain development and behavior*. New York: Academic Press, 1971.

Schapiro, S., & Norman, R. J. Thyroxine: Effects of neonatal administration on maturation, development, and behavior. *Science*, 1967, *155*, 1279–1281.

Schapiro, S., Vukovich, K., & Globus, A. Effects of neonatal thyroxine and hydrocortisone administration on the development of dendritic spines in the visual cortex of rats. *Experimental Neurology*, 1973, *40*, 286–296.

Schulenburg, C. J., Riccio, D. C., & Stikes, E. R. Acquisition and retention of a passive-avoidance response as a function of age in rats. *Journal of Comparative and Physiological Psychology*, 1971, *74*, 75–83.

Sereni, F., Principi, N., Perletti, L., & Sereni, L. P. Undernutrition and the developing rat brain. I. Influence on acetylcholinesterase and succinic acid dehydrogenase activities and on norepinephrine and 5-OH-tryptamine tissue concentrations. *Biology of the Neonate*, 1966, *10*, 254–259.

Slob, A. K., Snow, C. E., & de Natris-Mathot, E. Absence of behavioral deficits following neonatal undernutrition in the rat. *Developmental Psychobiology*, 1973, *6*, 177–186.

Smart, J. L. Activity and exploratory behavior of adult offspring of undernourished mother rats. *Developmental Psychobiology*, 1974, *7*, 315–321.

Smart, J. L., & Dobbing, J. Vulnerability of developing brain. II. Effects of early nutritional deprivation on reflex ontogeny and development of behavior in the rat. *Brain Research*, 1971, *28*, 85–95.

Smith, N. Effects of interpolated learning on the retention of an escape response in rats as a function of age. *Journal of Comparative and Physiological Psychology*, 1968, *65*, 422–426.

Spear, N. E. Retrieval of memory in animals. *Psychological Review*, 1973, *80*, 163–194.

Stanley, W. C., Bacon, W. E., & Fehr, C. Discriminated instrumental learning in neonatal dogs. *Journal of Comparative and Physiological Psychology*, 1970, *70*, 335–343.

Sterman, M. B., McGinty, D. J., & Adinolfi, A. M. (Eds.). *Brain development and behavior*. New York: Academic Press, 1971.

Tobach, E., Aronson, L. R., & Shaw, E. (Eds.). *The biopsychology of development*. New York: Academic Press, 1971.

Vernadakis, A., & Weiner, N. (Eds.). *Advances in behavioral biology. Drugs and the developing brain* (Vol. 8). New York: Plenum Press, 1974.

Wahlsten, D. Genetic variation in the development of mouse brain and behavior: Evidence from the middle postnatal period. *Developmental Psychobiology*, 1975, *8*, 371–380.

Walravens, P., & Chase, H. P. Influence of thyroid on formation of myelin lipids. *Journal of Neurochemistry*, 1969, *16*, 1477–1484.

Williams, R. A., & Campbell, B. A. Weight loss and quinine-milk ingestion as measure of "hunger" in infant and adult rats. *Journal of Comparative and Physiological Psychology*, 1961, *54*, 220–222.

Williamson, B., & Coniglio, J. G. The effects of pyridoxine deficiency and of caloric restriction on lipids in the developing rat brain. *Journal of Neurochemistry*, 1971, *18*, 267–276.

Winick, M., & Noble, A. Cellular response in rats during malnutrition at various ages. *Journal of Nutrition*, 1966, *89*, 300–306.

6 The Use of Psychopharmacological Procedures to Analyse the Ontogeny of Learning and Retention: Issues and Concerns

Linda Patia Spear[1]
State University of New York at Binghamton

Ontogenetic analysis has proved to be an excellent vehicle for examining principles of physiological and biochemical bases of brain function. With the progress that has been made in the area of the ontogeny of learning and memory exemplified by many of the chapters in this volume, a combined analysis of this area with that of the ontogeny of the nervous system may well lead to an elucidation of the physiological basis of learning and retention. As one possible means of such an elucidation I intend in this chapter to discuss some of the major issues in the field of psychopharmacological investigations of ontogeny and to offer some considerations for future work of this type.

There are at least three main approaches for determining which of the many developing physiological processes are critical for the ontogenetic maturation of learning and retention: (1) the amnesic approach, in which through some hormonal, drug toxin, nutritional or physiological insult on the developing brain one attempts to prevent the development of normal adult learning and retention abilities; (2) the hypermnesic approach, in which through a variety of experimental manipulations one tries to alleviate the typical retention deficits seen in developing animals; and (3) the correlative approach, in which one compares some aspects of brain development with ontogenetic patterns of development of learning, and especially memory, capabilities.

With respect to the last approach, there are many ways of assessing brain development in attempts to correlate brain development with the ontogeny of learning and memory capabilities. The development of the brain can be

---
[1]Previous work by this author has been published under the name of Linda Patia Lanier.

investigated anatomically by examining cell numbers of neurons and glia, rate of myelination, dendritic arborization, synaptogenesis, and so on. The developing brain can also be examined neurochemically, to determine the pattern of appearance of normal brain chemical constituents. But there is still the question of when any particular brain system becomes functional: For example, is 50% of adult levels of neurotransmitter sufficient for that neurotransmitter system to be functional, or does it have to be 70% to 80% or greater? Knowing the precise anatomical and neurochemical features of the brain during ontogeny still does not elucidate when the brain becomes functional. Consequently researchers have also used another approach, in which they attempt to assess the functional development of the brain. One example of this type of approach is to assess the development of spontaneous and evoked electrical activity. Another variation of this functional approach is to examine ontogenetic responsiveness to psychoactive drugs that affect in specific ways the known neurotransmitter systems and to use the data as indices of the functional development of those systems.

There are at least two ways of examining the ontogenetic effects of psychoactive drugs as a means of assessing functional maturation of the nervous system. One procedure is to examine the neurochemical changes that are associated with the administration of the psychoactive drug at different ages. In adult animals, administration of psychoactive drugs results in characteristic changes in the chemistry of the affected neurotransmitter system as well as indirect changes in other systems. There may be alterations in the rate of neurotransmitter synthesis, amount of neurotransmitter, turnover of the neurotransmitter, activity of postsynaptic enzymes associated with neurotransmitter action on postsynaptic membranes, and so on. One can examine the development of such neurochemical indices of functional maturation after ontogenetic administration of psychoactive drugs. Another approach is to examine the physiological or behavioral effects of ontogenetic administration of psychoactive drugs. It is this latter approach that is stressed in this chapter.

The behavioral responses to many psychoactive drugs administered to adult animals have been thoroughly studied. Much of this research has been directed toward assessing the "chemical coding" of behavior in the brain—that is, determining which neurotransmitter systems are utilized by neurons that form necessary (or "preferred") links in the elicitation of a particular pattern of behaviors. The developing animal may provide a unique opportunity in research of the chemical coding of behavior in the brain. If ontogenetic development of patterns of drug responsiveness reflects differential maturation of neuronal systems that are utilized by a psychoactive drug, then one may be more readily able to separate the relative contribution of individual neurotransmitter systems to normal and drug-induced behavior during ontogeny.

There are a multitude of psychoactive drugs that act on the nervous system to produce alterations in behavior. Some of the drugs have unknown, fairly nonspecific or varied modes of action on nervous tissue (for example, drugs of the depressant category such as barbiturates and minor tranquilizers), whereas others have a somewhat specific mechanism of action on one or more of the putative neurotransmitter systems (for example, amphetamine, cocaine, halo-peridal, clonidine, and apomorphine). It is generally of little interest to psycho-pharmacologists to utilize drugs of the first class in studies attempting to relate nervous system functioning to behavioral state. Little can be inferred about which brain changes are critical in producing the altered behavioral effects after such drug treatments. Rather it is the latter class of drugs that has been more of interest in research directed toward studying the chemical coding of behavior in the brain as well as in research that examines ontogenetic behavioral effects of psychoactive drugs as a means of assessing functional maturation of portions of the nervous system.

ONTOGENETIC BEHAVIORAL RESPONSES TO DRUGS

The classic simple "picture" of the development of drug responsiveness is that there is a gradual monotonic increase in the evidence of a particular drug-induced behavior with age (Fig. 6.1). At one age the drug does not have a noticeable behavioral effect; at an older age it begins to induce behavioral effects similar to, although of lower magnitude than, those seen in adults; and at a still later age the behavioral response to the drug is qualitatively and quantitatively similar to that seen in adults. This simplistic ontogenetic pattern does not hold true for many

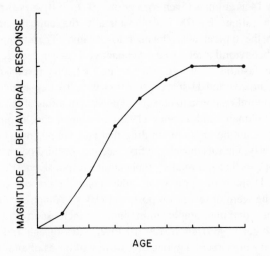

FIG. 6.1. Classic "picture" of the ontogeny of behavioral responsiveness to a psychoactive drug.

drugs. The behavioral effects of many psychoactive drugs differ quantitatively in a nonmonotonic fashion as well as qualitatively in animals of different ages. Variations from this classic picture of the ontogeny of drug responsiveness are presented in the next few pages. These types of variation are not mutually exclusive, and many drugs could be included in several of the following sections. However, for the sake of brevity not all drugs are discussed under each variation for which they might apply.

AGE-RELATED NONMONOTONIC RELATIONSHIPS
IN THE BEHAVIORAL RESPONSES TO DRUGS

The quantitative behavioral response to a drug may vary in a nonmonotonic fashion with age. Some examples of this type of age-related variation in drug responsiveness are given in this section.

One example of an extremely pronounced nonmonotonic alteration in the ontogenetic frequency of behaviors induced by a drug is with the noradrenergic uptake-inhibiting drug cocaine. We (Spear & Brick, in press) have examined, using a time-sampling behavioral categorization method, the behavioral effects of cocaine administered to rats on postnatal Day 7, 14, 21, 28, 35, or in adulthood. Of all the behaviors we recorded, activity (number of quadrants entered) was most markedly affected by age at time of injection. Cocaine produced the most pronounced stimulation of locomotor activity when administered on postnatal Day 7, 14, or 21 (Fig. 6.2). This stimulation of locomotor activity is most marked at Day 14 as animals given cocaine are 100 to 200 times as active as control animals given saline. By 28 days postnatally the animals are behaviorally responding in the typical adult manner to cocaine. These data illustrate how markedly the behavioral effects of a psychoactive drug can vary quantitatively in a nonmonotonic fashion with age. Age-related cocaine responsiveness can be expressed by an inverted U-shaped function with 14 day-animals showing the maximal behavioral response to cocaine expressed in terms of locomotor activity.

Sobrian, Weltman, and Pappas (1975) examined the locomotor stimulant effects of amphetamine (a stimulant drug that acts via potentiation of catecholaminergic pathways) in rats during the first, second, or third postnatal week. From their data it appears that age-related amphetamine responsiveness can be expressed by an inverted U-shape function because the maximal locomotor stimulant effects of amphetamine were observed on postnatal Day 4. Animals younger and older showed less of a maximal amphetamine-induced increase in activity. Campbell, Lytle, and Fibiger (1969) tested rats 10 to 25 days of age and adult rats in a stabilimeter cage after receiving one of a variety of doses of amphetamine. They observed that the maximally effective dose of amphetamine in increasing stabilimeter cage activity varied with age. From their graphs it appears that the absolute

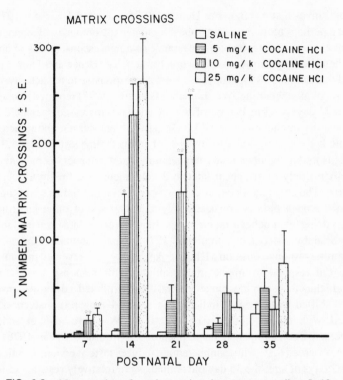

MATRIX CROSSINGS

□ SALINE
▤ 5 mg/k COCAINE HCl
▥ 10 mg/k COCAINE HCl
□ 25 mg/k COCAINE HCl

X̄ NUMBER MATRIX CROSSINGS ± S.E.

300

200

100

7   14   21   28   35

POSTNATAL DAY

FIG. 6.2. Mean number of matrix crossings in response to saline, 5, 10, or
25 mg/kg cocaine hydrochloride of rats tested on postnatal Days 7, 14, 21, 28, or
35. Animals were injected subcutaneously and placed into an open field for a
90-min test.

increase in activity at the maximally effective dose varied with age as well. Rats 10
and 15 days old appeared to show less, and rats 25 days old showed more, of an
increase in activity at the maximally effective dose than did adults. Although they
did not statistically examine cross-age comparisons, it is clear from their data that
there is no simple monotonic relationship in amphetamine-induced activity with
age. Similarly, we (Lanier and Isaacson, 1977) recently reported a study
examining responsiveness to amphetamine in rats beginning on postnatal Day 18,
34, 45, or in adulthood. Although, like Campbell et al. (1969), we did not
specifically analyze for differences in maximal responsiveness to amphetamine
across age, a cursory reexamination of our data indicates that the animals tested
during postnatal Days 18 to 22 may show a greater increase in activity in response
to amphetamine than adult animals and animals tested during postnatal Days
34−38 clearly show a lesser response (see the following). Clearly, the activity
increases induced by amphetamine at different ages is not a simple monotonic
function.

Several investigators (Bauer & Duncan, 1975; Lanier & Isaacson, 1977) have reported a perhaps more interesting phenomenon in the ontogeny of amphetamine-responsiveness—a post-weaning appearance of a nonresponsiveness to amphetamine when measured in terms of locomotor activity. Bauer and Duncan (1975) reported that animals 28 to 33 days old were nonresponsive to the activity-increasing effects of amphetamine. We (Lanier & Isaacson, 1977) reported that although rats 18 to 22 days or 45 to 49 days of age and adult rats increased open field activity in response to amphetamine, rats 34–38 days of age did not show increases in open-field activity in response to any dose of amphetamine tested (Fig. 6.3). Thus when measured in the open field, amphetamine responsiveness is present early in development, only to disappear later in development, and finally to reappear in adult form. The amphetamine nonresponsiveness seen in animals of this age when tested in the open field is not necessarily characteristic of other environmental situations using other behavioral measures. Indeed, recent data from my laboratory (Spear, Shalaby, & Brick, submitted, 1979), where animals were tested for amphetamine responsiveness in a "hole-poke" apparatus, revealed that animals of this age did respond to amphetamine, although the response was of a lesser magnitude than that seen in younger animals, and exhibited a dose-response curve that was shifted to the right (indicating a reduced drug responsiveness) when compared with older animals (see Fig. 6.4). We have also extended this phenomena to a consummatory-based phenomena (Infurna & Spear, 1978). In this study we observed that, while amphetamine induces taste aversions in animals 18, 35 and 52 days of age, the 35 day old animals were relatively resistant to forming the aversion when compared with younger or older animals.

A decreased behavioral responsiveness to a variety of other drugs is also seen in this time period around 35 days postnatally. Reinstein and Isaacson (1977, Reinstein, McClearn, & Isaacson, 1978) observed that the alpha-adrenergic receptor stimulating agent, clonidine, and the dopaminergic receptor stimulating agent, apomorphine, had no effect on locomotor activity when administered at postnatal Day 35. At younger ages and in adulthood, these drugs produce marked age-dependent effects on locomotor activity. Thus, it appears that this 35 day period is associated with a decreased responsiveness to drugs that potentiate the catecholamine systems (amphetamine, apomorphine, and clonidine). It is interesting that animals of this age also show an increased response to a catecholaminergic receptor blocking agent, haloperidol. Animals of this age are much more sensitive to haloperidol induced catalepsy than younger or older animals (Spear et al., see Fig. 6.4). Unfortunately, there is a dearth of information on the behavioral response to other drugs when administered at this age. However, this postnatal Day 35 adolescent age period may be a particularly critical time interval with which to examine psychoactive drug response. Animals of this age vary behaviorally from younger or older animals. Rats around 35 days of age are hyperactive (see Fig. 6.4) and exhibit an increase in hole-poke behavior when compared with younger or older animals (Spear et al., 1979).

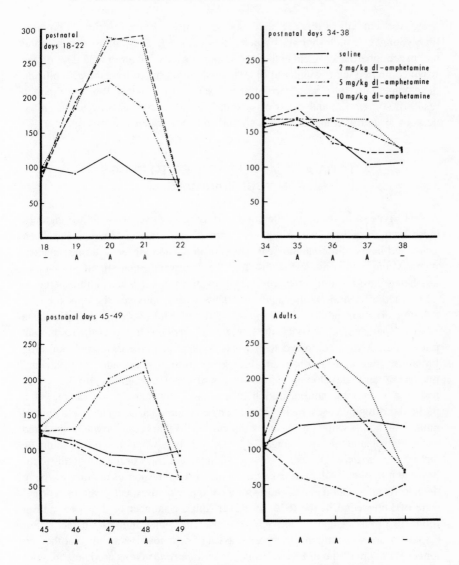

FIG. 6.3. Open-field activity in response to saline, 2, 5, and 10 mg/kg *dl*-amphetamine at four postnatal ages (postnatal Days 18−22, 34−38, 45−49, and in adulthood). Numbers on the abcissa refer to postnatal days. Rats were given a 5-min open-field test on 5 consecutive days. On the first and last day no drug injections were given (-). On the second, third, and fourth testing days animals in each injection group were given their appropriate injection intraperitoneally 15 min prior to the open-field test (A). Numbers on the ordinate refer to number of photocell counts in the automated open field. The adult animals were tested in a larger open field than that used to test the younger animals. (Adapted from Lanier and Isaacson, 1977.)

Moreover, animals of this age have more difficulty learning discrimination tasks than younger or older animals (Amsel, this volume). These unusual behavioral and psychopharmacological responses of animals tested at around 35 days of age when compared with younger or older animals suggest that something significant developmentally may be occurring at this stage of ontogeny. Whether this is a result of some hormonal factor or of some development events occurring in the nervous system is a matter of speculation and further experimentation.

"PARADOXICAL" RESPONSES TO DRUGS IN YOUNG ANIMALS

Another type of quantitative alteration in drug responsiveness with age includes those drug responses that have been termed *paradoxical*. Interest has been generated lately in the paradoxical effects of drugs administered during development. Much of this interest stems from the observation that stimulants such as amphetamine or ritalin often produce a calming effect when administered to "hyperactive" children. Because stimulants usually produce the opposite of a calming effect in adults, the response of these children to the drug has been labeled "paradoxical." To use the term *paradoxical* one has to assume a referent point—paradoxical compared with what? Typically, in the developmental drug literature, the term *paradoxical* has referred to a drug-induced behavioral response seen in developing animals that is of opposite magnitude to the typical response seen after administration of the drug to adults. For example, if a particular drug increases the incidence of a behavior when compared with control animals in adults while decreasing the incidence of that behavior when compared with control animals in younger animals, the behavioral response would be termed *paradoxical*. One can easily question the accuracy of the use of this term, because it implies by definition that these paradoxical responses to drugs in young deviate from common sense and from what one would expect given the current state of knowledge in the field. However, quite a number of drugs have been found to produce such paradoxical responses in young animals. In fact, these responses are so common for certain classes of psychoactive agents that they no longer seem out of the ordinary. Thus, the term *paradoxical* is used here in order to be consistent with the past literature and is not used to imply that such drug responses seen in developing animals are atypical in an ontogenetic sense.

Clonidine, an α-adrenergic receptor-stimulating drug, markedly stimulates locomotor activity of rats during the first two weeks of life with the most marked stimulation occurring during the first week (Kellogg & Lundborg, 1972; Reinstein & Isaacson, 1977). At 21 and 28 days of age, however, clonidine significantly decreases spontaneous activity, whereas at 35 days it has little effect on activity (Reinstein & Isaacson, 1977). Because clonidine produces a depression in motor activity in adult rats, the marked stimulation of motor activity seen in the first few weeks of life after clonidine administration may be viewed as a paradoxical drug effect.

Similarly, high doses of apomorphine and piribedil (Reinstein, McClearn, & Isaacson, 1978), both dopaminergic receptor-stimulating drugs, markedly stimulate locomotor activity in developing rats especially during the third and fourth postnatal weeks. Later in life high doses of these agents induce the typical adult response, which is characterized by a decrease in spontaneous motility associated with a marked induction of stereotyped behavior.

Amphetamine induces a number of paradoxical effects. It increases nipple attachment in 5- and 10-day-old rats while decreasing nipple attachment in older (15-day) rats (Randall & Campbell, 1977). Similarly, amphetamine increases conspecific aggregation in preweanling rats while decreasing conspecific aggregation in postweanling rats (Campbell & Randall, 1977). In a warm environment amphetamine induces hypothermia in developing mice (postnatal Days 13–16) and hyperthermia in adult mice (Alhava, 1975). However, amphetamine-induced hyperthermia during exposure to a high ambient temperature is present from birth in rats, whereas the development of amphetamine-induced hypothermia during exposure to a low ambient temperature develops at the onset of homeothermia (between postnatal Days 15–20) (Lytle & Keil, 1974).

With respect to drugs of the depressant category, Diaz and Schain (1977) briefly noted that neonates appeared behaviorally activated by low doses of phenobarbital. Similarly, a variety of informal sources have noted that children who accidently ingest quantities of minor tranquilizers are behaviorally stimulated instead of tranquilized or sedated.

Anticholinergic drugs such as scopolamine and atropine increase locomotor activity in adult rats and in rats 20 days of age and older (Campbell et al., 1969). However, a number of investigators have noted that these anticholinergic agents appear to suppress activity 15 to 17 days postnatally (Blozovski & Blozovski, 1973; Fibiger, Lytle, & Campbell, 1970; Smith, Spear & Spear, 1979).

AGE-RELATED QUALITATIVE DIFFERENCES IN THE BEHAVIORAL RESPONSE TO DRUGS

As was seen in the preceding two sections, there are a variety of psychoactive drugs that produce quantitative differences in the amount of drug-induced behavior when administered at different stages of ontogeny. Not only may psychoactive drug responses vary quantitatively with age along a single dimension of behavior, but they may also vary qualitatively in the type of behavior induced by the drug at different ages. For example, clonidine (Reinstein & Isaacson, 1977) induces pronounced wall-climbing during the first few weeks of life; later in life no evidence of drug-induced wall-climbing is seen. Clonidine also induces marked catalepsy in 21 to 28 day old rats and minimal catalepsy at

35 days. This drug-induced cataleptic behavior is characteristic only of animals of this age and is not seen after drug administration in younger or older animals (Reinstein & Isaacson, 1977). The anticholinergic drug atropine has little effect on spontaneous motility in rats older than 30 days; however, it decreases spontaneous activity in animals less than 25 days and increases spontaneous activity in animals between 26 and 30 days postnatally (Blozovski & Bachevalier, 1975).

Kellogg and Lundborg (1972) examined ontogenetic variations in the response to L-DOPA (a catecholaminergic precursor). They observed that L-DOPA induced marked hyperactivity in neonatal rats. Even at 1 day of age this drug induced intense forward-crawling behavior. This excitation response was much less marked at 14 days postnatally. In rats of this age L-DOPA induced periods of running interspersed with stuporous behavior and stereotyped behavior. At 21 days Kellogg and Lundborg noted that the behavioral response to L-DOPA appeared to be one of behavioral depression and placidity. It is interesting that the dose-response curve of L-DOPA in adult animals is apparently biphasic, with low doses of L-DOPA having a depressant effect and higher doses producing an excitatory effect on locomotion (Strömberg, 1970). Could it be that the comparatively low dose of L-DOPA (100 mg/kg) used by Kellogg and Lundborg was functionally equivalent to a high adult dose when administered during the first postnatal week and functionally equivalent to a low adult dose when administered at 14 or 21 days of age? Ontogenetic variables that might result in such an effect are discussed more fully in a later section.

DRUG-INDUCED "PRECOCIAL" BEHAVIORS

Some psychoactive drugs, when administered early in development, induce patterns of behavior that are not seen normally (under nondrug conditions) until later in ontogeny. For example, rats during the first week of life show little spontaneous activity. However, drugs potentiating the catecholaminergic neurotransmitters such as clonidine (Kellogg & Lundborg, 1972; Reinstein & Isaacson, 1977), cocaine (Spear & Brick, in press), L-DOPA (Kellogg & Lundborg, 1972), and amphetamine (Sobrian et al., 1975) induce marked increases in activity during this quiescent period that are reminiscent of the large activity increases that are normally seen in rats during development in the second and third postnatal week (Moorcroft, Lytle & Campbell, 1971). In addition, motor patterns that are normally seen at 6 to 7 days postnatally may be seen at 3 to 4 days postnatally after administration of amphetamine (Holmgren, Urbá-Holmgren, & Valdés, 1976), A proportion of infant rats show spontaneous head-shaking behavior between postnatal days 6 and 11. Amphetamine not only increases the frequency of head-shaking in infant rats but also advances the age at which head-shaking is first seen (Holmgren et al., 1976).

Spontaneous alternation (the tendency to explore alternate arms of a T or Y maze on successive trials) develops with age to reach an adult level of about 80%. Douglas (1975) has observed that young rats that have not yet developed spontaneous alternation behavior display typical adult levels of spontaneous alternation after receiving physostigmine (an anticholinesterase, which acts to increase acetylcholine levels by blocking enzymatic degradation of acetylcholine).

These examples illustrate that some psychoactive drugs may ontogenetically induce "precocial" behavioral responses that are not normally seen (under nondrug conditions) until later in development. It is interesting that all the drugs that induce precocial behaviors are drugs that potentiate the activity of the neurotransmitter system they are affecting. This point will be referred to again later.

COMMENTS

A variety of types of ontogenetic patterns of drug responsiveness have been discussed in the preceding sections. It is apparent that there are difficulties associated with attempts to infer from the ontogenetic pattern of drug responsiveness when the underlying neurotransmitter system(s) affected by the drug become functionally mature. Is the earliest behavioral response that can be elicited to a psychoactive drug a sign of the functional maturity of the affected neurotransmitter system? Or is it the earliest response that bears qualitative similarity to the adult behavioral response? Or is it the earliest drug response that quantitatively and qualitatively approaches adult levels? The definition of functional maturity one explicitly or implicitly accepts markedly affects the hypotheses one generates about the ontogeny of the underlying neurotransmitter system(s) that are affected by the psychoactive drug in question.

In the preceding section examples of drug-induced precocial behaviors were given. In these cases drug responses are obtained that might indicate that neurotransmitter systems are mature before the behavioral indices of maturation, thought to be chemically coded in adults at least in part by these neurotransmitter systems, reach maturity. Thus a neurotransmitter system may pass from a completely nonfunctional state through intermediate stages in which the partially developed system may be able to be stimulated by psychoactive drugs to produce behavioral responses that are typically only observed at later stages of maturation. The attainment of functional maturity may be a very gradual process. Drugs may be able to stimulate a partially mature system, but is this a sufficient condition to conclude that the system is functional? If so, then neurotransmitter systems may be termed "functionally mature" before they become ontogenetically involved in normal, non-drug-induced behavior. Thus even a comprehensive examination of the ontogeny of normal and drug-induced behaviors thought to be mediated by a particular neurotransmitter system does not readily lead to an easy determination of the time of functional maturation of that neurotransmitter system. Assignment of such a date is essentially a subjective decision based on one's own definition of functional maturity and extensive knowledge of ontogenetic patterns of drug-induced and normal behavior.

VARIABLES THAT MAY PLAY A ROLE IN THE ONTOGENESIS OF PATTERNS OF DRUG RESPONSIVENESS

The age-related alterations in drug responsiveness seen in the preceding sections are probably due to a conglomerate of many different factors. One such variable involves ontogenetic factors in the distribution and rates of metabolism of drugs. Most drug metabolism occurs in the liver by microsomal enzymes that show developmental increases in the capacity to metabolize drugs. Also there is only gradual development of the barrier systems between the brain and the blood, and these barrier systems may well show differential development in different brain areas. These factors together with others (development of drug-binding carrier proteins in the circulatory system, ontogenetic differences in general metabolic rate, etc.) act to influence drug distribution and rate of drug metabolism. Consequently one might expect that low doses of a drug in developing animals may induce brain concentration and half-life equivalent to that produced by a higher dose in older animals because of immaturity of catabolic enzyme systems and other related factors.

However, ontogenetic differences in drug distribution and metabolism do not account for all the age-related differences in the behavioral response to drugs. Symes, Lal, and Sourkes (1976) examined the half-life, brain concentrations, and behavioral effects of apomorphine after systemic injection of a single dose level into 7-day-old or adult rats. They observed that whereas there were no differences in peak brain concentration of apomorphine at the two ages, this peak concentration occurred later in the neonatal rats. The half-life of brain apomorphine was more than twice as great in the neonate as compared with the adult rat; by 30 minutes postinjection, brain concentrations of apomorphine were markedly greater in the neonates. However, interestingly enough they could not find a correlation between these indices and the observed behavioral effects of the drug at the two ages.

Another possible factor that might lead to ontogenetic differences in drug responsiveness is the ontogeny of hormonal systems that might influence cellular response to drugs, rate of metabolism or distribution of drugs, and so on. Another somewhat related factor involves development of circadian rhythms in drug responsiveness. Adults show circadian rhythms in drug responsiveness. A drug that produces one behavioral effect in the light phase may produce an effect of increased, decreased, or even opposite magnitude when administered in the dark phase. Development of circadian rhythms in drug responsiveness is an area that has not been carefully examined, although it appears to be a fruitful area of research.

Rate-dependent effects are another factor that might be related to ontogenetic differences in drug responsiveness. In adults the observed behavioral effects of some drugs are related to underlying baseline rates in frequency of spontaneous occurrence of behaviors. Because there are marked differences in frequency of baseline behavior patterns with age, this may alter the observed behavioral response seen after drug administration at different ages. For example, Sobrian et al. (1975) examined the motility-stimulating effects of amphetamine during the first three postnatal weeks in rats. They observed that baseline activity levels were higher at ages when drug effects were the smallest. Similarly, we (Spear, Shalaby, & Brick, 1979) examined rats from 23 to 30, 35 to 42, or 47 to 54 days postnatally with respect to baseline activity levels and responsiveness to amphetamine, scopolamine, and haloperidol (see Fig. 6.4). At the middle age range, rats were most active, most sensitive to the cataleptic effects of haloperidol, least sensitive to the effects of scopolamine, and showed less of an activity increase in response to amphetamine than the younger group and less amphetamine-induced stereotyped behavior than the older group.

Issues related to rate dependency are what might be called "behavioral–predispositional" and "situational" dependencies. Animals of different ages spontaneously emit different behaviors. For example, much of the behavior of the early altricial neonate is directed toward suckling and staying near the warmth of the mother. Later in life the young have a greater disposition toward exploring the environment and playing with conspecifics. Given these behavioral predispositions it would not seem surprising if psychoactive drugs differentially altered these age-related ongoing behavior patterns. Similarly, situational factors may influence the behavioral effects seen after drug administration in young and adult animals. For example, a situation in which an animal is tested solitarily in a strange chamber may create a very different internal state in neonates as compared with adult animals. This might influence the behavioral response to drugs when animals are tested in that situation.

These rate, situational, and behavioral–predispositional dependencies are one way of expressing that the "foundation" on which a drug acts may change with age. Because we may presume that behavior is ultimately mediated by the brain, another way to express these same phenomena is to suggest that the pattern of activity of the nervous system may vary with age, and this may alter the effect of a drug. Psychoactive drugs act to alter already ongoing nervous system activity. The patterns of this ongoing activity may change with age as new neuronal systems become functional. For example, nervous system response to the testing situation may change with age as new neuronal systems become functional, further altering baseline nervous system activity on which the drug must act. Thus another related factor that could result in ontogenetic differences in drug

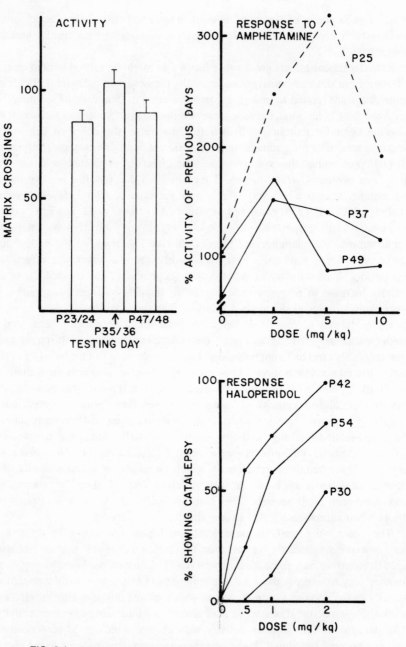

FIG. 6.4. Locomotor activity and behavioral response to *dl*-amphetamine in the open field and cataleptic response to haloperidol of rats of three different ages (postnatal Days 23–30, 35–42, and 47–54).

responsiveness is age-related nervous system alterations in baseline activity that may affect the net response of the nervous system to the drug.

There are a variety of other ways of viewing how the nervous system, through the process of maturation, may vary in its capacity to respond to drugs. Neuronal systems develop at different rates within the nervous system. This developmental interweaving of a multitude of maturing neuronal systems in a complex developmental symphony of interactions could affect the behavioral response to a psychoactive drug administered at any particular age during this process. For example, we (Lanier & Isaacson, 1977) postulated that the temporary non-responsiveness to amphetamine (when tested in the open field) seen in 34 to 38 day rats may be related to the delayed maturation of the hippocampus. Many behaviors characteristic of hippocampal damage in adult rats are present in the young rat of less than a month or so of age (Altman, Brunner, & Bayer, 1973; Douglas, 1975). The hippocampus, which thus appears to become functional at around this age, may temporarily override the still-maturing catecholaminergic systems that are stimulated by amphetamine. We did find that amphetamine increased locomotor activity at around 35 days of age in animals with prior hippocampal damage (although at this age and at younger ages, hippocampally damaged animals under nondrug conditions were not hyperactive). This type of approach, although it has not yet led to a conclusive answer to the issue, is important inasmuch as it stresses that during development there is a dynamic interplay among different brain areas that are maturing at different rates. The behavioral response to a drug at any given age is in part a function of the capacity of the nervous system to respond to the drug; this capacity may change markedly with age as the neuronal systems that respond to the drug and the neuronal systems that act in a net inhibitory or excitory fashion on these neuronal systems mature.

ADDITIONAL COMPLEXITIES IN ATTEMPTS TO CORRELATE BRAIN DEVELOPMENT WITH PSYCHOACTIVE DRUG RESPONSIVENESS

The complexities of the development of the nervous system present difficulties in interpretation of even simple monotonic developmental patterns of response to a drug. For example, assume that there is a gradual increase in the magnitude of a behavioral response to a drug affecting a neurotransmitter system during develop-ment (as seen in Fig. 6.1). Even so it cannot necessarily be concluded that the neurotransmitter system is gradually maturing. The neurotransmitter system affected by the drug might have fully developed early in ontogeny but have been prevented from inducing a behavioral effect when stimulated by the drug until an additional necessary brain system developed in series with the neurotransmitter system in question. For example, in general motor components of the nervous system develop before sensory components. However, interneurons, which connect such larger neurons that communicate between brain regions, are generally small neurons with short axons that develop relatively late in ontogeny. Thus the brain may be incapable of integrating changes in neuronal activity induced in certain brain regions by drug administration to produce a behavioral response until these interneurons are elaborated and reach functional maturity.

There is another issue that should be considered in attempts to relate ontogenetic differences in drug responsiveness to ontogeny of brain neurotransmitter systems. It is apparent that no given neurotransmitter system matures instantaneously; rather it undergoes a relatively protracted developmental process during which it may pass from a completely nonfunctional state through a variety of intermediate stages in which the partially developed system may be able to function under certain conditions. In its partially developed state the neurotransmitter system may not be able normally to mediate behaviors that are thought to be mediated in the adult at least in part by that system. However, although the neurotransmitter system may not play a role in non-drug-stimulated behavior in its partially developed state, it may be able to respond to drugs that potentiate the neurotransmitter system to result in a drug-induced behavioral response. For example, all the psychoactive drugs that were found to induce precocial behaviors were drugs that stimulate (potentiate) neurotransmitter systems. These early behavioral responses to such potentiating drugs may not indicate when that neurotransmitter system becomes functionally mature; rather they indicate that the immature system is at least capable of being stimulated into exerting some effect on behavior. However, one would not expect to observe a behavioral response to drugs that block the functioning of a neurotransmitter system until that system is significantly developed so as to exert some control over behavior (because blocking a nonfunctional system should be without observable effect.) In support of these suggestions it has been reported that although the catecholaminergic stimulating drug amphetamine markedly increases activity of rats during the first week of life (Sobrian et al., 1975), alpha-methyl-paratyrosine, a drug that blocks synthesis of the catecholamines, does not depress activity until about 15 days postnatally (Campbell & Mabry, 1973).

Psychoactive drugs can affect a given neurotransmitter system in one or more of a variety of ways; they can induce or prevent neurotransmitter release, block synthesis or degradation, act on neurotransmitter receptors to stimulate or block them, prevent reuptake, block neurotransmitter storage, and so on. The cellular mechanisms that they act on develop at different rates within a given neurotransmitter system, and thus caution must be exerted in generalizing from ontogenetic responses to one drug that affects a neurotransmitter system in a particular way to the ontogeny of that neurotransmitter system in general. For example, it appears that receptors are present prior to the time that presynaptic input is established

(Woodward, Hoffer, Siggins, & Bloom, 1971). Consequently one might expect to evoke behavioral responses with drugs that directly stimulate these receptors at an earlier point in development than with drugs that block these receptors or act on presynaptic mechanisms. Indeed, maximum locomotor stimulant effects were seen earlier in development with clonidine (postnatal Day 7) (Reinstein & Isaacson, 1977), a noradrenergic receptor-stimulating drug, than with cocaine (postnatal Day 14) (Spear & Brick, in press), a drug that exerts its effect presynaptically on the same neurotransmitter system.

Another issue that should be considered involves regional variation in the development of a particular neurotransmitter system. A given neurotransmitter system projects to many areas of the brain. Evidence indicates that these projections may develop at different times within a given neurotransmitter system, with generally more caudal brain areas developing before more rostral areas (see Lanier, Dunn, & Van Hartesveldt, 1976, for a review). So if the behavioral response to a drug affecting a given neurotransmitter system is mediated mainly via caudal projections, one might expect to observe a behavioral response to this drug earlier in ontogeny than to a drug that affects the same neurotransmitter system but is mediated via more rostral brain areas.

CONSIDERATIONS FOR FUTURE ONTOGENETIC PSYCHOPHARMACOLOGICAL RESEARCH

This chapter has presented some of the issues in the field of ontogeny of behavioral responsiveness to drugs. Although at the moment the field may seem beset by complexities, it is by no means inexorably so. Many of the apparent intricacies in the area may be due to an inadequate data base. There are only a few studies in this area, and such an insufficiency of information tends to encourage a false air of complexity. Much more research in this area is needed, but there are a variety of lessons that can be gained from the work of the past and applied to further research in the field.

First, one cannot draw conclusions about the state of maturity of a neurotransmitter system on the basis of observing the ontogeny of responsiveness to a single drug. Instead several drugs, each of which affects a given neurotransmitter system in a different manner, must be tested before suggestions can be generated as to the state of maturity of the underlying transmitter system.

Also, for any given drug, dose-response curves must be established at each of the different ages examined. The dose-response curves of drugs can vary markedly with age. For example, we have found marked age-dependent differences in responsiveness to haloperidol and amphetamine between 25 and 54 days postnatally (Fig. 6.4). One might note that these marked age-dependent alterations in drug responsiveness are evident during an interval of time that is not reknowned for marked ontogenetic brain or liver alterations, although it is a time of marked hormonal changes preparing for puberty. Because in adult animals a given drug may induce different behaviors, each with their own dose-response curve, it is doubly vital to determine the ontogenetic effects of a drug at a variety of different dose levels. One cannot infer from a dose-response curve established at one age what dose is a moderate dose for administration at other ages.

A related point is that studies examining the ontogeny of drug responsiveness should compare animals of several different ages. It is obvious from the studies reported in this chapter that the behavioral response to drugs can vary markedly with age. One clearly cannot discern the complete ontogenetic pattern of drug responsiveness by testing at only one or two developmental stages. There has been a trend in research of this type to test animals only up to the conventional age of weaning (21 days) or slightly thereafter. We have often found, however, that the postweaning periadolescent rat is by no means equivalent in drug responsiveness to either slightly younger or older animals. Thus it might be of value in future research to consider seriously this ontogenetic stage.

When examining animals of different ages, careful consideration should also be directed toward the relative benefits of cross-sectional and longitudinal research designs. Because injection of a particular drug does not affect subsequent sensitivity to that drug in adults, one cannot infer that the same will be true in younger animals. Consequently cross-sectional testing is crucial in research on the ontogeny of drug responsiveness. Although longitudinal testing certainly saves on expense of animals, it is only advisable if data obtained from longitudinally tested and cross-sectionally tested animals are equivalent for the particular drug and ages of animals being tested.

To understand the behavioral effects of a drug at any particular age, one must have a clear understanding of the normal behavioral patterns of animals of that age, not only in the particular testing situation that is being used but in other, more ethologically relevant situations as well. Species evolved not only because the adults of the species were subject to natural selection but because the young were as well. Behaviors may be manifested early in development not only as immature forms of the behavior of the adult but as evolutionarily important behaviors in and of themselves. Similarly, the nervous system has evolved owing to pressures, exerted both during ontogeny and in adulthood, to produce behaviors that were evolutionarily advantageous. The developing nervous system can be viewed as an immature adult nervous system or as a perfectly mature developing nervous system "evolutionarily designed" to produce appropriate behaviors at a particular stage in development. By examining whether drugs administered during development enhance or suppress these ethologically relevant behaviors, one arrives at a greater understanding of the ontogeny of drug responsiveness. In addition, such work may lead us to portions of the nervous system that are especially relevant to survival-dependent behaviors in infancy.

In psychopharmacological investigations of ontogeny, careful attention should also be paid to the drug testing situation. Using different behavioral responses and/or different testing procedures to measure a drug effect can give varying results for the ontogeny of drug responsiveness of a particular drug. For example, Campbell and associates have reported that the anticholinergic drug scopolamine increased stabilimeter cage activity only in animals 20 days of age and older (Campbell et al., 1969), whereas pilocarpine, a cholinomimetic drug, was not effective in inhibiting amphetamine-induced increases in stabilimeter cage activity prior to 20 days postnatally (Fibiger, Lytle, & Campbell, 1970). However, Blozovski, Cudennec, and Garrigou (1977) have reported that the anticholinergic drug atropine impaired passive-avoidance acquisition as early as 14 days postnatally and that scopolamine disrupted passive-avoidance acquisition in 17 day rats. Indeed, we (Smith et al., in press) have observed that scopolamine disrupted discrimination performance in 15-day rats while not increasing activity levels until 23 days postnatally. Thus the ontogenetic pattern of response to drugs affecting a given neurotransmitter system may vary with the type of testing situation used to assess the behavioral pharmacological response.

Initially it may be most advantageous to test for drug responsiveness in an unstructured situation. After the ontogeny of the behavioral responses to a drug is well understood in such unstructured situations, drug responsiveness can be meaningfully examined in more structured or automated tests. There are some problems, however, even in defining an appropriate unstructured testing situation. Campbell et al. (1969) have shown that during development, around postnatal day 15, rats pass through a period of intense hyperactivity. Randall and Campbell (1976) have suggested that this period of hyperactivity may be a response to isolation stress rather than reflecting a general phenomenon of maturation of caudal-excitatory before rostral-inhibitory brain areas. During this time period amphetamine has been shown to increase the activity of isolated rats (Campbell & Randall, 1977; Campbell et al., 1969; Sobrian et al., 1975) while decreasing activity of rats tested in the presence of a conspecific (anesthetized adult) (Campbell & Randall, 1977). These results have led researchers to reconsider the best strategy for psychopharmacological testing of animals during ontogeny. Is it better to test animals singly and perhaps induce isolation stress although avoiding possible confounds involving conspecific interaction? Or is it more appropriate to test animals in groups, testing possible conspecific inter-action problems but avoiding the problem of isolation-induced stress? In the latter case the drug may induce behavioral effects in the animal that may alter conspecific interaction that may in turn alter not only the behaviors emitted but also the actual physiological consequences of the drug. For example, toxic levels of amphetamine are much lower in grouped animals when compared with isolated animals (Höhn & Lasagna, 1960). We (Spear & Brick, in press) have used a testing situation wherein animals are tested in groups of four in individual but spatially adjacent testing chambers. In the testing situation, which allowed for no physical contact among conspecifics, there was no evidence of isolation-induced hyperactivity at any age (from postnatal Day 7 to adulthood). Our results suggest that testing animals in individual, spatially adjacent testing chambers may prove to be an effective strategy for testing developing animals. This procedure, although limiting conspecific interaction, may also prevent an isolation-induced stress effect, the behavioral manifestations of which may vary with ontogeny.

After careful analysis of the ontogeny of drug responsiveness for a variety of psychoactive drugs, drug responsiveness can next be tested in more complex situations. One example of a more complex testing situation is a situation in which an animal is tested for learning and retention. For instance, using the hypermnesic approach, psychoactive drugs can be used in developing animals to alleviate the typical retention deficits seen in developing animals. Conversely, other psychoactive drugs can be used during ontogeny to prevent the manifestation of learning and retention (the amnesic approach). The issues in administering drugs in these more complex situations are identical to those discussed previously in this section. In fact, since the nature of the interaction is much greater in these cases, even more attention should be directed toward careful consideration of issues involved in the ontogenetic administration of drugs.

Unfortunately, there are only so many variables that can be experimentally manipulated at one time. Consequently psychopharmacologists have tended to pick a single testing situation and manipulate drug variables enthusiastically. Conversely but not more insightfully, experimental psychologists have minimized drug manipulations (if they use drugs at all) and manipulated behavioral testing variables with at least as much enthusiasm. Although (and in a sense because) both approaches have been somewhat fruitful in the ontogenetic field, one can forsee a need for synthesis of such approaches to further our knowledge beyond what can be gained from either approach alone. This synthesis might be especially fruitful in elucidating the physiological basis of learning and memory.

The purpose of this chapter has been to present a frank discussion of psychopharmacological investigations of ontogeny and to offer some considerations for future work of this type. The hope is not to discourage the use of drugs in ontogenetic studies of learning and retention but to encourage work of a psychopharmacological nature, careful analytical work with an appreciation for the complexity of the ontogenetic development of the nervous system.

ACKNOWLEDGMENT

The research reported in this chapter was supported in part by Grant 1 RO3 MH29834-01 MSM from the National Institute of Mental Health and Grant 0005-02-040-76 0 from the Research Foundation of the State University of New York.

REFERENCES

Alhava, E. Body temperature responses induced by amphetamine isomers in adult and developing mice. *Acta Pharmacologica et Toxicologia*, 1975, *36*, 465–468.

Altman, J., Brunner, R. L., & Bayer, S. A. The hippocampus and behavioral maturation. *Behavioral Biology*, 1973, *38*, 557–596.

Bauer, R. H., & Duncan, D. L. Differential effects of *d*-amphetamine in mature and immature rats. *Physiology and Behavior*, 1975, *3*, 312–316.

Blozovski, D., & Bachevalier, J. Effects of atropine on behavioral arousal in the developing rat. *Developmental Psychobiology*, 1975, *8*, 97–102.

Blozovski, D., & Blozovski, M. Effects de l'atropine sur l'exploration, l'apprentissage et l'activité electrocorticale chez le rat au cours du développment. *Psychopharmacologica*, 1973, *33*, 39–52.

Blozovski, D., Cudennec, A., & Garrigou, D. Deficits in passive-avoidance learning following atropine in the developing rat. *Psychopharmacology*, 1977, *54*, 139–143.

Campbell, B. A., & Mabry, P. D. The role of catecholamines in behavioral arousal during ontogenesis. *Psychopharmacologia*, 1973, *31*, 253–264.

Campbell, B. A., Lytle, L. D., & Fibiger, H. C. Ontogeny of adrenergic arousal and cholinergic inhibitory mechanisms in the rat. *Science*, 1969, *166*, 635–636.

Campbell, B. A., & Randall, P. J. Paradoxical effects of amphetamine on preweanling and post-weanling rats. *Science*, 1977, *195*, 888–891.

Diaz, J., & Schain, R. J. Chronic phenobarbital administration: Effects upon brain growth and behavior of artificially reared rats. *Proceedings of the Western Pharmacological Society*, 1977, *20*, 153–157.

Douglas, R. J. The development of hippocampal function: Implications for theory and therapy. In R. L. Isaacson & K. H. Pribram (Eds.), *The hippocampus* (Vol. 2). New York: Plenum Press, 1975.

Fibiger, H. C., Lytle, H. D., & Campbell, B. A. Cholinergic modulation of adrenergic arousal in the developing rat. *Journal of Comparative and Physiological Psychology*, 1970, *72*, 384–389.

Höhn, R., & Lasagna, L. Effects of aggregation and temperature on amphetamine toxicity in mice. *Psychopharmacologica*, 1960, *1*, 210–220.

Holmgren, B., Urbá-Holmgren, R., & Valdés, M. Spontaneous and amphetamine induced head-shaking in infant rats. *Pharmacology, Biochemistry and Behavior*, 1976, *5*, 23–29.

Infurna, R. N., & Spear, L. P. Developmental changes in amphetamine-induced taste aversions. Paper presented at the annual meetings of the International Society for Developmental Psycho-biology, November, 1978, St. Louis, Missouri.

Kellogg, C., & Lundborg, P. Ontogenetic variations in responses to L-DOPA and monoamine receptor-stimulating agents. *Psychopharmacologica*, 1972, *23*, 187–200.

Lanier, L. P., Dunn, A. J., & VanHartesveldt, C. Development of neurotransmitters and their function in brain. In S. Ehrenpreis and I. J. Kopin (Eds.), *Reviews of Neuroscience*, (Vol. 2). New York: Raven Press, 1976.

Lanier, L. P., & Isaacson, R. L. Early developmental changes in the locomotor response to ampheta-mine and their relation to hippocampal function. *Brain Research*, 1977, *126*, 567–575.

Lytle, L. D., & Keil, F. C. Brain and peripheral monoamines: Possible role in the ontogenesis of normal and drug-induced responses in the immature mammal. In E. K. Fuxe, L. Olson, & Y. Zotterman (Eds.), *Dynamics of degeneration and growth in neurons*. New York: Pergamon Press, 1974.

Moorcroft, W. H., Lytle, L. D., & Campbell, B. A. Ontogeny of starvation-induced behavioral arousal in the rat. *Journal of Comparative and Physiological Psychology*, 1971, *75*, 59–67.

Randall, P. K., & Campbell, B. A. Ontogeny of behavioral arousal in rats: Effects of maternal and sibling presence. *Journal of Comparative and Physiological Psychology*, 1976, *90*, 453−459.

Randall, P. K., & Campbell, B. A. Effects of *d*-amphetamine on nursing behavior in the neonatal rat. The 48th annual meeting of the *Eastern Psychological Association*, 1977, p. 89 (Abstract).

Reinstein, D. K., & Isaacson, R. L. Clonidine sensitivity in the developing rat. *Brain Research*, 1977, *135*, 378−382.

Reinstein, D. K., McClearn, D., & Isaacson, R. L. The development of responsiveness to dopaminergic agents. *Brain Research*, 1978, *150*, 216−223.

Smith, G. J., Spear, L. P., & Spear, N. E. Behavioral effects of scopolamine in infant rats. *Journal of Comparative and Physiological Psychology*, in press.

Sobrian, S. K., Weltman, M., & Pappas, B. A. Neonatal locomotion and long-term behavioral effects of *d*-amphetamine in the rat. *Developmental Psychobiology*, 1975, *8*, 241−250.

Spear, L. P., & Brick, J. Cocaine-induced behavior in the developing rat. *Behavioral Biology*, in press.

Spear, L. P., Shalaby, I. A., & Brick, J. Chronic administration of neuroleptic drugs during development: behavioral and psychopharmacological effects. Manuscript submitted for publication, 1979.

Strömberg, U. DOPA effects on motility in mice: Potentiation by MK485 and dexchlorpheniramine. *Psychopharmacologica*, 1970, *18*, 58−67.

Symes, A. L., Lal, S., & Sourkes, T. L. Time-course of apomorphine in the brain of the immature rat after apomorphine injection. *Archives Internationales de Pharmacodynamie et de Thérapie*, 1976, *223*, 260−264.

Woodward, D. J., Hoffer, B. J., Siggins, G. R., & Bloom, F. E. The ontogenetic development of synaptic junctions, synaptic activation, and responsiveness to neurotransmitter substances in rat cerebellar Purkinje cells. *Brain Research*, 1971, *34*, 73−97.

7

Ontogeny of Associative Learning: Acquisition of Odor Aversions by Neonatal Rats

Jerry W. Rudy and Martin D. Cheatle
Princeton University

INTRODUCTION

An important belief shared by the contributors to this volume is that our understanding of learning can profit by studying its ontogeny in altricial animals such as mice, rats, cats, and dogs. As noted by many writers (Campbell & Spear, 1972; Campbell & Coulter, 1976; Kenny & Blass, 1977; Rosenblatt, 1971; 1972), altricial animals are attractive subjects for this purpose because at birth they are quite helpless; their nervous systems are markedly underdeveloped, and their sensory systems and behavioral repertoire are correspondingly primitive. Such animals, however, also mature in a relatively short time period. For example, by about 4 weeks of age the central nervous system of the rat in many ways approximates that of the adult, its sensory systems are functioning, and its behavioral repertoire is quite rich. Consequently by studying such animals at various ages, one might hope to discover important changes in their learning capabilities and possibly even identify neurological and neurochemical changes that are of functional significance to the learning processes.

In principal this research strategy has much potential as a source of ideas for the learning theorist and as a means of studying the biological basis of learning. When the current literature is examined from this perspective, however, one is forced to conclude that its promise is yet to be fulfilled (cf. Campbell & Coulter, 1976).

Progress in this domain has been hindered in part by the absence of adequate behavioral procedures for identifying learning in the neonatal animal, particularly during the first few days after birth. To be sure, there is evidence of learning in newborns of several altricial species. Rosenblatt (1972), for example, has shown the early involvement of learning in the control of the kitten's selection of the nipple from which it will nurse. Thoman, Wetzel, and Levine (1968) have reported that by 3 days of age tube-fed rat pups display anticipatory-conditioned reactions to experimenter-provided handling cues that preceded tube feeding. Although the procedures employed by these researchers are particularly appropriate to the study of learning in the newborn animal, they become much less so as the animal matures. Moreover they do not lend themselves easily to the task of systematically investigating the variables likely to influence the learning process. Consequently as of 1976 the only conclusion one could make about learning in the neonatal animal is that offered by Campbell and Coulter (1976): "Given that task demands are appropriate to the neonatal state, learning apparently occurs without difficulty [p. 211]." We know very little about either the principal variables that influence the learning processes of the infant or how these processes change as the organism matures.

Thus a central problem for the investigator interested in the ontogeny of learning is to develop behavioral methodologies that can be appropriately employed to identify the operation of associative-learning processes at the earliest possible age and that will remain appropriate as the animal makes the transition from infancy to adulthood. An additional desideratum of such a methodology is that it allows the researcher systematically to manipulate the experiential variables that are likely to influence the learning process.

To develop such a methodology, however, is no easy task. The researcher must overcome a number of problems that are a direct consequence of the fact that at birth the animal's nervous system is quite immature. On the one hand the neonate's sensory development is incomplete, and this restricts the class of stimulus events that it can be expected to learn to relate. On the other hand its behavioral repertoire is limited, and this makes it difficult to obtain a behavioral measure that can be used to index any learning that might have occurred.

Most recently, we (Rudy & Cheatle, 1977) have developed a behavioral task that has overcome some of these difficulties and may be a useful analytic tool for studying the ontogeny of associative-learning processes. Specifically, we have developed procedures that allow us to study in rats the acquisition of aversions to olfactory stimulation. The operation of associative-learning processes is revealed in this task by the pup avoiding a scent that it had previously experienced in conjunction with a drug-induced illness.

In choosing to develop a methodology for studying the acquisition of odor aversions in neonatal rats we were influenced by several existing facts. First, there is good evidence (Domjan, 1973; Lorden, Kenfield, & Braun, 1970; Taukulis, 1974) that adult rats display aversions to olfactory cues that have been paired with a drug-induced illness. Second, the recent research of Teicher and Blass (1976) has implicated a critical involvement of olfactory stimulation in the control of the rat pup's suckling behavior. For our purposes their work indicated that the olfactory system of the rat is functional shortly after birth and that therefore olfactory stimulation also might be an *appropriate* stimulus event to use with newborn pups in an associative-learning task. Third, since it has been established that adult rats acquire odor aversions, we felt that if we could successfully develop a behavioral task that would reveal the acquisition of odor aversions by the neonatal rat, then potentially we would have an analytic tool for tracking changes in the underlying associative processes throughout the rat's life span. In this chapter we review the progress we have made toward this goal.

In overview, we first describe the general methodology that we have developed to study the acquisition of odor aversions by neonatal rats. We then describe the results of several classes of experiments that have been obtained with this methodology. On the basis of the first set of experiments we will attempt to convince the reader that we have a powerful methodology that has implicated associative-learning capabilities in rats only 2 days of age. We then discuss our initial attempts to uncover some of the important experiential variables that influence the acquisition of odor aversions in pups trained at several ages. In one set of studies we varied the interstimulus interval between the pup's experience with the olfactory cues and the illness-inducing event, and in another set we varied the pup's experience with the olfactory cues prior to the training episode when the pup received the odor-illness pairing. Finally we describe several experiments in which we have extended our procedures to the study of second-order, conditioned-odor aversions.

METHODS AND PROCEDURES

The subjects were Sprague—Dawley-derived male and female pups bred in the Princeton University Psychology Department. All pups were at least 2 days old at the beginning of an experiment, where Day 0 is defined as the date of birth. When a new delivery was noted, the date of birth was recorded and the litter culled to 8 pups. Several different litters were used in each experiment, and an attempt was make to insure that each litter contributed equally to the composition of each treatment condition. On the day of the conditioning treatment the pups were taken from their maternity cage, weighed, and placed into a polyurethane bag (55 cm × 36 cm × 24 cm) containing 500 ml of fresh natural-pine shavings scented with the olfactory stimulus, 2.5 cc of McCormick's lemon extract. Generally 8 subjects were placed together into the same bag. Once all subjects were placed into the bag, the top was closed leaving an opening of about 2 to 3 cm in the top for ventilation. Approximately 5 minutes after being placed into this environment each pup was removed and injected intraperitoneally with the illness-inducing drug (2% body weight of a 0.15-M solution of lithium chloride, LiCl) and then returned to the odor environment for an additional 30 minutes prior to being returned to the maternity cage. In all the studies reported, the subjects received only a single such conditioning experience. The treatments administered to the various control groups are described in each of the separate experiments. In order to assess the acquisition of an aversion to the lemon scent, we employed a test procedure developed by Dr. Catherine Cornwell-Jones (1976)[1] to study the development of the olfactory system in neonatal hampsters and rats. The test apparatus consisted of a 30 cm × 20 cm × 10 cm Plexiglas compartment with a wire-mesh floor beneath which were two 15 cm × 9 cm × 3 cm containers. One container was always filled with lemon-scented shavings; depending on the test, the other was filled with either fresh natural-pine shavings or natural-pine shavings scented with a novel odor, McCormick's garlic juice (2.5 cc/500ml of pine shavings). On a test trial a single subject was placed into the center of the compartment for 150 seconds. The dependent variable of interest was the percentage of this time the pup spent over the lemon-scented shavings. The pup was judged to be over the lemon scent when its head and both forelegs were across a line dividing the two containers. After each pup was tested the wire-mesh floor was wiped with a damp cloth. After six animals were tested the shavings were discarded and replaced with appropriate fresh shavings and scent. These tests were conducted so that the experimenter had no knowledge of the treatment condition experienced by the pup prior to testing.[2]

ODOR-AVERSION LEARNING BY 2-DAY-OLD PUPS

Acquisition of the Aversion

The intent of our (Rudy & Cheatle, 1977) initial research was to determine if the procedures we have just described could be employed to reveal evidence of associative learning by 2-day-old pups. In the first experiment four treatment conditions were examined. The pups in the critical condition, Groups L-UCS (n = 12), received a single pairing of the lemon (L) scent and the unconditioned stimulus (UCS) LiCl in the manner just described. In order to assess the effects of this treatment, three additional treatment conditions were included to control for the influence of "nonassociative" factors that might influence the test results. The pups in Group L-Sham (n = 6) were treated exactly like those in Group L-UCS except that they experienced only an injection with the hyperdermic needle; they were not infused with the LiCl. This treatment thus controlled for the influence that the lemon scent experience might have on the test performance. The pups in Group UCS (n = 6) experienced the LiCl injection; however, olfactory stimulation in the polyurethane bag was provided by shavings from the pups' maternity cage. This treatment thus controlled for the possible influence of the LiCl treatment per se. Finally pups in Group N (n = 5) were naive (N) at the time of testing. They experienced neither the lemon scent nor the UCS nor the

---

[1]We are indebted to Dr. Cornwell-Jones for calling our attention to this test procedure.

[2]In each experiment where differences between groups are claimed, the reader can assume that they are statistically reliable, at least to the 0.025 level of significance.

injection. On the conditioning day they were simply placed into the polyurethane bag containing shavings from the maternity cage for 35 minutes. All subjects were subsequently tested twice. In one test the pups were allowed to choose between lemon-scented and garlic-scented shavings, and in the other they could choose between lemon-scented natural-pine and unscented natural-pine shavings. Half of the animals in each group were first given the choice between lemon- and garlic-scented shavings; the other half were first given the choice between lemon-scented and unscented shavings.

At this point it should be mentioned that our preliminary work had indicated that the pups were not active enough to display discriminative test behavior until they were about 8 days old. Thus we did not test them until they were this age. It also should be appreciated that this meant that in order to obtain evidence of associative learning in 2-day-old pups, the effect of the odor-conditioning treatment had to be retained by the pups for at least 6 days. This procedural necessity could have presented a problem. Potentially, the 2-day-old pup might be capable of associating the odor and illness episodes, but we might fail to detect this learning because of forgetting that occurred during the 6-day retention period.

It can be seen in Fig. 7.1, however, that the relatively long retention interval apparently did not produce this problem. From both of the test results displayed in this figure it is quite clear that the animals that had experienced the lemon−LiCl pairing, Group L-UCS, spent much less time over the lemon-scented shavings than did the pups in the three control conditions.

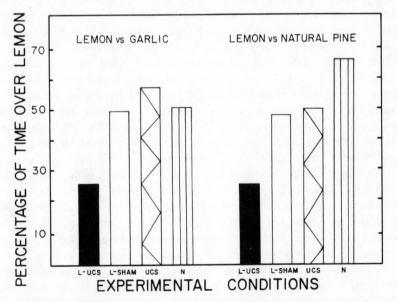

FIG. 7.1.   Mean percentage of time spent by each group over the lemon-scented shavings. (From Rudy and Cheatle, © (1977) by the American Association for the Advancement of Science).

The results of this study thus suggest that the 2-day-old pups have associative-learning capabilities, because the animals in Group L-UCS spent significantly less time over the lemon-scented shavings than did the animals in either of the "nonassociative" control groups. Before accepting this conclusion, however, one should be mindful of the fact that only the pups in Group L-UCS experienced both the lemon scent and LiCl-induced illness on the treatment day. The pups in the control groups experienced only the lemon scent (Group L-Sham), only the LiCl injection (Group UCS), or neither of these episodes (Group N). One could argue therefore that the behavior of pups in Group L-UCS was not the result of their associating the lemon scent and LiCl-induced illness but was due simply to their having experienced both of these events prior to testing. The conclusion that the lemon aversion displayed by pups in Group L-UCS was the product of association learning could be strengthened therefore by demonstrating that this aversion was dependent on the pups experiencing the lemon scent and LiCl injection in close temporal proximity and not simply a consequence of their having experienced both events on the treatment day.

In the next study we attempted to provide such a demonstration. Three treatment conditions were examined. One group of 2-day-old pups ($n = 9$) were treated much like the subjects in Group L-UCS of the first experiment. They experienced the lemon scent and LiCl injection in close temporal proximity. Subjects in two new conditions, Group L-60-UCS ($n = 10$) and Group UCS-60-L ($n = 8$), also experienced both the lemon scent and illness but not in close temporal proximity. Pups in Group L-60-UCS received their 35-minute exposure to the lemon-scented shavings 60 minutes prior to being injected with LiCl, whereas the pups in Group UCS-60-L experienced the LiCl injection 60 minutes prior to being exposed to the lemon-scented shavings.

The specific treatment-day experience for each group was as follows. The subjects in Group L-UCS were (a) placed into the polyurethane bag containing lemon-scented shavings for 5 minutes, (b) removed and injected with LiCl, (c) returned for 30 minutes to the lemon-scented environment, (d) removed and returned to their maternity cage for 55 minutes, (e) placed for 35 minutes into a bag containing maternity cage shavings, and (f) finally returned to the maternity cage. Subjects in Group L-60-UCS were treated exactly like those in Group L-UCS except that they were not injected with LiCl while in the lemon-scented environment. They received their LiCl injection 60 minutes later while they were in the bag containing the familiar maternity cage shavings. The subjects in Group UCS-60-L were treated exactly like those is Group L-UCS except that the order in which they were placed into the bags containing lemon-scented or maternity-cage shavings was reversed. As in the previous experiment the animals were not tested until they were 8 days of age. Since in the previous study the lemon versus garlic and lemon versus natural pine tests yielded similar results, the animals were given only a single lemon-aversion test in this experiment. They were allowed to choose between lemon- and garlic-scented shavings.

The results of this experiment are presented in Fig. 7.2. As in the first study, the animals that received the lemon and LiCl events in close temporal proximity, Group L-UCS, displayed a pronounced lemon aversion. If anything, the animals in Groups L-60-UCS and Group UCS-60-L appeared to display a slight preference for the lemon-scented shavings.

It is quite clear from this experiment that simply exposing the animal to both the lemon scent and the LiCl-induced illness on the treatment day does not result in the pup subsequently displaying an aversion to the lemon scent. Although the animals in both Group L-60-UCS and Group UCS-60-L experienced these two events, they displayed no evidence of avoiding the lemon scent. Only the animals in Group L-UCS, which experienced the lemon scent and LiCl-induced illness in close temporal proximity, displayed an aversion to the lemon scent. The lemon aversion displayed by Group L-UCS thus appears to depend on the temporal proximity of the animal's experience with the two events.

The results of the first two experiments thus appear to compel the conclusion that rat pups only 2 days of age have the associative processing capabilities necessary for acquiring illness-induced odor aversions. Indeed the 2-day-old appears to be remarkably equipped to acquire this aversion: The odor aversions seen in these two studies were acquired following only a *single* experience of the

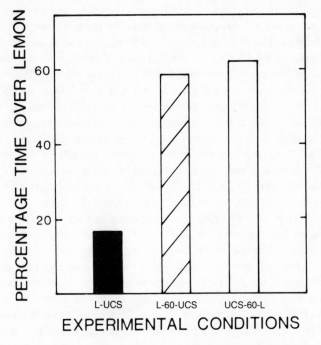

FIG. 7.2.   Mean percentage of time spent by each group over the lemon-scented shavings.

odor—illness episodes and was retained over the 6-day period that intervened between training and testing.

Extinction of the Aversion

The 2-day-old pups clearly behaved as if they in some sense associated the lemon scent with the LiCl-induced illness. If the conditioned-aversive properties of the lemon scent indeed reflect the operation of associative processes, one might also expect that the pup's aversion to the lemon scent can be extinguished. In our next experiment we attempted to determine if, following acquisition training, the pups' aversion could be removed by exposing them to nonreinforced presentations of the lemon scent.

The experiment itself was quite simple and included four treatment conditions. All animals were 2 days old at the start of the experiment. Pups in two of the conditions, Group L-UCS/L (n = 10) and Group L-UCS/MS (n = 9), each initially experienced the basic conditioning treatment necessary to establish an aversion to lemon-scented shavings. They received a single conditioning episode in which lemon-scented shavings were paired with an injection of LiCl. The pups in two additional groups, Group L-Sham/L (n = 6) and L-Sham/MS (n = 5), served as controls to determine if an aversion to the lemon scent was established. On the conditioning day these animals were exposed to the lemon scent but were not injected with LiCl. Over the next 5 days the pups in Group L-UCS/L were given a treatment calculated to extinguish their aversion to lemon. Once daily they were placed for 30 minutes into the bag containing lemon-scented shavings. The pups in the other conditioning group, Group L-UCS/MS, were treated exactly like those in Group L-UCS/L except that the bag in which they were placed contained familiar maternity-cage shavings (MS). Thus the aversion to the lemon scent should not be extinguished in these animals. Over this 5-day postconditioning phase, the pups in one control condition, Group L-Sham/L, were treated like those in Group L-UCS/L, whereas animals in the other control condition, Group L-Sham/MS, were treated like those in Group L-UCS/MS. On the test day the animals' aversion to the lemon scent was assessed by allowing them to choose between lemon- and garlic-scented shavings.

The results of this experiment are presented in Fig. 7.3. The first point to appreciate is that the animals in Group L-UCS/MS displayed a substantial aversion to the lemon scent. They spent much less time over the lemon-scented shaving than did either of the sham-injected control animals. The principal new finding revealed by this experiment, however, is seen by observing the performance of Group L-UCS/L. The animals in this condition displayed no evidence of an aversion to the lemon scent. They spent the same amount of time over the lemon-scented shavings as did the animals in the two sham-injected control groups.

The outcome of this experiment thus was quite clear. As a consequence of the

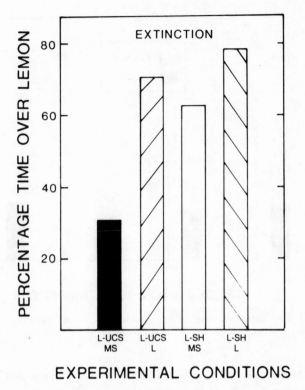

FIG. 7.3. Mean percentage of time spent by each group over the lemon-scented shavings. Subjects in Group L-UCS/L were extinguished prior to the test.

postconditioning, nonreinforced exposure to the lemon scent, the pups' aversion to the lemon scent was removed. Thus not only do neonatal rats acquire an aversion to odors experienced in a conditioning relationship to LiCl-induced illness; they also lose the aversion if the scent is subsequently experienced in the absence of illness.

Comparisons with Older Pups

We also have completed a number of experiments that permit the the comparison of 2-day-old pups with pups ranging in age from 4 to 14 days old at the time of odor-aversion training. The most notable finding of this research has been the failure to observe any age-related differences in the acquisition of the odor aversion when the training procedures and parameters were the same as those employed in the first two experiments.

The absence of any age-related effects can be seen in Fig. 7.4. This figure presents the results of the lemon-aversion test (lemon- versus garlic-scented

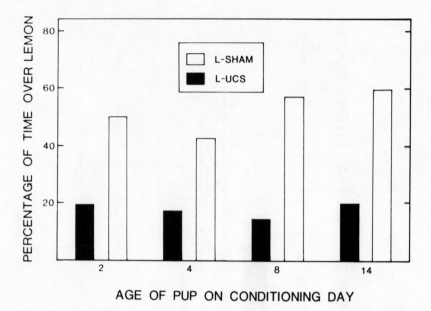

FIG. 7.4. Mean percentage of time spent over the lemon-scented shavings by subjects trained at either 2, 4, 8, or 14 days of age.

shavings) for pups given a single pairing of the lemon scent and the LiCl-induced illness at either 2, 4, 8, or 14 days of age. Control animals at each age also experienced the lemon scent but received a sham injection. The pups trained at 2 and 4 days of age were tested when 8 days old, whereas the pups trained at 8 and 14 days of age were tested when 9 and 15 days old, respectively. In spite of the fact that the retention interval between training and testing was shorter for the older pups, there is no evidence of any difference in the magnitude of the lemon aversion displayed by the various groups.

The studies that we have discussed have revealed several new and exciting findings. First, pups only 2 days of age will acquire an aversion to an olfactory stimulus paired with a LiCl-induced illness. Second, this aversion can be extinguished by exposing the pup to nonreinforced presentations of the scent. Third, under the training conditions that have been examined, the 2-day-old acquires the aversion as readily as do pups 4, 8, or 14 days of age. These results appear to leave little doubt that almost immediately after birth the rat pup is capable of associative learning. They also indicate that the methodology we have developed is remarkably sensitive to the associative capabilities of the neonatal rat and can be applied successfully to pups ranging from 2 to 14 days old.

The next step in this research program was to examine systematically some of the experimental variables that we thought might influence the learning processes engaged by this task.

THE ONTOGENY OF LONG-DELAY LEARNING

One of the most provocative findings of the last decade of animal learning research has been the discovery of what is commonly referred to as long-delay learning (Revusky, 1971; Revusky & Garcia, 1970). Rats easily learn to avoid novel-flavored solutions that have been sampled and followed by illness even when there is a delay of several hours between the time when the novel flavor was initially sampled and the onset of illness.

More relevant to our immediate concern is the recent finding by Taukulis (1974) that such long-delay learning is also observed when olfactory stimulation precedes illness. He has reported evidence that adult rats will acquire aversions to olfactory stimulation that precedes illness onset by as much as 4 hours.

It should be appreciated that in our initial experiments a set of learning parameters were selected that we hoped would maximize the likelihood of the neonatal pup acquiring an odor aversion. In particular we attempted to insure that the pups experienced the olfactory stimulation in close temporal contiguity with the induced illness. The animals were placed into the lemon-scented environment for 5 minutes prior to the injection of LiCl and returned to this environment for an additional 30 minutes following the injection. The results of these experiments to this point testify to the effectiveness of our training parameters. Not only did the 2-day-old pups acquire an aversion to the lemon scent; they did so as readily as pups 4, 8, or 14 days old. It remained to be determined, however, if the pups at any of the ages we have examined have the associative-processing capability necessary to demonstrate long-delay learning. Our next experiments therefore were calculated to investigate the long-delay learning capabilities of neonatal rats.

In the first experiment we examined pups that were either 2, 8, or 14 days old on the day of acquisition training. In order to assess the ability of these pups to acquire associations over long-delay intervals, pups at each age were trained at one of three delay intervals, 0, 0.25, or 15 minutes. Subjects in the 0-delay groups ($ns \times 8$ or 9) were given the standard treatment. They were placed for 5 minutes into the bag containing lemon-scented shavings, removed and injected with a 2% body-weight of a 0.15-M LiCl solution, and returned to the lemon-scented environment for an additional 30 minutes before being returned to the maternity cage. The subjects in the 0.25-minute delay groups ($ns = 7$ or 8) were also placed into the lemon-scented environment for 5 minutes. Upon being removed and injected with LiCl, however, these animals were returned to the maternity cage. They were not given any additional exposure to the lemon scent after being injected. A delay interval of about 0.25 minute intervened between their being exposed to the lemon scent and being injected with LiCl. The subjects in the 15-minute delay groups ($ns = 7$ or 8) were placed into the lemon-scented environment for 5 minutes, returned to the maternity cage for 15 minutes, whereafter they were injected with LiCl and returned again to the maternity cage.

Control animals that received sham injections at each of the three delay intervals when 2 (ns = 4 or 6) or 14 days (ns = 6) of age also were included in this experiment to permit an assessment of the magnitude of the odor aversion acquired by the animals injected with LiCl. The control animals were treated exactly like the experimental animals except that they were not infused with LiCl.

Since the animals that were trained at 2 days of age could not be tested until they were 8 days old, it was decided that animals trained at 8 and 14 days of age should not be tested until they were 14 and 20 days old, respectively. In this way we attempted to insure that any age-related differences that might be observed could not be attributed to variations in the retention interval between training and testing. Each subject was tested only once. In this test the pups were given a choice between lemon- and garlic-scent shavings.

The results of this experiment for each age group are presented in Fig. 7.5. We can thus examine the effect of the three training conditions on subjects trained at 2, 8, and 14 days of age. Note that pups at each training age displayed an odor aversion when they had been trained with the so-called "0-delay" procedure. Comparing across the three panels one also can see that there were no apparent age-related differences among the pups in the 0-delay condition.

Striking age-related differences can be seen, however, when one examines the influence of the 0.25- and 15-minute delay treatments. Note that the 8- and 14-day-old pups showed evidence of acquiring the aversion under both of these training conditions. In contrast, the 2-day-old pups failed to differ from sham-injected controls when trained with these procedures.

This experiment has revealed an intriguing set of findings. The 2-day-old pup apparently has the associative processing capability necessary for acquiring the odor aversion when it experiences the odor and illness in close temporal proximity but does not appear to be able to acquire the aversion when even a relatively brief delay, 0.25 minute, separates the odor experience and the LiCl injection. The 0-delay training procedure was calculated to insure that the pup was exposed to the scent at the time it was ill. This was accomplished by returning the pup to the scent for 30 minutes after it received the LiCl injection. Under these conditions it acquired the aversion. The 0.25- and 15-minute delay procedures were calculated to assess the acquisition of the aversion under conditions in which there was a nominal separation in time of the odor and illness experiences. The 2-day-old pup failed to display evidence of having acquired the aversion when trained with either of these conditions.

The 8- and 14-day-old pups, however, acquired the aversion when either the 0.25- or 15-minute delay procedure was employed. The net implication of this pattern of results is that the mechanisms necessary for mediating associative learning over long delays is not present at birth but develop between 2 and 8 days following birth.

We have replicated the basic finding that the acquisition of an odor aversion

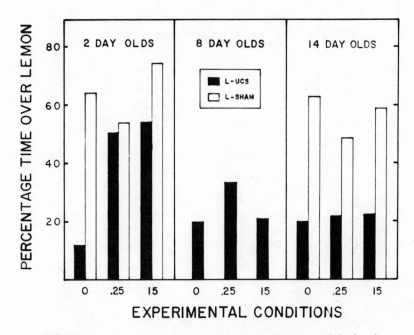

FIG. 7.5. Mean percentage of time spent over the lemon-scented shavings by pups trained at 2, 8, or 14 days of age as a function of the time interval separating the odor-illness events.

by 2-day-old pups is severely reduced by introducing very slight delays between the odor experience and LiCl injections. The same three delay conditions were examined, and there were 8 subjects in both the 0-delay and 0.25-minute delay conditions and 7 in the 15-minute delay group. Their mean percentage of time spent over the lemon scent was 20%, 42%, and 67%, respectively.

We also have further evidence bearing on the long-delay learning capabilities of the 8-day-old pups. In one experiment, 8-day-olds were trained with delays of either 15 or 90 minutes ($ns = 8$ or 12) separating their 5-minute exposure to the lemon scent and the LiCl injection. Sham-injected controls ($ns = 6$ and 7) were also included in this study to determine if the pups acquired aversions to the lemon scent even when a 90-minute delay interval separated the two events.

The results of the lemon- versus garlic-scent test are displayed in Fig. 7.6. It is quite clear from this figure that compared to sham-injected controls, the animals injected with the LiCl spent much less time over the lemon-scented shavings.

To assure ourselves of the reliability of this remarkable finding, we attempted to replicate the results of this experiment and, in addition, extended the delay interval to 240 minutes. In this experiment, four delay intervals, 0, 30, 90, and 240 minutes, were examined, and there were either 7 or 8 animals trained at each delay interval.

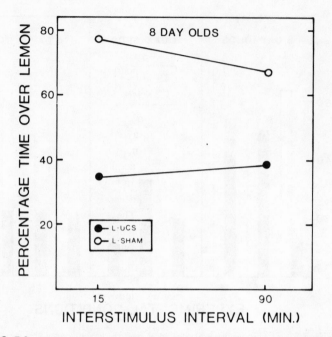

FIG. 7.6.   Mean percentage of time spent over lemon-scented shavings by pups trained at 8 days of age as a function of the time interval separating the odor and illness events.

The results of this study are presented in Fig. 7.7. They can be easily summarized. The animals in the 0-, 30-, and 90-minute delay groups behaved quite similarly, and each displayed an aversion to the lemon scent. In contrast, however, the animals in the 240-minute delay group displayed no evidence of an aversion to the lemon scent. If anything they appear to display a preference for the lemon scent.

This experiment thus confirms the finding that 8-day-old pups acquire the lemon aversion even when a 90-minute interval separates the experience of the lemon scent and the LiCl injection. No evidence of long-delay learning was obtained, however, when a 240-minute delay was introduced. Apparently, using these procedures, the boundaries of the 8-day-old pups' ability to associate the odor and illness lie between a 90- and 240-minute delay.

This set of experiments have revealed major age-related differences in the associative processing capabilities of neonatal pups. Exposed to the optimal training parameters afforded by the 0-delay treatment, 2-day-old pups easily acquired an aversion to the lemon scent. The introduction of a relatively brief delay between the odor experience and the LiCl injection, however, profoundly interfered with the acquisition of the aversion to the lemon scent. By 8 days of age, however, the pup apparently has developed the mechanisms necessary for long-delay learning. An aversion to the lemon scent was acquired by the 8-day-old even when as much as 90 minutes separated the odor and illness experiences.

Between 2 and 8 days of age the pup appears to develop the capacity to demonstrate long-delay learning. In the next experiment we attempted to determine more precisely at what age the processes mediating long-delay learning become functional. In this study pups 2, 4, 6, and 8 days of age were exposed to either the 0-delay or 15-minute delay conditioning procedure. There were 6 to 8 subjects in each treatment condition. All pups were given the lemon versus garlic scent test 6 days after the single acquisition trial.

The results of this experiment are presented in Fig. 7.8. It is quite clear from this figure that neither the 2- nor the 4-day old appears to have developed the processes necessary for long-delay learning. They displayed aversions to the lemon scent if trained under the 0-delay treatment but not if a 15-minute delay was employed. By 6 days of age, however, the pups acquired the aversion under both the 0- and 15-minute delay treatments.

On the basis of this experiment it would appear that between 4 and 6 days of age the processes involved have become sufficiently functional to allow for the acquisition of odor aversions even when the odor experience and LiCl injection are separated by 15 minutes.

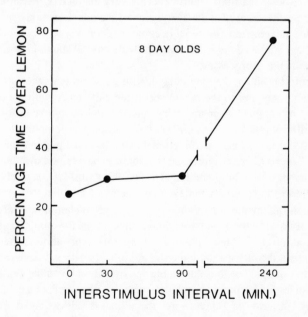

FIG. 7.7.   Median percentage of time spent over lemon-scented shavings by pups trained at 8 days of age as a function of the time interval separating the odor and illness events.

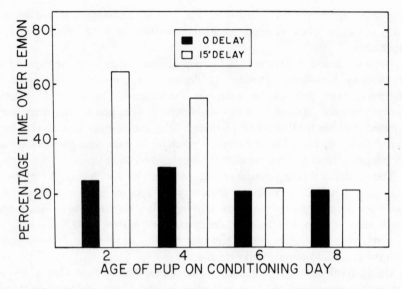

FIG. 7.8.   Mean percentage of time spent over lemon-scented shavings by pups trained at 2, 4, 6, or 8 days of age.

The long-delay learning experiments are very instructive, because they reveal that processes necessary for the acquisition of the odor aversion over long delays are not fully developed at birth but become functional only between 4 and 6 days of age. These studies do not, however, provide any substantial information about the nature of these processes.

The central problem the long-delay learning task presents the pup is that if it is to acquire an aversion to the lemon scent, the experience with the odor must in some way be retained over the delay interval and be available for association with the illness (cf. Revusky, 1971). It is particularly tempting to assume that some central process becomes functional that allows the pup to code its olfactory experience into a memory representation that can be retained over the delay inter-val. On this view, the failure of 2- and 4-day-olds to display long-delay learning is attributable to the relatively undeveloped status of this memory process.

Although this memory hypothesis is attractive, it should be appreciated that, in addition to structural and functional changes in the pup's central nervous system that might be taking place during this time period, there are other morphological developments. Notably, at birth, the pup is hairless; however, by about 6 days of age pelage is detectable and by 8 days it is quite evident. There is therefore a rather striking correlation between the appearance of pelage and long-delay learning. At 2 days of age the animal is hairless and does not display long-delay learning. By about Day 6 pelage is present and long-delay learning occurs. In point of fact there is reason to suppose that this correlation may be more than incidental. Recall that on the training day pups are placed directly onto shavings scented with lemon extract. It is also the case that when the pup is removed one can clearly detect the presence of the lemon scent on its body. The scent of lemon appears to diminish rapidly after the pup is placed into the shavings of the maternity cage, which are permeated with the scent of urine and feces. There is, however, the possibility that the presence of hair on the older pups might contribute to the retention of the lemon scent. In other words, what is being suggested is that the older animals have a peripheral "memory mechanism," hair, which allows them to retain the lemon scent over the delay interval and makes possible long-delay learning.[3]

Before seriously entertaining the view that long-delay learning depends on the development of a central process that allows the pup to code its olfactory experience into a memory, one must make a reasonable attempt to evaluate the alternative hypothesis—that the scent is retained in the hair. There are a variety of ways in which one can evaluate the latter position. In each case one would proceed by attempting to eliminate the advantage afforded the older pups by the presence of pelage. By removing this advantage one should also remove the ability of the older pups to display long-delay learning.

We have completed an experiment in which we attempted to remove the presumed advantage afforded the older pups by the presence of pelage. Our strategy was to remove the advantage by experimentally isolating the pup's hair from the lemon scent. To do this, we placed each pup into a small polyurethane bag (Glad sandwich bag) so that except for its head the pup's entire body and limbs were covered. The pups were then placed into the bag containing the lemon scented shavings. Instead of being placed directly on the shavings, however, they were layed onto a hardwire-floor platform about 3-inches above the shavings. The platform was introduced as an additional attempt to isolate the pup's body from the lemon extract.

The experiment included four treatment conditions. Two groups of pups were 2 days old and two were 8 days old at the time of training. One group of pups at each age ($ns = 7$ or 8) received training under standard or 0-delay conditions; the other two groups ($ns = 7$ or 8) received training under the 15-minute delay conditions. The pups in the 0-delay condition remained in their individual bags throughout the 35 minutes they were in the lemon-scented environment. In contrast, the pups in the 15-minute delay groups remained in the individual bags only for the 5-minute period in which they were exposed to the lemon scent. Immediately upon being removed from the lemon scent, the pup also was removed from its individual bag. To remove any lemon scent that might have attached to the pup's head, the entire head and face of the pup were gently wiped with a sponge containing warm water. The pups were then returned to maternity cages for 15 minutes, whereafter they were injected with LiCl.

On the view that the essential factor favoring long-delay learning in 8-day-old pups is the presence of hair, one would expect to see no evidence of long-delay learning in this experiment. As can be seen in Fig. 7.9, however, this was not the

---

[3]We thank Greg Christoph for pointing out this possibility to us.

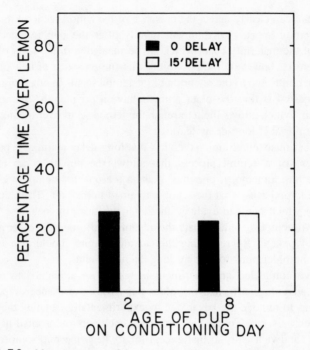

FIG. 7.9.   Mean percentage of time spent over lemon-scented shavings by pups trained at 2 or 8 days of age. In this experiment the bodies of the pups were isolated from the lemon scent.

case. To be sure, the pups trained at 2 days of age failed to display evidence of long-delay learning. The 2-day-old pups in the 0-delay group displayed an aversion to the lemon scent, whereas those in the 15-minute delay condition did not. In contrast, the pups trained at 8 days old displayed an aversion to the lemon scent whether they received the 0-delay or 15-minute delay treatment.

The results of this experiment provide no support for the notion that the factor that favored long-delay learning in 8-day-olds was the presence of hair that permitted the peripheral retention of the lemon scent. If this had been the mechanism of long-delay learning, then the isolation of the hair follicles from the lemon extract should have eliminated long-delay learning. Because the 8-day-olds displayed equivalent lemon aversions whether trained under the 0- or 15-minute delay condition, it would appear that this hypothesis is untenable.

THE ONTOGENY OF THE STIMULUS– PREEXPOSURE EFFECT

Given the failure to find evidence for the notion that the age-related differences in long-delay learning can be attributed to the presence of hair follicles on the older pups, an alternative view—that a central memory process develops that allows for the experience of olfactory stimulation to be retained over the delay interval—warrants further consideration. One approach to exploring the usefulness of this hypothesis is to examine other learning paradigms that one might also expect to depend on the pup's ability to code its experience with olfactory stimulation into a memory representation. If a memory process is becoming more functional as the pup ages then such tasks should also reveal differences in 2- and 8-day-old pups. The next set of experiments that we describe pursued this strategy by employing the paradigm that has often been employed to reveal the so-called "latent-inhibition" or stimulus–preexposure effect (Lubow, 1973).

A major parameter of virtually every conditioning paradigm employed to study animal learning is the subject's previous experience with the stimulus that is to serve as the conditioned stimulus. A *familiar* stimulus, one that the subject has experienced prior to the conditioning episode, is often retarded, relative to a *novel* or unexperienced cue, in acquiring conditioned properties as a consequence of being paired with a reinforcing event (see Lubow, 1973, for a review of this literature).

If an animal's prior experience with a stimulus is to interfere with its ability to acquire conditioned properties, it appears reasonable to assume that as a consequence of this prior experience the animal has in some sense acquired a memory representation that allows it to recognize the stimulus as familiar and that this recognition process in some manner interferes with the conditioning process (cf. Rudy, Rosenberg, & Sandell, 1977; Wagner, 1976). On the basis of this assumption we felt that the stimulus-preexposure paradigm might be fruitfully employed to provide additional evidence that 2- and 8-day-old pups differ in their ability to acquire a memory representation of an experience with olfactory stimulation. The logic is quite simple. If the 8-day-old's memory processes are more functional than the 2-day-old's, then prior exposure to olfactory stimulation should more strongly interfere with the acquisition of an aversion to that scent by 8-day-olds than by 2-day-olds.

In our initial empirical evaluation of this reasoning, 2- and 8-day-old subjects were examined under four treatment conditions. The subjects in Group MS/L-UCS ($n = 18$ and 17, respectively, for 2- and 8-day-old pups) were initially placed for 30 minutes in a bag containing maternity-cage shavings. They were then returned to their maternity cage for *4 hours*. Next they were placed into a bag containing lemon-scented shavings for 5 minutes, injected with LiCl, returned to the lemon-scented environment for 30 minutes, whereafter they were returned again to the maternity cage. Subjects in Group L/L-UCS ($n = 16$ and 19) were given a preexposure treatment calculated to interfere with the acquisition of an aversion to the lemon scent. Instead of being placed into a bag containing maternity-cage shavings, subjects in this group were initially placed into a bag containing lemon-scented shavings. Thereafter they were treated just like the subjects in Group MS/L-UCS. Two sham-injected controls, Group

MS/L-Sham (n = 11 and 10) and Group L/L-Sham (n = 11 and 12), were included to assess the acquisition of the aversion by Group MS/L-UCS and Group L/L-UCS. All subjects were tested for an aversion to the lemon scent by allowing them to choose between lemon- and garlic-scented shavings.

The results of this experiment are displayed in Fig. 7.10. The data for the 2-day-olds are presented in the left panel of this figure, that for 8-day-olds is presented on the right. Note first the data for the 8-day-old pups. It can be seen that the subjects in Group MS/L-UCS displayed an aversion to the lemon scent. Compared to pups in either of the sham-injected control groups they spent much less time over the lemon-scent shavings. In contrast, there is no evidence that the pups preexposed to the lemon scent, Group L/L-UCS, acquired an aversion to the lemon scent. These pups cannot be distinguished from the sham-injected animals. A quite different pattern of results were obtained for the 2-day-old pups. The pups in Group MS/L-UCS to be sure displayed an aversion to the lemon scent. It is also the case, however, that the pups in Group L/L-UCS displayed a comparable aversion. Preexposure to the lemon scent apparently did not interfere with the acquisition of an aversion to the lemon scent by 2-day-olds.

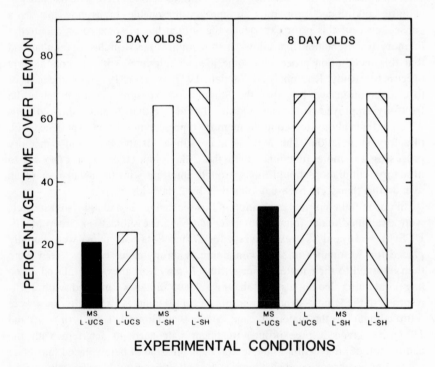

FIG. 7.10.   Mean percentage of time spent over the lemon-scented shavings by pups trained at 2 or 8 days of age. Subjects in Group L/L-UCS were exposed to the lemon scent 4 hours prior to conditioning.

We apparently have discovered another major difference between the 2- and 8-day-old pups. Exposing 8-day-olds to the lemon scent 4 hours prior to the conditioning episode interfered markedly with their acquiring an aversion to the lemon scent. In contrast, this same preexposure treatment had no detectable influence on the acquisition of the lemon aversion by the 2-day-old pup. This age-related difference is of course exactly what one might expect from the hypothesis that the memory mechanisms influenced by olfactory stimulation are more fully developed in 8- than in 2-day-old pups.

We have completed several additional experiments that provide useful information for characterizing the differences between 2- and 8-day-old pups when they are preexposed to the lemon scent. In the next study we examined subjects that were 8 days old when they experienced the conditioning treatment. They were exposed to the lemon scent, however, 24 hours prior to the conditioning experience. Thus they were 7 days of age when preexposed. Again four treatment conditions were examined: Group MS/L-UCS ($n = 19$), Group L/L-UCS ($n = 19$), Group MS/L-Sham ($n = 11$), and Group L/L-Sham ($n = 12$). The subjects in these groups were treated exactly like the corresponding groups of the previous experiment except that the preexposure experience occurred 24 instead of 4 hours prior to conditioning.

The results of this experiment are presented in Fig. 7.11. It can be seen that the stimulus-preexposure treatment given the subjects in Group L/L-UCS again prevented the acquisition of an aversion to the lemon scent, because the behavior of this group was quite similar to that of the sham-injected control groups. The nonpreexposed subjects in Group MS/L-UCS, in contrast, displayed a substantial aversion to the lemon scent.

Two new facts were provided by this experiment. First, by 7 days of age the pups appear to have developed the mechanisms responsible for the stimulus – preexposure effect. This finding is important, because it suggests a strong correlation between when the pup has developed the mechanisms for long-delay learning (about 6 days of age) and when the mechanisms for the stimulus-preexposure effect are functional. Second, the lemon-preexposure treatment interfered with conditioning even when a 24-hour interval separated preexposure and conditioning. This finding is important, because it suggests that the influence of the odor experience on the 7-day-old pup is quite durable.

It should be recalled that in contrast to the results obtained with older pups, we found no evidence of an effect of preexposure on the 2-day-old's acquisition of an aversion to the lemon scent. On the view that the absence of a stimulus-preexposure effect reflects the fact that the memorial processes mediating the effect of the lemon scent are relatively underdeveloped, one might expect, under conditions that place less demand on these processes, that a stimulus-preexposure effect could be demonstrated in the 2-day-old animal. In the previous experiment a 4-hour delay separated the 2-day-old's preexposure to the lemon scent and the conditioning episode. One way to reduce the demands on

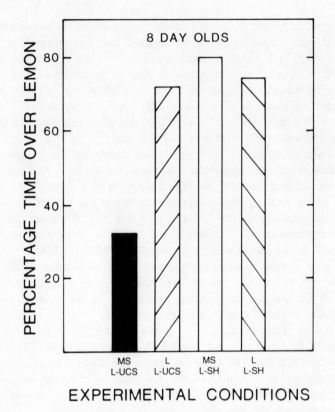

FIG. 7.11.   Mean percentage of time spent over the lemon-scented shavings by pups trained at 8 days of age. Subjects in Group L/L-UCS were exposed to the lemon scent 24 hours prior to conditioning.

the memory processes potentially mediating the stimulus-preexposure effect is simply to *reduce* the preexposure-conditioning delay interval. In another study we did just that. Instead of imposing a 4-hour delay, the preexposure treatment was separated from the conditioning episode by only *1 hour*. The study in all other respects was exactly like the previous one. There were 17, 16, 11, and 12 subjects, respectively, in Group MS/L-UCS, Group L/L-UCS, Group MS/L-sham, and Group L/L-sham.

The results of this study were most instructive. As shown in Fig. 7.12, a substantial aversion to the lemon scent was displayed by the nonpreexposed subjects receiving the conditioning treatment, Group MS/L-UCS. Note however that the pups preexposed to the lemon scent, Group L/L-UCS, displayed no evidence of such an aversion.

This experiment thus has revealed that the preexposure treatment given Group

L/L-UCS can interfere with the acquisition of an aversion to the lemon scent, provided a relatively brief, 1-hour interval separates the preexposure and conditioning treatments.

We should point out that 8-day-old pups also fail to acquire the aversion to the lemon scent when they are exposed to it only 1 hour prior to conditioning. The results of the experiment with 8-day-old pups is displayed in Fig. 7.13. It is quite clear that the preexposed pups, Group L/L-UCS ($n = 10$), did not differ from the sham-injected controls, Group MS/L-sham ($n = 6$) and Group L/L-sham ($n = 6$), and that the nonpreexposed pups, Group MS/L-UCS ($n = 8$), differed from each of the other three groups.

A remarkably clear pattern of results have emerged from these experiments. Prior exposure interfered with the acquisition of an aversion to the lemon scent by 8-day-old pups even when relatively long, 4- or 24-hour intervals, separated preexposure and conditioning. In contrast, exposure to the lemon scent 4 hours

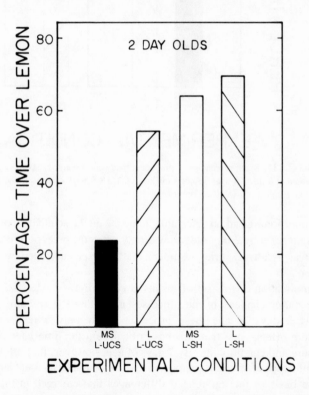

FIG. 7.12.   Mean percentage of time spent over lemon-scented shavings by pups trained at 2 days of age. Subjects in Group L/L-UCS were exposed to the lemon scent 1 hour prior to conditioning.

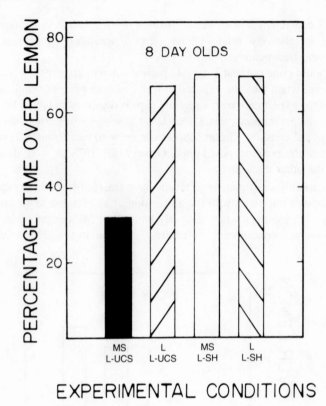

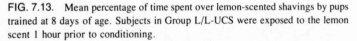

EXPERIMENTAL CONDITIONS

FIG. 7.13.   Mean percentage of time spent over lemon-scented shavings by pups trained at 8 days of age. Subjects in Group L/L-UCS were exposed to the lemon scent 1 hour prior to conditioning.

prior to conditioning had no detectable influence on the acquisition of an aversion to the lemon scent by 2-day-olds. It was only when the preexposure-conditioning interval was relatively brief, 1 hour, that preexposure interfered with their acquisition.

The implication of this set of results is clear. Between 2 and 7 days of age there are major changes in the processes mediating the stimulus-preexposure effect. At 2 days of age these processes allow only a relatively transient preexposure effect—one that depends critically on the time interval separating preexposure and conditioning. By 7 days of age, however, they allow for a quite durable influence of stimulus preexposure—one that persists for at least 24 hours.

On the basis of the age-related differences that emerged in the long-delay learning studies, it was suggested that 2- and 8-day-old pups may differ in their ability to code their olfactory experiences into a memory representation. The results of the stimulus-preexposure studies are quite compatible with this position. In the long-delay learning task the pup is exposed to the olfactory stimulus and some time later receives the LiCl-induced illness. In order for the pup to acquire an aversion to that odor it would appear to be necessary that it in some sense retain a memory for the olfactory experience over the delay interval. In the stimulus-preexposure paradigm the animal receives an initial exposure to the olfactory stimulus prior to experiencing a second exposure and the LiCl-induced illness. If the initial exposure to the odor is to interfere with the acquisition of an aversion to it, it is reasonable to assume that a memory of the initial experience must be retained over the preexposure-conditioning interval. In both the long-delay learning and stimulus-preexposure experiments, the 8-day-olds were much less affected than the 2-day-olds by increases in the retention interval between the odor experience and the subsequent training episode. That is to say, both long-delay learning and stimulus-preexposure effects were obtained over much longer retention intervals when 8-day-olds were examined than when 2-day-olds were employed. Given the common age-related effect produced in each task by variation in the retention interval, we thus find it difficult to resist the view that some aspect of the memory processes mediating the pups' experience with olfactory stimulation significantly matures between 2 and 8 days following birth.

There is a general discrepancy between the results of the stimulus-preexposure and long-delay learning studies that on the face of it, however, might appear at variance with the view that the development of a common memory process is implicated. At all ages the delay interval over which exposure to the scent would prevent conditioning was far longer than that which would support long-delay learning. For example, 2-day-olds failed to display long-delay learning when only 0.25-minute separated the odor exposure and LiCl injection, but a stimulus-preexposure effect was observed when 60 minutes separated preexposure and conditioning.

One might argue that the finding of a preexposure effect over a longer time interval than was functional for long-delay learning implies that different processes mediate the effects of odor exposure in these two tasks. Then it is instructive to appreciate the different demands these two tasks impose on the memory system. In long-delay learning the memory representation of the odor must be of sufficient strength to enter into association with the unconditioned stimulus. In the stimulus-preexposure task the memory representation of the first odor exposure must be sufficiently strong to allow the subject to recognize or code its second occurrence as familiar. To account for the discrepancy in the delay interval over which odor exposure will produce a preexposure effect as compared to that which will support delayed conditioning, one might reasonably assume that the strength of the memory representation necessary for producing a preexposure effect might be weaker than that necessary for allowing it to enter into an associative relationship with the unconditioned stimulus.

SECOND-ORDER CONDITIONING

The last set of experiments that we describe illustrate an attempt to determine if our procedures could be extended to reveal second-order conditioning in neonatal pups. Pavlov (1927) reported that a stimulus that has acquired the ability to evoke from the dog a conditioned salivary reaction also will promote the development of second-order or higher-order conditioned reaction. The paradigm he employed to reveal this phenomenon consisted essentially of two separate training phases. First, one neutral stimulus, S_1, was paired repeatedly with the unconditioned stimulus, food, until S_1 evoked the salivary reaction. In the second phase another neutral stimulus, S_2, was presented and followed by S_1. As a consequence of this second pairing operation, Pavlov observed that S_2 also acquired the ability to evoke the salivary reaction. More recently, Rescorla and his colleagues (Rescorla, 1973; Rizley & Rescorla, 1972; Holland & Rescorla, 1975) have demonstrated second-order conditioning using rats in a conditioned emotional response situation (Rizley & Rescorla, 1972) and in an appetitive, conditioned-activity task (Holland & Rescorla, 1975). Although we were not aware of any reports of second-order conditioning with adult rats in an odor-aversion task, we thought it would be of considerable value to determine if we could demonstrate second-order conditioning in the neonatal rat.

We attempted to demonstrate a second-order aversion by determining if the pup would acquire an aversion to a new odor, orange-scented shavings, if this scent were paired with the lemon scent that previously had been paired with the LiCl injection. As Rizley and Rescorla (1972) have noted, in order to demonstrate second-order conditioning it is necessary to show that the animal's test reaction to the second-order stimulus depends on both the pairing of S_1 and the unconditioned stimulus and on the subsequent pairing of S_2 and S_1. Thus the experiment included a number of comparison groups that allow one to conclude that such a dependency exist. The subjects were 7 days old at the beginning of the experiment.

Four treatment conditions were examined. Subjects in the second-order conditioning group, Group L-UCS/O-L, ($n = 10$), first received a single pairing of the lemon scent and the LiCl. They were placed into the lemon-scented shavings for 5 minutes, injected with LiCl (2% body weight of a 0.15-M LiCl solution), and returned to the lemon-scented environment for 30 minutes. Then, 24 hours later, they received the second-order conditioning treatment. They were placed into a bag containing orange-scented shavings (2.5 cc orange extract/500 ml of natural-pine shavings). After 5 minutes they were transferred directly into another bag that contained lemon-scented shavings, where they remained for 30 minutes. To control for the pairing operation of Phase 1, two control groups were included. Subjects in Group UCS/O-L ($n = 8$) received the LiCl injection after being placed in a bag containing shavings from the maternity cage. Thereafter they were treated exactly like pups in Group L-UCS/O-L. Subjects in the second control group, Group L-sham/O-L ($n = 8$), were treated exactly like those in Group L-UCS/O-L except they received a sham injection while being exposed to the lemon scent. Finally, to control for the pairing operation of Phase 2, subjects in Group L-UCS/O/L ($n = 8$) experienced both the orange scent and the lemon scent but 4 hours apart. Between their exposure to the orange and lemon scents they were returned to the maternity cages.

All subjects were subsequently tested for an aversion to the orange scent the next day. They were allowed to choose between the orange- and garlic-scented shavings.

The results of this test are displayed in the left panel of Fig. 7.14. First note that the animals in each of the three control groups appeared to display a preference for the orange-scented shavings. Observe however that the subjects given the second-order conditioning treatment displayed a mild aversion to the orange scent.

The comparison of Group L-UCS/O-L and Group L-sham/O-L, however, fell short of the conventional 0.05 level of significance. For this reason we replicated these two conditions in a subsequent experiment, the results of which are displayed in the right panel of Fig. 7.14. It is clear from this figure that Group

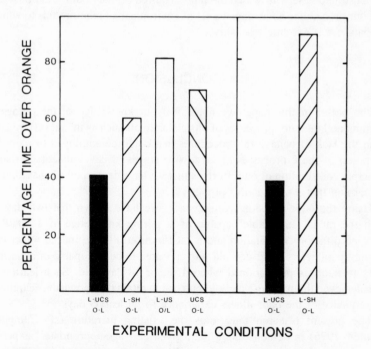

EXPERIMENTAL CONDITIONS

FIG. 7.14.   Mean percentage of time scent over orange-scented shavings by pups trained at 7 and 8 days of age. Subjects in Group L-UCS/O-L received a second-order conditioning treatment.

L-UCS/O-L ($n = 6$) spent less time over the lemon scent than did Group L-sham/O-L ($n = 5$).

Together, the results of these two studies suggest that we have a convincing demonstration of second-order conditioning. The subjects in Group L-UCS/O-L, which received both the pairing of the lemon scent and LiCl and the pairing of the orange and lemon scents, spent less time over the orange scent than either of the two controls, Groups UCS/O-L and Group L-sham/O-L, that received the pairing of the orange and lemon scents in Phase 2 but not the Phase 1 pairing of the lemon scent and LiCl. Group L-UCS/O-L also spent less time over the orange scent than the group that experienced only the Phase 1 pairing of lemon scent and LiCl but not the Phase 2 pairing of the orange and lemon scents, Group L-UCS/O/L.

It is perhaps worth noting that it was remarkably simple to demonstrate that neonatal pups will acquire second-order aversions. Only a single pairing of the lemon scent and LiCl in Phase 1 and only a single pairing of the orange and lemon scents in Phase 2 was necessary to modify the pup's reaction to the second-order stimulus. Moreover, this effect was produced without our having to explore a variety of parameters. These observations in conjunction with the demonstrated ease with which the pups acquired primary odor aversions suggest that our procedures have tapped a set of environmental relationships to which the neonatal rat is extremely sensitive.

CONCLUSION

At the outset of this paper we noted that our knowledge of the ontogeny of learning and memory processes of altricial animals such as the rat suffered in part from the lack of behavioral procedures that could be employed to identify the operation of these processes at successive stages of development. Perhaps the principal contribution of our efforts is that we have developed a behavioral assay of learning that possesses this property.

Using the odor-aversion learning task, we have shown that two days after birth the rat is remarkable capable of acquiring knowledge of a relationship between olfactory stimulation and a LiCl-induced illness. Indeed under certain training parameters the 2-day-old pup appeared to be as capable of acquiring an odor aversion as pups trained when 4, 8, or 14 days old. Such learning was revealed even though the 2-day-old pup had to retain the knowledge acquired as a consequence of the odor-illness experience for at least 6 days.

The present research thus joins the existing literature (cf. Campbell & Coulter, 1976) in demonstrating that, given an "age-appropriate" experience, the newborn altricial animal can learn. We have demonstrated, in addition, that the acquired odor aversion can be extinguished by providing the pup with nonreinforced presentations of the odor. The neonatal pup thus can learn not only that the odor presages illness; it also can learn that the odor no longer does so.

It also should be appreciated that an important feature of the odor-aversion learning task is that it allows the experimenter systematical control of the variables that are likely to affect the associative processes serving this task and to determine if there are important age-related changes in these processes. Although we have just begun to take advantage of these properties of the task, the initial effort in our view has revealed exciting age-related effects. First, we have seen that there appear to be significant age-related differences in the ability of the pups to demonstrate long-delay learning. The 8-day-old pups acquired the odor aversion even when a 90-minute delay was introduced between exposure to the odor and the LiCl injection. The 2-day-old pup, however, displayed little or no evidence of the odor aversion even when only a 0.25-minute delay separated the two events. Second, the research examining the effects of stimulus preexposure on odor-aversion learning revealed similar age-related differences. The 8-day-old pups failed to acquire the odor aversion when odor preexposure preceded the odor-LiCl episode by as much as 24 hours. The 2-day-old pups were similarly affected only if the odor exposure preceded the conditioning experience by 1 hour. If a 4-hour retention interval separated preexposure and conditioning, preexposure had no influence on the 2-day-old pup's acquisition of the odor aversion.

We have tentatively proposed that the age-related differences that emerged in both the long-delay learning and stimulus-preexposure experiments might reflect the maturation of a common process. More specifically we have suggested that between 2 and 8 days following birth, memory processes that allow the pup to retain its experience with olfactory stimulation become more functional.

We would also point out that the last set of experiments discussed suggest that the odor-aversion task may also prove to be a valuable analytic tool for studying the ontogeny of the associative processes involved in second-order conditioning (cf. Cheatle & Rudy, 1978).

We have reviewed the specific empirical contributions of our research. We would like to conclude with some general and cautionary remarks.

First, we will discuss some of the limitations of our work. It must be appreciated that our attempts to determine some of the important characteristics of the ontogeny of associative learning have been restricted to observations of a single animal, the rat, and to learning experiences involving only two classes of stimulus events—olfactory stimulation and illness induced by LiCl. To be sure, some intriguing ontogenetic effects emerged as we examined the ability of neonatal rats of various ages to "associate" these events. It would be imprudent however to presume that our findings tell us something quite general about the characteristics of the ontogeny of associative-learning processes or that any such set of restricted observations could do so. Indeed we must be doubly cautious about the general implications of the present research, because one of the events we employed, the LiCl-induced illness, is thought by some theorists (e.g., Garcia, McGowan, & Green, 1972; Rozin & Kalat, 1971; Seligman, 1970) to bring about associative learning through a set of specialized processes that evolved specifically to allow the rat to learn to identify and avoid toxic food sources. We suspect that such theorists would find our results to be quite consistent with their views. Consequently our findings may tell us only about the ontogenesis of these "specialized" learning processes. They may tell us very little about the ontogeny of the processes that allow the animal to learn about other environmental relationships, such as may be arranged by exposing pups of different ages to paired presentations of auditory or visual stimuli and appetitive or aversive reinforcers.

Regardless of the limitations of the present research, one must also appreciate that precious few data of any sort relevant to understanding the ontogeny of learning are available. Our research has revealed associative learning by rats only 2 days old and dramatic changes in the pup's ability to associate the stimulus events we have employed. To us this constitutes a promising approach to understanding the manner in which the mechanisms that allow animals to acquire knowledge of its world develop.

This brings us to our final comments. It is our impression that research on the ontogeny of the acquisition processes has been neglected especially in comparison with the research directed toward ontogenetic contributions to memory. The provocative demonstration of infantile amnesia by Campbell and Campbell (1962) and the subsequent finding by Campbell and Jaynes (1966) that it can be ameliorated by reinstating components of the original learning experience have motivated a great deal of developmental research on the posttraining variables that influence retention of a learned experience (Campbell & Coulter, 1976; Campbell & Spear, 1972; Spear & Parsons, 1976).

This latter work, to be sure, is of great importance for our understanding of memory retention processes. What apparently has been lost sight of, however, is the fact that it is equally important that we also ask systematic questions that will allow us more fully to understand the ontogeny of the acquisition processes that give birth to "memory". To do this, it may prove useful to develop other relatively simple Pavlovian conditioning procedures that will allow the investigation of learning induced by the neonatal's experience with stimulus arrangement provided by various combinations of auditory and visual stimuli and other aversive and appetitive reinforcers.

We hope that our initial attempts to investigate ontogenetic changes in the neonatal rat's ability to associate olfactory stimulation and illness will stimulate other researchers to consider addressing other facets of the acquisition problem. We are encouraged to believe that our understanding of the ontogeny of learning and memory may profit handsomely.

ACKNOWLEDGEMENT

This research was supported in part by a National Science Foundation Grant, GB-38322, to Jerry W. Rudy. We thank David Curry for his invaluable aid in maintaining our breeding operations and Joseph Gnandt for constructing the equipment.

REFERENCES

Campbell, B. A., & Campbell, E. H. Retention and extinction of learned fear in infant and adult rats. *Journal of Comparative and Physiological Psychology*, 1962, *55*, 1−8.

Campbell, B. A., & Coulter, X. The ontogenesis of learning and memory. In M. R. Rosenzweig & E. L. Bennett (Eds.), *Neural mechanisms of learning and memory*. Cambridge: MIT Press, 1976.

Campbell, B. A., & Jaynes, J. Reinstatement. *Psychological Review*, 1966, *1*, 71−74.

Campbell, B. A., & Spear, N. E. Ontogeny of memory. *Psychological Review*, 1972, *79*, 215−236.

Cheatle, M. D., & Rudy, J. W. Analysis of second-order odor-aversion conditioning in neonatal rats: Implications for Kamin's blocking effect. *Journal of Experimental Psychology: Animal Behavior Processes*, 1978, *4*, 237−249.

Cornwell-Jones, C. Selective exposure alters social and plant odor preferences of immature hamsters. *Behavioral Biology*, 1976, *17*, 131−137.

Domjan, M. Role of ingestion in odor-toxicosis learning in the rat. *Journal of Comparative and Physiological Psychology*, 1973, *84*, 507−521.

Garcia, J., McGowan, B. K., & Green, K. F. Biological constraints on conditioning. In A. H. Black & W. F. Prokasy (Eds.), *Classical conditioning II. Current theory and research*. New York: Appleton-Century-Crofts, 1972.

Holland, P. C., & Rescorla, R. A. Second-order conditioning with food unconditioned stimulus. *Journal of Comparative and Physiological Psychology*, 1975, *88*, 459−467.

Kenny, J. T., & Blass, E. M. Suckling as incentive to instrumental learning in preweaning rats. *Science*, 1977, *196*, 898−899.

Lorden, J. F., Kenfield, M., & Braun, J. J. Response suppression to odors paired with toxicosis. *Learning and Motivation*, 1970, *1*, 391−400.

Lubow, R. E. Latent inhibition. *Psychological Bulletin*, 1973, *79*, 398−407.

Pavlov, I. P. *Conditioned reflexes*. London: Oxford University Press, 1927.

Rescorla, R. A. Second-order conditioning: Implications for theories of learning. In F. J. McGuigan & E. B. Lumsden (Eds.), *Contemporary approaches to conditioning and learning*. Washington, D.C.: Winston, 1973.

Revusky, S. The role of interferences in association over a delay. In W. R. Honig & P. H. R. James (Eds.), *Animal memory*. New York: Academic Press, 1971.

Revusky, S. H., & Garcia, J. Learned associations over long delays. *The psychology of learning and motivation: Advances in research and theory, IV*. New York: Academic Press, 1970.

Rizley, R. C., & Rescorla, R. A. Associations in second-order conditioning and sensory preconditioning. *Journal of Comparative and Physiological Psychology*, 1972, *74*, 151−182.

Rosenblatt, J. S. Suckling and home orientation in the kitten: A comparative developmental study. In E. Tobach, L. R. Aronson, & E. Shaw (Eds.), *The biopsychology of development*. New York: Academic Press, 1971.

Rosenblatt, J. S. Learning in newborn kittens. *Scientific American*, 1972, *227*, 18−25.

Rozin, P., & Kalat, J. H. Specific hungers and poison avoidance as adaptive specializations of learning. *Psychological Review*, 1971, *28*, 459−486.

Rudy, J. W., & Cheatle, M. D. Odor-aversion learning by neonatal rats. *Science*, 1977, *198*, 845–846.

Rudy, J. W., Rosenberg, L., & Sandell, J. H. Disruption of a taste familiarity effect by novel exteroceptive stimulation. *Journal of Experimental Psychology. Animal Behavior Processes*, 1977, *3*, 26–36.

Seligman, M. E. P. On the generality of the laws of learning. *Psychological Review*, 1970, *77*, 406–418.

Spear, N. E., & Parsons, P. J. Analysis of a reactivation treatment: Ontogenetic determinants of alleviated forgetting. In D. L. Medin, W. A. Roberts, & R. T. Davis (Eds.), *Processes of animal memory*. Hillsdale, N.J.: Lawrence Erlbaum Associates, 1976.

Taukulis, H. Odor aversions produced over long CS-US delays, *Behavioral Biology*, 1974, *10*, 505–510.

Teicher, M. H., & Blass, E. M. Suckling in newborn rats: Elimination by nipple lavage, reinstated by pup saliva. *Science*, 1976, *193*, 422–424.

Thoman, E., Wetzel, A., & Levine, S. Learning in the neonatal rat. *Animal Behavior*, 1968, *16*, 54–57.

Wagner, A. R. Priming in STM: An information processing mechanism for self-generated or retrieval-generated depression in performance. In T. J. Tighe & R. N. Leaton (Eds.), *Habituation: Perspectives from child development, animal behavior, and neurophysiology*. Hillsdale, N.J.: Lawrence Erlbaum Associates, 1976.

8

The Ontogeny of Appetitive Learning and Persistence in the Rat

Abram Amsel
University of Texas at Austin

A very important consideration in the development of temperamental character-istics in mammals, including humans, is the interaction of inborn and learned factors in ontogeny. One such characteristic or trait is persistence (and its opposite, desistance) or perseverance. Behaviors that are characterized as persistent, perseverative, or fixated seem to be involved in many of the common personality disorders. The significance of the work reported in this chapter is that it provides a mammalian animal model for the study of the *development* of these emotional predispositions. The developmental model follows approximately twenty years of investigation of similar phenomena in adults of the same species. We have moved in our work from an early interest in the frustration effect (FE), the partial reinforcement extinction effect (PREE), discrimination learning, and related phenomena in adults (Amsel, 1958, 1962, 1967) to more general considerations of the role of frustrative and other disruptive factors in the invigoration, suppression, and persistence of behavior in adults (Amsel, 1972a, 1972b). Now we are involved in an examination of the learning, retention, and generality of such factors in the course of early development.

Some of the experimental work we report here involves close-to-natural interactions between infant and mother rats, and we have studied these interactions to identify a possible transitional period for the learning of long-lasting and perhaps highly generalizable persistence and desistence char-acteristics (traits?). If there are transitional, or even sensitive or critical, periods for the development of persistence in rats, we will of course be led to look for their counterparts in other mammals, including humans.

189

THEORETICAL–HISTORICAL INTRODUCTION

The experiments and analyses I present emerge out of a conceptualization of the relationship between frustration, persistence, and discrimination learning that has been developed in a series of theoretical papers (Amsel, 1958, 1962, 1967, 1972a).

In informal terms the theory assumes that following a number of rewarded trials, nonreward, reduced reward, or delayed reward results in an aversive motivational state, primary frustration. Primary frustration (R_F) will occur when the parameters of reward change so that the existing anticipation of reward ($r_R - s_R$) is greater than that which the reduced or delayed reward on that trial could support. For example, the size of $r_R - s_R$ established with a large reward is greater than with small reward. Accordingly the theory would require that R_F occur when, after training with a larger reward, a smaller reward or, in the limiting case, nonreward is presented. The theory then outlines a number of behavioral effects of frustration. Four properties of frustration have figured prominently in the theory. The first, R_F, is a hypothetical unconditioned reaction to the frustrating event, and the theory specifies that R_F will exert a transient energizing or activation effect on responses with which it coexists, increasing particularly the vigor with which these responses are performed. The behavioral manifestation of this immediate short-term consequence of R_F has been studied in a very large number of experiments and has been termed the frustration effect (FE). The second property of frustration to which some experimental attention has been given is the frustration drive stimulus (S_F), a feedback stimulus from *primary* frustration that acts like any other stimulus to cue, guide, and direct behavior— that is, it acts associatively (Amsel & Ward, 1954). It is important to note that this hypothetical stimulus (S_F) is not the result of conditioning, as is for example s_F, the feedback stimulus from r_F. The third property of frustration is conditioned (anticipatory) frustration ($r_F - s_F$). This factor refers to the manner in which frustration influences responses that *precede* the frustrating event, and here the theory relies on logic derived from its Pavlovian antecedents: With repeated occurrences, stimuli (CSs) accompanying primary frustration (R_F) should come to evoke a classically conditioned form of R_F, designated $r_F - s_F$. As with $r_R - s_R$, of which it is an aversive counterpart, $r_F - s_F$ is first evoked by stimuli in the region of the goal event and later by stimuli accompanying the instrumental response. The associative strength of r_F is assumed to grow as a function of number of conditioning trials, reaching an asymptotic value appropriate to the strength of its UCS (R_F). A fourth property, reinforcement through frustration reduction, has also been extensively investigated (see Daly, 1974, for a review).

For purposes of this paper perhaps the most relevant portion of the theory in its present form is the analysis of the partial reinforcement (PRF) and discrimination experiments in both of which reward for an instrumental response occurs only intermittently and, in the case of PRF, randomly. A four-stage hypothesis developed for both partial reinforcement and successive discrimination training outlines sequences of events leading to the occurrence of the partial reinforcement extinction effect (PREE) and the development of discrimination learning, respectively. These are shown in Fig. 8.1 and are described in the long caption.

The hypothesis that feedback stimuli from anticipatory frustration (s_F) are instrumentally counterconditioned to, and come to evoke, the instrumental response during extended training under partial reinforcement provides a plausible reason why responding is not immediately disrupted in extinction after partial reinforcement training: Extinction-induced anticipatory-frustration-produced stimuli continue to evoke the learned instrumental response. However, after continuous reinforcement training, responding deteriorates rapidly in extinction because of the strong buildup of r_F for the first time under conditions in which the s_F stimuli are not counterconditioned to the response but rather evoke strong avoidance of continued responding.

Our conditioning model theory is not restricted to the explanation of the FE and PREE but has integrated the explanations of a number of other phenomena as well, and this is perhaps its major strength. The theory has been extended to account for emotional–motivational factors in discrimination learning (Amsel, 1962; Amsel & Ward, 1965; Terrace, 1972), to generalization of persistence effects (Amsel, 1967), and to a variety of effects of prediscrimination exposure to stimuli on rate of subsequent discrimination learning (Amsel, 1962; Amsel & Ward, 1965; Brake, 1978). The theory has addressed the problem of trying to understand retention and durability of persistence (Amsel, Wong, & Traupmann, 1971), most recently, as we shall see, in a developmental context. Explanations in terms of frustration theory have been applied to a number of other phenomena, including successive and simultaneous contrast effects and operant behavioral contrast (Amsel, 1971a; Gonzales & Champlin, 1974); the overlearning–extinction effect, the overlearning–reversal effect in discrimination learning, and the paradoxical Haggard–Goodrich partial-reinforcement acquisition effect (PRAE) (Amsel, 1962); the action of certain drugs like alcohol and sodium amytal to attenuate the PRAE and the PREE (see Gray, 1975, chapter 9); the relation of the limbic system to the FE and to the PREE (Henke, 1973, 1974; Mabry & Peeler, 1972); transfer of persistence across situations and motivational-reinforcement conditions, including the effects of early experience on later behavior and "regression" to earlier successful modes of behavior (see Amsel, 1971b).

A recent extension of the theory (Amsel, 1972a) provides a more general account of persistence and views partial reinforcement as a special case of a more general rule. The more general theory proposes that stimuli that evoke responses disruptive to ongoing instrumental responding (e.g., stimuli to which subjects "habituate") eventually become associated through counterconditioning to the instrumental response they initially disrupt, with the consequence that instrumental responding is subsequently relatively unaffected by these and other

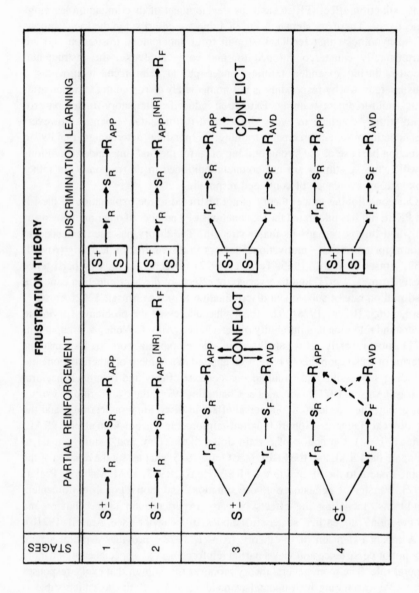

FIG. 8.1.

disruptive stimuli. For this reason there is transfer between behavioral habituation and appetitive persistence. This general position bears some similarity to
neo-Guthrian accounts of the PREE (Estes, 1959; Weinstock, 1954) and is
influenced importantly by the work of Terris and others (Terris, German, &
Enzie, 1969) and Wagner (1966) on fear–frustration commonality. It provides a
focus for some of our work on persistence, including some reported here from an
ontogenetic–developmental perspective.

In the last two or three years a major portion of our work has been with young
and infant rats. We have studied learning, extinction, persistence, desistance,
discrimination, and related phenomena. The ontogeny of persistence is broadly
defined to include developmental studies of the learning and retention of the
partial reinforcement extinction effect (PREE); developmental factors in discrimination learning and resistance to discrimination; transfer of persistence from
habituation training to appetitive extinction and from partial reinforcement (PRF)
training to resistance to habituation. We have also begun to examine the
reinforcing properties of various kinds of conspecific contact in infant rats and
have made some preliminary investigation of ultrasound emission in infant
learning and extinction.

LEARNING AND RETENTION OF PERSISTENCE IN
WEANLING AND OLDER RATS

In most of our experiments in this series, the behavior measured is a simple
approach response in a straight-alley runway to a positive (appetitive) reinforcer.
The alley, the reinforcer, and the response ("running" or "crawling") take
different forms depending on the age of the rats. As a first approximation to
answering questions about the age at which persistence can first be acquired and
retained, we reported differences in both partial reinforcement acquisition
(PRAE) and extinction (PREE) patterns between young rats whose straight-
runway training started at 30 days of age and weanling rats whose training started
at Day 18 (Chen & Amsel, 1975). The young but not the weanling rats showed a
PRAE. Extinction of running after continuous reinforcement (CRF) was very

---

FIG. 8.1. (*Opposite page*) Four-stage sequence of hypotheses relating primary
(R_F) and anticipatory (r_F) frustration to the development of persistence in partial
reinforcement training and to discrimination learning. The first three stages are
essentially the same in both. In the first stage an approach response mediated by
$r_R - s_R$ is formed to the partial ($S\pm$) or discriminative $\frac{S+}{S-}$ stimulus. In the second
stage, where nonreward elicits R_F, the conditioning of $r_F - s_F$ occurs. The third
stage involves conflict between r_R- and r_F-mediated approach and avoidance. In
the fourth stage persistence is built through counterconditioning of s_F to approach
in partial reinforcement training; in discrimination learning the conflict is resolved
when the discriminanda elicit appropriate instrumental responses.

slow and gradual in the weanling rats, but extinction in the older but still young rats was more like the adult pattern, abrupt and negatively accelerated. A comparison of extinction performance following CRF and PRF acquisition showed a PRE at both ages. Then, following a 45-day vacation period and a phase of continuous reinforcement (CRF) reacquisition, the PREE emerged clearly in the animals that had not undergone previous extinction (the retention of persistence groups). In those animals (half of each age group) that had been extinguished immediately after original acquisition training (the durability of persistence groups) the PREE reemerged in the later test (i.e., was durable) but was somewhat reduced in absolute size.

We recognize that these experiments were deficient in certain important respects. First of all, acknowledged procedural differences at the two ages make direct comparison even more risky than in the usual developmental experiment. Secondly, only two age ranges were investigated and these were rather grossly defined, making it difficult even to guess where transitions from one pattern to another might occur. In other words the age ranges in these preliminary experiments were so extended that they must surely have overlapped adjacent stages of development. In experiments that followed we concentrated on providing more precise information. In the first of these (Burdette, Brake, Chen, & Amsel, 1976) there were four age groups, and at each age original training was restricted to a 2½-day period, (e.g., evening of Day 18 to morning of Day 21). Half of each age group was trained in the runway under PRF and half under CRF conditions, followed by a 2-day extinction period that began 12 hours after terminal acquisition (e.g., evening of Day 21 to evening of Day 23). These experiments revealed remarkable persistence when the PRF and CRF treatments were given in the 18- to 21-day range, followed after 12 hours by an extinction test (Fig. 8.2). Our oldest group, trained from Days 36 to 39, showed less persistence. In a second experiment another group was added at each age to equate the PRF and CRF groups for rewards rather than trials. This rewards-equated group is designated PRF-R. Using only the two extreme age groups, trained at 18 to 21 or 36 to 39 days, the result was the same: although persistence was not different between PRF and PRF-R conditions at either age, the relative persistence due to PRF training was greater in the younger age group of rats when persistence was tested after 12 hours, and the overall level of persistence in this younger group was very high (Fig. 8.3).

In the experimental study of the ontogeny of learning, the factors of incentive (reward magnitude), level of motivation (hunger, thirst, pain), and their interactions are particularly troublesome, because there is no obvious way to equate them across ages. Because age-related differences in learning or persistence may be simply a function of such between-age variations in nondevelopmental factors, it is important to manipulate the level of such factors, a point stressed by Bitterman (1975) in his comparative analysis of reward effects.

In two experiments we have examined the effect of reward magnitude on

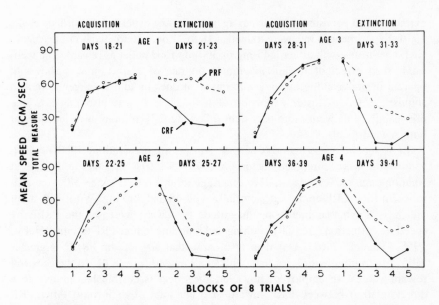

FIG. 8.2.   Acquisition under CRF and PRF conditions and extinction showing the PRE at four ages from preweanling to juvenile. (From Burdette, Brake, Chen, and Amsel, 1976.)

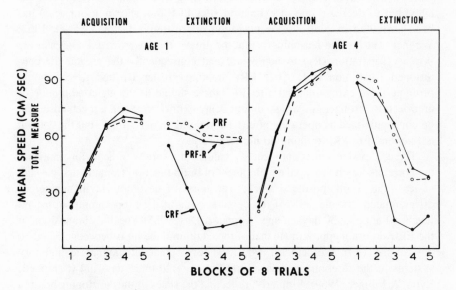

FIG. 8.3.   Acquisition under three conditions including PRF-R (a partial reinforcement condition with rewards equated to the CRF group). Acquisition is at Days 18−21 (Age 1) and 36−39 (Age 4). Extinction follows immediately in all cases (Days 21−23 and 39−41). (From Burdette, Brake, Chen and Amsel, 1976.)

extinction and persistence at various ages. In the first experiment (Burdette et al., 1976, Experiment 3) rats were trained at 18 to 21 or at 36 to 39 days of age under CRF conditions with either a 45-mg or 300-mg food pellet as reward. The well-established effect of reward magnitude on rate of extinction was shown to operate in preweanling and juvenile rats as it does in adults: Larger reward in acquisition led to faster extinction at both ages. It was also the case that preweanling rats were more persistent following CRF training than juveniles at both reward levels.

In a second experiment (Chen & Amsel, in preparation) PRF or CRF acquisition were combined factorially with 45-, 97-, or 300-mg reward at weanling age (17−20 days). Two other age groups (30−33, 55−58) were also run with PRF/CRF combined factorially with 45 and 300 mg. Work with adult rats has shown that increasing magnitude of reward increases the PREE by speeding extinction after CRF training and retarding it after PRF training (Hulse, 1958; Wagner, 1961). Our data also show that size of the PREE is greater following training with large than with small reward (Fig. 8.4). At the ages and reward values we employed, however, the effect is attributable entirely to a direct relation between CRF reward size and rate of extinction. After PRF training at each age there is greater, and about equal, persistence at all values of reward magnitude, and there is again a suggestion across ages of an inverse relationship between age and persistence. This paradoxical effect of magnitude of reward to increase rate of extinction following CRF training (shown at all our ages) but to decrease rate of extinction after PRF (not shown at our ages) has been attributed in adults to the operation of frustrative factors (Amsel, 1962; Wagner, 1961). The reasoning is that the greater the reward size the greater the primary frustration (R_F) to nonreward and consequently the greater the conditioned frustration (r_F). After CRF training greater R_F and r_F-s_F should promote rapid extinction; but after PRF there should be counterconditioning of approach to stronger s_F, which should delay extinction. Such a mechanism can be conceptualized as operating after CRF training in our groups, but the data on extinction after PRF training do not require it.

There is evidence that ontogenetic changes in a variety of behaviors in the rat are correlated with the rapid development of brain function from the first through at least the fourth postnatal week. The burst of development in number of differentiated granule cells of the dentate gyrus of the hippocampus in the rat levels off at about 30 days of age (Altman & Das, 1965); spectral composition of the EEG does not approximate that of the adult until the rat is between 25 and 30 days of age (Deza & Eidelberg, 1967); and development of cholinergic inhibitory systems in the forebrain is delayed until rats are 20 to 25 days old (Campbell, Lytle, & Fibiger, 1969). Similarly, reflecting the states of the developing brain, a number of experiments have revealed different behavioral patterns in young, especially in infant, as compared to adult rats in open-field activity (Bronstein, Neiman, Wolkoff, & Levine, 1974); in head-poke habituation (Feigley, Parson,

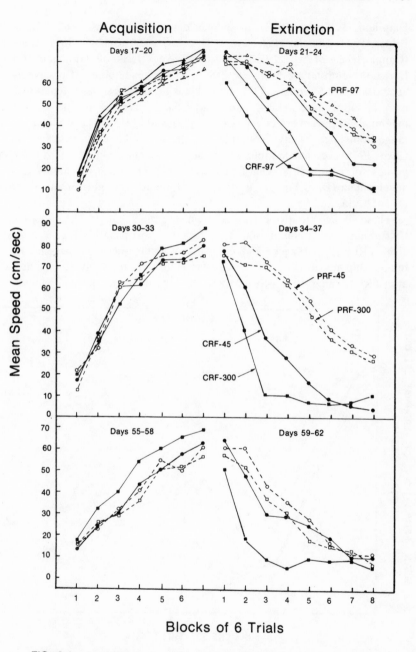

FIG. 8.4. Acquisition under CRF and PRF and various reward magnitudes followed by extinction. These data demonstrate not only the PRE but also the paradoxical magnitude–extinction effect at all three ages. (From Chen and Amsel, in preparation.)

Hamilton, & Spear, 1972); in spontaneous alternation (Bronstein, Dworkin, Bilder, 1974; Douglas, Peterson, & Douglas, 1973; Kirkby, 1967); in arousal (Campbell & Mabry, 1972); in suppressive effects of extinction (Ernest, Dericco, Dempster, & Niemann, 1975); and in conditioning of passive avoidance (Riccio & Marrazo, 1972). These kinds of considerations together with our own previous experiments, particularly the appearance of the paradoxical magnitude of reward effect in rats 17 to 20 days of age, led us to examine the age range from 17 to 30 days more minutely. In two further experiments (Amsel & Chen, 1976) we included four age groups in this range together with two older groups for comparison. Our first three age groups spanned only 4 days of development (Days 17−21) at the start of training. The other groups started at Days 28, 35, and 65.

These six age groups of rats were trained to run an alley under either PRF or CRF conditions. A comparison of age groups across panels in Fig. 8.5 shows a clear PREE at all ages, and comparison within panels shows an inverse relationship between immediate resistance to extinction and age, particularly after PRF training. In a second experiment long-term retention and durability of

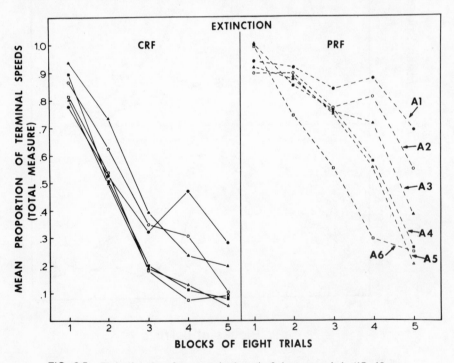

FIG. 8.5. Extinction data for rats trained at six 2-day age periods (17−18, 18−19, 21−22, 28−29, 35−36, and 65−66 for A1 to A6, respectively). Note, particularly for PRF conditions, the inverse relationship between persistence and age. (From Amsel and Chen, 1976.)

persistence, as well as immediate persistence, were tested following acquisition at three different ages. Recall that a retention condition is one in which CRF/PRF acquisition is followed by a retention interval, CRF reacquisition for both groups, and then extinction; whereas in a durability condition there is immediate extinction followed by retention interval, CRF reacquisition, and a second extinction. The immediate extinction tests confirmed our earlier results. In the long-term extinction tests, greater resistance to extinction following PRF (the PREE) was found in all age groups after both the retention and durability manipulations. In neither test did age in original acquisition affect the magnitude of adult persistence. These experiments confirm that rats trained with a PRF compared with a CRF schedule at weanling age show remarkable persistence in an immediate extinction test, that the persistence is even greater in preweanlings, and that it is retained into young adulthood.

Questions about Retrieval of Persistence

Before we leave this work on retention of persistence in preweanling and juvenile rats, I would like to address two questions that have occurred to us in considering these results. The first is: What is "remembered" when persistence is retained following a long retention interval? The second is: How should the retrieval process in this kind of memory be characterized?

The retention of persistence would seem to be different from the retention of, say, fear. Fear is said to be remembered when a situation and/or specific stimulus to which fear has been conditioned evokes fear after some retention interval. Fear is a direct reaction to the situation, a state that can be conceptualized as a simple response. Persistence, on the other hand, is not a specific reaction or response but has something of the characteristic of a trait or predisposition. It is a characteristic of behavior that emerges over a testing period and cannot readily be said to be present at any given point in time. This brings us to the second question—the manner of retrieval of persistence. The retrieval cues for persistence (the PREE) reside in the extinction procedure or in some interaction in our procedure between the CRF reacquisition and extinction. Perhaps if the retrieval cue is in the extinction procedure, the CRF reacquisition may have the status of a "reminder" or "reinstatement" treatment. An experiment by Chen (1978) addresses this possibility.

The experiment was performed with rats 45 to 56 days of age in acquisition. Following CRF or PRF acquisition, extinction is carried out *without interpolated CRF reacquisition* after 15, 60, or 72 days. This constitutes a direct test of retention of persistence. There is then a CRF reacquisition at the same age for all subjects followed by a second extinction. A control group trained at 45 to 60 days has CRF reacquisition after 80 days followed by extinction. The outline together wth the results are shown in Fig. 8.6. The control animals retain persistence perfectly after 80 days when CRF is given before the extinction test.

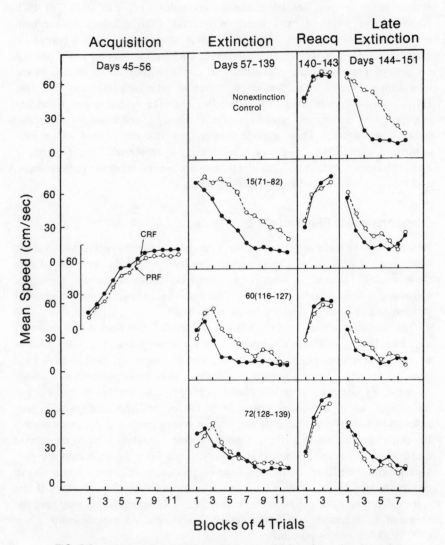

FIG. 8.6.   Acquisition under CRF or PRF and extinction after various intervals
followed by reacquisition and, in three cases, reextinction. In the second column
(Extinction) the number before the parentheses is the retention interval and the
number in the parentheses is the 12-day first-extinction period. A comparison of
the late extinction of the nonextinction control and the first extinction of the 72-day
retention group suggests a reinstatement function for the CRF reacquisition. (From
Chen, 1978.)

On the other hand the 72-day retention group without benefit of CRF reacquisition shows little or no retention of the PREE in their extinction test. The differential effects of the CRF versus PRF training 72 days earlier seem to have been forgotten. (There is good retention after 16 days and some after 60 days.) Clearly the persistence difference must reside somewhere in some form in these animals, but without the CRF reacquisition it is not expressed. The CRF reacquisition therefore seems to serve a reminding or reinstating function when the retention interval goes beyond some parameter-determined duration. We have always regarded the CRF reacquisition as simply a way of making the performance of PRF and CRF groups equivalent and of guaranteeing that the acquisition—extinction transition will be the same for both, so that the PREE will depend only on built-in historical factors. It now appears that in retention studies the CRF reacquisition may play the more crucial and active role of reinstating the memory for persistence.

LEARNING AND PERSISTENCE AT 10 TO 15 DAYS OF AGE

Our results showing extinction, persistence, and retention and durability of persistence in rats trained as young as 17 to 18 days of age suggested a reexamination of a common wisdom of some years' duration. In 1886, Hughlings-Jackson expressed the view that, during ontogenesis, neural centers responsible for inhibition develop more slowly than centers responsible for excitation. Through the years the working hypothesis has been that the later-developing, phylogenetically higher neural centers act to regulate (inhibit?) the excitation of the lower centers. There has been some behavioral and physiological support for this position. In altricial mammalian species the hippocampus and neocortex become functionally mature relatively late in development, and the hippocampus in particular has been implicated in the expression of behavioral inhibition (Altman, Brunner, & Bayer, 1973; Douglas, 1967; Kimble, 1968). Preweanling rats, in the third and fourth week of life, appear to lack maturity for tasks requiring suppression of responding; for example, they seem particularly deficient in passive avoidance learning and in habituating to novel stimuli (Bronstein, Neiman, Wolkoff, & Levine, 1974; Feigley et al., 1972). These task deficits resemble those shown in hippocampally lesioned adult animals (McCleary, 1966). If we regard extinction as involving a kind of passive avoidance, and if extinction and habituation involve common processes (Thompson & Spencer, 1966), we may well wonder why rats 17 to 18 days of age show substantial extinction and great persistence as a result of PRF training and retain this persistence into adulthood. It is of course natural also to ask how early in development these effects can be demonstrated in the rat. The very interesting question that arises is whether or not there is a transitional (or "critical") age range for extinction and persistence in the rat and if there is such an age range whether or not it corresponds to a period during which other significant behavioral and physiological changes are occurring. In the past year or so we have concentrated on the range from 10 to 15 days.

Because rat pups cannot be weaned much, if any, earlier than 16 days of age we needed to develop a procedure that would enable us to study reward-schedule effects in a seminatural setting. We found such a procedure and were able to demonstrate appetitive learning, patterned alternation, and extinction of an approach (crawling) response in 10-day-old rat pups (Amsel, Burdette, & Letz, 1976). In two experiments we showed that such behavioral plasticity in the 10-day-old rat could be controlled by using as the reinforcer the opportunity to suckle briefly on an anesthetized dam. The general procedure in these experiments is as follows: On the morning of Day 10 (or 11 or 14 in later experiments) pups from litters culled to 8 at birth are separated from their mother 8 hours prior to training and are placed in a plastic chamber partially filled with pine shavings. Temperature in the chamber is maintained at 37°C (the average temperature in an undisturbed nest) by means of thermostatically controlled commercial heating pads placed under the floor. Experimental training is in a clear Plexiglas alley (32 cm long and 8 cm wide) also maintained at 37° C. Approximately 20 minutes prior to the first trial the mother receives a 2 cc/kg IP injection of EquiThesin, a general anesthetic producing a surgical level of anesthesia and blocking milk release (Lincoln, Hill, & Wakerley, 1973; Wakerley & Lincoln, 1971). Preliminary training in these experiments consisted of a "priming" trial in which each pup is placed against the mother and allowed to attach to a nipple for 15 seconds. At the end of this interval the pup is gently detached from the nipple, carried by hand to the opposite end of the alley, and placed facing away from the mother. On reward (R) trials the mother is positioned on her side at the end of the alley, and the pup is permitted to attach to a nipple, in this first experiment for 15 seconds. On nonreward (N) trials in the first experiment the mother was removed from the alley, and the pup was picked up when it reached the end of the alley. The goal manipulations were varied in later experiments.

In the first experiment preliminary training was followed by five massed (3-second intertrial interval) R trials, a 15-minute retention interval during which the pup was returned to the deprivation chamber, and 25 massed trials in which R and N trials alternated (ALT) in blocks of 5 trials, starting and terminating with 5 R trials. In the second experiment the initial 5 R trials and the retention interval were not included, and two groups were formed: a 5-trial ALT group (as in the last 25 trials of Experiment 1) and a CRF group. Reward in each case was attachment to a nipple for 15 seconds. A 10-trial extinction phase began immediately after the last acquisition trial. Pups meeting an extinction criterion of 100 seconds on any trial were terminated and assigned a nominal latency of 100 for all remaining trials.

The results of the first experiment are shown in Fig. 8.7. Approach time decreased systematically over the first 5 R trials, there was significant savings in relearning after the retention interval, and there was also a systematic and significant influence on approach times of alternating blocks of R and N trials across the 25 trials following the retention interval. The first experiment established that infant rats will quickly learn to approach when the reward is an opportunity to attach to a nipple of an anesthetized dam for a brief period and that this learned tendency to approach can be successively weakened and strengthened by making the mother inaccessible and accessible on alternating blocks of five trials. In the second experiment we trained two groups of subjects, one on the alternating schedule, the other on a CRF schedule, and then extinguished both. The alternating pups showed patterned acquisition, the CRF pups a simple acquisition curve. In both groups removal of mother produced extinction, which was faster in the ALT than in the CRF group.

In these experiments employing the anesthetized-dam preparation, the dam was removed from the goal on nonreward trials, leaving the possibility that the approach and avoidance behavior was controlled by distance cues. In more recent experiments with infant rats in the 10- and 11-day range we have manipulated this and other factors (a) to show that the behavior we are observing reflects genuine learning and extinction and not simply "homing" on odor cues, (b) to examine the nature of the reinforcing agent we are employing, and (c) to determine whether or not a PREE can be demonstrated in 10- to 11-day-old rats.

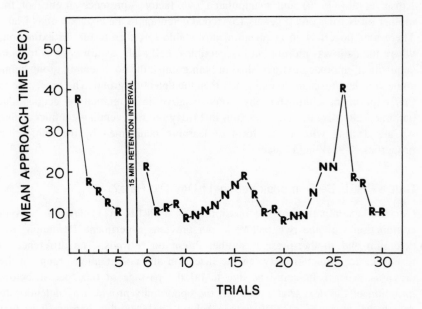

FIG. 8.7. Acquisition, reacquisition after a 15-minute interval, and 5-trial alternation behavior of 10-day-old rat pups run to an anesthetized dam with nonlactating suckling as reward. (From Amsel, Burdette, and Letz, 1976.)

Is It Genuine Learning?

Because of the possibility of differential distance cues related to the presence and absence, respectively, of the dam on R and N trials (the homing factor to which we have alluded), we changed the apparatus and the procedure in later experiments so that the dam was in the goal box on all trials but was inaccessible to the pup on N trials. This was accomplished with an apparatus in which the anesthetized dam was in the rear portion of the goal box and could be made accessible or inaccessible to the pup by a door that bisected the box. The most important feature of the procedure was that there was no possible differential stimulation from the mother's presence or absence while the pup was in the runway and the approach response was being measured (Amsel, Letz, & Burdette, 1977).

In this and in other experiments in this series subjects were albino rat pups of the Sprague–Dawley strain, bred and reared in our laboratory. Within 3 days after birth, litter size was reduced to 8 pups, and the litter was left undisturbed until the experimental treatment began on the morning of Day 11 postpartum. Body weight of the pups on Day 11 averaged 30 g (range 26.2 g to 33.4 g). In this and other experiments pups from at least three litters were involved in every condition.

Using this changed procedure we repeated the 5-trial ALT experiment of Amsel et al. (1976) and manipulated two factors—presence/absence of the mother on N trials and 0 versus 15-second detention in the goal box on N trials. There was no effect in acquisition attributable to either factor. In extinction, where the dam was present but inaccessible on all trials, as it was on N trials in acquisition, approach extinguished in both groups, the no-detention group being somewhat less resistant to extinction than the detention group. The procedure in this experiment eliminates any nonassociative interpretation of acquisition, patterned alternation, and extinction in 11-day-old rats, lending confidence that we are dealing with a true form of learning maintained by the reinforcing properties of suckling/contact.

Can a PREE Be Demonstrated in 11-Day-Old Rats?

Our first examination of the possibility of a PREE in 11-day-olds was in conjunction with the two factors in our previous experiment: Detention–no-detention and mother-present–mother-absent on N trials. The difference in resistance to extinction between the detention and no-detention groups in the previous experiment could be due to (a) the passage of time per se before initiation of the next trial and/or (b) the opportunity provided by detention to detect the presence of the mother behind the Plexiglas barrier. The first alternative suggests a memory-deficit notion to account for slower extinction in the detention group. If memory processes, especially for aversive events, are easily disrupted by the passage of time, perhaps a 15-second interval in the goalbox on N trials is long enough to produce a decrement in retention of the nonreward experience. On the basis of this factor the No-detention group should extinguish faster, because the memory traces of preceding nonreward trial(s) have not had a chance to dissipate to the same extent as in the detention group. The second interpretation is that detention provides differential information to the pups about the mother's presence via olfactory-based or other proximal stimuli. Although such information would be minimally available to pups in the no-detention group because they were quickly removed from the goal box on N-trials, pups in the detention group have 15 seconds to detect such cues. If the cues are available even with a door separating pups from the dam and if the cues have reinforcing properties, they may serve to attenuate the aversive effects of nonreward. Detention subjects would then have some basis for greater persistence in extinction than no-detention subjects.

We studied detention—no-detention and presence—absence in factorial combination with PRF and CRF in acquisition (Amsel, Letz, & Burdette, 1977). Detaining subjects on N-trials slowed the rate of extinction if the mother was present, but increased the rate of extinction when she was absent (Fig. 8.8). There was no evidence of a partial reinforcement extinction effect in any of these

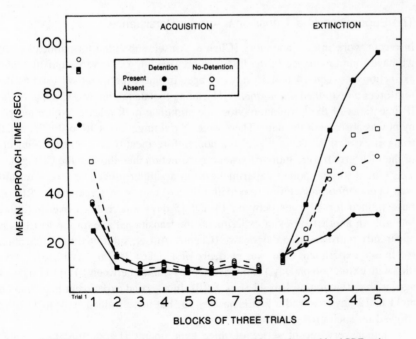

FIG. 8.8.   Acquisition and extinction in 11-day-old pups for combined PRF and CRF data varying factorially mother present—absent on N trials and detention—no detention in goal box on N trials. (From Amsel, Letz, and Burdette, 1977.)

11-day-old groups, and so the groups were combined for this factor.

The results of this experiment are more in line with an explanation of detention effects based on some feature of the dam's presence than with a memory-deficit interpretation. If it were the case that the increased persistence in the detention condition was due solely to rapid forgetting of the preceding nonrewarded trial, the dam's presence or absence should make little difference to the pups' extinction performance. In fact with mother absent the least persistent pups were in the detention group, which suggests that detaining the pups enhances the aversiveness of nonreward (primary frustration, R_F) and the subsequent anticipatory frustration (r_F), as reflected in the faster rate of extinction in the detention−absent group. This suggests in turn that a small but still effective source of (reinforcing?) stimulation is provided by the dam's presence, even under otherwise frustrative−extinctive circumstances. We return to the consideration of the presumed emotional properties of frustration in infant behavior in our later discussions of the nature of the reinforcer and ultrasound emission in rats of this age. But first I should like to present additional data that suggest a transitional age for learned persistence (PREE) in rats. (We have already established that the PREE is easily demonstrable in 17−18 days of age and that there is even retention of this persistence into adulthood.)

The Suggestion of a Transitional Age for Persistence

In recent work in our laboratory (Chen & Amsel, submitted for publication a), we have found evidence of the PREE in preweanling rats given acquisition and extinction between 14 and 15 days of age. In one experiment we used as the reinforcer a restrained *unanesthetized* lactating female rat that was given periodic IP injections of the hormone oxytocin to stimulate milk release. Nonreinforcement was absence of the dam. There were 28 training trials, CRF or PRF, and 20 trials of extinction. There was also a nonreinforcement (NRF) control. Subjects in the PRF group were more persistent in extinction than those in the CRF group (see Fig. 8.9). In another experiment using a similar procedure where reward was an *anesthetized* lactating (oxytocin-injected) female we found that a PREE in pups trained for 40 trials between 14 and 15 days was retained over a 13-day interval. In another series of experiments the transitional age for the PREE was apparently narrowed to a day or two (Chen & Amsel, submitted for publication b). In one experiment there was evidence of a clear PREE in rats 12 to 13 days old, with extinction on Day 13, but not in pups trained between 10 and 11 days of age, with extinction on Day 11 (Fig. 8.10). In a second experiment pups trained at 11 to 12 days showed a PREE on Day 13, but those trained at 10 to 11 days showed no such effect on Day 13.

Another very recent series of three experiments (Letz, Burdette, Gregg, Kittrell, & Amsel, 1978), probing the interval between 11 and 14 days of age, leads to the same conclusion about the approximate transitional age for learned

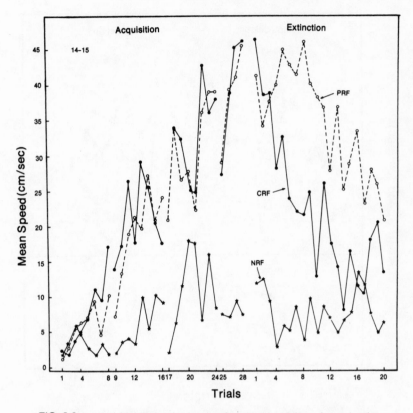

FIG. 8.9.   Acquisition and extinction data for pups 14–15 days of age, showing the PREE at this age in extinction. The NRF control shows the "operant" rate of responding in the runway at this age. (From Chen and Amsel, submitted a.)

persistence. In these experiments the reinforcer was either 30 seconds of dry suckling or 5 seconds of milk from an anesthetized dam induced to lactate by oxytocin injection. In the first experiment we used a spaced-trial procedure (10–12 min ITI) and manipulated schedule of reward (PRF versus CRF) at two ages and, under two of the reward conditions, dry suckling and suckling with milk. We were of course interested in the possibility of an interaction among the effects of schedule of reward, type or reward, and age. Some details of this experiment follow. The subjects were 80 albino rat pups from 20 litters, culled to 8 pups on Day 3 postpartum. The apparatus was the plastic runway described earlier. The general procedure was also the same. Four pups were tested from each litter, and of the four pups from each litter two were assigned to each reward-schedule condition. Each litter was assigned unsystematically to either the milk or no-milk reward condition and tested at either 11 or 14 days of age. Thus the data for each age-reward group (e.g., 14-day-old milk) were collected on 5 litters with 2 PRF and 2 CRF subjects per litter. All groups received 24

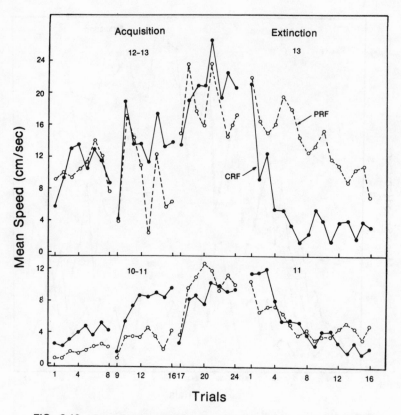

FIG. 8.10. Data showing PREE when acquisition is at Days 12−13 and extinction is at Day 13 but not when acquisition is at Days 10−11 with extinction at Day 11. (From Chen and Amsel, submitted b.)

acquisition trials and 16 extinction trials in 3 sessions within a single day at each age. Each of the first 2 sessions consisted of 8 acquisition trials; in the third session there were 8 acquisition and 16 extinction trials. All subjects were removed from the nest 16 hours prior to the beginning of the first session. Milk subjects were allowed 5 seconds suckling after the stretch reflex on an oxytocin-treated anesthetized dam. No-milk subjects were allowed 30 seconds suckling on the dry nipple of an anesthetized dam. Nonreward for all subjects consisted of 30 seconds detention in the outer portion of the goal box while the dam remained in the rear portion of the goal box behind the unopened gate. Milk subjects ran faster than no-milk subjects, this latter effect being greater for 14- than for 11-day-olds. The reward-schedule effect was significant in acquisition, the occurrence of nonreward trials reducing level of performance of the PRF relative to CRF groups. This schedule effect did not interact with either age or type of reward.

The most interesting extinction effect for our purposes was the occurrence of a PREE in 14- but not 11-day-olds. As Fig. 8.11 shows, 11-day-olds were made, if anything, less persistent by PRF training. Another interesting result was that at both ages and reinforcement schedules the Milk groups extinguished more *slowly* than no-milk groups, and in fact the 11-day-old milk groups showed little evidence of extinction. If suckling with and without milk can be regarded as two reward "magnitudes," which seems reasonable on the basis of the acquisition data, then the well-known paradoxical reward-magnitude-extinction effect—the larger the reward the more rapid the extinction—might have been expected to occur in the CRF groups. Earlier in this chapter, I described such an effect in rats as young as preweanling age, 17 to 20 days, where the reward was dry food rather than milk (Burdette et al., 1976, Experiment 3: Chen & Amsel, in preparation).

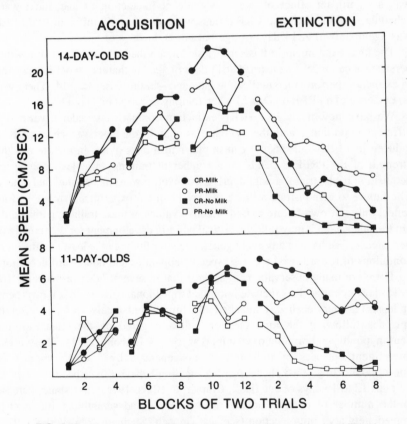

FIG. 8.11. Data showing the PREE under two conditions of reward (milk and dry suckling) in 14-day-olds but not in 11-day-olds when acquisition and extinction training are conducted within a single day at each age. (From Letz, Burdette, Gregg, Kittrell, and Amsel, 1978.)

In summary, this one experiment shows the following: The PREE occurs at 14 but not at 11 days of age with two different types of reward. Acquisition speeds are faster at both ages when suckling with milk is used as reward than when dry suckling is used. Acquisition is greater with CRF than with PRF training. At both ages there is a direct relationship between the effectiveness of these two rewards in acquisition and resistence to extinction, a result not characteristic of adult animals or even of weanling rats rewarded with two magnitudes of dry food.

In a second experiment (Letz et al., 1978) we asked whether or not the occurrence of the PREE in 14-day-olds but not in 11-day-olds is specific to spaced-trial testing conditions. Returning to our original massed-trial procedure (Amsel, Letz, & Burdette, 1977, Experiment 2), in which it is not possible to use milk reward, we manipulated the dry-suckling reward schedule in pups 11 and 14 days of age. The results were very much the same as with spaced trials. There was a significant effect of age, a significant interaction of age and reward schedule, and the PRF and CRF groups were significantly different (the PREE was again shown) at 14 days of age but not at 11 days of age.

The final experiment in this series tested again the interesting possibility that persistence can indeed be learned at 11 days of age but that it cannot be expressed in extinction performance until some later age—in this case, Day 14. There was no evidence of a PREE on Day 14 when training occurred on Day 11.

We have now made PRF−CRF extinction comparisons under a variety of different conditions, and the evidence is that learned persistence cannot be induced in 11-day-old rats but can in rats 1 to 3 days older. In mature rats the strength of the PREE depends on a number of training variables—number of acquisition trials, trial spacing, deprivation level, reward magnitude, and others. The failure to demonstrate a PREE at Day 11 in our experiments may therefore reflect only our own failure to find effective values of these training parameters. On the other hand it may reflect a critical point in development for the training of persistence. We have in any event generalized our finding to at least two different conditions of reward, trial-spacing, specific apparatus and nonreward definition.

There are many observations to suggest that in several other respects the 10- to 15-day age range does include important transitional periods. Infant rats spend at least 12 hours each day attached to a nipple but receive milk in discrete episodes following the milk ejection reflex triggered by the release of the neurohypophysial hormone oxytocin (Wakerley & Lincoln, 1971). These brief, intermittent episodes of milk release are separated by 5 to 15 minutes of non-milk-suckling. Two changes in the suckling behavior have been reported in rat pups 12 to 14 days of age (Hall, Cramer, & Blass, 1975): (a) a sharp increase in the number of pups detaching from a nipple and scrambling for another immediately after milk ejection (see also Drewett, Statham, & Wakerley, 1974) and (b) an inverse relation between duration of food deprivation and latency to attach to a nipple beginning at this age but not at younger ages. At about 14 days of age pups first open their eyes, gain the ability to thermoregulate, begin to leave the nest, and begin to meet their nutritional needs in ways other than suckling (Bolles & Woods, 1964). In addition, this age range includes the age at which the maternal pheromone is first reported to appear (Holinka & Carlson, 1976; Leon, 1974; Leon & Moltz, 1972).

It seems to be the case then that the mechanisms responsible for maintaining the mother–infant bond undergo a change at about 2 weeks of age. Up to about 2 weeks of age, suckling, even during the long no-milk intervals, and contact with the mother may be viewed as involving a kind of built-in persistence essential for survival. We suggest—and plan to examine further—the possibility that as eating and drinking come more and more under direct instrumental control of the pup, externally imposed differential-reward schedules may become more and more effective determinants of learned persistence.

Implications for Acquisition, Extinction, and Inhibition in Neonates

In addition to suggesting a transitional period for the PREE, these experiments have demonstrated that infant rat pups, 10, and 11 days of age will learn, under a number of schedules, a simple approach response rewarded by nonnutritive suckling and/or contact with an adult conspecific (this latter result is discussed in a later section). This approach response can be successively strengthened and weakened by blocks of rewarded and nonrewarded trials. With several con-secutive nonreward trials, as in alternating acquisition or in extinction, the pups show evidence of actively suppressing the approach response. When the mother is in the goal box but inaccessible during extinction trials, rate of extinction is slower if the pup is detained in the goal box for 15 seconds than if it is not detained. Removing the mother on extinction trials increases rate of extinction generally, and now detention produces *faster* extinction than no detention.

Extinction of the approach response in 11-day-old rats is interesting in the light of current theories about the ontogeny of learning in altricial organisms. Several investigators (e.g., Altman et al., 1973; Douglas, 1972) have noted that learning involving "response inhibition," such as in passive avoidance and spontaneous alternation, is much slower in young than in adult rats. The "young" rats in these experiments are 1 week to 2 weeks older than our pups. These observations have led to the proposition that until certain structures (e.g., hippocampus) and systems (e.g., cholinergic) are fully matured, young rats lack, or at least are severely impaired in, the ability to inhibit responding. We have argued elsewhere (e.g., Burdette et al., 1976) that this inhibition-deficit hypothesis is at most only partially supported by appetitive extinction data from rats between 18 and 36 days of age. From our present vantage point, although it is the case that older animals do extinguish faster than younger ones, there is no question that 10- and 11-day-old pups are capable of extinguishing a learned response. And if extinction, which is a form of response suppression, is an example also of the operation of "inhibition" (as is, say, passive avoidance), then 11-day-old rats would not seem to lack inhibitory mechanisms. My own view (Amsel, 1972b) is that neither instrumental extinction nor passive shock avoidance reflects the operation of inhibition mechanisms and that if we are looking for transitional periods for true inhibition, we may have to look for other behavioral indicants.

DISCRIMINATION AND PREDISCRIMINATION EFFECTS IN INFANT RATS

Recent work in our laboratory (Brake, 1978) has addressed itself to developmental considerations in the context of an appetitive go−no-go discrimination. The particular emphasis in this work has been on effects of a variety of prediscrimination exposures to the discriminative stimuli on rate of discrimination learning. In this respect Brake has begun to deal in a developmental way with theoretical considerations introduced earlier in this paper that were derived from work on adult rats (see Fig. 8.1).

Rats in two age groups were trained under either PRF or CRF conditions or on a successive discrimination (D). The apparatus was a simple runway, and the intertrial interval was 10 to 15 minutes. In Phase 1, rats 11 or 15 days of age received 128 training trials over 4 days, reinforcement being the opportunity to suckle the dry nipples of an anesthetized dam for 15 seconds. The discriminative stimuli were two floor surfaces, either wire mesh or Plexiglas, inserted into the alley. For the D subjects these tactile stimuli were perfectly correlated with the presence or absence of reinforcement; for the other groups they were uncorrelated. Phase 2, which followed 10 days after the completion of Phase 1 for each age, consisted of 128 trials of training over 4 days on a successive discrimination that was the reversal of the earlier discrimination for the D subjects but was the first exposure to discrimination for the other two groups. Food pellets were used as reinforcement in this phase. Two control groups at each age were trained on the Phase 2 discrimination after receiving either a handling treatment or no treatment in Phase 1. In Phase 1 the results of which are shown in Fig. 8.12, the D subjects of both ages showed behavioral discrimination. The PRF subjects of both ages ran significantly slower than CRF subjects, with a suggestion that PRF subjects of Age 2 actually extinguished over "acquisition" trials. In Phase 2 (see Fig. 8.13) only the CRF subjects of Age 1 discriminated. The PRF subjects did not learn the discrimination in 128 trials, nor did the D subjects reverse their discrimination. All three Age 2 groups formed a discrimination in Phase 2, the CRF discrimination developing earliest, the PRF discrimination latest. These results, and particularly the retardation of discrimination learning following PRF training, provide some developmental evidence for a frustration-theory analysis of certain discrimination and prediscrimination effects (Amsel, 1962).

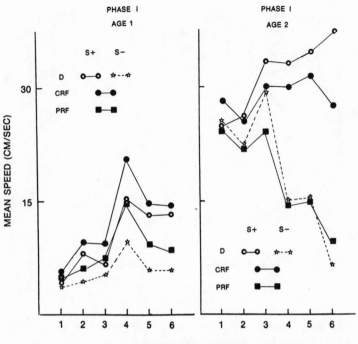

FIG. 8.12. CRF, PRF, and discrimination performance at two ages, Age 1 (11−14 days) and Age 2 (15−18 days). Data from the first 32 preliminary trials run in a smaller alley are not shown. (Adapted from Brake, 1978.)

Both Age 1 control groups showed a late-developing discrimination in Phase 2, but neither of the Age 2 control groups showed any sign of discrimination. This apparently paradoxical failure of the older of the two sets of control groups to learn the tactile discrimination at about 30 days of age corresponds to our observations, and personal communications from others, that there is something peculiar about rats at this age. They are extremely excitable and often fail to learn as well as rats a little older or a little younger, possibly because of what seems to be a high level of distractability. Certainly rats are extraordinarily active at this age, so much so that the term "popcorn" stage of development (especially if the pups are white) seems to describe them very well. Adult rats learn a tactile discrimination in 50 to 90 trials, but there is other evidence that 33-day-old rats have difficulty with a simple spatial discrimination (Bronstein & Spear, 1972). Brake thinks one possibility is that rats at this age are overloaded with sensory information, and for this reason first exposure to discriminanda at this age is not effective for learning. However, experience with discriminanda of any kind (PRF, CRF, D) during infancy somehow renders these stimuli more salient to the 30-day-old than they otherwise would be. Hence discrimination learning and

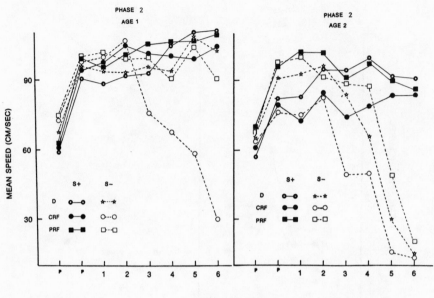

FIG. 8.13. Discrimination learning at Age 1 (25–28 days) or Age 2 (29–32 days) for groups previously run in CRF, PRF, or the reverse discrimination. (The P designation of the first two blocks of 8 trials has no particular importance here and can be read as Blocks 1 and 2 of 8 blocks of trials. (Adapted from Brake, 1978.)

even reversal is possible at this age *for pretrained groups* but not for controls. (c.f. Livesey & Dawson, 1977, who feel that although inhibition in the context of discrimination of bar-pressing begins to be demonstrated at a certain age regardless of amount of previous training, experience with the discrimination task prior to the age at which performance will show improvement produces dramatic facilitation of later discriminative–inhibitory performance in these rats.)

REINFORCING PROPERTIES OF CONSPECIFIC
CONTACT IN 11-DAY-OLDS

Although our data indicate that suckling, with or without milk, is reinforcing, we need to know more for example about the relative importance of contact alone as compared to contact combined with suckling as factor(s) affecting this reinforcing property. Rats of all ages interact intensively with conspecifics. When placed in novel situations, even mature rats increase the time they spend in direct contact with conspecifics (e.g. Latane, Cappell, & Joy, 1970), and of course they huddle together while resting or sleeping. Almost from birth, then, rats manifest conspecific contact, and although the mechanisms controlling such behaviors may change as the rat matures, social environment undoubtedly exerts a potent influence on behavior, even during the preweaning period of life (Randall & Campbell, 1976). A perhaps extreme example of sociability in young rats comes from experiments showing that 15-day-old rats will follow and, if injected with amphetamine, maintain contact with an anesthetized adult rat who is moved about in an open field (Campbell & Randall, 1975).

The purpose of one of our experiments (Amsel, Letz, & Burdette, 1977, Experiment 3) was to examine the relative reinforcing values of the various goal box stimuli. Acquisition and extinction were studied in six groups of 11-day-old rats. The rewards were suckling a lactating dam (suckling), contacting a lactating dam not suckling (no-suckling), contacting a nonlactating female rat (non-lactating), contacting a mature male rat (male), contacting a single littermate (pup), or absence of conspecific contact (nothing). The method and apparatus were as previously described.

Although our main interest in this experiment was to compare reinforcing agents in acquisition, we decided to extinguish all groups but the nothing group, which had already reached a 100-second criterion of extinction during acquisition. Extinction trials immediately followed acquisition training. In extinction, pups were detained in the goal box for 15 seconds on each trial with the acquisition goal object inaccessible behind the barrier during the detention interval. The extinction data are only suggestive of course, because these differences in goal condition during extinction made direct comparison impossible.

Subjects in the pup and nothing groups failed to reduce approach times across acquisition training much below operant levels (Fig. 8.14); the suckling, no-suckling, nonlactating, and male groups all showed evidence of good acquisition that was sustained until the end of acquisition training, and these four groups were not significantly different from each other. Subjects in the pup groups were significantly better at performing the approach response than the nothing group. These acquisition data suggest that at this age and under these conditions, any one of our anesthetized adult rat conditions is more or less equivalent to any other in terms of its reinforcing value in supporting approach behavior. All groups extinguished but at significantly different rates. The suckling and no-suckling groups were not different, nor were the male and nonlactating groups, but the first two were significantly slower to extinguish than the latter two, suggesting again that the presence behind a barrier of a lactating female may be sufficiently reinforcing to retard extinction; the presence of a male or nonlactating female has no such effect. All of this is of course subject to the limitations imposed by the confound that is operating in the extinction phase of the experiment.

This last experiment did not involve the obvious extreme positive condition: a suckling-with-milk condition. The reason was that such a condition cannot be

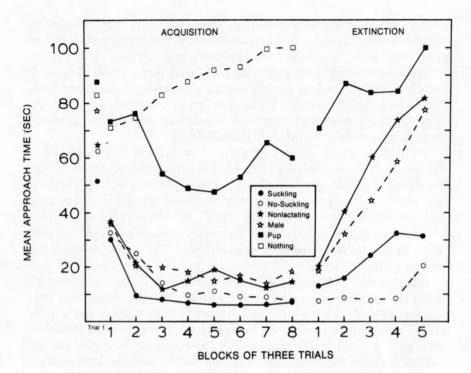

FIG. 8.14.   Acquisition and extinction of an approach response in 11-day-old
pups under six conditions of reward. (From Amsel, Letz, and Burdette, 1977.)

run with massed trials. Infant rats spend at least 12 hours of each day suckling,
and milk ejections are sporadic but fairly widely spaced, with 5 to 15 minutes
separating each brief (20–25 second) episode of milk release (Wakerley &
Lincoln, 1971). Thus in order to run a milk-reinforcement condition under
something like normal rates of milk ingestion, we ran a preliminary experiment
at a 5-minute ITI. We compared three groups: suckling–milk, suckling–no
milk, and no suckling. Milk letdown in the anesthetized dam was induced by IP
injection of oxytocin (2 ml/kg). The same dam served for all three conditions for
Ss of a given squad (litter). We have run this experiment at two ages—11 days
and 14 days. At each age 10 acquisition and 10 extinction trials were run on a
single day. The results are that at neither age is there a difference in acquisition
or in extinction with this few trials. There is a nonsignificant suggestion,
particularly at the older age, of faster extinction following the suckling-milk
condition. (The Letz et al. experiments reported earlier were actually performed
after this one, and they show differential effects of these two rewards at these
ages when more trials are run.)

These experiments and others have demonstrated that infant rat pups 11 and 14
days of age will learn under a number of schedules a simple approach response

rewarded by nutritive, nonnutritive suckling, and/or contact with an adult conspecific. They are the merest beginnings of a research program to relate the effectiveness of specific reinforcers to stages of ontogeny. (See Chapters 1 and 2 in this volume.)

ULTRASOUNDS AND AROUSAL IN EXTINCTION OF INFANT RATS

Infants of most rodent species emit sounds at frequencies above the range of human hearing. These ultrasonic vocalizations, investigated in a number of species, typically occur when the infants are exposed to conditions of environmental stress (Noirot, 1972; Sales & Pye, 1974). Thermal and tactual stressors, unusual odors, pain, and hunger evoke the ultrasonic calls of infant rats (Bell, 1974; Noirot, 1972; Okon, 1970; Oswalt & Meier, 1975). Developmentally the rate of ultrasound production decreases as homeothermy is attained (Okon, 1970). Indeed, recent work in our laboratory (Graham & Letz, in press) has confirmed that although there are litter differences in this regard, on the average ultrasounding to cold stress decreases systematically after 11 days of age.

Ultrasounds appear to be an important signaling system in altricial infant rodents. They seem, for example, to be important for initiating infant retrieval by the dam in rats (Allin & Banks, 1972) and for the coordination of maternal behaviors in mice (Noirot, 1966, 1969, 1970). Bell (1974) has emphasized that ultrasounds reflect a high level of arousal in infants and induce arousal in the dam. At a time when the infant is unable to thermoregulate, to see, or to ambulate efficiently, the infant ultrasound seems to serve as a distress signal to the dam. In the rat, ultrasounds diminish at the age when the pup gains the ability to thermoregulate, opens its eyes, and begins to leave the nest, at which time a chemical signaling system involving a maternal pheromone (Leon, 1974; Leon & Moltz, 1972) begins to predominate.

Some of our previous work (Amsel et al., 1976; Amsel, Letz, & Burdette, 1977) has demonstrated that 10- and 11-day-old rat pups can learn to approach an anesthetized dam in a heated alley with dry suckling as reward and that the approach behavior is extinguished with successive nonrewarded trials. As I have pointed out, extinction in these experiments may indicate that at least one kind of response-suppressive mechanism is operating at an age when centers responsible for inhibition are said not to be well developed in rat pups (Altman et al., 1973; Douglas, 1967). It could be the case that the extinction we find in rats 10 to 11 days of age reflects decreased arousal or excitation resulting from some decrease in incentive to approach the dam. We know, however, that in adult animals extinction following appetitive learning is an active process that involves increasing arousal, presumably because of the primary and conditioned frustrative effects of nonreward following a history of reward (Amsel, 1967). If appetitive extinction in infant rats is similar to that in older rats, involving active suppressive—inhibitory processes and conflict and if ultrasounds are an indicant of arousal in the pup (Bell, 1974), then one would expect ultrasounds to increase during extinction of a learned appetitive response. A recent experiment in which we measured ultrasound production in learning and extinction provides evidence for an active conception of appetitive extinction in 11-day-old rats (Amsel, Radek, Graham, & Letz, 1977).

The subjects, 8 albino rat pups bred in our laboratory but originally of Holtzmann stock, weighed 25 to 30 gm. The training apparatus is the Plexiglas alley described earlier, as are the deprivation, training procedure, and anesthetized-dam (reward) preparation.

Ultrasounds were detected by a Bruel and Kjaer condenser microphone with cathode follower, a Bruel and Kjaer microphone amplifier, and a Krohn—Hite bandpass filter. The filtered microphone output was monitored visually on a Tektronix oscilloscope, and any ultrasound pulses in the range of 20 kHz to 50 kHz (above 30 db.) were counted by a specially constructed digital counter. The microphone was positioned over the point at which the alley intersected the goal box in such a way that ultrasounds anywhere in the apparatus were detected.

For each pup, 25 successive rewarded trials were followed immediately by 15 unsignaled nonrewarded trials. Reward in this experiment was 30 seconds of dry suckling. Nonreward was a 30-second detainment in the outer portion of the goal box with dam present in the other portion but inaccessible because the gate was not raised. Between trials the pup was placed in a 12 cm × 12 cm × 10 cm Plexiglas holding box for approximately 5 seconds. In addition to the usual time measures of learning and extinction, number of ultrasounds emitted during those times were recorded for each trial. In addition, ultrasounds emitted in 30 seconds in the goal box during extinction were recorded. During acquisition ultrasounds in the goal box were not recorded, because the pups sometimes emitted ultrasounds when the experimenter guided the pup, on occasion, in nipple attachment. During extinction pups were tested until they failed to reach the goal box in 100 seconds.

The approach-time data for acquisition and extinction were quite similar to those reported in earlier studies with this age and reinforcer (Amsel et al., 1976; Letz et al., 1978). What is new are the data on ultrasound production by infant rats in an appetitive learning situation, ultrasounds decreasing (habituating?) across acquisition and increasing across extinction trials. Figure 8.15 presents, for the extinction phase, the mean start and run times, the constant 30-second goal time, and the corresponding mean frequencies of ultrasounds emitted during those times. Although the time and ultrasound means for the start and run measures are strikingly parallel (i.e., number of ultrasounds increase as approach times increase), ultrasounds also increased significantly in the goal box where the detention interval was constant (30 seconds) for all trials. The increase in goal box ultrasounds and an additional fact argue against attributing increased

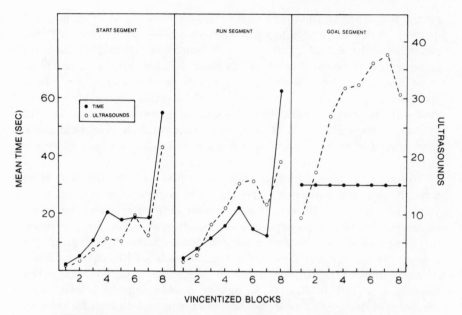

FIG. 8.15. Extinction performance (approach time) and frequency of ultra-sounds in three segments of the crawlway. In the goal segment, the 11-day-old pup was detained for a constant 30 seconds. (From Amsel, Radek, Graham, and Letz, © (1977) by the American Association for the Advancement of Science.)

ultrasounds in extinction simply to time spent in the runway: The correlation between ultrasounds in the alley and time spent there on the last interval (when both were highest) was −0.25.

If one accepts that ultrasounds reflect arousal (Bell, 1974), the increase in ultrasounds in extinction, particularly over the fixed 30-second interval of goal box detention, argues against a simple arousal–decrement interpretation of extinction, even in infant rats. Our findings of increased ultrasounds and other indicants of arousal in the appetitive extinction of infant rats do not fit the idea that the infant rat is lacking in suppressive mechanisms nor that it is similar to the adult with a nonfunctioning hippocampus (Altman, Brunner, & Bayer, 1973; Douglas, 1967). Extinction in these pups involves active suppression of behavior (the pup learns not to approach the nonrewarding goal box), as it does in adults.

CONCLUDING COMMENTS

I have described a number of experimental developments from our laboratory, whose major common focus is the study of ontogeny of appetitive learning. In this respect our work, together with some recent work from the laboratories of Blass, Rosenblatt (see Chapters 2 and 1, respectively, in this volume), and others, is a departure from most of the work on the ontogeny of learning and memory, which has tended to stress aversive conditioning and learning and, particularly, the use of electric shock as reinforcer. Although I have not addressed the particular question in this paper, it is possible that there will be some divergence between the general results developed from the use of appetitive and aversive reinforcers: Clearly the appetitive interaction we have used with our youngest pups, although not completely natural, is more relevant to the developing ecology of the young mammal than is electric shock stimulation and for this reason may produce different—for example, longer-lasting—effects.

To summarize the experimental work of the past few years, the work is on appetitive learning, extinction, persistence, and discrimination learning in the young, weanling, and infant rat. If we look at the weanling to juvenile age range, there seems little difference in patterns of acquisition, extinction, and persistence (the PREE) across ages, and there is some suggestion that the PREE is greater the younger the age. It is also the case that larger rewards in CRF acquisition result in faster extinction (the paradoxical reward−magnitude−extinction effect) when acquisition is at 17 to 20 days, as they do in older animals. Working with somewhat older animals, we are developing experimental methods for studying the retention and reinstatement of persistence, and we hope to apply these methods to younger and younger animals.

The age range on which we have concentrated in the infant work has been 11 to 14 days. Here we have demonstrated appetitive instrumental learning and extinction in the 11-day-old, using as reward dry suckling, milk suckling, and contact with lactating and nonlactating adult females and males. We have also begun to examine a possible transitional period for the learning and retention of persistence in infants. In a number of experiments using as reward dry suckling as well as milk suckling from both anesthetized and nonanesthetized females, we have shown that the PREE can be found in 14-day-olds but not in 11-day-olds under all the various reinforcement conditions and under both massed- and spaced-trial conditions. It may be possible under our conditions to delimit this transitional period to a day or two of developmental age, somewhere between 11 and 13 days in rat pups raised in litters of 8 from the Day 3 of life.

To go back to my introductory statement, the most important long-term consideration in these investigations has to do with the development of a temperamental characteristic, persistence, in mammals, including humans. The work is in the context of the frustration-theoretic approach to the study of persistence, its retention, and durability. The difference between these experiments and those reported over the past 20 years or so is that this experimental program may enable us to say with some confidence that a general temperamental disposition (as contrasted with a particular response or memory) can be learned "at mother's breast." When in the present context we say "general temperamental disposition," we refer to some kind of learned system that transcends particular constraints of situation and response to affect later behavior. We are still some way from identifying the boundary conditions for generality of persistence, but a beginning has been made in this direction. I refer here not only to the work described in this chapter but to transfer experiments involving habituation to electric shock and stimulus change. This line of developmental investigation is not so far along as the work contained in this chapter, but some beginnings have been made in a doctoral dissertation by David Burdette (1977) and in work with Jaw-Sy Chen (Chen & Amsel, 1977 and unpublished).

The significance of this kind of work is that it provides a mammalian model for identifying periods in which certain hypothetical processes, inferred from work with adults of the same species, begin to appear in infancy. It may ultimately be possible to identify the underlying physiological and anatomical substrates of such processes by relating behavioral development to the development of the nervous system, particularly at certain identifiable transitional stages.

ACKNOWLEDGEMENT

The preparation of this chapter and all the experimental work reported therein were supported by Grants BMS74-19696 and BNS74-19696 from the National Science Foundation. My indebtedness to the many students who contributed to this work will be obvious, but I want especially to thank Stephen Brake, David Burdette, Jaw-Sy Chen, and Richard Letz. My thanks also to Mark Stanton for a very helpful critical reading of the manuscript.

REFERENCES

Allin, J. T., & Banks, E. M. Functional aspects of ultrasound production by infant albino rats. *Animal Behavior*, 1972, *20*, 175–185.

Altman, J., Brunner, R. L., & Bayer, S. A. The hippocampus and behavioral maturation. *Behavioral Biology*, 1973, *8*, 557–596.

Altman, J., & Das, G. D. Autoradiographic and histological evidence of postnatal hippocampal neurogenesis in rats. *Journal of Comparative Neurology*, 1965, *124*, 319–336.

Amsel, A. The role of frustrative nonreward in noncontinuous reward situations. *Psychological Bulletin*, 1958, *55*, 102–119.

Amsel, A. Frustrative nonreward in partial reinforcement and discrimination learning: Some recent history and theoretical extension. *Psychological Review*, 1962, *69*, 306–328.

Amsel, A. Partial reinforcement effects on vigor and persistence: Advances in frustration theory derived from a variety of within-subjects experiments. In K. W. Spence and J. T. Spence (Eds.), *The psychology of learning and motivation* (Vol. I). New York: Academic Press, 1967.

Amsel, A. Positive induction, behavioral contrast, and generalization of inhibition in discrimination learning. In H. H. Kendler and J. T. Spence (Eds.), *Essays in neobehaviorism*. New York: Appleton-Century-Crofts, 1971. (a)

Amsel, A. Frustration, persistence, and regression. In H. D. Kimmel (Ed.), *Experimental psychopathology: Recent research and theory*. New York: Academic Press, 1971. (b)

Amsel, A. Behavioral habituation, counterconditioning, and a general theory of persistence. In A. H.

Black & W. F. Prokasy (Eds.), *Classical conditioning II*. New York: Appleton-Century-Crofts, 1972. (a)

Amsel, A. Inhibition and mediation in classical, Pavlovian and instrumental conditioning. In R. Boakes & S. Halliday (Eds.), *Inhibition and learning*. London: Academic Press, 1972. (b)

Amsel, A., Burdette, D. R., & Letz, R. Appetitive learning, patterned alternation, and extinction in 10-day-old rats with non-lactating suckling as reward. *Nature*, 1976, *262*, 816–818.

Amsel, A., & Chen, J. Ontogeny of persistence: Immediate and long-term persistence in rats varying in training age between 17 and 65 days. *Journal of Comparative and Physiological Psychology*, 1976, *90*, 808–820.

Amsel, A., Letz, R., & Burdette, D. R. Appetitive learning and extinction in 11-day-old rat pups: Effects of various reinforcement conditions. *Journal of Comparative and Physiological Psychology*, 1977, *91*, 1156–1167.

Amsel, A., Radek, C. C., Graham, M., & Letz, R. Ultrasound emission in infant rats as an indicant of arousal during appetitive learning and extinction. *Science*, 1977, *197*, 786–788.

Amsel, A., & Ward, J. S. Motivational properties of frustration: II. Frustration drive stimulus and frustration reduction in selective learning. *Journal of Experimental Psychology*, 1954, *48*, 37–47.

Amsel, A., & Ward, J. S. Frustration and persistence: Resistance to discrimination following prior experience with the discriminanda. *Psychological Monographs*, 1965, *79*, (4, whole No. 597).

Amsel, A., Wong, P. T. P., & Traupmann, K. L. Short-term and long-term factors in extinction and durable persistence. *Journal of Experimental Psychology*, 1971, *90*, 90–95.

Bell, R. W. Ultrasounds in small rodents: Arousal-produced and arousal-producing. *Developmental Psychobiology*, 1974, *7*, 39–42.

Bitterman, M. E. The comparative analysis of learning. *Science*, 1975, *188*, 699–709.

Bolles, R. C., & Woods, P. J. The ontogeny of behavior in the albino rat. *Animal Behavior*, 1964, *12*, 427–441.

Brake, S. C. Discrimination training in infant, preweanling and weanling rats: Effects of prior learning experiences with the discriminanda. *Animal Learning & Behavior*, 1978, *4*, 435–443.

Bronstein, P. M., Dworkin, T., & Bilder, B. H. Age-related differences in rats' spontaneous alternation. *Animal Learning & Behavior*, 1974, *2*, 285–288.

Bronstein, P. M., Neiman, H., Wolkoff, F. D., & Levine, M. J. The development of habituation in the rat. *Animal Learning & Behavior*, 1974, *2*, 92–96.

Bronstein, P., & Spear, N. E. Acquisition of a spatial discrimination by rats as a function of age. *Journal of Comparative and Physiological Psychology*, 1972, *78*, 208–212.

Burdette, D. R. *Behavioral habituation and persistence in the rat*. Unpublished doctoral dissertation, University of Texas, 1977.

Burdette, D. R., Brake, S., Chen, J. S., & Amsel, A. Ontogeny of persistence: Immediate extinction effects in preweanling and weanling rats. *Animal Learning & Behavior*, 1976, *4*, 131–138.

Campbell, B. A., Lytle, L. D., & Fibiger, H. C. Ontogeny of adrenergic arousal and cholinergic inhibitory mechanisms in the rat. *Science*, 1969, *166*, 635–636.

Campbell, B. A., & Mabry, P. D. Ontogeny of behavioral arousal: A comparative study. *Journal of Comparative and Physiological Psychology*, 1972, *81*, 371–379.

Campbell, B. A., & Randall, P. K. Paradoxical effects of amphetamine on behavioral arousal in neonatal and adult rats: A possible animal model of the calming effect of amphetamine on hyperkinetic children. In N. R. Ellis (Ed.), *Aberrant development in infancy*. Hillsdale, N.J.: Lawrence Erlbaum Associates, 1975.

Chen, J. S. *Mechanisms and limits of durable persistence*. Unpublished doctoral dissertation, University of Texas at Austin, 1978.

Chen, J. S., & Amsel, A. Retention and durability of persistence acquired by young and infant rats. *Journal of Comparative and Physiological Psychology*, 1975, *89*, 238–245.

Chen, J. S., & Amsel, A. Prolonged unsignalled, inescapable shocks increase persistence in subsequent instrumental learning. *Animal Learning & Behavior*, 1977, *5*, 377–385.

Chen, J. S., & Amsel, A. The paradoxical effect of magnitude of reward on extinction in preweanling and older rats. Manuscript in preparation.

Chen, J. S., & Amsel, A. Retention under changed-reward conditions of persistence learned by infant rats. Manuscript submitted for publication (a).

Chen, J. S., & Amsel, A. Learned persistence at 11–12 days but not at 10–11 days in infant rats. Manuscript submitted for publication (b).

Daly, H. B. Reinforcing properties of escape from frustration aroused in various learning situations. In G. H. Bower (Ed.), *The psychology of learning and motivation*. New York: Academic Press, 1974.

Deza, L., & Eidelberg, E. Development of cortical electrical activity in the rat. *Experimental Neurology*, 1967, *17*, 425–438.

Douglas, R. J. The hippocampus and behavior. *Psychological Bulletin*, 1967, *67*, 416–442.

Douglas, R. J. Pavlovian conditioning and the brain. In R. A. Boakes & M. S. Halliday (Eds.), *Inhibition and learning*. New York: Academic Press, 1972.

Douglas, R. J., Peterson, J. J., & Douglas, D. P. The ontogeny of a hippocampus-dependent response in two rodent species. *Behavioral Biology*, 1973, *8*, 27–37.

Drewett, R. F., Statham, C., & Wakerley, J. B. A quantitative analysis of the feeding behavior of suckling rats. *Animal Behavior*, 1974, *22*, 907–913.

Ernest, A. J., Dericco, D., Dempster, J. P., & Neimann, J. Developmental differences in rats of suppressive effects of extinction as a function of extinction sessions. *Journal of Comparative and Physiological Psychology*, 1975, *88*, 633–639.

Estes, W. K. The statistical approach to learning theory. In S. Koch (Ed.), *Psychology: A study of a science* (Vol. 2). New York: McGraw-Hill, 1959.

Feigley, D. A., Parson, P. A., Hamilton, L. W., & Spear, N. E. Development of habituation to novel environments in the rat. *Journal of Comparative and Physiological Psychology*, 1972, *79*, 443–452.

Gonzales, R. C., & Champlin, G. Positive behavioral contrast, negative simultaneous contrast and their relations to frustration in pigeons. *Journal of Comparative and Physiological Psychology*, 1974, *87*, 173–187.

Graham, M., & Letz, R. Within-species variation in the development of ultrasonic signaling of preweanling rats. *Developmental Psychobiology*, in press.

Gray, J. A. *Elements of a two-process theory of learning*. London: Academic Press, 1975.

Hall, W. G., Cramer, C. P., & Blass, E. Developmental changes in suckling of rat pups. *Nature*, 1975, *258*, 318–320.

Henke, P. G. Lesions in the amygdala and the frustration effect. *Physiology and Behavior*, 1973, *10*, 647–650.

Henke, P. G. Persistence of runway performance after septal lesions in rats. *Journal of Comparative and Physiological Psychology*, 1974, *86*, 760–767.

Holinka, C. F., & Carlson, A. D. Pup attraction to lactating Sprague–Dawley rats. *Behavioral Biology*, 1976, *16*, 489–505.

Hulse, S. H., Jr. Amount and percentage of reinforcement and duration of goal confinement in conditioning and extinction. *Journal of Experimental Psychology*, 1958, *56*, 48–57.

Kimble, D. P. Hippocampus and internal inhibition. *Psychological Bulletin*, 1968, *70*, 285–295.

Kirkby, R. J. A maturation factor in spontaneous alternation. *Nature*, 1967, *215*, 784.

Latane, B., Cappell, H., & Joy, V. Social deprivation, housing density, and gregariousness in rats. *Journal of Comparative and Physiological Psychology*, 1970, *70*, 221–227.

Leon, M. Maternal pheromone. *Physiology and Behavior*, 1974, *13*, 441–453.

Leon, M., & Moltz, H. The development of the pheromonal bond in the albino rat. *Physiology and Behavior*, 1972, *8*, 683–686.

Letz, R., Burdette, D. R., Gregg, B., Kittrell, E. M. W., & Amsel A. Evidence for a transitional period for the development of persistence in infant rats. *Journal of Comparative and Physiological Psychology*, 1978, *92*, 856—866.

Lincoln, D. W., Hill, A., & Wakerley, J. B. The milk-ejection reflex of the rat: An intermittent function not abolished by surgical levels of anesthesia. *Journal of Endocrinology*, 1973, *57*, 459—476.

Livesey, D. J., & Dawson, R. G. A learning-performance distinction during development. *Behavioral Biology*, 1977, *20*, 25—31.

Mabry, P. D., & Peeler, D. F. Effect of septal lesions on response to frustrative nonreward. *Physiology and Behavior*, 1972, *8*, 909—913.

McCleary, R. A. Response modulating functions of the limbic system: Initiation and suppression. In E. Stellar & J. M. Sprague (Eds.), *Progress in physiological psychology* (Vol. 1). New York: Academic Press, 1966.

Noirot, E. Ultrasounds in young rodents. I. Changes with age in albino mice. *Animal Behavior*, 1966, *14*, 459—462.

Noirot, E. Changes in responsiveness to young in the adult mouse. *Animal Behavior*, 1969, *17*, 542—546.

Noirot, E. Selective priming of maternal responses by auditory and olfactory cues from the mouse pup. *Developmental Psychobiology*, 1970, *2*, 273—276.

Noirot, E. Ultrasounds and maternal behavior in small rodents. *Developmental Psychobiology*, 1972, *5*, 371—387.

Okon, E. E. The effect of environmental temperature on the production of ultrasounds by isolated non-handled albino mouse pups. *Journal of Zoology, London*, 1970, *162*, 71—83.

Oswalt, G. L., & Meier, G. W. Olfactory, thermal, and tactual influences on infantile ultrasonic vocalization in rats. *Developmental Psychobiology*, 1975, *8*, 129—135.

Randall, P. K., & Campbell, B. A. Ontogeny of behavioral arousal in rats: Effect of maternal and sibling presence. *Journal of Comparative and Physiological Psychology*, 1976, *90*, 453—459.

Riccio, D. C., & Marrazo, M. J. Effects of punishing active avoidance in young and adult rats. *Journal of Comparative and Physiological Psychology*, 1972, *79*, 453—458.

Sales, G., & Pye, D. *Ultrasonic communication*. London: Chapman and Hall, 1974.

Terrace, H. S. By-products of discrimination learning. In G. H. Bower (Ed.), *The psychology of learning and motivation* (Vol. 5). New York: Academic Press, 1972.

Terris, W., German, D., & Enzie, R. Transsituational resistance to the effects of aversive stimulation. *Journal of Comparative and Physiological Psychology*, 1969, *67*, 264—268.

Thompson, R. F., & Spencer, W. A. Habituation: A model phenomenon for the study of neuronal substrates of behavior. *Psychological Review*, 1966, *73*, 16—43.

Wagner, A. R. Effects of amount and percentage of reinforcement and number of acquisition trials on conditioning and extinction. *Journal of Experimental Psychology*, 1961, *62*, 234—242.

Wagner, A. R. Frustration and punishment. In R. N. Haber (Ed.), *Current research in motivation*. New York: Holt, Rinehart & Winston, 1966.

Wakerley, J. B., & Lincoln, D. W. Intermittent release of oxytocin during suckling in the rat. *Nature*, 1971, *233*, 180—181.

Weinstock, S. Resistance to extinction of a running response following partial reinforcement under widely spaced trials. *Journal of Comparative and Physiological Psychology*, 1954, *47*, 318—322.

9 Sources of Infantile Amnesia

Ralph R. Miller and Alvin M. Berk
Brooklyn College of the City University of New York

Infantile amnesia, the rapid forgetting of acquired information by very young organisms relative to adults, is commonly assumed to occur in both humans and animals. Its existence in infrahuman species is of particular interest because it suggests that anthropomorphic mechanisms like sexual repression, linguistic development, or hemispheric dominance do not completely account for human infantile amnesia. Using rats and frogs, we are presently exploring a mechanism that could contribute to infantile amnesia in *all* species: retroactive interference with retention by environmental events.

METHODOLOGICAL ISSUES

Unfortunately, many of the demonstrations of infantile amnesia in infrahumans have been both of limited generality and inconclusive. Generality is limited because most of the published studies have used a narrow range of tasks. For example, in an effort to equate motivation across age levels, aversive motivation has been employed almost exclusively, which leaves unanswered questions about amnesia for appetitive situations. Moreover, many demonstrations of infantile amnesia tend to be inconclusive because ontogenetic differences in retention often are not adequately differentiated from inferior initial acquisition by infants relative to adults, claims of comparable original learning notwithstanding.

Certainty of equal acquisition of a learning task across age groups is an unachievable goal that can at best be approximated by subjecting all animals to

225

the same training experience (e.g., equal number of training trials) and by demanding that regardless of amount of training all animals meet some common performance criterion. However, in practice only one or the other of these goals is usually attainable. When this is the case equal performance is the preferred criterion, because learning–performance functions are less apt to be age-dependent than are experience–learning functions, provided an appropriate choice of response measure is made.

A number of investigations of infantile amnesia have attempted to bypass the initial acquisition problem by employing retention ratios in which retention scores are weighted by acquisition scores or by the scores of age-mates tested soon after training (e.g., Kirby, 1963). However, interpretation of such retention scores depends strongly on the particular transformation chosen; ratios, differences, and complex sum—difference ratios can lead to entirely different conclusions if the original raw scores differ appreciably (Lea & Morgan, 1972), as is often the case in developmental comparisons. This presents particular problems when secondary phenomena such as "spontaneous" forgetting, generalization, or extinction are to be compared across age groups.

Even when performances are matched across age groups in an effort to equate initial acquisition, comparisons can be strongly biased by "ceiling" effects. These can arise either from experimenter-imposed time limitations placed on latency scores, as in the case of escape, avoidance, or suppression tasks, or from limits inherent in the dependent variable itself, such as Kamin-type suppression ratios (Annau & Kamin, 1961), or when number of errors in a discrimination task approaches zero. For example, Campbell and Campbell (1962, Experiment 1) trained young and adult rats to avoid a shuttlebox compartment where they had previously experienced equivalent footshock. Acquisition and retention were assessed by 60-minute shock-free position preference tests begun on the shock side. When tested immediately after training, *all* animals avoided the shock compartment for almost the entire hour, thereby permitting a ceiling effect to be mistaken for equal acquisition. The likelihood that such a confound occurred is supported by the observed difference in initial latency to exit from the shock compartment.

In conditioned suppression tasks comparing responses during the conditioned stimulus (CS) to those preceding it, age differences in initial learning can be obscured by the impossibility of achieving a suppression ratio of less than zero, as is the case with a Kamin ratio. Kamin ratios near zero, which necessarily incorporate ceiling effects, can be avoided through the use of long CS presentations during testing provided that the long CS presentations do not yield differential within-test rates of extinction. This appears to be the case at least across age levels in rats (Campbell & Campbell, 1962). Another alternative is to measure latency to emit some small number of responses after CS onset using a liberal time allotment to avoid ceiling problems.

One of the first decisions that a researcher concerned with the ontogeny of memory must make is when to conduct the initial acquisition test. Tests during or immediately following acquisition (e.g., Campbell & Campbell, 1962; Riccio, Rohrbaugh, & Hodges, 1968) seem the obvious choice but are not necessarily desirable and may be quite misleading, particularly for aversively motivated tasks. The short-lived systemic changes in excitability and hormone levels that result from shock or other trauma can differ widely across ages; behavior on an immediate test may reflect changes in these performance variables in addition to associative learning. Thus initial acquisition is best equated at some later time. Unfortunately, transient postacquisition perturbations in information accessibility, such as the Kamin effect (e.g., Klein & Spear, 1969), persist long enough to suggest that the ideal short-interval train-test interval is no less than 24 hours, and diurnal rhythms argue for intervals that are exact multiples of 24 hours.

The dominant role of aversively motivated tasks in this research area is due to two factors: the ease and speed with which such tasks can be mastered, allowing the time of acquisition to be sharply defined, and the difficulty of equating appetitive motivational levels across ages. The traditional operational definition of equal hunger or thirst,—that is, equal hours of food or water deprivation— appears inappropriate because it produces substantially more percentage weight loss and activity increase in young pups than it does in adults (Campbell & Cicala, 1962; Campbell, Teghtsoonian, & Williams, 1961). Even equal percent weight loss is an unsatisfactory criterion for equal motivation across ages because adult weight is relatively stable and pups are growing rapidly. A number of studies employing deprivation (e.g., Frieman, Frieman, Wright, & Hegberg, 1971) have calculated weight loss in pups by comparisons with undeprived age-mates; however, there is no basis for assuming that comparable percentages of weight loss ensures motivational equivalence. In another attempt to minimize age differences in appetitive drive level, Campbell, Jaynes, and Misanin (1968) housed their animals continuously in experimental operant chambers for 5 days of acquisition of a bar-press discrimination. Although prolonged periods of total food deprivation were thus avoided, food receipt was contingent on acquisition of the bar-press response, and the pup groups actually lost weight during the first day of training, whereas adult rats gained. Our own partial solution (Berk, 1977) is to maintain all age groups on ad lib. food and water and to offer them sweetened condensed milk as a reward for the desired response. In truth, rats treated this way are "deprived" of condensed milk between experimental sessions, but the physiological consequences of such deprivation are presumably minimal, especially because our pups are exposed to pellets and water for 3 days prior to weaning at 17 days of age and 2 postweaning days prior to training. Nevertheless, similarity to mother's milk may imbue condensed milk with extra incentive value for recently weaned pups. In a simple appetitively motivated task this could lead to pup performance comparable to adults', albeit with inferior learning, which would introduce a bias in favor of finding infantile "amnesia." Our solution to this problem is to use the *cessation* of an appetitively motivated response as the measure of acquisition, thereby turning the bias *against* the hypothesized infantile memory deficit.

Studies using escape and avoidance tasks to assess age-related retention deficits invariably focus on associations to spatial cues. Unfortunately the changes in visual and tactual perspective undergone by rapidly growing animals over extended retention intervals can attenuate their recognition of the location in which they were trained, causing the test performance of younger subjects to suffer more than that of adults independently of any long-term retention differences. This so-called "generalization decrement" can be avoided by using nonspatial cues such as auditory stimuli in a conditioned suppression paradigm (Coulter, Collier, & Campbell, 1976). But conditioned suppression is not without its own difficulties. It requires a steady baseline behavior—which introduces some of the same problems faced by appetitive tasks. Even when the motivation for the baseline response is equated, as we have tried to do with condensed milk, the baseline task must be one that yields equal response rates in infants and adults. Otherwise the same ambiguities that exist with retention ratios appear. Fortunately the rat comes equipped with a prewired baseline behavior that changes little with age, sex, or religious persuasion. Although perhaps not as invariant as once believed, momentary lick rat in rats remains between 5.5 and 7.0 licks per second over much of their lifetime (Wells & Cone, 1975) and is remarkably constant between animals of comparable age. Lick suppression is additionally useful in developmental studies, because no lengthy shaping is necessary, allowing pups to be tested at younger ages than alternative responses such as bar-pressing would ordinarily permit.

Because conditioned suppression is measured by resistance to extinction, it is a valid measure of acquisition only if on-baseline extinction itself does not differ with age. Campbell and Campbell (1962, Experiment 3) have presented data supporting this assumption. Extinction as conventionally practiced in conditioned suppression tasks is on-baseline; we have evidence indicating that extinction is not equivalent across ages when off-baseline stimulus exposure is given prior to testing.

CONDITIONED LICK SUPPRESSION: RETENTION, EXTINCTION, AND INTERFERENCE

We are currently using a conditioned lick-suppression paradigm with a pure tone CS and a footshock unconditioned stimulus (US) to investigate infantile amnesia. The shock intensity titration studies done by Campbell and his colleagues (Campbell, 1967; Campbell & Teghtsoonian, 1958) allowed us to choose current values equally aversive to pups and adults—about 1.5 mA. for a duration of 2.0 sec. Without any food or water deprivation, our animals are adapted to licking diluted Magnolia Brand of sweetened condensed milk in the test apparatus over the 4 days prior to training, which for pups starts at 15 days of age. Off-baseline CS—US pairings are given in a Plexiglas-walled grid-floored apparatus, and initial testing occurs 24 or 48 hours later in the animal's home cage, inserted into a sound-attenuating chamber. Thus spatial cues are completely irrelevant. Pre-CS lick rates in pups and adults are virtually identical, eliminating any problems of scaling. Suppression is indexed by measuring latency to recover licking after CS onset. A 60-minute test limit ensures that age differences are not obscured by ceiling effects; 50 licks in the presence of the CS are required to indicate extinction.

The pups are weaned and individually caged at 17 days of age, about 4 days earlier than conventional American practice. Weaning 2 days prior to training permits passage of the retention interval in similar familiar surroundings independent of age. The pup and adult housing differ only in that the pups require a warmer environment for survival and are given glass nesting bowls in their cages to block circulating air currents and provide a comfortable sleeping location. By placing food pellets directly in the breeding cage 3 days prior to weaning, we manage to avoid any difference in weight between these prematurely weaned animals and unweaned age-mates at 21 days of age, the time of testing.

Using these techniques, we have successfully trained rat pups and adults to an equal performance criterion. Following the example of Dr. Coulter, we chose a pure-tone CS to avoid growth-induced spatial generalization decrements. Our 2400-Hz CS has been shown to produce adult-like cochlear potentials in pups as young as 16 or 17 days of age (Crowley & Hepp-Reymond, 1966), suggesting that the ears of our 19-day-old weanlings have no problem registering the CS. Nevertheless we have found that this tone 12 dB above background does not produce regular startle responses or adult rapidity of learning in the pups, implying some age-related difference in perception or attention. However, when the tone intensity was increased to 18 to 20 dB above background, learning could easily be equated across age levels. Figure 9.1 shows lick suppression in 21-day-old pups and adults as a function of the number of off-baseline tone—foot-shock pairings received 48 hours earlier. It is apparent that learning rates are not identical, but by 3 trials pups and adults do not differ significantly, $p > 0.20$. Both age levels displayed significant suppression, $ps < .01$, and neither group approached ceiling performance (Ln latency = 8.19 Ln sec). This implies that the parameters used can yield an appropriate point of departure for developmental comparisons of retention, extinction, or generalization. However, in our own investigations of these phenomena we have eliminated the nonsignificant trend toward superior adult acquisition (retention at 48 hours) after 3 pairings in favor of an even smaller nonsignificant bias toward *better* acquisition by the pups, achieved by giving them 3 training trials and the adults only 2.

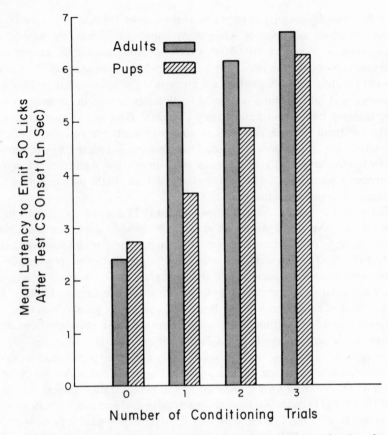

FIG. 9.1. Lick suppression in 21-day-old pups and adults as a function of number of CS–US pairings 48 hours earlier. All $ns = 12$. Groups receiving no training trials were given either 2 (adults) or 3 (pups) explicitly unpaired presentations of the CS and US. Suppression for the full 60-minute test limit would result in a score of 8.19 Ln sec. Uninterrupted licking yields a score of about 2.00 Ln sec.

With 3 training trials for pups and 2 for adults, lick-suppression tests at retention intervals longer than 48 hours reveal a reliable infantile amnesia effect. In a study recently completed, independent groups at each age level were trained and were tested either 2, 8, 16, 32, or 64 days later. The results are shown in Fig. 9.2. Pups displayed significant retention deficits at 8, 16, 32, and 64 days after conditioning compared to others tested 48 hours after conditioning, all $ps < 0.05$. Animals trained as adults failed to forget even after 64 days, $p > 0.10$. ANOVA and subsequent t-tests found pups and adults equivalent in acquisition as defined by the 48-hour test, $p > 0.10$, and to differ from one another at all other retention intervals, all $ps < 0.05$.

Our choice of a 48-hour retention test to define "initial" acquisition is somewhat unusual. We selected this interval in preference to the customary immediate or 24-hour test because we are interested in the effects of interposing CS exposures between conditioning and a test at which pups and adults ordinarily show equal performance. Such exposures in the absence of the to-be-tested baseline behavior could be termed off-baseline extinction treatments, whereas our test procedure itself, which involves recovery of licking after interruption, is conventional on-baseline extinction. In a recent study (Berk & Miller, 1977) designed to explore the effects of off-baseline stimulus exposure, pups and adults were trained and then returned to the training apparatus the next day, where they received either 0, 2, 4, 8, or 12 15-second nonreinforced exposures to the same 2400-Hz CS used in conditioning. The interstimulus interval was 40 minutes. Retention, illustrated in Fig. 9.3, superficially resembled the long-interval retention functions of Fig. 9.2. With increasing nonreinforced postconditioning CS exposures as with increasing time, pups significantly attenuated their suppression, whereas within the limits explored, adults did not. We are presently

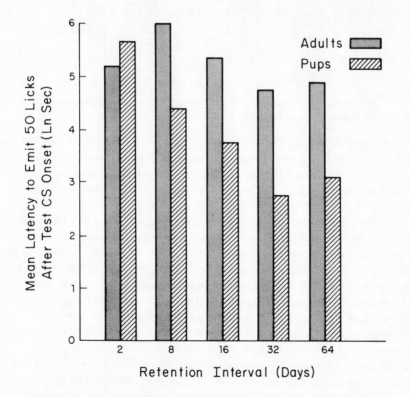

FIG. 9.2.   Long-term retention of fear in pups conditioned at 19 days of age and adults. All $ns = 8$.

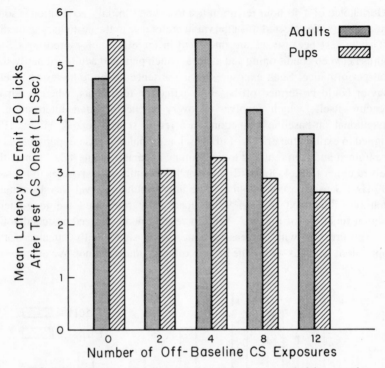

FIG. 9.3.   Lick suppression 48 hours after training by pups and adults exposed to off-baseline, nonreinforced CS presentations during the retention interval.

exploring the possibility that the infants' performance decrement over time and their susceptibility to off-baseline extinction represent a single process. The underlying assumption is that off-baseline extinction is the extreme, specific case of a more general phenomenon: retroactive interference from environmental events.

Our theoretical interest is in the sources of infantile amnesia. The hypothesized origins of juvenile retention deficits are usually classified as those of maturational origin and those deriving from specific experience. Because this division is yet another restatement of the nature−nurture question, it is appropriate to attempt to partition variance between age levels. Indeed, the age-related coding differences alluded to by Dr. Coulter and Dr. Gordon (Chapters 10 and 11, respectively) could be partitioned into maturational, experiential, and interactional components, depending on the factors that precipitate the change in coding.

The first behavioral study emphasizing the importance of maturational factors in producing infantile amnesia was one by Campbell, Misanin, White, and Lytle (1974), which contrasted the presence of juvenile retention deficits in the altricial albino rat with an absence of juvenile deficits in the precocial guinea pig. The authors concluded that the rapid development undergone by rats but not by guinea pigs produced accelerated infantile forgetting. Interesting as this comparison is, it suffers from the many problems of cross-species comparisons, including equating acquisition, motivation, and effective task in addition to the previously discussed problems of ontogenetic comparisons. It is not clear which of the innumerable differences between the two species was responsible for the disparity in infantile amnesia. To properly exploit this approach, guinea pigs must be trained in additional tasks, and other species, precocial and altricial, should be added to the comparison.

Our previously described studies of CER retention in rats found pups to be more susceptible to off-baseline extinction than adults. This is consistent with the suggestion that specific stimulus events during the retention interval contribute to the production of infantile amnesia and is in contrast to the conclusions of Campbell et al. (1974). Despite physically identical retention interval environments for pups and adults, some stimuli can be more detrimental to retention in pups than adults. Possibly this is true because environmental stimuli are more novel to the newcomers and therefore more likely to be attended to and processed. Such processing may interfere with the retention of previously acquired information, perhaps the more so if the interfering information and target information are similar. This last qualification is consistent with the more rapid off-baseline extinction we have observed in pups. Our manipulations during the retention period are off-baseline rather than on-baseline in order to approximate the dissimilarity between the training situation and the retention environment in conventional demonstrations of infantile amnesia. The difficulty in separating this kind of experientially dependent mechanism from purely maturational factors is that stimulus novelty (and therefore, presumably, retroactive interference) decreases with age at a rate that is ordinarily paralleled by a decreasing rate of neurological development.

EFFECTS OF METAMORPHOSIS ON RETENTION

Another of our attempts to categorize the sources of infantile amnesia (Miller & Berk, 1977) took advantage of the unique features of metamorphosis. During metamorphosis the rate of neural maturation is enhanced, but motor activity and interaction with the environment are diminished, so that fewer potentially interfering stimuli are encountered. These relationships are shown in Fig. 9.4. Good retention over metamorphosis relative to retention just before and just after metamorphosis would suggest that maturational changes are relatively unimportant in diminishing memory in young animals. On the other hand, poor retention over metamorphosis compared to retention prior to and following metamorphosis would imply that purely maturational changes are significant in producing infantile amnesia.

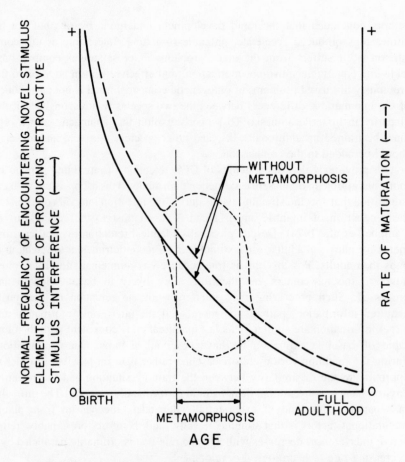

FIG. 9.4. Representation of hypothesized rate of maturation relative to frequency of encountering novel stimulus elements in a typical, unchanging laboratory or field environment. Relative starting points, terminal points, and the exact slopes of the curves are arbitrary; only approximate parallelism is important to make the point that both curves predict infantile amnesia. Because of this, forgetting due to intrinsic maturational changes is difficult to distinguish from forgetting due to retroactive stimulus interference in developmental studies using nonmetamorphosing species (heavy lines). Metamorphosis, which elevates rate of neural maturation and depresses interaction with potential sources of retroactive interference (light dashed lines), or alternatively manipulation of the retention environment (not illustrated) offers potential solutions to this problem.

Although several attempts have been made at studying retention over metamorphosis, only recently have studies been sufficiently well controlled to permit firm conclusions. One of the best is by Alloway (1972), who observed appreciable retention in the mealworm, *Tenebrio*, despite its enormous neurological reorganization over metamorphosis. Unfortunately neither he nor any other investigator included a measure of retention over equal intervals just before and after metamorphosis to provide the necessary basis for comparison. Our own study (Miller & Berk, 1977) included such groups. The subjects were African claw-toed frogs, *Xenopus laevis*, presumably phyletically closer to humans than Alloway's mealworms are but considerably less transformed by metamorphosis than are *Tenebrio*. We chose *Xenopus* because they spend most of their adult life under water, which permitted us to retain the same environmental medium before and after metamorphosis. Our choice might have been different if we had known how lethargic and slow-witted these beasties are.

After two years of seeking a situation in which *Xenopus* tadpoles would show both acquisition and retention, we finally devised the trapezoidal water-filled trough illustrated in Fig. 9.5. Half of its translucent white Plexiglas floor, illuminated from beneath, was covered by black emery cloth that obscured the illumination and provided tactile cues to further differentiate the two halves. The central regions of the two sides, labeled A and B, were defined by removable nylon mesh screens that were ordinarily absent. Stainless steel plates lining the converging walls of the trough served as electrodes to deliver electric shock, pulsed 0.5 second on, 0.5 second off, through the water. Shock density varied inversely with the distance between the plates so that animals at the narrow end

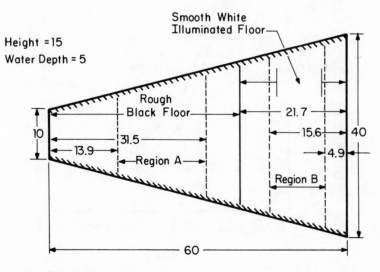

\\\\\\\\ Electrodes

- - - - - Removable Nylon Screens

FIG. 9.5.   Top view of apparatus used in *Xenopus* experiments. Dimensions are in centimeters. The removable nylon screens were the only obstacles to animals' freedom to explore the water-filled part of the apparatus. (From Miller and Berk. Reprinted by permission of the American Psychological Association © 1977.)

of the apparatus received shock 4 times as intense as at the wide end. We chose electric shock because *Xenopus* changes from a filter-feeding larval form to a predatory adult, ruling out the possibility of equating appetitive motivation across developmental stages.

The behavioral task was a position preference motivated by the shock density gradient. Retention of this preference was to be measured over metamorphosis, defined for our purposes as the period between Stage 54, when first indications of fingers and toes appear on limb buds, and Stage 63, when only small size and a vestigial tail externally distinguish the animal from a full-grown adult (Nieuwkoop & Faber, 1967). In our laboratory this transition took about 35 days,

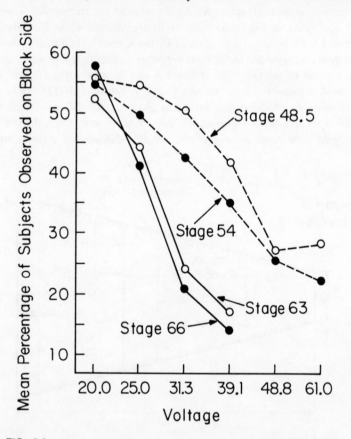

FIG. 9.6. Mean percentage of subjects observed on the black side of the apparatus as a function of applied voltage (log scale) and stage of development in Experiment 2 of the *Xenopus* series. The acquisition session ran for 24 hours with observations every 2 hours starting 2 hours into the session. Each data point represents 6 squads of 6 subjects. Some animals at Stages 63 and 66 tetanized at 48.8 V and 61.0 V; therefore these data are omitted. (From Miller and Berk. Reprinted by permission of the American Psychological Association © 1977.)

thereby determining the length of the retention intervals to be used with larvae and adults. Thus 35 days before Stage 54 our average tadpole was in Stage 48 or 49 (which we will refer to as Stage 48.5), and 35 days after metamorphosis ended at Stage 63, our average animal was in Stage 66. Thus retention before metamorphosis was measured in animals trained at Stage 48.5 and tested at Stage 54, retention during metamorphosis required that animals be trained at Stage 54 and tested at Stage 63, and retention after metamorphosis was measured in animals trained at Stage 63 and tested at Stage 66. Animals differing from these standards by more than 1 stage at the end of their retention interval were discarded. Extra subjects were routinely trained to compensate for these losses, which ran about 15%, as well as for losses caused by death.

The study included five experiments. Experiment 1 determined position preference as a function of age before any shock was imposed. The animals were tested 6 at a time for 24 hours with observations every 2 hours. All subjects were started in the central region of the black side. Tadpoles always had an abundance of powdered nettle-leaf food suspended in the water; the adults had none. This dissimilarity was necessitated by the difference in feeding patterns between larvae and adults. The results of this study indicated a mild but significant preference for the black side that other studies showed not to be the result of starting

TABLE 9.1

Xenopus Experiment 3: 24-Hour Nonreinforced Retention
of Acquisition

		Mean % Observed on Black Side[a]	
Stage	*Voltage*	*Acquisition*[b]	*Retention*
48.5	39.1	40.7*	56.3*
48.5	48.8	27.3*	50.2
48.5	61.0	28.2*	46.8*
54	39.1	35.2	52.1
54	48.8	25.7*	44.7*
54	61.0	22.2*	44.7*
		Metamorphosis	
63	31.3	24.1*	49.3
63	39.1	17.4*	46.8*
66	31.3	20.8*	51.4
66	39.1	14.1*	48.1*

[a]Each condition represents 6 squads of 6 *Xenopus* each.

[b]The acquisition data are from Experiment 2.

*Significantly different from nonshocked age-mates in Experiment 1, $ps < 0.02$. (All other groups failed to differ from Experiment 1 age-mates, ($ps > 0.05$.)

TABLE 9.2
Xenopus Experiment 4: Acquisition and 24-Hour Reacquisition

		Mean % Observed on Black Side[a]	
Stage	*Voltage*	*Acquisition*	*Reacquisition*
48.5	39.1	37.7	22.0
48.5	48.8*	27.6	15.0
48.5	61.0	25.2	13.9
54	39.1	31.9	20.1
54	48.8*	21.8	15.0
54	61.0	17.8	13.0
	Metamorphosis		
63	31.3*	21.3	14.8
63	39.1	19.7	8.3
66	31.3*	19.9	13.7
66	39.1	15.5	7.2

[a]Each condition represents 6 squads of 6 *Xenopus* each. All means differed from nonshocked age-mates in Experiment 1, all $ps < 0.001$. Within groups all reacquisition means differed from acquisition means, all $ps < 0.05$.

*Voltages selected for Experiment 5.

position. More important, there was no difference in preference between age groups.

Experiment 2 varied the applied voltage in order to achieve equal acquisition across ages. Again all subjects were started in groups of 6 in Region A on the black side and were observed every 2 hours for 24 hours. As shown in Fig. 9.6, adults were found to be more sensitive to shock than larvae, although there was considerable overlap between individual thresholds. Within-group variance was large enough that a shock too weak to evince an immediate response in one animal was above the tetanization threshold for another. Based on this fact, further studies were conducted using 24-hour-long training sessions and low shock levels that produced little or no immediate responding.

Based on the acquisition data, we decided to do a further study (Experiment 3) of acquisition, this time with a short-term retention test, using 31.3 V or 39.1 V for adults and 39.1 V, 48.8 V, and 61.0 V for tadpoles. With a 1-day interval between training and nonreinforced testing, we found little significant evidence of retention, as illustrated in Table 9.1. This suggested that with a 35-day retention period we could expect to see virtually no retention even among the adults. Consequently we decided to switch to a relearning test procedure with shock present.

Experiment 4, summarized in Table 9.2, was identical to the preceding study except for the presence of shock during testing. The acquisition data paralleled acquisition in Experiment 3; however, evidence for retention was far more robust. The short-term retention test—that is, relearning after an interval of one day—yielded highly significant retention in all groups. Unfortunately under equal shock conditions neither acquisition nor retention scores could be equated between tadpoles and adults. Because we required equal acquisition in order to study age-related retention differences over long intervals, we thought it best to sacrifice equal shock levels and strive for similar performance in both acquisition and short-term retention testing. Therefore the shock levels selected for the final experiment in this series were 48.8 V for tadpoles and 31.3 V for adults.

To give the reader some idea of the behavior of a typical squad, the performance of the median score squads from Experiment 4 at each of the voltages selected for Experiment 5 are illustrated in Fig. 9.7. It should be noted that nowhere in this series of experiments did we ever differentiate individual animals.

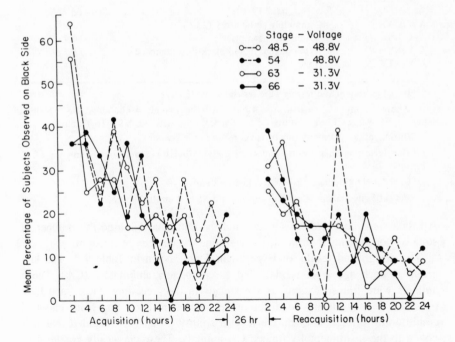

FIG. 9.7.   Mean percentage of subjects on the black side on each bihourly observation in Experiment 4 of the *Xenopus* series. For purposes of legibility only those age level–voltage groups selected for Experiment 5 are represented. Each data point corresponds to the mean of 6 squad means. Each squad contained 6 animals. (From Miller and Berk. Reprinted by permission of the American Psychological Association © 1977.)

TABLE 9.3

Xenopus Experiment 5: Design and Mean Percentage Subjects
Observed on Black Side[a]

Group[b]	Initial Treatment[c]	Test Score[d]
	Stage 48.5 (48.8 V)	Stage 54 (48.8 V)
L-L (CA)	Completely ambulatory (26.1)	19.6
L-L (NS)	Nylon screens in place	20.8
L-L (NS+FR)	Nylon screens in and black floor removed	23.8
L-L (NT)[e]	None	23.7
	Stage 54 (48.8 V)	Stage 63 (31.3 V)
L-A (CA)	Completely ambulatory (24.2)	13.3*
L-A (NS)	Nylon screens in place	17.8
L-A (NS+FR)	Nylon screens in and black floor removed	19.2
L-A (CA+FS)	Completely ambulatory with floor switched (12.8)	31.7*
L-A (NT)[e]	None	22.7
	Stage 63 (31.3 V)	Stage 66 (31.3 V)
A-A (CA)	Completely ambulatory (23.1)	12.2*
A-A (NS)	Nylon screens in place	16.4
A-A (NS+FR)	Nylon screens in and black floor removed	18.1
A-A (NT)[e]	None	20.4

[a]Initial treatment and testing were separated by 35 days.

[b]Abbreviations: L = Larva, A = Adult, CA = Completely Ambulatory, NS = Nylon Screen, FR = Black Floor Removed, FS = Black Floor Switched, NT = To Training.

[c]During initial treatment each squad consisted of 8 *Xenopus*.

[d]During testing all subjects were completely ambulatory; each squad consisted of 6 *Xenopus*.

[e]Data for NT groups are from Experiments 2 and 4.

*$p < 0.05$, two-tailed, relative to appropriate NS+FR control group.

All data were collected by squads, and the data analysis used the number of squads, not individual animals, to determine the degrees of freedom.

The design and results of Experiment 5 are shown in Table 9.3. The key group at each age level is identified as completely ambulatory (CA). These animals were trained exactly as the squads in the preceding studies and then retrained 35 days later. To differentiate instrumental learning from classical conditioning effects, at each age level a control group was included that was yoked to the instrumentally trained CA animals. These classically conditioned animals were placed in Region A on the black side with the nylon screens (NS) in place. They were left there until *more* than half of the subjects in the corresponding CA group were observed on the white side, at which time the NS animals were transferred to Region B and confined there by nylon nets. The sensitization controls, Groups NS+FR, were also yoked to instrumentally trained squads and were treated identicaly to the NS animals except that the black floor was removed from the apparatus, leaving them only a homogeneous white translucent floor. Removal of the floor should have prevented any associations to differential floor cues as a function of shock density. A final group (CA+FS), only present across metamorphosis, was added to assess the value of the floor cues to the instrumentally trained animals. These subjects were trained as the CA groups were but with the black and white halves of the floor switched. During initial treatment all squads contained 8 animals to compensate for any later losses but were tested with only 6 animals each. Squads larger than 6 at the time of testing were culled to 6 by randomly eliminating animals.

The statistical analysis is summarized in Table 9.3. Groups are ordered by the extent of black-side avoidance on the retention test. No retention was evident after 35 days in any of the groups both trained and tested as tadpoles. Looking at the animals that metamorphosed over retention (L-A) and those that metamorphosed prior to initial training (A-A), we see a trend of improving performance going from no initial training (NT, data from Experiments 2 and 4), to the sensitized animals (NS+FR), to the classically conditioned animals (NS), to the instrumentally trained animals (CA). However, *over* metamorphosis, only the instrumentally trained animals differed significantly from the naive animals. The animals tested with the floor switched (CA+FS) performed worst of all, suggesting the importance of the floor cues to the CA groups. Most critical, the difference between age levels in savings due to instrumental learning relative to controls was significant. When the animals trained and tested as larvae were compared to animals trained and tested as adults or to animals trained as larvae and tested as adults, they were found to have performed significantly worse. However, these latter two groups did not differ among themselves.

The results suggest that at least in *Xenopus* the maturational processes undergone during metamorphosis are not important determinants of amnesia. Whether or not this conclusion can be generalized to mammals is a matter for further research. One way to investigate this is by systematically manipulating the level of potentially interfering stimuli in the retention interval environment of young and adult animals. If immature rats, for example, show more amnesia for a tone – footshock pairing under high stimulation conditions than adults do but show equal forgetting when retention interval stimulation is low, environmentally induced retroactive interference will be implicated as a significant factor in infantile amnesia. Such a result is suggested by our observation of rapid off-baseline extinction in weanling rats relative to adults and would be entirely consistent with the outcome of our experiments with *Xenopus*.

SUMMARY

The study of developmental differences in retention by animals ideally requires that initial acquisition be equated across ages under conditions of comparable motivation. Difficulty in matching motivational levels in appetitive tasks has caused most researchers to use escape, avoidance, or conditioned suppression paradigms, tasks that are particularly prone to ceiling effects obscuring developmental differences in initial acquisition. A conditioned lick-suppression task is described that minimizes this problem and is currently being used in our laboratory to probe the sources of infantile amnesia, with specific attention to distinguishing endogenous maturational factors from environmentally induced interference factors. Equating acquisition, we have found more rapid off-baseline extinction in rat pups than adults, a result that speaks for the importance of environmental sources of infantile amnesia. Work recently completed using the African claw-toed frog, *Xenopus laevis*, aimed at the same problem by investigating retention of a learned position preference across metamorphosis, which is a time of low environmental stimulation and rapid neural reorganization. Retention by metamorphosing animals equaled that of adults over an identical time interval, whereas memory in tadpoles was inferior to both. The results indicate that maturational processes are not important determinants of infantile amnesia in *Xenopus* relative to experiential factors. Collectively these studies suggest, at least in some situations, that specific experiential factors can account for an appreciable part of the retention difference between young and adult animals. Further research is necessary to fully appraise these factors. Moreover, separating maturational from experiential sources of age-dependent differences in forgetting is only a first step toward understanding infantile amnesia. The specific nature of the contributing maturational and experiential factors will still have to be identified.

ACKNOWLEDGMENT

This research was supported by National Science Foundation Grant BMS75-03383 and a grant from the CUNY Faculty Research Award Program. Ralph R. Miller was supported by Research Scientist Development Award K2-MH00061. Michael Vigorito assisted with the data collection. Nancy Marlin, John Sullivan, and Michael Vigorito were kind enough to give a critical reading to a preliminary version of this chapter. Thanks are due Joan Wessely for her help in preparing the manuscript.

REFERENCES

Alloway, T. M. Retention of learning through metamorphosis in the grain beetle (*Tenebrio molitor*). *American Zoologist*, 1972, *12*, 471–477.
Annau, Z., & Kamin, L. J. The conditioned emotional response as a function of the intensity of the US. *Journal of Comparative and Physiological Psychology*, 1961, *54*, 428–432.

Berk, A. M. Developmental deficits in acquisition of the CER: Implications for studies of infantile amnesia. Paper presented at the meeting of the Eastern Psychological Association, Boston, April 1977.

Berk, A. M., & Miller, R. R. *A developmental comparison of CER extinction in the rat.* Paper presented at the meeting of the Psychonomic Society, Washington, D.C., November 1977.

Campbell, B. A. Developmental studies of learning and motivation in infra-primate mammals. In H. W. Stevenson, E. H. Hess, & H. L. Rheingold (Eds.), *Early behavior: Comparative and developmental approaches.* New York: Wiley, 1967.

Campbell, B. A., & Campbell, E. H. Retention and extinction of learned fear in infant and adult rats. *Journal of Comparative and Physiological Psychology,* 1962, *55,* 1–8.

Campbell, B. A., & Cicala, G. A. Studies of water deprivation in rats as a function of age. *Journal of Comparative and Physiological Psychology,* 1962, *55,* 763–768.

Campbell, B. A., Jaynes, J., & Misanin, J. R. Retention of a light–dark discrimination in rats of different ages. *Journal of Comparative and Physiological Psychology,* 1968, *66,* 467–472.

Campbell, B. A., Misanin, J. R., White, B. C., & Lytle, L. D. Species differences in ontogeny of memory: Support for neural maturation as a determinant of forgetting. *Journal of Comparative and Physiological Psychology,* 1974, *87,* 193–202.

Campbell, B. A., & Teghtsoonian, R. Electrical and behavioral effects of different types of shock stimuli on the rat. *Journal of Comparative and Physiological Psychology,* 1958, *51,* 185–192.

Campbell, B. A., Teghtsoonian, R., & Williams, R. A. Activity, weight loss, and survival time of food-deprived rats as a function of age. *Journal of Comparative and Physiological Psychology,* 1961, *54,* 216–219.

Coulter, X., Collier, A. C., & Campbell, B. A. Long-term retention of early Pavlovian fear conditioning in infant rats. *Journal of Experimental Psychology: Animal Behavior Processes,* 1976, *2,* 48–56.

Crowley, D. E. & Hepp-Reymond, M. Development of cochlear function in the ear of the infant rat. *Journal of Comparative and Physiological Psychology,* 1966, *62,* 427–432.

Frieman, J. P., Frieman, J., Wright, W., & Hegberg, W. Developmental trends in the acquisition and extinction of conditioned suppression in rats. *Developmental Psychology,* 1971, *4,* 425–428.

Kirby, R. H. Acquisition, extinction, and retention of an avoidance response in rats as a function of age. *Journal of Comparative and Physiological Psychology,* 1963, *56,* 158–162.

Klein, S. B., & Spear, N. E. Influence of age on short-term retention of active-avoidance learning in rats. *Journal of Comparative and Physiological Psychology,* 1969, *69,* 583–589.

Lea, S. E. G., & Morgan, M. J. The measurement of rate-dependent changes in responding. In J. R. Millenson & R. M. Gilbert (Eds.), *Reinforcement: Behavioral analyses.* New York: Academic Press, 1972.

Miller, R. R., & Berk, A. M. Retention over metamorphosis in the African claw-toed frog. *Journal of Experimental Psychology: Animal Behavior Processes,* 1977, *3,* 343–356.

Nieuwkoop, P. D., & Faber, J. (Eds.). *Normal table of Xenopus laevis (Daudin)* (2nd ed.). Amsterdam: North-Holland, 1967.

Riccio, D. C., Rohrbaugh, M., & Hodges, L. A. Developmental aspects of passive and active avoidance learning in rats. *Developmental Psychobiology,* 1968, *1,* 108–111.

Wells, R. N., & Cone, A. L. Changes in the burst lick rate of albino rats as functions of age, sex, and drinking experience. *Bulletin of the Psychonomic Society,* 1975, *6,* 605–607.

10 The Determinants of Infantile Amnesia

Xenia Coulter
State University of New York at Stony Brook

PROBLEMS IN THE EMPIRICAL STUDY OF INFANTILE AMNESIA

There is a considerable body of evidence suggesting that infantile amnesia is not restricted to man but can be observed in a number of species (for recent reviews, see Campbell & Coulter, 1976; Campbell, Riccio, & Rohrbaugh, 1971; Campbell & Spear, 1972). It is not known whether or not the mechanism(s) that underly this inability to remember early events is the same in all species. It is not even clear if this apparently similar deficit is really the same phenomenon. For example, humans seem to have complete amnesia for events occurring before 3 to 4 years of age with adult-like memory abilities for events occurring very shortly thereafter (Waldfogel, 1948). In contrast, rats (as well as dogs and monkeys) show, over relatively long periods of development, only slow and gradual improvements in long-term retention (Campbell & Campbell, 1962). However, this difference could be explained by differences in the way these memory effects have been measured: Human data are all largely unverified anecdotal recollections, unlike the infrahuman data, which consist of retests or of some kind of controlled recognition tests. Thus many researchers, including myself, feel justified in accepting the working hypothesis that infantile amnesia is a general enough phenomenon that it can be fruitfully studied in a nonhuman species such as the rat.

It is easy to see why such a stance is almost a necessity. Few researchers can afford the enormous commitment in time, money, and personnel required for longitudinal human studies over the time span presumably necessary for establishing infantile forgetting. These difficulties are compounded by the special problems attendant upon working with infants and preschool children. What kinds of nontrivial yet noncontroversial experiences can these subjects be exposed to that we can be certain will not be experienced again as uncontrolled reminders (or as interference) during the long retention interval? With the rat most of these difficulties simply do not arise. Even the problem of time is greatly reduced, because roughly analogous periods of development last only for weeks in the rat rather than for years, as required for human maturation.

Even though the study of infantile amnesia may be more feasible if infrahuman subjects are used, it is still not particularly easy (see in particular Chapter 9). Despite many years of studying this problem in the rat alone, we do not yet know why early experiences are forgotten, in part because it was necessary first to collect a great deal of data simply to establish the generality of the effect. Merely to demonstrate and assess the extent of infantile amnesia requires, ideally, a minimum of eight experimental groups. For the age (i.e., "infantile") factor, at least two groups at different stages of development (e.g., infants and adults) must be exposed to some kind of experience, usually a task that can be easily learned by both groups. To measure the memory (i.e., "amnesia") factor, separate groups from each age must then be tested at at least two different times after learning, immediately afterward and again after an appropriate retention interval. Because it is the retention of learning that is nearly always of interest, not just the nonspecific effects of early experience, nonlearning control groups for each age and at every retention interval should also be included. If more than the minimum values of the basic factors is desired (as is often the case), the number of groups begins to multiply rapidly. If still more factors are included in the design, a necessary step if we wish to do more than demonstrate the phenomenon, the "ideal" experiment ends up being much too cumbersome, not only to execute but also to interpret. Thus it is not very surprising that data have accumulated slowly and that they are as yet too limited to provide us with a definitive account of why early experiences are so readily forgotten.

THEORETICAL AND EMPIRICAL BACKGROUND

Given the insufficiencies of existing data, we must acknowledge the possible validity of most of the many theories that have been put forth to explain early memory deficits. One exception to this rule is, ironically enough, the original explanation of infantile amnesia as presented by Freud. His account, which views the amnesia as the result of active repression by adults of the memory of sexual conflicts in infancy, is not seriously considered by most researchers because it was clearly intended as relevant only to human experiences (for an exception see Stein & Berger, 1969). However, most other theories, regardless of whether they were developed out of a consideration of human or infrahuman evidence, have been or can be formulated so as to be reasonably applicable to all living organisms. In reviewing these theories it will be useful to adhere to the dichotomy that originated with Campbell and his associates (e.g., Campbell & Spear, 1972; Campbell, Riccio, & Rohrbaugh, 1971), not just as an organizational device but because in the research to be described shortly this dichotomy was given serious empirical consideration. In any case these writers noted that the study of infantile amnesia could be approached from one or the other of two different perspectives. From a behavioral point of view, explanatory emphasis is centered upon theories, in large part extensions of S−R (stimulus−response) theory, that define and analyze forgetting processes at a behavioral level. In nearly all these theories early memory deficits are postulated to arise from processes already identified in the adult but thought to be exaggerated for the infant by the number, novelty, and other aspects of experiences intimately tied to development. In contrast, a neurological approach to the problem of infantile forgetting centers upon organismic determinants, namely, the central nervous system. Theories derived from this vantage point view infantile amnesia as the result of a process unique to the developing organism, an inevitable outcome of the neurologically immature state of the organism at the time of the experience that is later forgotten.

Behavioral Theories

Interference effects.   Of all the behavioral theories, perhaps the best known is interference theory, which states that memory deficits arise when various other events and experiences in some way interfere with the particular event to be recalled. Proactive interference, studied extensively by Underwood (1957), is said to occur when events prior to the target experience interfere with subsequent recall. In contrast, retroactive interference occurs when it is the events that follow a target experience that interfere with recall. Because the younger the organism the fewer the absolute number of prior events, a simple version of proactive interference theory does predict what is contrary to fact—namely, that memory capacity should improve with decreasing age (see, for example, Underwood, 1957). By the same logic one can see that the younger the organism the larger the number of subsequent events that must occur before adulthood; hence there is an increasing opportunity for retroactive interference. Thus in contrast to the proactive case, a simple version of retroactive interference theory predicts exactly what we are trying to explain, a decrease in memory capacity with decreasing age. For that reason at this point we consider further only the retroactive interference account, even though it is possible and in some ways desirable to qualify both of these theories so that each appears equally viable (see in particular Campbell & Spear, 1972).

Although in its apparent simplicity it is theoretically appealing, retroactive interference, has in fact only limited direct empirical support. No data have been reported showing that organisms deprived of normal learning experiences during development (e.g., Harlow, Harlow, & Suomi, 1971; Sackett, 1970) are better able to recall infantile experiences than organisms not so deprived. On the other hand Parsons and Spear (1972), approaching the problem from the opposite direction, have reported that with a greater number of learning experiences (i.e., with an enriched environment) during development, retention of early learning by rats is poorer than without such experiences. However, they also found a comparable impairment in retention by adult rats exposed to a similar environment. Thus these results show only that young rats are susceptible to retroactive interference but not that the basic deficit is in itself due to such interference.

Although direct support for a theory of retroactive interference is minimal, there is other evidence that provides at least inferential support for the theory. If retroactive interference is a primary source of infantile amnesia, one would expect that the longer the interval between the target event and the retention test, the greater the opportunity for interference and therefore the greater the likelihood of forgetting. In those studies that have tested for retention over increasingly longer intervals (e.g., Campbell & Campbell, 1962), this result is precisely what has been obtained (see also Fig. 10.1). Another result predicted by a retroactive interference theory is that events occurring just prior to periods of great change in development will be more poorly retained than if the retention interval spans a less active time in the life of the organism. Certain data have been described that support this expectation. Fox (1971), for example, reports that puppies trained at the onset of a "period of socialization" (i.e., at 6 weeks of age) later show no memory of the early training, whereas puppies trained at the end of the socialization period (i.e., at 12 weeks of age) show no such retention deficits after a comparable period of time. If one were willing to grant that the period during which children develop language is also a period of great opportunity for interference, it is clear that a theory of retroactive interference is also able to account for the very early memory deficits seen in man.

The problem with a theory of retroactive interference is that it does not in itself predict that interference might be differentially effective. There is no a priori reason to expect language development, for example, to interfere more with retention than the development and/or learning of other skills. Taken at face value a retroactive interference theory suggests that although memory for events occurring late in development will be better than for events occurring earlier, memory should on balance be poorer for events occurring any time during development other than during adulthood. With humans, although memory for very early events seems to be nonexistent, there is very little evidence that major or even minor deficits exist for events occurring after 5 or 6 years of age, even though they are followed by important developmental changes. Even with the rat, retention deficits have been reported only for experiences occurring prior to 30 days of age, despite the fact that sexual development, which represents a major period of change, occurs several weeks later. Once it becomes necessary to specify why certain developmental events but not others may retroactively interfere with retention, the theory no longer appears to be sufficient in itself to account for infantile amnesia.

Size change effects.   A behavioral theory of a somewhat different nature has a similar problem in accounting for the selectivity of early memory deficits. Originally expounded by Perkins (1965), who described his hypothesis as a special case of "stimulus generalization decrements," this theory can be more generally regarded as one that attributes age-related retention failures to increases in the organism's size during the retention interval. By this account organisms fail to perform appropriately when tested for retention because they either fail to recognize the relevant cues owing to a change in perspective, because they are much larger than when they were originally trained, or because the method of responding learned as an infant is no longer appropriate to a much larger organism. As with the theory of retroactive interference, this account predicts that retention deficits will be seen as long as the organism is growing (i.e., throughout development). Furthermore, the amount of deficit is thought to be proportional to the amount of growth. Thus a size-change theory cannot explain any better than the interference theory why a child of 10, even though he may have grown considerably since he was 5, can still recall events from 5 years before with seeming ease, whereas a child of 5 has no recollection of events

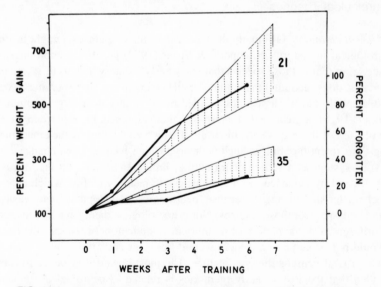

FIG. 10.1.   Percent increase in weight by male (upper line of shaded areas) and female (lower line) rats after 1 to 7 weeks relative to their original weight at 21 days of age or at 35 days of age. (From Sprague-Dawley weight chart prepared by Charles River.) Also, percent forgotten of a spatial-avoidance task 1, 3, and 6 weeks later by rats trained originally at 21 or 35 days of age. (From Campbell and Campbell, 1962.)

occurring less than 2 years before, despite the fact that the amount of growth is considerably less. On the other hand a size-change theory is not incompatible with much of the evidence arising from studies with infrahuman species. As can be seen in Fig. 10.1, the gradual loss of memory seen in the rat does correlate remarkably well with increases in the size of the rat during development. In addition, it is noteworthy that many studies of infant rats, including the one represented in Fig. 10.1, have required the organism to learn and then later recognize spatial (i.e., apparatus) cues that might be particularly susceptible to perceptual changes by increased size. Several investigators have attempted to eliminate this possibility by increasing the size of the apparatus during the retention test (Feigley & Spear, 1970; Thompson, Koenigsberg, & Tennison, 1965). Although this procedure has not been shown to reduce the retention deficits (thus suggesting that size change may not be important), these investigators have also noted that changes in apparatus size produce retention deficits in themselves, as indicated by the performance of various control groups. Thus it seems clear that a size-change hypothesis cannot be easily ruled out as an explanation of many of the laboratory demonstrations of infantile amnesia even though it seemingly cannot account for the pattern of forgetting that apparently exists in man.

Neurological Theories

Neural change.   Originally the theory that infantile amnesia might be due to neurological immaturity (Campbell & Spear, 1972) was based upon the simple observation that in those species that show early memory deficits (e.g., humans, monkeys, dogs, and rats) the infants are all born with immature nervous systems. As Campbell and his associates pointed out then and later (e.g., Campbell & Coulter, 1976), a great deal of neurological development takes place in the early life of each of these species, any or all of which could underly the emergence of long-term retention ability. Such a theory, which focuses upon changes in the nervous system as a source of forgetting, unlike environmental theories is not embarrassed by evidence of abrupt changes in memory ability, which appear to be characteristic of man, because neurological development can easily be postulated to mirror those changes. Nor is neurological theory at a loss to account for differences in the pattern of memory development between species, because it would not be surprising if there were differences among species in the rate at which critical neural structures mature. The most powerful evidence to support the idea that the loss of early memories is related to neurological immaturity comes from a study (Campbell, Misanin, White, & Lytle, 1974) in which it was shown that guinea pigs, animals that are born with a mature nervous system, in contrast to rats do not have any difficulty in remembering early experiences, even those occurring as early as 3 to 4 days of age.

In describing this theory, Campbell and Spear (1972) suggest at least two different mechanisms by which changes in the nervous system could produce a deficit in retention. In one account they suggest that structures that normally mediate long-term memory may simply not be functioning at the time of the early experience. As a result memories of that experience are not consolidated or stored and are no longer available at the time of recall. In an alternative account they suggest that structures that continue to develop after the initial experience, such as the cortex, may during the course of development come to inhibit the functioning of whatever structure mediates the memory of the original experience. In this case, although memory might be available at the time of recall, it would be essentially inaccessible. The distinction between memories that are "unavailable" and those that are "inaccessible" (e.g., Tulving & Pearlstone, 1966) is one that is quite current in recent investigations of human adult memory. In these investigations the procedure used to distinguish between these two processes is to present the subject with a reminder (i.e., some fractional part of the target experience) some time after that experience. If, with a reminder, memory is restored, it is assumed that the forgetting observed in the absence of such reminders must be due to a failure in retrieval rather than a failure in storage (see Spear, 1973, for application of these concepts to animal memory). There is some evidence in studies of infantile amnesia that brief reminders during the retention interval, which in themselves have no noticeable effect, are nonetheless frequently sufficient to "reinstate" those early memories that would otherwise be forgotten (Campbell & Jaynes, 1966). Thus on logical grounds it would seem that of the two neurological processes suggested by Campbell and his associates, the inhibition account may be the more likely. On empirical grounds, although there is no direct neurological evidence bearing on these two accounts, clinical reports indicate that reflexes seen only in infancy occasionally do reappear in aged (senile) patients suffering from cortical damage, which suggests that the disappearance of early behaviors and/or memories could be due to some kind of inhibitory process.

Change in learning. The two neurological theories just described, in common with the behavioral theories, assume that infantile amnesia, as the name implies, is a forgetting phenomenon that results from processes (or the absence of processes) that occur *after* the initial experience. However, it is reasonable to consider the possibility that what we call a memory deficit could in fact be the result of processes (or their absence) that occur *during* the original experience itself. Indeed, many casual observers (e.g., Rousseau, as quoted in Kessen, 1965, p. 83; Miller & Buckhout, 1973, p. 208) view infantile amnesia solely as evidence for deficiencies in the encoding of early experiences that reveal themselves only indirectly by affecting the storage or retrieval of those experiences. By this view infantile amnesia is defined primarily as a learning, not a forgetting, phenomenon. Although an account of infantile forgetting in terms of deficient processing is not typically discussed at a neurological level, it is a reasonable (although not essential) assumption that if such a deficiency exists, it stems from the immature neurological state of the infant. On this basis it seems appropriate to consider the learning-deficiency hypothesis as another example of a neurological theory, even though the central nervous system is not usually invoked.

It seems obvious that anything an organism fails to learn, it will certainly not remember. To the extent that infants are considered incapable of learning, infantile amnesia would then be a foregone conclusion. Nonetheless there are several lines of evidence that indicate that the matter cannot be so simply resolved. In the first place there is considerable evidence that neural tissue is inherently plastic (e.g., Von Baumgarten, 1967). Given that learning can be demonstrated in simple organisms (Eisenstein, 1967) and even in single cells (Kandel, 1967), it stands to reason that regardless of maturational level, any living organism should show a certain amount of plasticity. Secondly, as researchers have become more skilled at designing tasks that accommodate to the sensorimotor capacities of immature organisms, they have been increasingly successful in demonstrating that learning can take place even in the neonate (e.g., Lipsitt, 1971). Finally, even if it were the case that very young infants are unable to learn, infantile amnesia has been reported for experiences that have taken place much later than during the neonatal period, at an age (i.e., up to 3 years in man, 30 days in the rat, 12 weeks in the puppy) where there is really no question about the ability to learn.

The issue then is not really whether or not the infant has learned, but if it has learned in sufficient quantity to retain the experience. Ever since Ebbinghaus, it has been known that retention is a direct function of amount of learning. If, for example, infants learn less rapidly than adults, then with an equivalent amount of exposure to some experience they may subsequently show forgetting relative to adults simply because they have learned less. As it happens, many developmental studies of memory have assessed learning and retention in relation to performance only after a fixed number of learning trials (e.g., Campbell & Campbell, 1962). Although both young and adult subjects were reported to perform similarly immediately afterward, it is possible that during the unmeasured period of acquisition the adults attained asymptote sooner and thus, at the end, were overtrained relative to the younger subjects. However, this procedure has not been used in all infantile amnesia studies. In many other experiments, subjects have been exposed to as many trials as were necessary to attain some particular performance criterion. In those cases overlearning presumably could not occur, because the investigator observed the actual course of learning and terminated it at the appropriate time. Most investigators using this procedure have reported no differences in the rate at which young and adult subjects attain asymptote (e.g., Crockett & Nobel, 1963; Frieman, Frieman, Wright, & Hegberg, 1971; Green, 1962; Smith, 1968). Although in some instances younger subjects were observed to learn more slowly (e.g., Feigley & Spear, 1970) and in at least one case more rapidly than adults (Fox, 1971), the important point is that no matter how long it reportedly took them to attain peak performance, the youngest subjects always forgot most. Such inconsistencies in the relationship between learning rate and forgetting suggest that differences in rate of learning or in amount learned are, if not irrelevant, at least insufficient to account for the ubiquitous retention failures of immature animals.

On the other hand differences in quality of learning, as opposed to quantity, may be better able to account for those failures. It is probable that immature organisms, regardless of efficiency, learn by strategies that are different in kind from those used by adults. Within the same situation they may be predisposed to attend to different stimuli, develop different response patterns, or acquire different associations than do adults, all of which may be equally successful for attaining asymptotic performance in the immediate situation but prove to be inappropriate, inadequate, or even disruptive after a delay. As an illustration of an inappropriate strategy, suppose that young animals confronted with a spatial-avoidance task, unlike adults, are predisposed to associate footshock with the odor of the aversive compartment rather than its appearance (in particular, color, the stimulus of importance to the investigator). After a delay, forgetting—that is, a failure to avoid the appropriate compartment—would result simply because the odor cues are no longer present. An inadequate strategy might occur in a classical conditioning situation where, for the infant, apparatus cues may be as salient as the conditioned stimulus (CS) and relatively more important as a signal for the unconditioned stimulus (US) than for an adult. Over a delay period, apparatus cues may be equally susceptible to forgetting for both age groups, but if they were more important to the younger subjects, forgetting would obviously be greater for them as well. Another possibility is that developmentally induced changes in strategy may in themselves disrupt retention performance. Having learned a task by one strategy, subjects whose predispositions have changed during the retention interval not only may know nothing about the task in adult terms, but their adult-like predispositions may now interfere with their ability to recover their original infantile strategy.

However reasonable the possibility that developmental changes in learning strategy underly infantile forgetting, there is no direct evidence to support it. With humans, there are considerable data relating to the nature of changes in learning with development (from Piaget) but none that relates to the effect of these changes upon long-term retention. As mentioned earlier, such research requires not only observations made over intervals of years but also controls over extraexperimental experiences that are very difficult to achieve, especially with children. With infrahumans, ethologists (Lehrman, 1970) have influenced the study of development so that researchers now seek to characterize different ages as different in kind rather than as deficient relative to adult standards (see Kessen, 1965). But how these differences might relate to traditional learning tasks, to say nothing of the retention of these tasks, is simply unknown.

Infantile amnesia as a learning rather than a forgetting phenomenon, although a theoretically interesting possibility, has not been vigorously pursued at an empirical level. In part this may be because researchers have interpreted such a hypothesis to mean that infants suffer from learning *deficiencies*. With that meaning the hypothesis has been essentially rejected, because even though young animals do occasionally find certain tasks harder to learn than do adults (e.g., passive avoidance, delayed response, complex visual discriminations, etc.; see Campbell & Coulter, 1976), these have not been the tasks used to establish the generality of early memory deficits. If, however, infantile amnesia is a result of age-related learning *differences*, the hypothesis remains essentially untested. As such, it is one more viable explanation of infantile amnesia that needs to be taken into account as we seek out concrete evidence to bear upon the question of why early experiences are forgotten.

RECENT INVESTIGATIONS

General considerations

Rationale.   Of all the theories just described, the neurological hypotheses, especially those relating to neural change, were of particular interest to me and my colleagues at Princeton and later in Stony Brook. Intrinsic to these theories is the assumption that the forgetting of early experiences is not due to processes seen in the adult. The implication is that if these theories are true our understanding of memory, based almost entirely upon research with adults, must be incomplete. Another implication that arises from these theories is that if they are true the emergence of long-term memory should correlate with the maturation of certain structures in the central nervous system so that it should ultimately be possible, by studying infant memory, to specify the biological substrates of long-term memory in general. Given these possibilities, however remote, it seemed to us that a primary goal of any further research in this area should be to assess the extent to which neurological factors are truly responsible for infantile forgetting.

One way of measuring the importance of neurological factors is to determine how much is forgotten of an early experience for which the importance of behavioral factors is minimal. Specifically this would require an assessment of memory for a learning task that is unlikely to be affected by interference or by increases in size during the retention interval. A situation that seemed to us to meet these criteria was the "off-baseline" Pavlovian fear conditioning procedure. In this situation subjects are first exposed in one setting to a number of tone presentations that signal shock. Then the subjects are tested in an entirely different setting, either immediately after the conditioning experience or after a relatively long delay period, by being exposed to tone alone while engaged in some ongoing behavior. The usual behavioral outcome, tone-elicited suppression of the ongoing behavior, which apparently stems from a predisposition of animals to freeze when confronted with a fear-arousing stimulus, is extremely robust (Davis, 1969; Lyons, 1968). As such it appears to be particularly well insulated against the effects of extraexperimental responding that might otherwise interfere with less primitive behaviors. Similarly, size change was not expected to have much of an effect upon the ease of executing such a simple response (i.e., nonresponding). In our analysis of the stimulus situation we did not expect an auditory stimulus such as tone or a pain-inducing stimulus such as footshock to be subject to interference from extraexperimental stimulus events in the rat colony. Nor did it seem likely that the perception of these particular stimuli would be altered by changes in subject size. The perception of stimuli that were likely to be affected by increased size, specifically spatial cues such as those represented by the apparatus, were eliminated from consideration by testing the subjects in a setting other than the one in which they were originally conditioned.

Basic procedures.   Subjects were all Sprague–Dawley rats, born in local institutional colonies and raised with their mothers in litters of 8 (culled at 3 days of age). Unless it was not feasible, each pup of a given litter was randomly assigned to a different experimental group, until each contained, in some cases 8 but usually 10 subjects in all. Conditioning took place for each pup individually in a small, dark chamber where the pup was exposed, usually during 3 hourly sessions, to 3 or 4 presentations per session of a 2-minute, 80-db., 1600-Hz tone (in later studies, white noise) that coterminated with 0.75-second, 2-mA scrambled footshock. These stimulus pairings occurred on a variable time schedule that was changed for each session. With the "random" control procedure, tone (or white noise) was presented on the same variable time schedule as in conditioning. Shock, however, was presented on an independent although similarly spaced schedule, such that out of 9 trials, shock occurred at least once in conjunction with the presentation of tone or white noise. The "unpaired" control procedure was the same as the random procedure except that no shocks were programed to occur within 3 minutes of the auditory stimulus.

Acquisition and retention of conditioning were assessed by measuring the extent to which tone or noise (without shock) disrupted rates of bar-pressing by each subject in a standard operant chamber. Thus all animals, at some point during the experiment, had to be trained to bar-press. If animals were to be tested only after a delay, bar-press training took place several weeks after conditioning and consisted of 1 hourly session of training to press a bar for 45-mg (P. J. Noyes) pellets on a continuous reinforcement schedule and 5 additional 1½-hour sessions of training on a variable interval (VI) 90-second schedule. If the experiment required an immediate assessment of learning as well as a retention test, then all animals, after being weaned at 16 days of age, were trained to bar-press for 20-mg pellets in twice daily 1½-hour sessions with gradually increasing VI schedules up to VI 90 from 16 to 21 days old. All animals received supplementary food such that their weight was maintained at approximately 75% of what their weight would have been if they were given ad lib. access to food (as determined by observing weight changes in free-feeding control animals).

The principal measure of bar-press disruption was a ratio, $A/(A+B)$, calculated for each subject for each test trial, where A equals the number of bar presses made during the 2-minute tone or noise stimulus and B equals the number of bar presses made during the 2-minute period that immediately preceded the onset of that stimulus. Thus a score of .00 indicates that bar-pressing was totally suppressed by the stimulus and that conditioning and/or retention was excellent, whereas 0.50 indicates that bar-pressing was unaffected by the stimulus and that conditioning and/or retention was poor or nonexistent. In some instances we also calculated suppression ratios for each 30-second segment of the stimulus and recorded for each subject latency to resume bar-pressing with each tone or noise termination.

The original demonstration

With this off-baseline conditioning procedure, one that we felt would reduce or eliminate major behavioral sources of forgetting, we conducted our first studies (Coulter, Collier, & Campbell, 1976). Subjects were 20- to 22-day-old pups, which other researchers had shown rapidly forget spatial avoidance (Campbell & Campbell, 1962), passive avoidance (Feigley & Spear, 1970), active avoidance (Kirby, 1963), escape (Smith, 1968), and discriminated bar-press training (Campbell et al., 1968). Our subjects were all exposed to 12 tone−shock pairings over the 3-day conditioning period and then tested for bar-press suppression either 1 day or 42 days after conditioning. What we found was that the presentation of tone elicited almost total suppression of bar-pressing as much 42 days after conditioning as only 1 day later. In other words in contrast to what had been reported for other tasks, these animals experienced no difficulty in remembering early fear conditioning. To eliminate the possibility that these rats responded to tone because of some nonassociative factor such as early sensitization, a second study (see also Coulter et al., 1976) was conducted that measured the long-term retention of rats that experienced at 20 to 22 days of age either tone−shock pairings or unpaired tones and shocks. Once again the conditioned animals showed strong evidence of memory, whereas there was no evidence of bar-press suppression in the unpaired group, suggesting that nonassociative factors did not contribute significantly to the excellent retention exhibited by the conditioned animals. It was difficult not to conclude that if by eliminating behavioral factors infantile forgetting is also eliminated, then all the forgetting hitherto reported for rats of this age must have been due largely to behavioral factors.[1] In other words

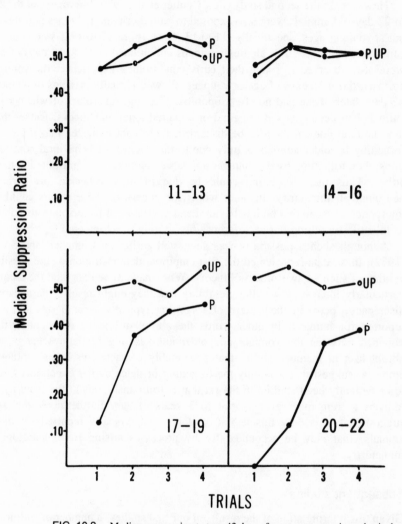

FIG. 10.2.   Median suppression to tone 42 days after rat pups experienced paired (P) or unpaired (UP) tones and shocks when 11 to 13, 14 to 16, 17 to 19, or 20 to 22 days of age. (From Coulter et al., 1976.) Suppression, as shown in this and all other figures, was assessed by comparing bar-press rates during the 2-minute stimulus to bar-press rates both during and before the stimulus. Thus, 0.00 represents total suppression (i.e., no bar-pressing during the stimulus) and 0.50 represents no suppression (i.e., no change in bar-pressing during the stimulus).

these results suggested that the contribution of neurological immaturity to infantile amnesia may be relatively unimportant.

However, in the second study (i.e., Coulter et al., 1976) littermates of the 20- to 22-day-old animals were also exposed to paired or unpaired tones and shocks but at younger ages, specifically, 11 to 13, 14 to 16, or 17 to 19 days of age. As can be seen in Fig. 10.2, although animals conditioned at 17 to 19 days of age were also observed to retain their early conditioning experience, the younger animals, those 16 days of age or younger, showed virtually no signs of memory 42 days later. Tone had no effect upon bar-pressing, regardless of whether the animals had been exposed to paired or unpaired tones and shocks. Rather than that the neurological theories be discarded, these data indicated that if lack of forgetting by older animals is truly due to the absence of behavioral contributions, then forgetting by the younger animals cannot be easily attributed to them either. Thus their forgetting could be due to some other factor, perhaps neurological immaturity. In other words the pattern of these results could be interpreted to mean that both behavioral and neurological factors may contribute to infantile forgetting but at different times during development.

Although such a possibility was suggested earlier by Campbell and Spear (1972), these data represented the first empirical demonstration of the possible validity of such a "two-process" theory. What made these data (and the theory) particularly interesting was the possibility that they might resolve the apparent discrepancy between the pattern of forgetting typically seen in rats and that reported for humans. In other words the abrupt difference in retention that obtained between the younger and older animals, highly reminiscent of the abrupt loss in memory ability that presumably characterizes human infantile amnesia, suggest that it is only the forgetting of much earlier experiences than have typically been studied in the rat that is truly analogous to the inability of humans to remember events prior to 3 years of age. Furthermore, the data suggest that it is only this deficit, and not that typically reported for older animals, that may be accounted for by processes arising from neurological immaturity.

Subsequent studies

Given this interpretation of the results of our first studies, a number of additional studies were conducted that were designed to test further the two-process theory of infantile forgetting. Our goal was to elucidate the nature of those neurological factors that might underly the forgetting of very early fear conditioning and to

---

[1]Results of a recent study by Alberts (1976), who observed excellent retention by rats poisoned at 18 days of age, are not incompatible with the foregoing conclusion, inasmuch as the taste aversion paradigm, like Pavlovian fear conditioning, would tend to minimize behavioral factors, particularly the effects of size change.

verify that behavioral factors are responsible for the forgetting of somewhat later experiences as reported by other investigators.

Retention of conditioning at 14 to 16 days.   Initially our interest focused upon the younger animals. Our first question was whether the inability to remember events experienced at 14 to 16 days of age was a retention effect or due to the absence of learning. To answer this question, we (Coulter et al., 1976) exposed rats 14 to 16 days old either to paired or random tones and shocks and then tested their response to tone while bar-pressing for food either 5, 10, or 20 days later. The results, shown in Fig. 10.3, clearly indicate that the animals had learned: 5 days after conditioning tone elicited marked suppression, even though 10 days later suppression was less and, within 20 days, absent.

Because these results indicated that forgetting by animals conditioned when very young was not due to the absence of learning, our attention turned to the two neurological theories of forgetting proposed by Campbell and Spear (1972). We reasoned that if retention failures by young animals were due to the absence of some critical structure for long-term storage, the forgetting curve (see Fig. 10.3) must reflect a gradual loss of memory and its eventual absence (i.e., unavailability) within 20 days. Following this reasoning we expected that a reminder given to these animals 20 days after conditioning, when memory was presumably gone, would have no greater effect on retention than a reminder given without

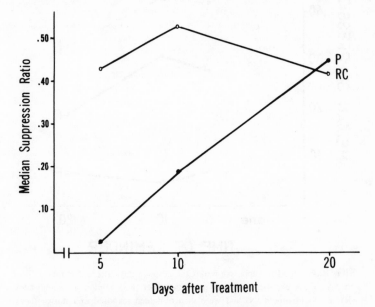

FIG. 10.3.   Median suppression to tone on the first test trial 5, 10, and 20 days after infant rats were exposed to tone−shock pairings (P) or random tones and shocks (RC) when 14 to 16 days old. (From Coulter et al., 1976.)

any conditioning experience. On the other hand if forgetting was due to subsequent development of, say, the cortex, the forgetting curve must represent a gradual increase in the inhibitory functioning of that structure (i.e., a gradual increase in the inaccessibility of memory). In that case we expected that a reminder given 5 days after conditioning, when that structure was presumably not yet functional, would be no more effective than if no reminder were given at that time. These expectations led Sharon Murrel, a graduate student at Stony Brook, and myself to design a study in which we exposed 14- to 16-day-old rats either to paired or random presentations of another 2-minute auditory stimulus, white noise, and shock or to no conditioning at all, testing the animals for retention 28 days later with or without having exposed them to a reminder (a single noise–shock pairing) either 5, 10, or 20 days after conditioning. The results of this study, as seen in Fig. 10.4, were surprising but clearcut: Although animals conditioned without reminders or subject only to reminders showed no signs of memory, all subjects that were both conditioned and reminded clearly remembered, regardless of when during the retention interval the reminder was presented. In essence these results did not support either of the neurological

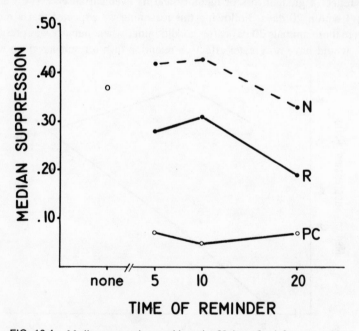

FIG. 10.4.   Median suppression to white noise 28 days after infant rats at 14 to 16 days of age experienced paired noise and shock (PC), random noise and shock (R), or no treatment (N) and were then reminded (exposed to 1 noise–shock pairing) either 5, 10, or 20 days after treatment. Animals with no reminder were exposed to noise–shock pairings (P) when 14 to 16 days of age and were then simply tested for suppression 28 days later.

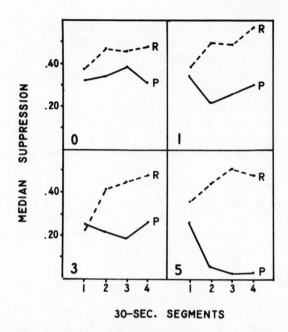

30-SEC. SEGMENTS

FIG. 10.5.   Median suppression ratios during successive 30-second segments of the first presentation of white noise 28 days after rats experienced at 14 to 16 days of age noise—shock pairings (P) or random noise and shocks (R) and were then reminded (exposed to 1 noise—shock pairing) 1, 3, or 5 days after treatment or not at all (0).

forgetting theories, because at the very least both theories predict that reminders will be differentially effective depending on the state of memory at the time they are presented.

Although it might be possible to rescue either the memory-inhibition theory by postulating certain unobservable processes or the memory-loss theory by assuming a noncorrespondence between performance and memory, we decided first to determine how soon after conditioning a reminder would fail to reinstate later memory. Once again rat pups were exposed at 14 to 16 days of age to paired or random presentations of noise and shock, but in this study before being tested for retention 28 days later, they were given a reminder (again, a single noise—shock pairing) either 1, 3, or 5 days after conditioning, or not at all. These results were also somewhat surprising. As shown in Fig. 10.5, all conditioned animals that received a reminder suppressed more in response to the noise stimulus than animals exposed to random presentations of noise and shock plus a reminder. The effect was not large, but it was significant. We also examined latency to resume bar-pressing after the termination of the noise stimulus during the test, and the results were similar. Bar-press recovery time was short and the same for animals that did not receive a reminder and for those that received a reminder after previously being exposed to random noise and shock. However, recovery took significantly longer for all animals that experienced a reminder in conjunction with conditioning, although unlike what was observed with suppression, the latency effect increased the longer the interval between conditioning and reminder.

The results of this study, our most recent with 14- to 16-day-old pups, are not easily explicable.[2] Although at least by one measure reminders did increase in effectiveness the longer the time after conditioning, all reminders were more effective than none at all. Yet our earlier study established that during the time these reminders were given, subjects are easily able to recall their conditioning experience. Why should a reminder whose function is presumably to help the subject retrieve an "inaccessible" memory have any effect at all during a period when memory is perfectly accessible? It is not at all clear how any of the forgetting theories, behavioral or neurological, would have predicted this effect.

Retention of conditioning at 18 to 20 days. At the same time that these studies were being conducted, Pearl Kessler, a recent Ph.D. from Stony Brook, completed a set of studies for her dissertation (1976) designed to examine more closely the absence of forgetting previously observed in rats conditioned at a somewhat older age. We had noted elsewhere (Campbell & Coulter, 1976; Coulter et al., 1976) that although it was reasonable to assume that Pavlovian fear conditioning is remembered by somewhat older rat pups because it is not readily susceptible to behavioral sources of forgetting, other differences exist between that procedure and the many other learning tasks that rats of this age do later forget. Specifically, with our conditioning procedure the temporal parameters were relatively long. Instead of a conditioned stimulus measured in seconds, its duration in our studies was 2 minutes; instead of intertrial intervals

---

[2]One aspect of these data seemed potentially troublesome. Although there were no statistically significant differences between random and paired groups that received no reminder, noise did appear to elicit some suppression in both groups and somewhat more in the paired group than had been observed in the previous study. The only major procedural difference between the two studies was that in the first study infants were weaned immediately after the last conditioning trial on Day 16 (i.e., before any reminders were given), whereas in the second study the pups were not weaned until 22 days of age (i.e., after all reminders were given). To determine whether or not late weaning might in some way have enhanced the memory capacity of pups in the second study, we conducted a 3-group study to assess the effects of weaning age upon memory. There were 30 pups conditioned when 14 to 16 days of age and tested for retention 28 days later. One-third of these animals were weaned immediately after the last conditioning trial (on the morning of their 16th day), one-third was weaned 12 hours after their last trial (on the evening of their 16th day), and the last third was weaned 5 days later (when the pups were 21 days old). Regardless of when they were weaned, the three groups showed no evidence of memory later—tone elicited virtually no suppression in any of the groups, just as had been observed in the first study. Therefore we concluded that, despite apparent differences, the absence of statistical differences between the random and paired groups without reminders in the second study was not misleading.

(ITI's) of less than 1 minute, the average time between tone– or noise–shock pairings was 15 minutes; and instead of receiving all trials in 1 day, even though the total number of trials (i.e., conditioned stimulus–unconditioned stimulus pairings) was relatively small (i.e., 9 or 12), rats in our studies experienced the pairings over a period of 3 days. There is some evidence that young animals may require more time for memory consolidation than adults (Caldwell & Werboff, 1962; Doty & Doty, 1964; Dye, 1969; Thompson, 1957), and Kessler reasoned that in addition to the elimination of environmental factors, it may have been a fortuitous choice of long temporal parameters by Coulter et al. (1976) that was responsible for the excellent retention shown by rats conditioned at 17 days of age or older.

In all, Kessler's dissertation consisted essentially of four studies. In the first the major variable of interest was number of days over which conditioning took place. Although all experimental subjects experienced a total of 9 noise–shock pairings, one-third of the subjects received all 9 trials on 1 day when they were 20 days old, another third received 4 or 5 trials a day when 19 and 20 days old, and the final third received 3 trials a day when 18, 19, and 20 days, this last condition being what is typically the case in my laboratory. In the second study the major variable of interest was the length of time between trials. In this case all pups experienced 9 trials over 3 days, and for one-third of the subjects the ITI was, as in the previous study, an average of 12 minutes. However, for another third of the subjects the ITI was 6 minutes and, for the final third, 1 minute. The third and fourth studies involved adults. In the first of the adult studies subjects were exposed to 9 trials of conditioning either on 1 or over 3 days, and in the second of these studies subjects were exposed to 9 trials over 3 days but with an average ITI of either 1 or 12 minutes. In all four studies retention was assessed by comparing the degree to which noise elicited bar-press suppression in groups tested 1 day after conditioning and in groups tested 28 days later. In addition, retention was measured by comparing after a delay the conditioned groups to groups that had been initially exposed to random presentations of noise and shock with temporal parameters comparable to that of the experimental groups.

The results were that with 9 noise–shock pairings presented over 3 days, long-term retention by rats conditioned when 18 to 20 days old was excellent, just as had been observed earlier by Coulter et al. (1976). Moreover, a reduction in ITI had no adverse effect on performance either immediately or after a delay. However, the surprising result, as shown in Fig. 10.6, was that if conditioning took place over only 2 days, retention was significantly less, and if the original conditioning took place in 1 day, there was no evidence of memory at all 28 days later. In contrast, retention by rats conditioned as adults was excellent under all conditions.

That number of days of conditioning in pups should have such a marked effect on long-term retention has profound implications for the meaning of our previous work. The fact that pups conditioned when 17 days of age or older had been

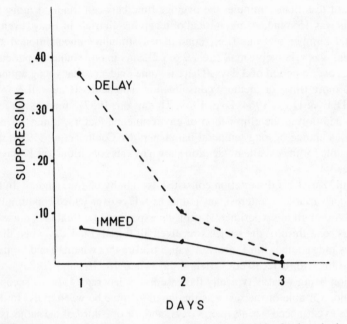

FIG. 10.6.   Median suppression to white noise by rats exposed to 9 noise—shock pairings when they were 18 to 20 days old (3 days), 19 and 20 days old (2 days), or 20 days old (1 day) and then tested while bar-pressing for food either 1 day later or after a delay of 28 days. (From Kessler, 1976.)

found previously to show no forgetting may not have been necessarily due to the elimination of behavioral factors but to a fortuitous choice of conditioning parameters. That rats can be made to forget merely by changing the value of a learning parameter, particularly when other sources of forgetting have presumably been minimized, means that an important determinant of memory must reside within the learning situation itself. Thus infantile amnesia, even for relatively late experiences, may well be due to neurological factors, at least if one is willing to grant that an age-related need for special conditions during learning can be attributed to neurological immaturity.

In any event, what is the nature of that learning requirement? And why does it affect only long-term memory? Perhaps immature rats need 24-hour rest periods during the course of conditioning, or perhaps they simply need to spend certain periods of time in the home cage. Assuming that rest and/or exposure to the home environment is somehow necessary for memory consolidation (Agranoff, 1967; Hartmann, 1973), it is still the case that differences in amount of consolidation should have been evident in the days immediately after conditioning. Yet on the 1st day after conditioning all pups showed marked suppression to the noise stimulus regardless of whether the 9 noise—shock pairings had taken place during the previous 1, 2, or 3 days. Furthermore, it took all three groups at least 4 days (i.e., 16 presentations of noise alone) before they stopped suppressing, ample time for any submerged differences among the groups to appear. Since they did not, the question arises as to why deficits in memory consolidation, presumably produced by massed conditioning, should become evident only after several weeks. Perhaps a more straightforward way of accounting for the effect of number of conditioning days on retention is to postulate that pups need to be exposed repeatedly to the onset of a conditioning session. It could be that, in contrast to adults, young rats use session onset as an important predictor of shock. Whereas 1 exposure to session onset as provided by 1 day of conditioning may be sufficient for learning, it may not be sufficient for long-term retention (i.e., a kind of underlearning effect, only with respect to session onset). Or it could be that session onset is equally important to both pups and adults as a predictor of aversiveness but that it is more susceptible to forgetting by pups than by adults, an effect that in itself would still have to be explained.[3]

In any case, a critical distinction between a memory consolidation and a session-onset hypothesis is that in the former case some finite amount of time is important whereas in the latter case it is only the removal and replacement of the subjects out of and and into the chamber that is important. Because this distinction can be easily tested, we proceeded to do so in order to follow up Kessler's major findings. Once again older pups (in this case, 19- to 21-day-olds) were all exposed to 9 noise—shock pairings, just as in Kessler's dissertation. For all subjects the last 3 of these pairings occurred the morning of their 21st day, exactly 1 or 28 days before they were to be tested for the effect of the white noise stimulus on bar-pressing. What distinguished the different groups was what occurred after the 3rd and 6th noise—shock pairing. For one group, nothing unusual took place: The animals remained in the conditioning chamber, where they simply experienced 9 noise—shock pairings over a 3-hour period. Another group was exposed to exactly the same schedule of pairings over the same 3-hour period, except that after the 1st and again after the 2nd hour (i.e., after the 3rd and the 6th pairing), the animals were removed from the chamber for 5 minutes. The remaining four groups were also removed from the chamber after the 1st and 2nd hour but for increasingly longer times: One group was taken out for ½ hour each time; another group for 6 hours at a time; and the remaining two groups for either 12 or 24 hours. In essence the group that was never removed from the

---

[3]It may be important that in Kessler's study the apparatus used for conditioning was more similar to the bar-press (i.e., test) chamber than in the earlier study by Coulter et al. (1976). If placement in the chamber is the principal cue that defines session onset, and if there was significant generalization between the two chambers, one could attribute some of the forgetting by the pups to size-change effects—that is, to the fact that the chamber appeared to be different after a delay. The problem with this explanation is that if the chamber was such an important predictor of shock, the random control groups should have showed significant amounts of suppression when in fact they performed no differently than rats that had never experienced either noise or shock.

chamber and the one removed twice for 24 hours were replications of the 1-day and 3-day groups in Kessler's dissertation.

The results, as shown in Fig. 10.7, were quite clearcut. First of all, as was found by Kessler, animals that were conditioned in 1 day, without being removed from the chamber, clearly forgot their conditioning experience 28 days later, whereas those exposed to conditioning over 3 days (having been removed twice for 24 hours each time) did not. However, number of days of conditioning and/or length of time outside the chamber were seemingly irrelevant features, because the other groups, in which these parameters were varied, were all strikingly similar. None forgot, not even the group that experienced the same conditioned stimulus – unconditioned stimulus schedule as the group that did forget. In other words the critical variable appeared to be, simply, removal from the chamber. This result is what would be expected if, as was suggested earlier, repeated exposure to session onset is what is essential for the long-term retention of conditioning by immature subjects. Although we have speculated somewhat seriously about possible mechanisms that might account for this requirement, it

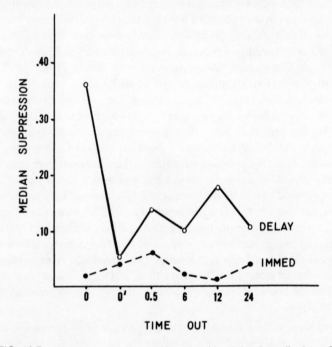

FIG. 10.7. Median suppression to white noise either 1 day (immediately) or 28 days later (delayed) by rats exposed at 19 to 21 days of age to 9 noise–shock pairings either without interruption (0), or with removal from the conditioning chamber for 5 minutes (0'), or for 0.5, 6, 12, or 24 hours after the 3rd and the 6th noise–shock pair.

is clear that more data and further thought should be brought to bear on this issue before much more can be said. But it worthwhile pointing out that, even though the major effects can be seen only after several weeks, the manipulations and mechanisms we are speaking about are relevant primarily to the learning process. None of the retention data from the older animals that have been described are incompatible with a theory that attributes infantile amnesia to differences in the way immature organisms learn as compared to adults.

SUMMARY REMARKS

In our original study (Coulter et al., 1976) we found that rats conditioned when very young show rapid forgetting, whereas rats conditioned at a somewhat older (although hardly mature) age do not. Since then we have found that we can attenuate the rapid forgetting seen in the younger animals merely by exposing them to an extra abbreviated learning session, which we call a reminder. Now we have found that we can induce rapid forgetting in the somewhat older pups—that is, those that we have otherwise shown to have good memories—merely by preventing them from experiencing more than one session of learning. It is noteworthy that the manner in which we have gained control over memory in both the younger and older pups appears to be similar. Being exposed to a reminder before forgetting is evident is not unlike experiencing the last of several learning sessions; both situations involve reexposure or repetition. Obviously the comparison is limited, because the younger pups that were not reminded and later forgot did nonetheless experience more than one session of trials. On the other hand, if the salutary effect of reminders on young pups is even remotely related to the salutary effect of repeated exposure to session onset on older pups, our initial interpretation of the apparent difference in memory ability between these two age groups may have to be revised. It may be that the difference between the older and younger pups simply reflects the degree to which increasingly immature animals are susceptible to the same process rather than, as we suggested earlier, to the operation of different processes.

Taken as a whole, these studies suggest that the role of learning may be more important in the forgetting of early experiences than has hitherto been considered. In a sense, none of the forgetting theories can easily explain any of our more recent findings. Even attempts directly to test the two neurologically based forgetting theories when they were most likely to be true resulted in data not readily predicted by either. What does seem to be critical for the long-term retention of early experiences is more than one exposure to that experience. Whether this reexposure must take place only after a certain level of neurological maturity has been attained is possible but as yet unknown. However, since reexposures can effectively enhance memory even if they occur before any memory deficits can be detected, it is hard to see how theories that focus only upon forgetting processes can account for infantile amnesia without serious modification.

ACKNOWLEDGMENTS

Much of the research described in this paper was conducted in Stony Brook and was supported in part by a National Institutes of Health Biomedical Support Grant (RR07067-09) and two State University of New York Foundation awards. Some of the earlier work described herein, which was conducted at Princeton University, was supported by a National Institutes of Health Grant (MH-01562) to Byron A. Campbell.

REFERENCES

Agranoff, B. W. Memory and protein synthesis. *Scientific American*, 1967, *216*, 115–112.

Alberts, J. *The retention of taste aversions established in infant rats*. Paper given at the meeting of the Eastern Psychological Association, May 1976.

Caldwell, D. F., & Werboff, J. Classical conditioning in newborn rats. *Science*, 1962, *136*, 1118–1119.

Campbell, B. A., & Campbell, E. H. Retention and extinction of learned fear in infant and adult rats. *Journal of Comparative and Physiological Psychology*, 1962, *55*, 1–8.

Campbell, B. A., & Coulter, X. Ontogeny of learning and memory. In M. R. Rosenzweig (Ed.), *Neural mechanisms of learning and memory*. Cambridge: MIT Press, 1976.

Campbell, B. A., & Jaynes, J. Reinstatement. *Psychological Review*, 1966, *73*, 478–480.

Campbell, B. A., Jaynes, J., & Misanin, J. R. Retention of a light–dark discrimination in rats of different ages. *Journal of Comparative and Physiological Psychology*, 1968, *66*, 467–472.

Campbell, B. A., Misanin, J. R., White, B. C., & Lytle, L. D. Species differences in ontogeny of memory: Support for neural maturation as a determinant of forgetting. *Journal of Comparative and Physiological Psychology*, 1974, *87*, 193–202.

Campbell, B. A., Riccio, D. C., & Rohrbaugh, M. Ontogenesis of learning and memory: Research and theory. In M. E. Meyer (Ed.), *Second Western Washington Symposium on learning: Early learning*. Bellingham, Wash.: Western Washington State College Press, 1971.

Campbell, B. A., & Spear, N. E. Ontogeny of memory. *Psychological Review*, 1972, *79*, 215–236.

Coulter, X., Collier, A., & Campbell, B. A. Long-term retention of Pavlovian fear conditioning by infant rats. *Journal of Experimental Psychology: Animal Behavior Processes*, 1976, *2*, 48–56.

Crockett, W. H., & Nobel, M. E. Age of learning, severity of negative reinforcement, and retention of learned responses. *Journal of Genetic Psychology*, 1963, *103*, 105–112.

Davis, H. Conditioned suppression: A survey of the literature. *Psychonomic Monograph Supplements*, 1969 (2), No. 14 (Whole No. 30), 283–291.

Doty, B. A., & Doty, L. Effects of age and chlorpromazine on memory consolidation. *Journal of Comparative and Physiological Psychology*, 1964, *57*, 331–334.

Dye, C. J. Effects of interruption of initial learning upon retention in young, mature, and old rats. *Journal of Geronotologica*, 1969, *24*, 12–17.

Eisenstein, E. M. The use of invertebrate systems for studies on the bases of learning and memory. In G. C. Quarton, T. Melnechuk, & F. O. Schmitt (Eds.), *The neurosciences: A study program*. New York: Rockefeller University Press, 1967.

Feigley, D. A., & Spear, N. E. Effect of age and punishment condition on long-term retention by the rat of active- and passive-avoidance learning. *Journal of Comparative and Physiological Psychology*, 1970, *73*, 515–526.

Fox, M. *Integrative Development of Brain and Behavior in the Dog*. Chicago: University of Chicago Press, 1971.

Frieman, J. P., Frieman, J., Wright, W., & Hegberg, W. Developmental trends in the acquisition and extinction of conditioned suppression in rats. *Developmental Psychology*, 1971, *4*, 425–428.

Green, P. C. Learning, extinction, and generalization of conditioned responses by young monkeys. *Psychological Reports*, 1962, *10*, 731–738.

Harlow, H. F., Harlow, J. K., & Suomi, S. J. From thought to therapy: Lessons from a primate laboratory. *American Scientist*, 1971, *59*, 538–549.

Hartmann, E. L. *The Functions of Sleep*. New Haven: Yale University Press, 1973.

Kandel, E. R. Cellular studies on learning. In G. C. Quarton, T. Melnechuk, & F. O. Schmitt (Eds.), *The neurosciences: A study program*. New York: Rockefeller University Press, 1967.

Kessen, W. *The Child*. New York: John Wiley & Sons, 1965.

Kessler, P. *Effects of temporal conditioning parameters upon long-term retention by infant rats*. Unpublished doctoral dissertation, State University of New York at Stony Brook, 1976.

Kirby, R. H. Acquisition, extinction, and retention of an avoidance response as a function of age. *Journal of Comparative and Physiological Psychology*, 1963, *56*, 158–162.

Lehrman, D. S. Semantic and conceptual issues in the nature–nurture problem. In L. R. Aronson, E. Tobach, D. S. Lehrman, & J. S. Rosenblatt (Eds.), *Development and evolution of behavior*. San Francisco: Freeman & Company, 1970.

Lipsitt, L. P. Infant learning: The blooming, buzzing confusion revisited. In M. E. Meyer (Ed.), *Second Western Washington symposium on learning: Early learning*. Bellingham, Wash.: Western Washington State College Press, 1971.

Lyons, D. O. Conditioned suppression: Operant variables and aversive control. *The Psychological Record*, 1968, *18*, 317–338.

Miller, G. A., & Buckhout, R. *Psychology: The science of mental life*. New York: Harper & Row, 1973.

Parsons, P. J., & Spear, N. E. Long-term retention of avoidance learning by immature and adult rats as a function of environmental enrichment. *Journal of Comparative and Physiological Psychology*, 1972, *80*, 297–303.

Perkins, C. C. A conceptual scheme for studies for stimulus generalization. In D. I. Mostofsky (Ed.), *Stimulus generalization*. Palo Alto: Stanford University Press, 1965.

Sackett, G. P. Innate mechanisms, rearing conditions, and a theory of early experience effects in primates. In M. R. Jones (Ed.), *Miami symposium on the prediction of behavior, 1968: Effects of early experience*. Coral Gables: University of Miami Press, 1970.

Smith, N. Effects of interpolated learning on the retention of an escape response in rats as a function of age. *Journal of Comparative and Physiological Psychology*, 1968, *65*, 422–426.

Spear, J. E. Retrieval of memory in animals. *Psychological Review*, 1973, *80*, 163–194.

Stein, L., & Berger, B. D. Paradoxical fear-increasing effect of tranquillizers: Evidence of fear repression in the rat. *Science*, 1969, *166*, 253–256.

Thompson, R. W. The effect of ECS on retention in young and adult rats. *Journal of Comparative and Physiological Psychology*, 1957, *50*, 644–646.

Thompson, R. W., Koenigsberg, L. A., & Tennison, J. C. Effects of age on learning and retention of an avoidance response in rats. *Journal of Comparative and Physiological Psychology*, 1965, *60*, 457–459.

Tulving, E., & Pearlstone, Z. Availability versus accessibility of information in memory for words. *Journal of Verbal Learning and Verbal Behavior*, 1966, *5*, 381–391.

Underwood, B. J. Interference and forgetting. *Psychological Review*, 1957, *64*, 49–60.

Von Baumgarten, R. J. Plasticity in the nervous system at the unitary level. In G. C. Quarton, T. Melnechuk, & F. O. Schmitt (Eds.), *The neurosciences: A study program*. New York: Rockefeller University Press, 1967.

Waldfogel, S. The frequency and affective character of childhood memories. *Psychology Monographs*, 1948, *62* (4, Whole No. 291).

11
Age: Is It a Constraint on Memory Content?

William C. Gordon
University of New Mexico

As adults we are capable of remembering very few of the specific events that occurred in our early childhood. This phenomenon, labeled "infantile amnesia," is evident not only to those of us who attempt to recall our childhood past (Schachtel, 1947) but also to the numerous researchers who have documented a similar effect in the retentive capacity of infrahumans (Campbell & Spear, 1972). Moreover it is clear that this failure to recall events experienced during early development is not simply a function of the long retention interval separating infancy and adulthood. Although forgetting may be relatively minimal over a given period of time in adulthood, this same period of time often results in massive forgetting if it occurs contemporaneously with the period of transition between infancy and maturity.

Clearly the mere occurrence of infantile amnesia has a variety of implications not only for descriptive models of development but also for models of learning and memory in the adult organism. If the factors underlying this instance of forgetting can be identified, such a finding should contribute to our understanding of the necessary and sufficient conditions for learning and retention in the mature individual. Based on this assumption research concerning the bases of infantile amnesia has intensified in recent years (Campbell & Coulter, 1976; Campbell & Spear, 1972). Nevertheless the question of why we forget our earliest experiences has remained largely unresolved, despite the fact that numerous hypotheses concerning infantile amnesia have been advanced and tested. The purpose of the present chapter is to suggest a source of forgetting that may well contribute to the poor retention of early events by infrahuman species but which has not as yet been explored extensively. Prior to discussing this possible source of forgetting, however, it is useful as a point of departure to describe briefly some of the

271

alternative hypotheses concerning the causes of infantile amnesia. A more complete review of hypotheses and data relevant to infantile amnesia in infrahumans is available elsewhere (cf., Campbell & Coulter, 1976).

HYPOTHESIZED SOURCES OF INFANTILE AMNESIA

The typical demonstration of infantile amnesia in altricial animals such as the rat involves training the animals to perform some task prior to or around the time of weaning (usually within the first 25 days postpartum) and then testing for retention of the learned task after an interval of several days (i.e., in adolescence or adulthood). Such animals normally exhibit poorer retention performance than animals that have a comparable retention interval but are both trained and tested during adulthood. Likewise, in many studies those animals trained prior to the weaning period exhibit long-term retention performance that is indistinguishable from that of same-age animals that were never trained at all (Spear & Parsons, 1976). Hypotheses designed to isolate the causes of this deficit have clustered around three critical stages in the information processing sequence: (1) acquisition or storage of information; (2) maintenance of information in storage; (3) retrieval of stored information.

Storage or Acquisition Deficits

Early experiments suggested that a probable cause of infantile amnesia is the relative lack of learning capacity possessed by immature organisms (Cornwall & Fuller, 1961). These kinds of studies appeared to demonstrate that neonates are incapable of learning even simple responses and therefore cannot be expected to show evidence of retention at a later time. The mass of evidence in recent years, however, contradicts the view that neonates lack the capacity for learning and suggests that many of the earlier studies might have been assessing sensory or motor deficits of neonates rather than deficits in associative processes (Cornwall & Fuller, 1961). It is now known, for example, that under appropriate stimulus conditions and response requirements rats younger than 25 days are capable of acquiring both active- and passive-avoidance responses (Feigley & Spear, 1970), shock-escape responses (Campbell, Misanin, White, & Lytle, 1974), classically conditioned responses based on aversive unconditioned stimuli (UCSs) (Caldwell & Werboff, 1962), and conditioned aversions to both odor and taste cues (Campbell & Alberts, in press; Rudy & Cheatle, 1978). Similarly, rat pups as young as 7 days have been shown to be capable of acquiring a spatial discrimination when the reward for a correct response is the nonlactating nipple of an anaesthetized mother rat (Kenny & Blass, 1977). Such studies leave little doubt that very young animals possess the capacity for learning and can even exhibit evidence of acquisition at 1 day of age as long as appropriate stimuli and response measures are used (Caldwell & Werboff, 1962).

Of course the fact that neonates possess the capacity for learning does not imply that acquisition deficits do not contribute to the young animal's poor long-term retention. It is possible that neonates learn less efficiently or less completely than adults and that such a deficiency might result in poor retention performance. The data pertaining to this hypothesis are equivocal, especially if one assesses degree of learning by the rate at which an animal approaches asymptotic performance (Underwood, 1964). For example, there is general agreement that preweanling rats reach criterion performance on a passive-avoidance task more slowly than an adult animal (Riccio & Schulenberg, 1969; Schulenberg, Riccio, & Stikes, 1971). It is unclear, however, the degree to which this performance deficit results from less efficiency in learning the passive-avoidance contingency as opposed to reflecting a general deficiency in the ability of a neonate to inhibit responding (Campbell, Riccio, & Rohrbaugh, 1971). Likewise, although some studies have suggested that preweanling rats are slightly inferior to adults in the rate of active avoidance acquisition (Klein & Spear, 1969), many such studies have required that the animals make an avoidance response within a relatively short conditioned stimulus (CS) period. Therefore it is possible that these results may be reflecting the neonate's inferior motor performance rather than any difficulty in learning the active-avoidance response.

The point of these examples is that although some studies have suggested that young animals reach acquisition criteria more slowly than adults on some tasks, the reasons for this performance difference are not always evident. What is evident, however, is that even in those studies in which no age-related acquisition differences have been found, infantile amnesia still occurs (Kirby, 1963; Smith, 1968). These studies suggest that a slower rate of acquisition by the neonate is not a necessary condition for the neonate's poor long-term retention. This conclusion is reinforced by results from studies that have specifically overtrained young rats relative to adults in an effort to assure that the degree of learning for the young animals was at least equivalent to that of the adults (Feigley & Spear, 1970; Schulenberg, et al., 1971). In these types of studies evidence of infantile amnesia persists, despite the attempt to bias degree of learning in favor of the younger animals.

Maintenance of Information in Storage

With little direct evidence to suggest that learning deficits cause the poor long-term retention of neonates, the question arises as to how well young animals maintain information that has been stored at an early age. Is it possible, for example, that young, maturing animals are more susceptible to sources of forgetting such as proactive and retroactive interference than animals that learn in a mature state? Such questions thus far have received little attention in the infrahuman literature. Although at least one study does suggest that immature rats are more susceptible to the effects of experimentally induced proactive interference (PI) than adults (Spear, Gordon, & Chiszar, 1972), it would seem unlikely that PI differences could be responsible for the inferior long-term retention of young animals. For PI to act as a major source of forgetting in most experiments it would be necessary to assume that extraexperimental events experienced prior to training constitute the main interfering influence. Yet the notion that extraexperimental events produce PI is questionable at best (Underwood & Keppel, 1963). Furthermore, even if this were the case one would probably predict that older, not younger, animals would be most affected by PI, because they would be expected to have had more experiences than neonates prior to a training task.

Logically then it would seem that retroactive interference (RI) is a better candidate as a source of infantile amnesia than PI. At least there is some reason to believe that younger animals experience a broader range of events during a given retention interval than mature animals. This assumption is based on numerous experiments that demonstrate that preweanling rats exhibit higher levels of activity than mature animals (Bronstein, Neiman, Wolkoff, & Levine, 1974; Feigley, Parsons, Hamilton, & Spear, 1972). On the other hand there is presently some question as to whether or not this heightened activity level actually represents increased exploration of the environment by the neonate (Douglas, Peterson, & Douglas, 1973; Williams, Hamilton, & Carlton, 1975). So it is unclear if neonates actually acquire more conflicting information during a given retention interval than do adults. It is interesting that in one of the few studies designed to compare the influence of RI on the retention of neonates and adults, Parsons and Spear (1972) found no evidence to suggest that neonates are more susceptible to interfering events than adults. On balance there is little evidence to suggest that younger animals are any more susceptible to the interfering effects of prior and intervening events than are adults.

Retrieval of Information

Certainly one of the most plausible interpretations of infantile amnesia is that although information concerning early experiences may be stored and maintained as efficiently as information acquired during adulthood, the memories of early events are particularly difficult for an organism to access or retrieve. This interpretation derives from the view that a memory is stored as a collection of attributes, each representing important stimulus or response elements noticed by an organism during learning (Spear, 1971, 1973; Underwood, 1969). According to this view the target attributes (i.e., those attributes representing the critical elements or contingencies in learning) can be retrieved only if a sufficient number of attributes are activated. Activation occurs via contact with stimuli similar to those noticed during learning. Within this framework there are a number of potential mechanisms by which infantile amnesia might occur. For example, it is probable that as an animal matures its perception of the world changes because of growth-induced changes in perspective. Thus it is quite possible that stimulus generalization decrements will be more pronounced across a period of rapid maturation than across a comparable period in adulthood. According to the retrieval deficit position, the greater the generalization decrement the greater should be the difficulty in retrieving a previously acquired memory with the aid of contemporary cues.

Although this line of reasoning is clearly logical, the data suggest that stimulus generalization decrements, at least for those external stimuli in a testing situation, may not play a major role in infantile amnesia. Feigley and Spear (1970), in a specific test of this notion, trained weanling rats in either a scaled-down avoidance apparatus or an apparatus designed for adults. After a retention interval of approximately 1 month all animals were tested for retention in the adult version of the apparatus. If infantile forgetting is due to stimulus generalization decrement one would predict that changing the size of the apparatus as the size of the animal changes should reduce forgetting by reducing generalization decrement. However, both groups exhibited a high degree of forgetting, and there were no differences between the groups in retention performance.

A similar explanation of infantile amnesia has been suggested by Campbell and Spear (1972). The essence of this proposal is that in rats and other altricial organisms, early life is characterized by a period of rapid central nervous system (CNS) maturation (e.g., increased myelinization, growth of dendritic spines) and that this period of growth might act to produce numerous changes both in the animal's internal cue state and its perception of external cues. Should an animal learn some task during or before the period of rapid maturation and then be tested for retention after this period is over, massive stimulus generalization decrements should occur between the time of training and testing, and retrieval should be difficult. Although this hypothesis is relatively intractable to experimental test, indirect evidence in support of this view exists. It has been shown, for example, that guinea pigs, which are born with a relatively well developed CNS and do not undergo a period of rapid CNS change in early life, do not exhibit evidence of infantile amnesia (Campbell, et al., 1974). Obviously this correlation between the occurrence of marked CNS change and infantile amnesia is interesting and warrants further investigation.

One final hypothesis concerning retrieval deficits as a basis for infantile amnesia can be derived from a number of recent experiments concerning reinstatement or memory reactivation in the neonate. Inherent in such experiments is the assumption that young animals do not encode or elaborate information to the same degree as adults at the time of learning. Therefore even though the appropriate information is stored, the lack of sufficient encoding makes later retrieval difficult. To eliminate this proposed deficit, several experimenters have attempted to induce further elaboration by young animals via reinstatement or reactivation treatments. Such treatments normally involve confronting animals with cues from the learning situation during the retention interval with the hope that young animals will retrieve and further process previously stored information (Spear & Parsons, 1976). Such procedures have been shown to alleviate some long-term retention deficits in weanling rats (Campbell & Jaynes, 1966). However, recent evidence suggests that the long-term retention deficits exhibited by animals trained at an earlier age (16 days) may be particularly difficult to influence via reactivation (Spear & Parsons, 1976). Whether these failures to alleviate infantile amnesia are due to the use of ineffective reactivation treatments or to the fact that elaboration problems play little role in infantile forgetting is difficult to assess at the present time.

An Alternative Position

Although the present review of hypotheses is not intended to be exhaustive, even a brief treatment of the explanations of infantile amnesia should reveal an important fact. One common assumption that underlies all of the hypotheses discussed thus far is that young and adult organisms acquire the same kinds of information when confronted with the same experimenter-defined contingencies. Inherent in all of these hypotheses is the notion that infantile amnesia reflects the relative inability of the young animal to deal with the identical information that an adult handles easily. This assumption concerning the equivalence of acquired information across ages is certainly a reasonable starting point for the study of infantile forgetting. Also it is an important assumption to make if one wishes to understand learning and memory processes in the adult by studying deficiencies in these processes as they occur in the neonate. It is interesting to note, however, that if we make a different assumption—that is, that the kinds of information acquired in a given situation and under a given contingency change as a function of age—alternative explanations of infantile amnesia soon become evident.

To amplify this point of view let me describe more fully what is meant here by "acquiring different kinds of information in the same learning situation." When an animal is confronted with a compound (CS) or with multiple discriminative stimuli in a learning situation, the degree of stimulus control attained by each element of the compound is not always predictable solely on the basis of the reinforcement schedules and parameters in effect. The stimulus control obtained by one stimulus element often depends on an animal's prior experience with other elements in the compound (Kamin, 1969). Likewise, the amount of stimulus control acquired by one element may well be contingent on the intensity or perceived salience of that element relative to other parts of the compound (Miles & Jenkins, 1973). Such phenomena suggest that animals that have different learning histories or perceive the salience of stimulus elements differentially (e.g., animals of different species) may well form a different set of associations within the same learning situation. Stated in another way, two animals that acquire a response in the same context may, under some circumstances, carry memories of the situation that differ substantially in terms of the specific attributes or elements that make up those memories.

Although the occurrence of stimulus selection phenomena has caused a reexamination of traditional views of conditioning (Rescorla & Wagner, 1972; Sutherland & Mackintosh, 1971), there has been little work to date concerning the degree to which a variety of subject and treatment variables might influence cue selection in animals. The importance of such information for the study of retention in animals should be obvious, because any subject or treatment variable that alters stimulus selectivity might also be expected to affect the retention performance of an animal depending on the type of retention test situation employed.

Following this line of reasoning, some recent work in our laboratory, done in conjunction with Michael Brennan, has begun to look at the degree to which certain subject and treatment variables modify an animal's selection of stimuli. In all these studies we trained 60-100-day-old mice (Binghamton Heterogeneous Stock) to traverse a 6-unit maze to receive dilute saccharine solution in a goal compartment. Each unit in the maze consisted of an entryway leading to two separate alleyways. One alleyway always led to the entryway of the next unit (or to the goal box in the case of the last unit), whereas the other alleyway was always blocked at the end by a piece of clear vinyl. One alleyway in each unit was white and the other was black. The white and black alleyways remained in the same position in each unit on all training trials. Thus animals could learn to reach the goal box by utilizing either brightness or sequence (position) cues.

In the earliest study using this paradigm, both male and female mice were trained for 4 days (3 trials per day) with a simple sequence (i.e., the correct brightness was located on the same side of all units for a given animal). Then, 24 hours later, each animal was tested for retention under one of two conditions: brightness reversal (BR)—the correct brightness was the reverse of that used in prior training, but the correct positions or sequence remained the same; sequence reversal (SR)—the correct sequence was the reverse of that used in prior training, but the correct brightness remained the same. Each animal received 3 retention test trials per day for 4 days. Figure 11.1 represents the mean errors made during training and testing as a function of sex and testing condition. As can be seen, both males and females reduced their number of errors substantially during the course of training and by the end of training were performing with relatively few errors. However, on Day 1 of retention testing, dramatic differences between the male and female animals were evident. The females exhibited good retention under both BR and SR conditions. On the other hand the males performed well only in the BR condition. When the originally correct sequence was reversed, the performance of the males decreased dramatically. These data suggested to us that the females had acquired information concerning both brightness and sequence during original training and were able to utilize one set of cues when the other

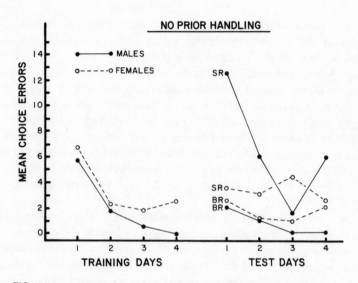

FIG. 11.1.   Mean choice errors during training and testing as a function of sex and reversal conditions.

offered incorrect choices during retention testing. On the other hand the performance of the males suggested that they had acquired mainly sequence information during training because reversal of brightness caused few errors whereas reversal of sequence decremented performance substantially.

Even more surprising than this initial finding were the data from a second study that was identical to the first except that all animals in the second experiment underwent a handling experience just prior to the beginning of training. Handling consisted of picking up each animal and holding it for 30 seconds each day for 7 consecutive days prior to the initiation of training. Results of this study, represented in Fig. 11.2, suggest that the prior handling abolished the differential selectivity of the males and females, because both showed evidence of strong reliance on sequence but not on brightness cues on Day 1 of retention testing. These findings, as well as those in the first experiment, are preliminary in nature and require further work to determine how generalizable such phenomena are. However, these data do suggest that subject variables such as sex and subtle treatment variables such as handling may influence the kinds of information an animal stores concerning a learning experience.

We have reached a similar conclusion in another line of research dealing with the effects of CNS stimulants on retention performance. It is well documented that the postlearning administration of drugs such as strychnine sulphate enhance later retention test performance in a variety of learning paradigms (Calhoun, 1971). This phenomenon is normally explained as an effect of the drug on the processing of information from a learning trial, resulting in enhanced storage or encoding of information (Gordon, 1977; McGaugh & Dawson, 1971). We became interested in the question of whether drugs such as strychnine act to enhance all attributes of a memory equally or whether certain elements of a memory are enhanced selectively. In a recent experiment examining this question (Brennan & Gordon, 1977, Experiment 2) we trained male mice in the same maze task described earlier except that these mice received only 2 training trials (1 per day) and a complex sequence was used: The correct brightness appeared in a L (left), R (right), R,L,L,R sequence in the 6 maze units. Half of the animals were injected with strychnine (1 mg/kg., I.P.) immediately following the second training trial, and the remaining animals were injected with an equal volume of a 0.9% saline solution. Then, 24 hours later, all animals were tested under either brightness or sequence reversal conditions. Only 1 test trial per day was given for 4 consecutive days.

The results of this experiment are shown in Fig. 11.3, which represents the mean choice errors (initial errors upon entrance to any unit) by the strychnine (ST)- and saline (SA)-injected animals under the BR and SR conditions. As can be seen in this figure, animals injected with saline performed at essentially a chance level (3 errors in 6 units) under both BR and SR conditions on Test Day 1. The same was true of the strychnine-treated animals when sequence cues were reversed and brightness cues remained as in training. However, animals treated with strychnine and tested under a reversal of the brightness cues exhibited excellent retention performance, suggesting that the original sequence cues were being utilized by these animals on the first retention-test trial. It should be noted

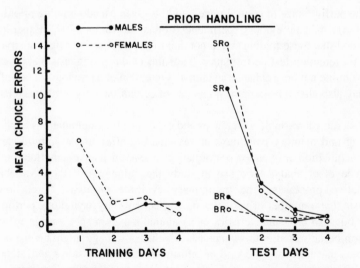

FIG. 11.2.   Mean choice errors during training and testing as a function of sex and reversal conditions.

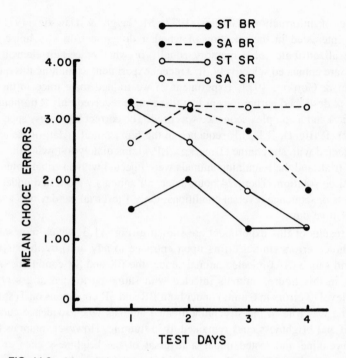

FIG. 11.3. Mean choice errors during testing as a function of drug treatment and reversal condition. (Reprinted with permission from *Pharmacology Biochemistry & Behavior*, © 1977, Vol. 7, Brennan, M. J. and Gordon, W. C.).

that the performance of control mice (animals given pseudo training prior to drug injection) run in a previous experiment (Brennan & Gordon, 1977, Experiment 1) suggested that these findings were not due to some proactive effect of strychnine alone on retention-test performance. Thus this evidence suggests that drugs such as strychnine not only enhance an animal's retention of a previously learned event but may also alter the strength or salience of certain memory attributes relative to others.

Most subject-variable differences and experimental manipulations explored in learning and memory paradigms are assumed to affect the asymptotic level of either acquisition or retention performance; at least such an assumption is implicit in the level of analysis we use to study the influences of these variables on associative processes. The preliminary evidence discussed here, however, suggests that a number of variables may affect not only asymptotic performance levels but also the characteristics of an animal's memory for a prior event. The question being raised in this chapter is whether or not age might be one of those variables that influence the kind of information an animal stores and, if so, how such differential selectivity might affect retention performance. The remainder of this chapter addresses these questions more directly.

AGE AS A DETERMINANT OF MEMORY CONTENT

Learning has long been viewed, even by the most traditional theorists, as a biologically adaptive process (Hull, 1943). In other words, presumably organisms process information because such an endeavor allows them best to cope with their own particular needs in a flexible yet effective manner. Let us assume for a moment that young animals are as capable of learning and remembering information as adults. However, because young animals have different needs than adults and because they have less experience both with external stimuli and with the use of their own sensory apparatus, they tend to be "sensitive" to different features of a given stimulus complex than are adults. This differential sensitivity might be expressed as something as simple as a preference for using one sensory modality over another. It might also mean that within a sensory modality certain stimulus dimensions are preferred over others. Such differential sensitivity to stimulus features would be expected to influence not only the dimensional information an animal stores about the critical elements in an association (c.g., CS or UCS) but also the kinds of contextual stimuli selected by an animal to become part of its memory for an event. In short the content of an animal's memory should depend to a great degree on which stimulus dimensions and stimulus categories an animal is most sensitive to in a given situation.

Before attempting to extend this line of reasoning to look at the implications of such a view for long-term retention, it becomes necessary first to determine whether or not the basic assumptions of this view are plausible. Although there is no direct evidence to show that animals of different ages store different types of information, at least three lines of evidence support the plausibility of the idea.

Stimulus Selection Based on Relevance of Stimuli for Behavioral Adaptations

As noted previously, when animals are confronted with compound CSs or redundant discriminative stimuli in a learning situation, a certain amount of stimulus selection often occurs. One factor that appears to influence which particular stimuli gain control in a given situation is the species of the animal being tested. For example, rats quite obviously form associations between taste cues and illness but do not acquire food aversions based on visual cues (Garcia & Koelling, 1966). On the other hand there is substantial evidence that birds come to associate visual cues with illness quite readily (Brower, 1969; Wickler, 1968). In a particularly elegant demonstration of this phenomenon, Wilcoxon, Dragoin, and Kral (1971) confronted both rats and Japanese quail with a solution that had both a distinctive color (blue) and taste (sour). Thirty minutes later all animals were poisoned and then subsequently tested for aversion to the different stimulus components of the solution. The rats exhibited aversion to the sour taste but not the color, whereas the quail developed greater aversion to the color and some evidence of aversion to the taste.

Though there are a variety of possible interpretations of these kinds of data, one explanation that has been offered is of particular interest in the present context. Rozin and Kalat (1971) suggest that poison-based aversion learning probably will occur only to "eating related-cues." Thus species may differ in the types of cues that will become associated with illness, because various species use different cues in the identification and acquisition of food. In other words animals show not only a tendency toward stimulus selection, but the cues that are selected in a certain situation may depend on which cues an animal views as relevant, given its history of adapting to its environment. This supposition, although derived from data concerning different species, might also be expected to apply to animals of different ages. Such a view is certainly not original with this author. For example, the failure of many researchers to demonstrate classic heart-rate conditioning in human infants (Hirschman & Katkin, 1974) has been explained by some writers as a failure to employ CSs that have "biological significance" for the infant (Pomerleau-Malcuit, 1974). However, if we are to explain age-related differences in stimulus selection via concepts such as "relevance" or "biological significance," we must be able to define these concepts independent of the learning situation in which stimulus selection is measured. Otherwise we run the risk of becoming circular in our definitions and simply equating the terms "stimulus selection" and "relevance." The question thus arises as to whether or not there are in fact identifiable age-related differences in the stimuli animals rely upon in adapting to their normal environments. If so, this would strengthen the case that animals of different ages find different sets of stimuli to be particularly relevant for their behavioral adaptations.

Stages of Stimulus Utilization

Evidence presented in a recent review by Rosenblatt (1976) clearly indicates that different sensory modalities play a predominant role in an animal's behavioral organization at different stages in the animal's development. For example, in the early days of a rat pup's development such behaviors as suckling, huddling with littermates, and orienting toward the nest appear to be controlled primarily by thermal and tactile cues. By the second week of life these same behaviors begin to be organized by olfactory cues. Finally, visual cues begin to play a predominant role in these behaviors about days 14 to 16.

In one sense these stages of stimulus utilization are not surprising, because, for example, it would be unlikely for visual cues to play a role in behavioral adjustments prior to the time an animal's eyes open. What is more interesting, however, is that just because a sensory system is functional does not mean that it will play an important part in an animal's adaptive behaviors. Rat pups, for instance, exhibit both behavioral and EEG responses to olfactory cues such as maternal odor between days 3 and 5 postpartum (Math & Desor, 1974; Tobach, Rouger, & Schneirla, 1967). However, it is not until an animal is approximately 14 days of age that olfaction plays a critical role in approach responses to a lactating mother (cf. Rosenblatt, 1976). Likewise it is obvious that once the visual system begins to predominate in an animal's behavioral organization, systems relied on earlier, such as the tactile and olfactory senses, are fully functional. Regarding these early-maturing sensory systems, Rosenblatt suggests that they do not cease to function as other systems develop. However, these systems are replaced by later developing systems as the predominant organizer of behaviors. Clearly these observations of the developing animal do not indicate that different sensory systems are relied upon totally at different ages. This evidence does suggest, however, that there are age-related changes in the sensory systems that predominate in an animal's attempt to adapt behaviorally to its environment.

Age-Related Changes in Human Memory Attributes

The first two lines of evidence discussed have suggested that it may be plausible to assume (1) that animals select stimuli for processing partly on the basis of how relevant certain stimuli are to their behavioral adaptations and (2) that there are age-related changes in the types of stimuli animals use to adapt behaviorally. The third area that appears relevant to the question of whether or not animals of different ages store different information is that of human learning as a function of age.

Several studies concerning the development of human verbal learning suggest that when children of different ages are exposed to the same set of stimulus items, different features of the stimulus items are stored. In one of the earlier studies of this phenomenon, Bach and Underwood (1970) presented lists of words to second- and sixth-grade students and later required that the children recognize the target items from a larger list. In measuring false alarms on the test (i.e., false positive responses) Bach and Underwood found that the younger children exhibited a greater tendency to respond incorrectly to items that were acoustically similar to the test items. False alarms by the older children consisted mainly of verbal associates of the original items. The conclusion drawn from this work was that younger children store mainly acoustic information concerning words, whereas older children store information having to do with word meanings or associations (see also Freund & Johnson, 1972).

In a second study, Hasher and Clifton (1974) demonstrated that free recall of a word list was facilitated in second graders if the words in the list were phonemically related. However, semantically related words were recalled no better than unrelated words. The reverse of this facilitory influence was found for sixth graders, whereas college students were able to use both kinds of relation-ships to facilitate recall. Again there is the suggestion of the presence of age-related differences in the utilization of certain stimulus features during learning.

Another study of particular relevance to the present discussion was conducted by Odom and Guzman (1972). These experimenters involved children 5 to 12 years old in a problem-solving task that required them to select two of three cards that were most similar. The figures on the cards varied along form, color, number, and position dimensions, and cards were presented such that all possible two-dimensional combinations occurred during the task. It was found that the performance of the 5- to 7-year-olds was best when form and color could be used to solve the problem, whereas for older children the task was easiest when number and position were the relevant dimensions. The findings suggest that there may be age-related differences in the stimulus features a human subject finds important in solving problems.

Implications for Long-Term Retention

As stated earlier, most of the explanations of infantile amnesia share the assumption that animals of all ages store the same information when placed in the same learning situation. In the present chapter an attempt is made to determine whether or not an alternative view is plausible. This alternative is that there may be age-related differences in the stimulus features that an animal finds relevant for adapting to its environment. As a result animals of different ages may select different stimulus features from a learning situation as being relevant for storage. Although the data cited in support of such a notion are far from conclusive, they do suggest that such an assumption is feasible and warrants further investigation.

If we do assume then that animals of different ages store different types of information, how might one explain the phenomenon of infantile amnesia? Actually such a view suggests a variety of alternatives. Probably the most appealing explanation is one that is analagous to the retrieval-deficit hypotheses already discussed. Animals trained at an early age should view certain stimulus features as being particularly relevant or significant and should therefore store information regarding the learning experience in relation to these stimulus features. However, when tested as adults these same animals should find a different set of stimulus features to be of maximal relevance and be maximally attentive to these features. Since the newly relevant features do not match the features relevant at an earlier time, activation of the appropriate memory attributes should not occur, and a retrieval deficit should result.

There is also the possibility that information concerning some stimulus dimensions is forgotten more rapidly than information about other dimensions. Although such a possibility is difficult to test and has only recently been considered experimentally (Farthing, Wagner, Gilmour, & Waxman, 1977), such a possibility might provide an alternative explanation of infantile amnesia. It is possible, for example, that the particular stimulus elements that are most relevant to younger organisms may be the same stimuli that are forgotten most rapidly by organisms of all ages. Such a circumstance would suggest that younger animals forget more rapidly than older animals when in fact rates of forgetting might be more dependent on particular memory attributes than on developmental level of the organism.

Such interpretations of infantile amnesia are obviously difficult to test experimentally. One starting point would be to determine whether or not animals of different ages do in fact exhibit differential stimulus selection strategies in the same learning situation. Work presently underway in our laboratory is directed at this question. If this should be the case, the present view suggests that in order to understand learning and memory functioning in the young animal, it may be most useful to understand the purposes such processes serve in an animal's attempts to adapt behaviorally to its environment.

REFERENCES

Bach, M. J., & Underwood, B. J. Developmental changes in memory attributes. *Journal of Educational Psychology*, 1970, *61*, 292–296.

Brennan, M. J., & Gordon, W. C. Selective facilitation of memory attributes by strychnine. *Pharmacology Biochemistry & Behavior*, 1977, *7*, 451–457.

Bronstein, P. M., Neiman, H., Wolkoff, F. D., & Levine, M. J. The development of habituation in the rat. *Animal Learning & Behavior*, 1974, *2*, 92–96.

Brower, L. P. Ecological chemistry. *Scientific American*, 1969, *220*, 22–29.

Caldwell, D. F., & Werboff, J. Classical conditioning in newborn rats. *Science*, 1962, *136*, 1118–1119.

Calhoun, W. H. Central nervous stimulants. In E. Furchgott (Ed.) *Pharmacological and biophysical agents and behavior*. New York: Academic Press, 1971.

Campbell, B. A., & Alberts, J. R. Ontogeny of long-term memory for learned taste aversions. *Behavioral Biology*, in press.

Campbell, B. A., & Coulter, X. The ontogenesis of learning and memory. In M. R. Rosenzweig & E. L. Bennett (Eds.), *Neural mechanisms of learning and memory*. Cambridge: MIT Press, 1976.

Campbell, B. A., & Jaynes, J. Reinstatement. *Psychological Review*, 1966, *73*, 478–480.

Campbell, B. A., Misanin, J. R., White, B. C., & Lytle, L. D. Species differences in ontogeny of memory: Support for neural maturation as a determinant of forgetting. *Journal of comparative and Physiological Psychology*, 1974, *87*, 193–202.

Campbell, B. S., Riccio, D. C., & Rohrbaugh, M. Ontogenesis of learning and memory: Research and theory. In M. E. Meyer (Ed.), *Second Western symposium on learning: Early learning*. Bellingham, Wash.: Western Washington State College Press, 1971.

Campbell, B. A., & Spear, N. E. Ontogeny of memory. *Psychological Review*, 1972, *79*, 215–236.

Cornwall, A. C., & Fuller, J. L. Conditioned responses in young puppies. *Journal of Comparative and Physiological Psychology*, 1961, *54*, 13–15.

Douglas, R. J., Peterson, J. J., & Douglas, D. P. The ontogeny of a hippocampus-dependent response in two rodent species. *Behavioral Biology*, 1973, *8*, 27–37.

Farthing, G. W., Wagner, J. M., Gilmour, S., & Waxman, H. M. Short term memory and information processing in pigeons. *Learning and Motivation*, 1977, *8*, 520–533.

Feigley, D. A., Parsons, P. J., Hamilton, L. W., & Spear, N. E. Development of habituation to novel environments in the rat. *Journal of Comparative and Physiological Psychology*, 1972, *79*, 443–452.

Feigley, D., & Spear, N. E. Effect of age and punishment condition on long-term retention by the rat of active- and passive-avoidance learning. *Journal of Comparative and Physiological Psychology*, 1970, *73*, 515–526.

Freund, J. S., & Johnson, J. W. Changes in memory attribute dominance as function of age. *Journal of Educational Psychology*, 1972, *63*, 386–389.

Garcia, J., & Koelling, R. A. Relation of cue to consequence in avoidance learning. *Psychonomic Science*, 1966, *4*, 123–124.

Gordon, W. C. Susceptibility of a reactivated memory to the effects of strychnine: A time-dependent phenomenon. *Physiology and Behavior*, 1977, *18*, 95–99.

Hasher, L., & Clifton, D. A developmental study of attribute encoding in free recall. *Journal of Experimental Child Psychology*, 1974, *17*, 332–346.

Hirschman, R., & Katkin, E. S. Physiological functioning, arousal, attention, and learning during the first year of life. In H. W. Reese (Ed.), *Advances in child development and behavior* (Vol. 9). New York: Academic Press, 1974.

Hull, C. L. *Principles of behavior*. New York: Appleton-Century-Crofts, 1943.

Kamin, L. J. Predictability, surprise, attention and conditioning. In B. A. Campbell & R. M. Church (Eds.), *Punishment and aversive behavior*. New York: Appleton-Century-Crofts, 1969.

Kenny, J. T., & Blass, E. M. Suckling as an incentive to instrumental learning in pre-weanling rats. *Science*, 1977, *196*, 898–899.

Kirby, R. H. Acquisition, extinction, and retention of an avoidance response as a function of age. *Journal of Comparative and Physiological Psychology*, 1963, *56*, 158–162.

Klein, S. B., & Spear, N. E. Influence of age on short-term retention of active avoidance learning in rats. *Journal of Comparative and Physiological Psychology*, 1969, *69*, 583–589.

Math, F., & Desor, D. Évolution de la réaction d'arrêt de l'électroencéphalogramme consécutive aux stimulations olfactives naturelles chez le Rat blanc élevé en semi-liberté. *Comptes rendus hebdomadaire des séances de l'Académie des sciences*, 1974, *279*, 931–934.

McGaugh, J. L., & Dawson, R. G. Modification of memory storage processes. In W. K. Honig & H. James (Eds.), *Animal memory*. New York: Academic Press, 1971.

Miles, C. G., & Jenkins, H. M. Overshadowing in operant conditioning as a function of discriminability. *Learning and Motivation*, 1973, *4*, 11–27.

Odom, R. D., & Guzman, R. D. Development of hierarchies of dimensional salience. *Developmental Psychology*, 1972, *6*, 271–287.

Parsons, P. J., & Spear, N. E. Long-term retention of avoidance learning by immature and adult rats as a function of environmental enrichment. *Journal of Comparative and Physiological Psychology*, 1972, *80*, 297–303.

Pomerleau-Malcuit, A. Activité cardiaque et comportement: Mesures des premiers processus d'interaction entre l'organisme naissant et son environnement. *Canadian Psychologist*, 1974, *15*, 43–60.

Rescorla, R. A., & Wagner, A. R. A theory of Pavlovian conditioning: Variations in the effectiveness of reinforcement and nonreinforcement. In A. H. Black & W. F. Prokasy (Eds.), *Classical conditioning II: Current research and theory*. New York: Appleton-Century-Crofts, 1972.

Riccio, D. D., & Schulenberg, C. J. Age-related deficits in acquisition of a passive avoidance response. *Canadian Journal of Psychology*, 1969, *23*, 429–437.

Rosenblatt, J. S. Stages in the early behavioural development of altricial young of selected species of non-primate mammals. In P. P. G. Bateson & R. A. Hinde (Eds.), *Growing points in ethology*. Cambridge: Cambridge University Press, 1976.

Rozin, P., & Kalat, J. W. Specific hungers and poison avoidance as adaptive specializations of learning. *Psychological Review*, 1971, *78*, 459–486.

Rudy, J. W., & Cheatle, M. D. *Odor-aversion learning in infant rats*. Manuscript submitted for publication, 1978.

Schachtel, E. G. On memory and childhood amnesia. *Psychiatry*, 1947, *10*, 1–26.

Schulenberg, C. J., Riccio, D. C., & Stikes, E. R. Acquisition and retention of a passive avoidance response as a function of age in rats. *Journal of Comparative and Physiological Psychology*, 1971, *74*, 75–83.

Smith, N. Effects of interpolated learning on retention of an escape response in rats as a function of age. *Journal of Comparative and Physiological Psychology*, 1968, *65*, 422–426.

Spear, N. E. Forgetting as retrieval failure. In W. K. Honig & P. H. R. James (Eds.), *Animal memory*. New York: Academic Press, 1971.

Spear, N. E. Retrieval of memory in animals. *Psychological Review*, 1973, *80*, 163–194.

Spear, N. E., Gordon, W. C., & Chiszar, D. A. Interaction between memories in the rat: Effect of degree of prior conflicting learning on forgetting after short intervals. *Journal of Comparative and Physiological Psychology*, 1972, *78*, 471–477.

Spear, N. E., & Parsons, P. J. Analysis of a reactivation treatment: Ontogenetic determinants of alleviated forgetting. In D. L. Medin, W. A. Roberts, & R. T. Davis (Eds.), *Processes of animal memory*. Hillsdale, N.J.: Lawrence Erlbaum Associates, 1976.

Sutherland, N. S., & Mackintosh, N. J. *Mechanisms of animal discrimination learning*. New York: Academic Press, 1971.

Tobach, E., Rouger, Y., & Schneirla, T. C. Development of olfactory function in the rat pup. *American Zoologist*, 1967, *7*, 792–793.

Underwood, B. J. Degree of learning and the measurement of forgetting. *Journal of Verbal Learning and Verbal Behavior*, 1964, *3*, 112–129.

Underwood, B. J. Attributes of memory. *Psychological Review*, 1969, *76*, 559–573.

Underwood, B. J., & Keppel, G. Retention as a function of degree of learning and letter-sequence interference. *Psychological Monographs*, 1963, *77* (4, Whole No. 567).

Wickler, W. *Mimicry in Plants and Animals*. New York: McGraw-Hill, 1968.

Wilcoxon, H. C., Dragoin, W. B., & Kral, P. A. Illness-induced aversions in rat and quail: Relative salience of visual and gustatory cues. *Science*, 1971, *171*, 826–828.

Williams, J. M., Hamilton, L. W., & Carlton, P. L. Ontogenetic dissociation of two classes of habituation. *Journal of Comparative and Physiological Psychology*, 1975, *89*, 733–737.

12

Some Approaches to the Alleviation of Ontogenetic Memory Deficits

David C. Riccio and Vahram Haroutunian
Kent State University

That immature organisms do not retain learned responses as well as adults has been well established by Campbell and others (for reviews see Campbell & Coulter, 1976; Campbell, Riccio, & Rohrbaugh, 1971; Campbell & Spear, 1972; see also Nagy, Chapter 5). The age-related changes in memory are not limited to infrahuman species or laboratory experiments; the inability of human adults to remember events of the first few years of life ("infantile amnesia") represents a similar phenomenon (Campbell & Coulter, 1976). This memory deficit in the developing organism is of particular interest from several perspectives. On the one hand the phenomenon poses an intriguing paradox for "early experience" studies: How do events during infancy modify later adult behavior if retention of these early experiences is so limited? On the other hand the relatively rapid forgetting in young animals provides a convenient type of preparation with which to study memory. Thus, determining the events that can eliminate or alleviate infantile amnesia should serve to advance our understanding of the ontogeny of memory and, more generally, add to our understanding of memorial processes.

One paradigm to alleviate developmental forgetting has been described by Campbell & Jaynes (1966). These authors demonstrated that, following Pavlovian fear conditioning in weanling rats, periodic exposure to an abbreviated form of the training regime during the retention interval maintained the fear response at a high level. Pairing a brief exposure to the fear cues with a single shock once per week for four weeks significantly reduced retention loss, although the same treatment given to untrained subjects was too weak to produce new learning. This evidence of *reinstatement*, as the phenomenon was termed, subsequently was replicated and extended to other learning tasks (Campbell &

Jaynes, 1969; Hoving, Coates, Bertucci, & Riccio, 1972; Shubat & Whitehouse, 1968). A finding from our laboratory suggested that reinstatement could also be produced by exposure to the conditioned cues alone (Silvestri, Rohrbaugh, & Riccio, 1970). This "conditioned reinstatement" seemed of particular interest because it greatly expanded the opportunities for a developing organism to make contact with a reminder situation. However, as might be expected, the improvement in retention was considerably weaker when the reminder consisted of the presentation of the conditioned fear stimuli alone (i.e., in extinction) than when a complete re-pairing of cues and shock was provided. This raised the interesting question of whether there are manipulations that might amplify the effect of a cue-only exposure and provide a strengthening of memory more comparable to that obtained with a complete conditional stimulus to unconditioned stimulus (CS–UCS) trial.

Our basic strategy followed from Spear's (1973) analysis of memory failures. Presumably the target memory consists of a multiplicity of attributes. Only a portion of these attributes would be present during a conditioned reinstatement treatment. If pain, arousal, and internal changes associated with a strong emotional state are important concomitants of the original fear-conditioning experience, then reeliciting some of these components in conjunction with exposure to fear cues might increase the effectiveness of reinstatement. Accordingly we have conducted several studies employing either drugs or noncontingent footshock in an attempt to induce some of these internal attributes at the time of cue exposure. Although our techniques for mimicking the internal state associated with original training have not been elaborate, the data appear promising. Before describing the experiments, however, we will outline the methodology.

GENERAL PROCEDURES

Similar training and testing procedures were used in most of the studies to be discussed. Departures from the general method outlined in the following will be indicated where appropriate.

Training consisted of Pavlovian discriminative fear conditioning given when the rats were 20 to 21 days of age. Conditioning took place in a two-compartment black–white shuttle box with grid floors in both compartments. A guillotine door that separated the two compartments remained closed throughout the conditioning phase. Each rat was placed inside the black compartment of the shuttle box for one 5-minute period, where it received a total of six 2-second, 150-V scrambled footshocks. Shocks were programed on a variable-interval time schedule. The rat was then confined for a comparable period in the white compartment of the shuttle box but was not shocked. This treatment was then repeated. Thus during a single 20-minute session fear was conditioned to the black chamber (brightness and other contextual stimuli), and safety (or at least less danger) was established to the shock-free white compartment.

A single reinstatement treatment was typically administered after 1 week of a 2-week retention interval. Although the nature of the reinstatement experience varied among experiments, it consisted generally of administration of either a drug or aversive stimulation in conjunction with the presence or absence of the conditioned fear cues.

Then 1 week later (i.e., at the end of the 2-week retention interval) subjects were tested for retention. A passive-avoidance procedure was used to assess retention of fear. The rat was placed in the white chamber of the shuttle box, the guillotine door leading to the black compartment was raised, and the latency of the subject to step into the black chamber was recorded. Unlike many experiments using passive-avoidance testing, latencies were measured for each subject until a cross-through response occurred. This was intended to preclude the possibility that indeterminate scores produced by an artificial ceiling would obscure differences in retention.

REINSTATEMENT WITH DRUG-INDUCED CHANGES

Epinephrine

In our initial experiment to examine the potential role of internal cues in activating memory during a nominal extinction treatment, we chose epinephrine (EPI) as the agent to mimic fear-related changes (Haroutunian & Riccio, 1977). The endogenous secretion of epinephrine from the adrenal medulla during fear and stress states is well known (Turner & Bagnara, 1976), and the variety of changes induced by exogenous administration of epinephrine is well established (e.g., Grossman & Sclafani, 1971; Innes & Nickerson, 1975). When we began there was also some evidence that a posttrial injection of epinephrine could enhance retention of a weakly learned passive-avoidance response (Gold & Van Buskirk, 1975; Kamano, 1968).

The procedure was straightforward. Four groups of 21-day-old rats received Pavlovian fear conditioning (described in the foregoing) followed by a single reinstatement treatment 1 week later. Rats in the drug condition received a 0.05-mg/kg dose of epinephrine (adrenalin chloride) injected subcutaneously at the nape of the neck. Then 20 minutes later half of these subjects were placed for 1 minute each in the black and then the white compartment of the training apparatus; the remaining rats were handled briefly but not exposed to the apparatus cues. As a control for injection effects, two other groups were given saline (SAL), followed either by cue exposure or handling. To determine the degree of forgetting that could be expected without reinstatement, an additional group of retention controls received Pavlovian fear conditioning, but its only treatment 1 week later was a brief period of handling.

The results of the passive-avoidance test, given 2 weeks after original training, are presented in the left panel of Fig. 12.1 Long latencies are interpreted as reflecting the presence of memory—that is, fear of returning to the shock compartment. It is clear that exogeneous administration of epinephrine succeeded in reinstating or maintaining fear but only when provided in the context of the appropriate cues. Neither the drug alone nor the injection procedure with or without cues proved effective. Since the epinephrine administration occurred 1 week prior to testing, long latencies cannot be attributable to sensorimotor impairments induced by the drug. Similarly the finding that the effectiveness of epinephrine was contingent on training cues at reinstatement argues against drug-related performance artifacts. There was no evidence of a conditioned-reinstatement effect without the drug; about the only hint of such an effect is that cue-alone groups were not lower than the retention control, as might be expected on basis of extinction. The improved retention in the epinephrine-cues condition does demonstrate that the UCS (shock) is not a necessary condition for the reinstatement effect.

We viewed these outcomes as generally consonant with the notion that increasing the number of memory attributes available at the time of reinstatement treatment will enhance subsequent retention performance. Presumably a more potent collection of memory attributes is present when an epinephrine-injected rat is returned to the original fear cues. In addition the importance of the external

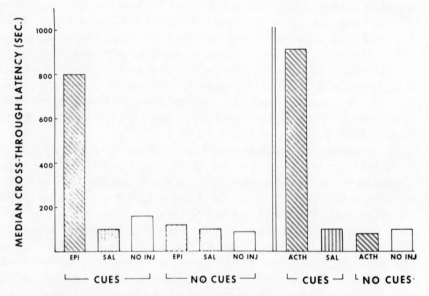

FIG. 12.1.   Effect of interpolated reinstatement treatment without shock upon passive-avoidance latencies at testing. EPI = epinephrine; SAL = saline; ACTH = adrenocorticotropic hormone; NO INJ = no injection.

cues as well as internal state is intriguingly reminiscent of Schacter's finding that human subjects receiving epinephrine tended to label their presumably identical emotional state in keeping with certain experimenter-induced expectations (Schacter & Singer, 1962). Depending on the particular information previously presented, for example, the drug induced either "gregariousness" or "anger." Could it be that even in rats the changes induced by epinephrine are perceived as "fear" only if the appropriate redintegrative stimuli for that experience are present?

Adrenocorticotrophic Hormone (ACTH)

In order to confirm and extend these findings with epinephrine, our next experiment employed ACTH, another hormone intimately involved in the organism's response to a stressor (Sayers & Travis, 1970). In addition to its role in controlling the output of adrenal cortical steroids, several studies indicated that ACTH can influence acquisition and extinction of avoidance (see de Wied, 1974, for review).

Four groups of subjects ($N = 8$), differing only in their treatment at the time of reinstatement, were used. Two drug groups received subcutaneous injections of corticotropin gel: For one group this was followed 30 minutes later by placement in the fear-conditioning chamber; for the other group handling was substituted for cue exposure. The third group received a saline injection prior to cue exposure, and retention controls were neither injected nor exposed to cues. The results, depicted in the right-hand panel of Fig. 12.1, were strikingly similar to those obtained with epinephrine.

These data appear to support our earlier supposition that exogenous administration of hormones associated with stressful experience can reestablish important internal attributes of the target memory. When these are then linked with appropriate external cues, a powerful reminder effect is obtained. This interpretation also seems consistent with evidence of induced recovery of memory in retrograde amnesia studies. For example, it has been reported that retrograde amnesia is alleviated when ACTH (Keyes, 1974; Rigter & van Riezen, 1975) or the original amnestic treatment (Thompson & Grossman, 1972; Hinderliter, Webster, & Riccio, 1975) is given shortly prior to testing. Presumably the drug as well as the amnestic agent induces many of the internal concomitants of the original training–treatment episode. To the extent that the memory is embedded in these "contextual cues" (Hinderliter et al., 1975; Jensen, Riccio, & Gehres, 1975) the response is retrievable and the amnesia reduced.

Analeptic Agents: Amphetamine and Strychnine

We assumed initially that "arousal," as a component of the drug-induced changes, was an attribute important to obtaining memory reinstatement. For example, although epinephrine does not easily cross the blood–brain barrier and is not regarded as a potent Central Nervous System (CNS) stimulant (Innes & Nickerson, 1975), it seemed possible that activation might be achieved indirectly through feedback from peripheral changes. Accordingly, using drugs that directly increase CNS arousal should produce comparable or perhaps stronger reinstatement effects. We chose to use amphetamine, which in addition to its sympathomimetic function readily crosses the blood–brain barrier to stimulate the CNS (Innes & Nickerson, 1975), and strychnine, the classic example of a convulsant agent, which stimulates the CNS by blocking inhibition (Franz, 1975). Both agents have been used in an enormous variety of behavioral experiments (e.g., see Calhoun, 1971; Grossman & Sclafani, 1971; and McGaugh & Dawson, 1971, for reviews). Of particular interest to us was the report that passive-avoidance memory is enhanced if strychnine is administered shortly after a reactivation treatment (Gordon & Spear, 1973).

For brevity, the two separate experiments will be described together. In the amphetamine study, groups of rats at the time of reinstatement received subcutaneous (nape of neck) injections of either 0.0 (Saline), 0.5, 1.0, or 3.0 mg/kg of drug approximately 20 minutes prior to cue exposure. A similar procedure was used in the strychnine experiment, except that the drug dosages were 0.5 and 0.75 mg/kg. Various control groups received saline followed by cues, drug not followed by cues, or no treatment during the retention interval.

The findings were uniformly disappointing. There was no evidence that these arousal-inducing drugs influenced retention under any condition. Among the experimental groups the best retention score was a rather paltry median latency of 41 seconds for the intermediate dose level of amphetamine. This performance did not approach being reliably different from the retention controls.

One obvious explanation for these negative results is that values of the parameters for dose level, time delay, cue exposure, and so forth were less than optimal. A more interesting possibility is that directly evoked arousal of the CNS is not as important to reinstating fear memory as the peripheral changes linked with a stressful state (changes that are presumably then detected by the CNS). A problem for this second alternative is that in addition to its arousal effects, amphetamine produces many of the same peripheral changes as does epinephrine. In this connection, however, it is interesting to note that tonic immobility, a response presumably reflecting fear, is enhanced by epinephrine but not by amphetamine (Boren & Gallup, 1976).

These few experiments represent only a beginning effort to delineate the attributes that are necessary and sufficient for the reinstatement of memory. At a more general level, however, the findings with epinephrine and ACTH add to the growing body of evidence implicating hormonal involvement in the modulation of memory.

REINSTATEMENT WITH ENVIRONMENTAL
MANIPULATIONS

Arrangements of UCS and CS

If presentation of a CS in conjunction with injections of stress-related hormones could facilitate long-term retention, then it seemed reasonable to expect a similar outcome using the original UCS rather than drugs. As mentioned earlier, direct re-pairing of the CS with the UCS is a highly effective treatment. Our interest was in the possibility that the aversive stimulation need not occur in the presence of the fear cues in order for the reinstatement phenomenon to be obtained. Despite the questionable adequacy of the backward conditioning procedure in establishing acquisition (Hall, 1976), we presumed that delivery of a noncontingent footshock (NCFS) followed by a CS exposure might be an effective reminder. As many investigators have discovered to their chagrin, a shocked rat is an agitated rat, even when the shock has terminated. Thus it seemed to us that persistence of emotional–arousal responses following shock should, if combined with fear stimuli, serve to prevent or reduce ontogenetic retention loss.

Accordingly we carried out an experiment in which one group of rats received a NCFS in a neutral area and, 30 seconds later, was briefly exposed to the training cues with no further shocks. Because the shock-elicited changes should subside, we gave a second group the same treatment except for a 20-minute interval between noncontingent shock and cue exposure. To provide an estimate of the maximum reinstatement to be expected, a third group received the same shock in the presence of fear stimuli—that is, the type of reinstatement treatment originally described by Campbell & Jaynes (1966). A fourth set of rats was administered noncontingent shock and returned to home cages without the cue exposure. This group was designed to serve as an "arousal" control, much like the epinephrine-alone group discussed earlier. The degree of forgetting to be expected without any reinstatement episode was provided by a fifth group. (Because this experiment was run concurrently with the epinephrine study, the same retention control group was used for both.)

Figure 12.2 presents the findings. As the figure suggests, all three types of reinstatement enhanced memory relative to the no-reinstatement control group. Furthermore, exposure to cues shortly after the NCFS was as effective as regular reinstatement in maintaining memory. And, as expected, degree of reinstatement was less with a 20-minute "cooling off" period between NCFS and cues. Again these findings seem to parallel the epinephrine and ACTH outcomes in suggesting that memory retrieval is greatly facilitated when the appropriate internal milieu is available during presentation of learned fear cues.

The other salient outcome is the potency of the UCS alone as a reinstating agent. This is consistent with results recently reported by Spear and Parsons

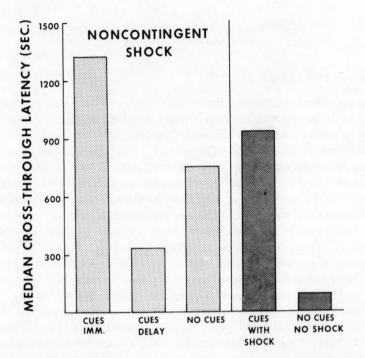

FIG. 12.2.   Effect of type of reinstatement condition upon retention. In the left-hand portion NCFS was followed immediately (0.5 minute) or after a delay (20 minutes) by cue exposure or cue presentation was omitted. The group receiving cues with shock (right-hand portion) represents the traditional reinstatement treatment.

(1976), who utilized footshock in a rather similar reactivation paradigm. In addition, unsignaled UCS presentations appear to activate memory in a variety of other circumstances. For example, noncontingent footshock has been reported to alleviate electroconvulsive shock (ECS)-induced amnesia (Miller & Springer, 1973; Quartermain, McEwen, & Azmitia, 1972); to re-establish a Pavlovian fear response following extinction (Rescorla & Heth, 1975); and to reactivate stimulus control of a conditioned emotional response (CER) in pigeons (Hoffman, Selekman, & Fleshler, 1966). We find it intriguing that in all these diverse paradigms a noncontingent UCS proved effective in restoring the learned response. Presumably such treatment elicits a large proportion of the attributes necessary for memory retrieval.

In the context of the current study, however, we are faced with the problem of why retention performance should be significantly better in the NCFS group than in the group receiving NCFS followed, after a delay, by the CS. Given the notion of multiple attributes of memory, it seems puzzling that any condition incorporating both the fear cues and the shock should be less effective than the shock alone.

In order to explore more fully the relationship between amount of retention and the sequencing of reinstating events, we carried out an experiment in which the interval between noncontingent shock and cue exposure was systematically varied. It seemed likely that if exposure to fear cues were sufficiently delayed after UCS presentation, we would approximate the effects of the UCS-alone condition. Because the order of presentation of stimuli also might be important, we included parallel manipulations in which exposure to the contextual CS preceded the noncontingent footshock. Thus, following standard training and a 1-week retention interval, three groups of subjects were exposed to the discriminative cues of the training apparatus for a total of 2 minutes, followed either 60, 20, or 5 minutes later by NCFS, and another three groups received the NCFS treatment followed 60, 20, or 5 minutes later by the brief exposure to training stimuli. In addition we included a group run under conditions of the preceding study—that is, the NCFS was delivered and shortly afterward (0.5 min.) subjects were given cue exposure.

Figure 12.3 presents the passive-avoidance scores from the retention test 1 week after reinstatement. The functions indicate that imposing the intermediate intervals between stimulus presentations, regardless of order, provides less effective reinstatement than when the delay is very brief. The other striking aspect of the data is their nonmonotonicity. As we had predicted (but not really

STIMULUS SEQUENCE AND TEMPORAL RELATIONS

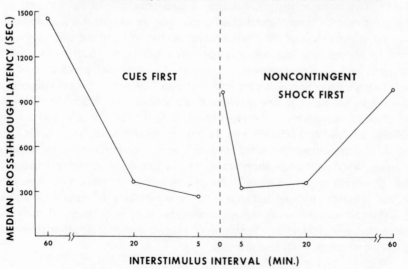

FIG. 12.3.   Retention performance as a function of the interval between stimulus events during reinstatement. Left panel: Brief exposure to training cues was followed by NCFS after the designated interval. Right panel: Noncontingent shock occurred first and cue presentation was delayed as indicated.

expected), with a very long interval between the two stimulus events, retention is comparable to that produced by the NCFS alone.

These findings are not inconsistent with the view that memory is represented by a collection of attributes, but they do suggest that the cues may not combine additively. Otherwise, if memory retrieval depended on the total number of cues presented at reactivation, any condition that incorporated CS and UCS should have been at least as beneficial as a condition with only one of these events. It may be that forgetting in immature organisms reflects as much the loss of memory for the UCS as it does the failure of associative linkages between cues and UCS (cf. Rescorla, 1973, 1974). Thus even in the absence of original fear stimuli the NCFS could activate an internal representation of the UCS (Rescorla & Heth, 1975) that has degraded during the developmental span of the retention interval. It also seems necessary to assume that under certain conditions the original cues may have inhibitory or extinction-like effects that reduce the effectiveness of reminder treatment.

The implicit Pavlovian conditioning features of the reminder treatment constitute a further consideration that may be important. The term "noncontingent footshock" is a misnomer, albeit a popular and rather convenient one. Clearly, shocks (or any other aversive stimuli for that matter) are administered in the presence of various stimuli, even if these contextual stimuli are not designated by the experimenter as "CS." The UCS-alone manipulation can be seen as a classical conditioning episode with cues that are different from original training. These considerations suggest that lack of discriminability of the noncontingent reminder episode from original training may play an important role in determining the effectiveness of the reinstatement. As forgetting of the attributes of the original fear-training situation develops over time, the NCFS trial may come to be perceived as a continuation of training. An interesting implication of this still-roughhewn notion is that the effectiveness of the noncontingent treatment as a reminder should be inversely related to the amount of retention. Thus, shortly following training, while the characteristics of the conditioning trial are still salient, an episode of NCFS may be readily distinguished from training and would thus contribute little to the enhancement of retention. Later in the retention interval, when only a few attributes of the conditioning situation can be recalled (cf. Thomas & Riccio, in press), subjects may be unable to differentiate between stimuli present at training and stimuli that now constitute the reminder situation. Under these circumstances the noncontingent shock may be functionally and perceptually equivalent to a repetition or extension of training, thus promoting retention of the original fear response.

Other Aversive Stimuli

The potency of the noncontingent shock in reinstating memory encouraged us to consider the possibility that other aversive treatments also might serve as reminders. If aversiveness is encoded as an attribute of the target memory, then a variety of stressor agents or noxious stimuli might share enough commonality to permit access to memory. Indeed, Klein and Spear (1970) have provided a classic example of this approach in their analysis of the Kamin effect as a retrieval failure. They demonstrated that cold water exposure is as effective as NCFS in eliminating depressed active-avoidance performance at intermediate intervals after training. Their study suggests that the internal attributes evoked by either type of aversive stimulation allows retrieval of the original memory. With the help of Cindy Legin and Chris Papantonakis, we have begun to compare the reinstating potency of footshock, tailshock, and mild hypothermia treatments. All of these are clearly stressful but differ in loci and type of sensory receptors activated. In a factorial manner the stress manipulations have been crossed with either the presence or absence of training cues at reinstatement. Although we have consistently obtained a reinstatement effect, it is not possible to conclude which, if any, are the more effective treatments. The variability of these data has sensitized us to some potential difficulties. For example, if cues can detract from the magnitude of the reinstatement phenomenon, as they clearly seem to do with intermediate intervals between CS and footshock, then similar interactions may occur here as well. In short, complex relationships among type of unconditioned stimulus duration and intensity of the unconditioned response, and timing of conditioned stimulus presentation may be partly responsible for the variability in our data. For the moment, however, we continue to believe that the issue of generality of reinstating events is an important one.

It has been demonstrated in several paradigms that reminder treatments modify performance only if there had been prior associative learning (e.g., Campbell & Jaynes, 1966; Hinderliter et al., 1975; Spear & Parsons, 1976). However, because we were using passive avoidance as an index of retention, it seemed especially important to obtain independent evidence that elevated response latencies were not simply an artifact of exposure to repeated shocks. Therefore we conducted an ancillary experiment in which, instead of Pavlovian fear conditioning, 21-day-old rats received an equivalent amount of noncontingent shock experience. Ideally, a truly random control procedure would have been employed with respect to the correlation between CS and shocks. With apparatus cues as a contextual CS, however, such a procedure is difficult to implement without introducing additional confoundings. As a compromise strategy, one group received the NCFS and never was exposed to the apparatus cues; a second group, after receiving the NCFS, was confined for 10 minutes in the black and 10 minutes in the white compartments with no further shocks. The second group thus matched trained subjects with respect to total exposure to cues and shocks except for the contingency between them; the potential disadvantage was that for the controls the cues might acquire "safe" properties. Both groups received a single NCFS as a "reinstatement" treatment at 28 days of age, followed 1 week later by the passive-avoidance test. The cross-through latencies in these control conditions were well below those of animals that had received similar reinstatement after having been fear conditioned. Interestingly, these two control groups did differ from each other; the shock-only group had a significantly longer median latency (200 seconds) than the group in which cue exposure followed shock (13 seconds). It is possible that the score of one group is elevated owing to the fact that these shocked subjects are hesitant to move about when tested in a novel stimulus situation; alternatively, the "safety" aspects of cue exposure in the other condition may have elicited exploratory activity and unusually short latencies. But the major point is that the passive-avoidance levels obtained in reinstatement studies are attributable primarily to improved retention rather than to generalized emotionality, systemic stress, or other performance variables.

ALLEVIATION OF FORGETTING THROUGH PROACTIVE EXPERIENCE

Prior Footshock

This line of investigation, although in some respects the converse of the reinstatement paradigm, originated rather directly from evidence that retrograde amnesia can be attentuated by pretraining experience. For example, Lewis, Miller, and Misanin (1968) reported that prior exposure to training cues (familiarization, or FAM) would reduce the severity of later electroconvulsive shock-induced amnesia. Several subsequent studies extended this work by showing that prior exposure to the eventual UCS (Hinderliter, Smith, & Misanin, 1973; Jensen & Riccio, 1970) or to the amnestic agent (Hinderliter et al., 1973; Hinderliter & Riccio, 1976) would also protect subjects from amnesia. Indeed we have suggested that these findings represent a paradox in that retrograde amnesia is an extremely reliable phenomenon, which can be obtained across a diversity of experimental conditions, yet it can be eliminated (or attenuated) surprisingly easily by these seemingly minor or irrelevant manipulations (Riccio, 1975).

Although the theoretical basis for the familiarization effect is not clear, it seemed of interest to determine whether or not a similar phenomenon occurs with respect to developmentally related memory failure; that is, would infantile amnesia be altered as a function of experiences prior to the criterion task? This experimental issue can be seen more broadly as an extension of the early experience paradigm. In contrast to the variety of studies concerned with the effects of early experience upon adult behavior, there has been relatively little assessment of the consequences of early treatment on still-unfolding ontogenetic processes. The following experiments focus on the impact of prior experience on the memory system of the immature organism.

As a starting point we chose noncontingent shock as the type of prior experience to be used. In the first study the experimental treatment consisted of a single NCFS administered on each of 3 days. Somewhat arbitrarily we selected 16 to 18 days of age as the treatment period. Each NCFS was delivered at a randomly selected time during a 60-second session while the rat was in a wooden box. This noncontingent shock box differed from the Pavlovian conditioning chamber in size, illumination, and construction material. The training and testing procedures were identical to those used in the reinstatement studies: Pavlovian discriminative fear conditioning at 20 days of age and a passive-avoidance test for retention 2 weeks later.

Of three control groups, one was given handling instead of the noncontingent shocks at 16 to 18 days of age. Because the treatment variable resulted in the experimental subjects receiving slightly more total shocks, we included a second control group, which received three "extra" shocks as part of the classic conditioning session. A third group received NCFS but was not given fear conditioning. These subjects provided a check on the possibility that elevated response latencies were not simply a function of early shock experience.

During testing, the experimental group refrained from entering the shock compartment for a median of 767 seconds. This contrasted with cross-through latencies of controls receiving regular training (88 seconds), extra footshocks in training (83 seconds), or noncontingent shock without training (49 seconds). Thus noncontingent shocks prior to training markedly enhanced the retention of fear, but the difference does not appear to be based simply on total shock experience. It is also clear that noncontingent shocks per se have little effect on cross-through latencies. Under these conditions weanling rats without the prior experience show drastic retention loss in 2 weeks, and their test performance is indistinguishable from untrained controls.

The finding did seem analogous to the familiarization effect obtained in retrograde amnesia experiments. However, one important methodological concern in the present paradigm is whether or not the improved retention is a by-product of stronger initial learning. Before presenting our attempts to address that issue, we will describe briefly a replication experiment in which the effects of massed versus distributed noncontingent shocks were compared. The distributed group received the same schedule of shocks (1 per day for 3 days) as in the earlier study; the massed group received the 3 shocks during a 3-minute session at 17 days of age; and a baseline group received handling. Subsequently, Pavlovian fear conditioning was administered to all three groups at 20 days of age. Mean passive-avoidance latencies at the end of the 2-week retention interval were 524, 430, and 152 seconds for the distributed, massed, and control conditions, respectively. The distributed preshock group differed significantly from the control condition, thus replicating the earlier finding. The massed preshock group did not differ reliably from either of the other groups. As the efficacy of the massed preshock treatment was left open to question, we decided to use the spaced condition in our subsequent experiments.

As indicated earlier, it is possible that the prior shock experience facilitates or potentiates acquisition of fear and thus only indirectly modifies retention. The finding that extra shocks during conditioning (i.e., a form of overtraining) did not eliminate the retention deficit casts doubt on such an interpretation. However, prior experience may have had a more subtle effect on response strength. Accordingly, we carried out several experiments to evaluate the effect of our proactive manipulation on strength of learning, assessed independently of the degree of retention. In one study, resistance to extinction was used as an index of original response strength. That resistance to extinction may be sensitive to prior shock effects is indicated by data showing that in adult rats preshock enhanced the effects of punishment and augmented resistance to extinction of fear (Anderson, Cole, & McVaugh, 1968). In the present experiment one group of rats received preshock treatments on Days 16, 17, and 18 of age, whereas the second group was handled but not shocked on these days. At 20 days of age all the rats in both groups received the previously described Pavlovian discriminative fear-conditioning treatment. One day later all subjects received a latent extinction treatment consisting of confinement in each compartment of the apparatus for 10 minutes without shocks. A passive-avoidance test administered 24 hours following the extinction treatment did not reveal any significant differences between the preshocked and handled controls: Mean cross-through latencies for preshocked and handled subjects were 257 and 221 seconds, respectively. This outcome, although hardly definitive, is consistent with the view that initial response strength did not differ markedly between the groups.

Apart from the problems inherent in proving the null hypothesis, it is possible that a more direct measure of acquisition strength would reveal differences. We attempted to assess this possibility by testing "incompletely" conditioned rats that had received either 0 or 3 noncontingent shocks prior to Pavlovian training. A third group received preshock but was not conditioned. The conditioning procedure of the previous experiments was modified by reducing the number of UCS presentations from 12 to 2. This weaker training was intended to reduce the likelihood of ceiling scores obscuring differences in acquisition. The two UCS presentations were apparently sufficient to establish fear conditioning, because both trained groups showed significantly more passive avoidance than the untrained animals. There was no significant difference between the two trained groups. Thus we again found no evidence that preshocks substantially altered the acquisition of fear in young rats. Although we cannot assert or expect that acquisition is totally unaffected, we tentatively conclude that prior noncontingent shocks can enhance retention in young rats relatively independently of the acquisition process.

Other Prior Stimulation: Hypothermia and Restraint

In the studies described thus far we used the same UCS as the aversive agent in both pretraining and training treatments. Although the preshock and training apparatus cues were quite dissimilar, the nature of footshock as a UCS made certain commonalities in the contextual CS (e.g., grid floor, etc.) inevitable. Perhaps stimulus generalization along these broad categories of cues facilitated acquisition of the criterion task in the preshock subjects. This argument could be tempered, however, if a qualitatively different form of noncontingent aversive stimulation also alleviated the retention decrement. Examination of a different form of prior noxious stimulation would also address the more general question: Can proactive stress experience unrelated to the training episode modify the retention of that event? To explore this possibility we compared the retention of fear in rats that received either footshocks or hypothermia prior to conditioning. For one group the procedure for noncontingent prior shock treatment was identical to that previously described. For another group three hypothermia treatments were administered during the same period (Days 16−18) that

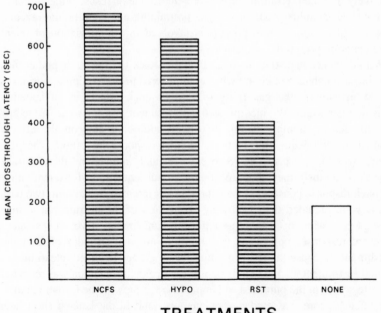

FIG. 12.4.   Effect of noncontingent shock, hypothermia, and restraint prior to Pavlovian fear conditioning upon long-term retention.

preshocks were administered. Hypothermia was induced by restraining rats in wire mesh cylinders and partially immersing them in a water bath (4°C) until their colonic temperature dropped to about 27.5°C (approximately 2.5 minutes). A third group was confined in the restraining cylinders for the same duration but was not cooled. Finally, to provide a baseline, some rats did not receive any pretraining treatments at all. All animals received the Pavlovian discriminative fear-conditioning treatment at 20 days of age and were tested for retention of fear 14 days later using the passive-avoidance test.

Figure 12.4 shows the mean cross-through latencies for all four groups following the 14-day retention interval. The results of this experiment replicated our earlier findings with noncontingent preshocks and, in addition, showed that cold stress during Days 16 to 18 enhanced retention of fear learned at 21 days. Under these particular conditions, both shock and cooling produced an effect of similar magnitude. Furthermore, even the relatively mild stress of restraint produced some enhancement of retention. It is noteworthy that these results are similar to data reported by Hinderliter and Riccio (1976), who unexpectedly found that adult "control" rats given restraint treatment prior to training showed a significant reduction in hypothermia-induced amnesia. The present results make it unlikely that the pretraining effects on retention are a result of the similarity in the physical stimulus properties of the pretraining and conditioning agents but suggest that a more central process is involved in the alleviation of retention decrements by pretraining experiences.

With evidence that stressors other than the shock UCS (e.g., hypothermia and restraint) can enhance retention when administered prior to training, our next step was to investigate the generality of the preshock effects in an appetitively motivated paradigm. We incorporated a punishment task for some of the groups into the design, hoping thereby to obtain additional data on the effects of preshock on the acquisition and retention of response inhibition. The general scheme was to give prior NCFS to experimental animals and then to train all subjects on an instrumental approach task. A subsequent test for retention of the approach response constituted the data of major interest. In addition, two parallel groups were included that, following acquisition of the instrumental response, received a session of response-contingent punishment. Two weeks later the degree of response suppression or inhibition provided an index of retention of punishment. Because the test procedure for all groups involved relearning of the original instrumental approach response, the degree of retention was reflected by opposite scores in the punished and unpunished groups. In the former condition a long latency score was evidence of memory, and in the latter a short latency would indicate retention of the response.

More specifically, pre- and nonpreshocked rats received approach training for appetitive reinforcement in the two-compartment black–white apparatus. Approach training consisted of placing the rat in the white compartment, raising the access door to the black compartment, and allowing the rat to drink sweetened milk (Eagle Brand) from a drinking spout placed in the black compartment. The latency from the opening of the door until 10 licks occurred was taken as the dependent measure. As the left-hand panel of Fig. 12.5 suggests, we did not find any significant differences between the preshocked and handled controls in the acquisition of the approach response. All rats learned this response with comparable ease. Once the approach response was learned, half the rats in each of these groups was punished for the approach response by shock administration. The punishment trials continued until a passive-avoidance criterion of two consecutive 300-second avoidances was met. Once again the preshocked rats did not differ significantly from the nonpreshocked handled controls in their rate of acquisition of the passive-avoidance response.

The retention test was given 14 days following acquisition and consisted of 20 reacquisition approach trials, all of which were reinforced with sweetened milk. Thus previously punished subjects were tested in extinction with respect to aversive consequences for responding. The mean latencies to approach and lick as a function of trials are shown in the right panel of Fig. 12.5. Although relearning occurs very rapidly for all groups, the noncontingent shock experience significantly enhanced retention of both classes of response. Because relearning

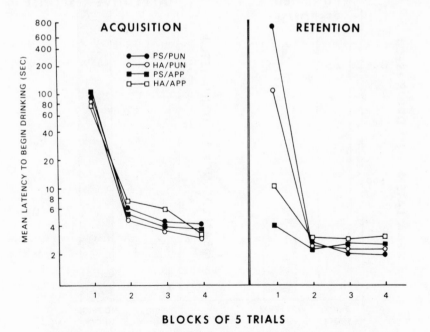

FIG. 12.5.   Left panel: Acquisition of the approach response in preshocked (PS) and handled (HA) groups. Right panel: Reacquisition of approach behavior in groups punished (PUN) or not punished (APP) during initial learning.

was so rapid we thought it instructive to examine the latency on the initial trial of the retention test, that is, before the subject made contact with the existing reinforcement contingency. These data, presented in Fig. 12.6, indicate that the preshocked rats approached the spout more slowly than their control counterparts if they had been punished but more quickly if they had not. The bidirectional nature of these outcomes makes it unlikely that the performance is attributable to generalized motor or emotionality effects produced by the early noncontingent shock experience.

SUMMARY AND CONCLUSIONS

Exposure to the footshock employed in fear conditioning, either prior to or following training, enhanced the long-term retention of fear in weanling rats. In the reinstatement paradigm a single exposure to the UCS during the retention interval substantially improved retention over untreated controls. A similar degree of improvement occurred when the rats were exposed to the conditioned fear cues while under the influence of either an epinephrine or ACTH injection

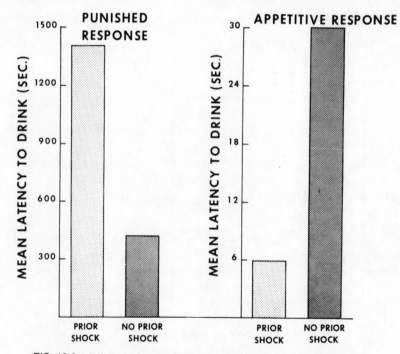

FIG. 12.6.   Effect of prior experience upon retention of aversively and appetitively motivated responses. Data shown are from the first test trial. Note that the two
ordinates have different scales.

but not when given amphetamine or strychnine. These data suggest that the activation of at least some endocrine systems specifically associated with stress-induced arousal is an important attribute of the target memory. The reinstatement of these internal conditions in association with more peripheral or external cues leads to a powerful reminder effect.

Preconditioning stressful experiences appear to have a priming effect on the later retention of the conditioned fear response. When immature rats were exposed to the UCS or to other dissimilar stressful experiences prior to conditioning, retention of fear was enhanced whereas the degree of response acquisition appeared unaffected.

In chapter 10 Coulter has described some of her work on the conditions necessary for obtaining infantile amnesia. Of particular relevance to the present topic is her finding that the usual memory deficit of young rats is abolished when they are exposed to the training contingencies over several days rather than within a single session. Despite the obvious procedural differences between Coulter's work and our own, in both cases the distribution of experience over days was shown to have a potent effect on retention. If as Coulter proposes repeated exposure to the training episode is the key element to producing long-term retention in the immature organism, then our data indicate that one need only to repeat a component of the training episode. Prior exposure to the UCS or other noxious events appears sufficient to permit later establishment of a durable memory. In connection with reinstatement studies described earlier, we followed an analysis offered by Rescorla and Heth (1975) and suggested that NCFS might alleviate memory loss because it reactivated a representation of the UCS. Extending this notion to the present design it seems possible that distributed trials, or exposures to the UCS component of training, may "prime" the system to allow a more adequate representation of the reinforcing stimulus. Regardless of how this enhanced retention is explained, we think the proactive paradigm may have heuristic value. The approach incorporates features of early experience research but emphasizes the way in which these experiences may modulate behavioral processes (such as retention) during ontogeny.

ACKNOWLEDGMENT

The research reported here was supported by NSF Grant GB41488 and NIMH Grant MH30223-01. Preparation of this chapter was supported by the latter grant.

REFERENCES

Anderson, D. C., Cole, T., & McVaugh, W. Variations in unsignalled and inescapable preshock as determinants of responses to punishment. *Journal of Comparative and Physiological Psychology*, 1968, *65*, 1−17. (Monograph supplement)

Boren, J., & Gallup, G., Jr. Amphetamine attenuation of tonic immobility in chickens. *Physiology Psychology*, 1976, *4*, 429−432.

Calhoun, W. C. Central nervous system stimulants. In E. Furchtgott (Ed.), *Pharmacological and biophysical agents and behavior*. New York: Academic Press, 1971.

Campbell, B. A., & Coulter, X. Ontogeny of learning and memory. In M. R. Rosenzweig & E. L. Bennet (Eds.), *Neural mechanisms of learning and memory*. Cambridge, Mass.: MIT Press, 1976.

Campbell, B. A., & Jaynes, J. Reinstatement. *Psychological Review*, 1966, *73*, 478−480.

Campbell, B. A., & Jaynes, J. Effect of duration of reinstatement of a visual discrimination learned in infancy. *Developmental Psychology*, 1969, *1*, 71−74.

Campbell, B. A., Riccio, D. C., & Rohrbaugh, M. Ontogenesis of learning and memory: Research and theory. In M. E. Meyer (Ed.), *Second Western symposium of learning: Early learning*. Bellingham, Wash.: Western Washington State College Press, 1971.

Campbell, B. A., & Spear, N. E. Ontogeny of memory. *Psychological Review*, 1972, *79*, 215−236.

de Wied, D. Pituitary−adrenal system hormones and behavior. In F. O. Schmitt & F. G. Worden (Eds.), *The neurosciences* Vol. 3. Cambridge, Mass.: MIT Press, 1974.

Franz, D. N. Central nervous system stimulants. In L. S. Goodman & A. Gilman (Eds.), *The pharmacological basis of theraputics*. New York: Macmillan, 1975.

Gold, P. E., & Van Buskirk, R. B. Facilitation of time-dependent memory processes with post-trial epinephrine injections. *Behavioral Biology*, 1975, *13*, 145−153.

Gordon, W. C., & Spear, N. E. The effects of strychnine on recently acquired and reactivated passive avoidance memories. *Physiology and Behavior*, 1973, *10*, 1071−1075.

Grossman, S. P., & Sclafani, A. Sympathomimetic amines. In E. Furchtgott (Ed.), *Pharmacological and biophysical agents and behavior*. New York: Academic Press, 1971.

Hall, J. F. *Classical conditioning and instrumental learning*. Philadelphia: Lippincott, 1976.

Haroutunian, V., & Riccio, D. C. Effect of arousal conditions during reinstatement treatment upon learned fear in young rats. *Developmental Psychobiology*, 1977, *10*, 25−32.

Hinderliter, C. F., & Riccio, D. C. Retrograde amnesia: State-dependency and contextual cues. Paper presented at the meeting of the Midwestern Psychological Association, Chicago, May, 1976.

Hinderliter, C. F., Smith, S. L., & Misanin, J. R. Effects of pretraining experience on retention of a passive avoidance task following ECS. *Physiology and Behavior*, 1973, *10*, 671−675.

Hinderliter, C. F., Webster, T., & Riccio, D. C. Amnesia induced by hypothermia as a function of treatment−test interval and recooling in rats. *Animal Learning & Behavior*, 1975, *3*, 257−263.

Hoffman, H. S., Selekman, W., & Fleshler, M. Stimulus aspects of aversive controls: Long term effects of suppression after equal training to two stimuli. *Journal of the Experimental Analysis of Behavior*, 1966, *9*, 659−662.

Hoving, K. L., Coates, L., Bertucci, M., & Riccio, D. C. Reinstatement effects in children. *Developmental Psychology*, 1972, *6*, 426−429.

Innes, I. R., & Nickerson, M. Norephinephrine, epinephrine, and the sympathomimetic amines. In L. S. Goodman & A. Gilman (Eds.), *The pharmacological basis of therapeutics*. New York: Macmillan, 1975.

Jensen, R. A., & Riccio, D. C. Effects of prior experience upon retrograde amnesia produced by hypothermia. *Physiology and Behavior*, 1970, *5*, 1291−1294.

Jensen, R. A., Riccio, D. C., & Gehres, L. Effects of prior aversive experience upon retrograde amnesia induced by hypothermia. *Physiology and Behavior*, 1975, *15*, 165−169.

Kamano, D. K. Enhancement of learned fear with epinephrine. *Psychonomic Science*, 1968, *12*, 331−333.

Keyes, J. B. Effect of ACTH on ECS-produced amnesia of a passive avoidance task. *Physiological Psychology*, 1974, *2*, 307−309.

Klein, S. B., & Spear, N. E. Reactivation of avoidance—learning memory in the rat after intermediate retention intervals. *Journal of Comparative and Physiological Psychology*, 1970, *72*, 498–504.

Lewis, D. J., Miller, R. R., & Misanin, J. R. Control of retrograde amnesia. *Journal of Comparative and Physiological Psychology*, 1968, *66*, 48–52.

McGaugh, J. L., & Dawson, R. G. Modification of memory storage processes. In W. Honig & P. H. R. James (Eds.), *Animal memory*. New York: Academic Press, 1971.

Miller, R. R., & Springer, A. D. Amnesia, consolidation, and retrieval. *Psychological Review*, 1973, *80*, 69–79.

Quartermain, D., McEwen, B., & Azmitia, E. Recovery of memory following amnesia in the rat and the mouse. *Journal of Comparative and Physiological Psychology*, 1972, *79*, 360–379.

Rescorla, R. A. Effect of US habituation following conditioning. *Journal of Comparative and Physiological Psychology*, 1973, *82*, 137–143.

Rescorla, R. A. Effect of inflation of the unconditioned stimulus value following conditioning. *Journal of Comparative and Physiological Psychology*, 1974, *86*, 101–106.

Rescorla, R. A., & Heth, C. D. Reinstatement of fear to an extinguished conditioned stimulus. *Journal of Experimental Psychology: Animal Behavior Processes*, 1975, *104*, 88–96.

Riccio, D. C. The paradox of retrograde amnesia. Paper presented at the meeting of the Midwestern Psychological Association, Chicago, May, 1975.

Rigter, H., & Van Riezen, H. Anti-amnesic effect of ACTH 4-10: Its independence of the nature of the amnesic agent and the behavioral test. *Physiology and Behavior*, 1975, *14*, 563–566.

Sayers, G., & Travis, R. H. Adrenocorticotropic hormone; adrenocortical steroids and their synthetic analogs. In L. S. Goodman & A. Gilman (Eds.), *The pharmacological basis of therapeutics*. New York: Macmillian, 1970.

Schacter, S., & Singer, J. Cognitive, social, and physiological determinants of emotional state. *Psychological Review*, 1962, *69*, 379–399.

Shubat, E. E., & Whitehouse, J. M. Reinstatement: An attempt at replication. *Psychonomic Science*, 1968, *12*, 215–216.

Silvestri, R., Rohrbaugh, M., & Riccio, D. C. Conditions influencing the retention of learned fear in young rats. *Developmental Psychology*, 1970, *2*, 389–395.

Spear, N. E. Retrieval of memory in animals. *Psychological Review*, 1973, *80*, 163–194.

Spear, N. E., & Parsons, P. J. Analysis of a reactivation treatment: Ontogenetic determinants of alleviated forgetting. In R. T. Davis, D. L. Medin, & W. A. Roberts (Eds.), *Coding processes in animal memory*. Hillsdale, N.J.: Lawrence Erlbaum Associates, 1976.

Thomas, D. A., & Riccio, D. C. *Forgetting of a CS attribute in a conditioned suppression paradigm. Animal Learning and Behavior*, in press.

Thompson, C. I., & Grossman, L. B. Loss and recovery of long-term memories after ECS in rats: Evidence for state-dependent recall. *Journal of Comparative and Physiological Psychology*, 1972, *78*, 248–254.

Turner, C. D., & Bagnara, J. T. *General endocrinology*. Philadelphia: Saunders, 1976.

Author Index

The numbers in *italics* refer to the pages on which the complete reference is cited.

311

Subject Index